Fodor's

D1397502

BUENOS AIRES

1st Edition

Where to Stay and Eat
for All Budgets

Must-See Sights
and Local Secrets

Ratings You Can Trust

Fodor's Travel Publications   New York, Toronto, London, Sydney, Auckland
www.fodors.com

FODOR'S BUENOS AIRES

Editors: Laura M. Kidder (Lead Project Editor); Erica Duecy (Restaurants & Hotels Editor); Kelly Kealy; Alexis Kelly

Editorial Production: Tom Holton
Editorial Contributors: Brian Byrnes, Andy Footner, Victoria Patience
Maps & Illustrations: David Lindroth, *cartographer*; Rebecca Baer, Bob Blake and William Wu *map editors*
Design: Fabrizio LaRocca, *creative director*; Guido Caroti, Siobhan O'Hare, *art directors*; Tina Malaney, Chie Ushio, Ann McBride, *designers*; Melanie Marin, *senior picture editor*; Moon Sun Kim, *cover designer*
Cover Photo (Sunday market, San Telmo): SIME s.a.s/eStock Photo
Production/Manufacturing: Matthew Struble

1st Edition

ISBN 978–1–4000–1965–6

ISSN 1941–0182

SPECIAL SALES

This book is available at special discounts for bulk purchases for sales promotions or premiums. Special editions, including personalized covers, excerpts of existing books, and corporate imprints, can be created in large quantities for special needs. For more information, write to Special Markets/Premium Sales, 1745 Broadway, MD 6-2, New York, New York 10019, or e-mail specialmarkets@randomhouse.com.

AN IMPORTANT TIP & AN INVITATION

Although all prices, opening times, and other details in this book are based on information supplied to us at press time, changes occur all the time in the travel world, and Fodor's cannot accept responsibility for facts that become outdated or for inadvertent errors or omissions. So **always confirm information when it matters,** especially if you're making a detour to visit a specific place. Your experiences—positive and negative—matter to us. If we have missed or misstated something, **please write to us.** We follow up on all suggestions. Contact the Buenos Aires editor at editors@fodors.com or c/o Fodor's at 1745 Broadway, New York, NY 10019.

PRINTED IN THE UNITED STATES OF AMERICA
10 9 8 7 6 5 4 3 2 1

Be a Fodor's Correspondent

Your opinion matters. It matters to us. It matters to your fellow Fodor's travelers, too. And we'd like to hear it. In fact, we need to hear it.

When you share your experiences and opinions, you become an active member of the Fodor's community. That means we'll not only use your feedback to make our books better, but we'll publish your names and comments whenever possible. Throughout our guides, look for "Word of Mouth," excerpts of your unvarnished feedback.

Here's how you can help improve Fodor's for all of us.

Tell us when we're right. We rely on local writers to give you an insider's perspective. But our writers and staff editors—who are the best in the business—depend on you. Your positive feedback is a vote to renew our recommendations for the next edition.

Tell us when we're wrong. We're proud that we update most of our guides every year. But we're not perfect. Things change. Hotels cut services. Museums change hours. Charming cafés lose charm. If our writer didn't quite capture the essence of a place, tell us how you'd do it differently. If any of our descriptions are inaccurate or inadequate, we'll incorporate your changes in the next edition and will correct factual errors at fodors.com immediately.

Tell us what to include. You probably have had fantastic travel experiences that aren't yet in Fodor's. Why not share them with a community of like-minded travelers? Maybe you chanced upon a beach or bistro or B&B that you don't want to keep to yourself. Tell us why we should include it. And share your discoveries and experiences with everyone directly at fodors.com. Your input may lead us to add a new listing or highlight a place we cover with a "Highly Recommended" star or with our highest rating, "Fodor's Choice."

Give us your opinion instantly at our feedback center at www.fodors.com/feedback. You may also e-mail editors@fodors.com with the subject line "Buenos Aires Editor." Or send your nominations, comments, and complaints by mail to Buenos Aires Editor, Fodor's, 1745 Broadway, New York, NY 10019.

You and travelers like you are the heart of the Fodor's community. Make our community richer by sharing your experiences. Be a Fodor's correspondent.

¡Buen viaje!

Tim Jarrell, Publisher

CONTENTS

BUENOS AIRES IN FOCUS

ABOUT
THIS BOOK

Our Ratings

Sometimes you find terrific travel experiences and sometimes they just find you. But usually the burden is on you to select the right combination of experiences. That's where our ratings come in.

As travelers we've all discovered a place so wonderful that its worthiness is obvious. And sometimes that place is so unique that superlatives don't do it justice: you just have to be there to know. These sights, properties, and experiences get our highest rating, **Fodor's Choice**, indicated by orange stars throughout this book.

Black stars highlight sights and properties we deem **Highly Recommended**, places that our writers, editors, and readers praise again and again for consistency and excellence.

By default, there's another category: any place we include in this book is by definition worth your time, unless we say otherwise. And we will.

Disagree with any of our choices? Care to nominate a place or suggest that we rate one more highly? Visit our feedback center at www.fodors.com/feedback.

Budget Well

Hotel and restaurant price categories from ¢ to $$$$ are defined in the opening pages of each chapter. For attractions, we always give standard adult admission fees; reductions are usually available for children, students, and senior citizens. Want to pay with plastic? **AE, D, DC, MC, V** following restaurant and hotel listings indicate whether American Express, Discover, Diners Club, MasterCard, and Visa are accepted.

Restaurants

Unless we state otherwise, restaurants are open for lunch and dinner daily. We mention dress only when there's a specific requirement and reservations only when they're essential or not accepted—it's always best to book ahead.

Hotels

Hotels have private bath, phone, TV, and air-conditioning and operate on the European Plan (aka EP, meaning without meals), unless we specify that they use the Continental Plan (CP, with a continental breakfast), Breakfast Plan (BP, with a full breakfast), or Modified American Plan (MAP, with breakfast and dinner) or are all-inclusive (including all meals and most activities). We

always list facilities but not whether you'll be charged an extra fee to use them, so when pricing accommodations, find out what's included.

Many Listings

★	Fodor's Choice
★	Highly recommended
✉	Physical address
↔	Directions
⌂	Mailing address
☎	Telephone
🖷	Fax
⊕	On the Web
✉	E-mail
🎫	Admission fee
☉	Open/closed times
Ⓜ	Metro stations
▭	Credit cards

Hotels & Restaurants

🏨	Hotel
🛏	Number of rooms
⌂	Facilities
❢⦿❢	Meal plans
✗	Restaurant
⌂	Reservations
⦙	Smoking
⦿⦿	BYOB
✗🏨	Hotel with restaurant that warrants a visit

Outdoors

🏌	Golf
⛺	Camping

Other

☺	Family-friendly
⇨	See also
✉	Branch address
☞	Take note

1

Experience
Buenos Aires

Dorrego Café, San Telmo

WORD OF MOUTH

I'm a *big* fan of BA. It's a huge city with lots to do. We've been there a few times, most recently for a couple of weeks to study Spanish. Nightlife? You bet. Culture? Yes. Locals? Friendly and outgoing. Food? Great. Prices? Dollar is still OK. Architecture? Sweet. Safe? Yes. Tango? Why not.

—JKinCALIF

BUENOS AIRES TODAY

They say the only thing certain in life is change, and no one knows it like porteños (citizens of Buenos Aires) do. A decade of political uncertainty and financial instability has left this city's inhabitants wondering what tomorrow might bring. But from the ashes of economic burnout, a vibrant, global, more-progressive Buenos Aires is rising. At times, uncertainty can be worrying. But it can be exciting, too.

Today's Buenos Aires . . .

. . . is getting a face-lift. Cobbled streets, wrought-iron billboards, and cafés that don't seem untouched since 1940 are all part of Buenos Aires' trademark time-warp look. But though *porteños* are nostalgic, even they've had enough of exquisite stone facades crumbling (sometimes plain plummeting) through lack of maintenance. Suddenly, scaffolding is everywhere; private investment and public spending is seeing old buildings all over town revamped. The Teatro Colón, the MAMBA (a San Telmo–based modern art museum), and other major buildings have all benefited. Meanwhile, savvy developers are transforming century-old houses into slick apartments or shops. Erstwhile mansions and warehouses are reopening as hotels, some boutique, others behe-moth (witness the ex-grain-silo Faena Hotel + Universe). Like other aging local beauties, Buenos Aires' historical buildings are looking younger by the minute.

. . . is less smoky. Whenever the government tries to increase cigarette prices, porteños protest vociferously that smoking is one of the few pleasures they can afford. And, indeed, this was a town where lights were for sissies as real men smoked *negras,* harsh black cigarettes. But all this is, well, going up in smoke: at the end of 2006—ahead of many European countries—the city banned smoking from most indoor spaces, including shops, bars, and restaurants. Flouting laws is something most Argentines take pride in, so the really astonishing part is that people are largely obeying: the classic porteño breakfast of a *cafecito y un pucho* (espresso and a smoke) is no more. Of course, true to local ways, there's a loophole: restaurants and cafés are allowed smoking areas if they're over a certain size and have the correct ventilation equipment. Instead, most owners have opted just to move more tables onto the sidewalk (where smoking is allowed).

WHAT'S HOT IN BUENOS AIRES NOW

Forget Recoleta, forget Palermo: trend spotters agree that south is the new north. Neighborhoods below Avenida Rivadavia are the ones to watch. Designers and restaurateurs are upping sticks to San Telmo, and those in the know tip run-down Barracas, packed with abandoned factories just begging for loft conversion, as the next big real-estate bubble.

Being out has never been this in. Buenos Aires looks set to become Latin America's gay capital. It's not just bars and clubs, either: we're talking travel agencies, tango schools, *milongas* (tango dance halls), and now Axel, a posh gay hotel. The local community has plenty to cheer about, too: same-sex civil unions have been legal since 2003, and the Marcha del Orgullo Gay (Gay Pride March) attracts thousands of revelers each November.

. . . is full of free speech. Forget writing to your political representatives when you've got a gripe with the system—in Buenos Aires, you take to the streets. Strikes, marches, and rallies have long been a fixture of daily life. They reached new levels after December 19, 2001, when the country's economy crashed. The state froze all private bank accounts, and ensuing demonstrations escalated into riots due to the violence of police response. Although things have calmed considerably since then, Plaza and Avenida de Mayo still fill regularly with drum- and banner-toting crowds chanting in a tuneful unison that can only come from practice. Sometimes they're protesting low salaries or police repression; other times they're marking an event, such as March 24, when thousands gather to mourn the anniversary of the start of Argentina's last, and bloodiest, dictatorship, which lasted from 1976 to 1982.

. . . is going global. Argentina is a long, long way from a lot of places. In the years leading up to and immediately after the 2001 economic crisis, Buenos Aires felt very isolated: first, high prices and poor infrastructure kept people away, and then political instability did. Things couldn't have changed more. And though most porteños are descended from immigrants, they just can't get over the number of out-of-towners there are today. (Thankfully, compared to many big capitals, the numbers are still small enough to keep sightseeing from being a competitive sport.) And more and more of the 2.3 million annual foreign visitors are staying. The number of exchange students at city universities has soared, and there's a thriving expat scene complete with how-to blogs and magazines. Low property prices and living costs mean many of these European and North American newcomers can afford not to work: would-be novelists, painters, and musicians abound. International bands that have already made the big time are back to play the stages they abandoned in the late '90s. Even the urban landscape is affected: architects Norman Foster (New York's Hearst Headquarters, London's Swiss RE Building) and local-boy-gone-global César Pelli (Kuala Lumpur's Petronas Towers) both have projects being constructed in Puerto Madero, one of the city's swankiest neighborhoods.

Some of the city's best food is served *a puertas cerradas,* or behind closed doors. These small, informal "restaurants" are often in people's homes and open just one or two nights a week. Expect top-quality tasting menus at places like Casa Saltshaker (*www.casasaltshaker.com*); others, like Almacén Secreto (11/4775–1271) have à la carte menus. On reserving (by phone or e-mail) you're given the address.

Listening to *cumbia* (a local tropical-style rhythm) was once as trashy as it got. But now Buenos Aires' hottest club nights spin around electronic cumbia remixes. Some call it "electrotropical" or "electrocumbia," others "cumbiatrónica": whatever its name, its trademark "shh-chicki-shh" beat has clubbers hooked. Club Night Zizek at the happening nightspot Niceto is *the* place to go.

EXPERIENCE BUENOS AIRES PLANNER

No Time Like the Present

Fabulous wine, endless nightlife, friendly locals, the best steak, rock-bottom prices . . . shaking off a stereotype can be hard. But when yours reads like a shopping list for indulgence, why bother? Whether they're screaming for a soccer team or enjoying an endless barbecue with friends, porteños are always demonstrating that enjoying the here and the now is what life is all about.

Visitor Info

The Web site of the city tourist board, **Turismo Buenos Aires** (⊕*www.bue.gov.ar*) has lively, downloadable MP3 walking tours in English. Bright orange info booths at the airports and seven other locations provide maps and have English-speaking personnel.

The **South American Explorer's Club** (⊠*Estados Unidos 577, San Telmo, C1101AAK* ☎*11/4307–9625* ⊕*www.saexplorers.org*) is an American nonprofit that aims to help independent travelers in the region. Membership gives you access to its clubhouses and its extensive online resources. The Buenos Aires' clubhouse has a map library; a book exchange; and a bulletin board.

Get Around Just Fine

Intriguing architecture, an easy-to-navigate grid layout (a few diagonal transverses aside), and ample window-shopping make Buenos Aires a wonderful place to explore on foot. Street cafés abound for when your feet tire.

Public Transit. Service on the *subte* (subway) is quick, but trains are often packed and strikes are common. Four of the six underground lines (A, B, D, and E) fan out west from downtown; lines C and H (only partly open) connect them. Single-ride tickets cost a flat 90¢. The subte shuts down around 11 PM and reopens at 5 AM.

Colectivos (city buses) connect the city's barrios and the greater Buenos Aires area. Ticket machines on board only accept coins (fares within the city are a flat 90¢). Bus stops are roughly every other block, but you may have to hunt for the small metal route-number signs: they could be stuck on a shelter, lamppost, or even a tree. Stop at a news kiosk and buy the *Guía T*, a handy route guide.

Taxis. Black-and-yellow taxis fill the streets and take you anywhere in town and short distances into greater Buenos Aires. Fares start at 3.10 pesos with 31¢ per 650 feet. You can hail taxis on the street or ask hotel and restaurant staffers to call for them.

Safety

Although Buenos Aires is safer than most Latin American capitals, the country's unstable economy means crime is a concern. Pickpocketing and mugging are common, so avoid wearing flashy jewelry, be discreet with money and cameras, and be mindful of bags. Take taxis as much as possible after dark. Police patrol most areas where you're likely to go, but they have a reputation for corruption, so locals try to avoid contact with them.

Protest marches are a part of life in Buenos Aires: most are peaceful, but some end in confrontations with the police. They often take place in the Plaza de Mayo, in the square outside the Congreso, or along the Avenida de Mayo connecting the two.

Tours

Ghosts, crimes, and spooky urban legends are the focus of the Buenos Aires Misteriosa tours run by **Ayres Viajes** (☎11/4383-9188 ⊕www.ayresviajes.com.ar). The super-personalized service—for tours in town and out—you get from Isabel at **Buenos Aires Tours** (⊕www.buenosaires-tours.com.ar) is almost heroic. For a local's perspective, contact the **Cicerones de Buenos Aires** (☎11/4431-9892 ⊕www.cicerones.org.ar), a free service that pairs you with a porteño to show you parts of town you might not see otherwise. Highly informed young historians from the University of Buenos Aires lead the cultural and historical tours at **Eternautas** (☎11/5031-9916 ⊕www.eternautas.com). It offers orientation tours, neighborhood walks, themed outings (e.g., Evita, the literary city, Jewish Buenos Aires), and excursions outside town.

A dynamic way to see the city's sights is on two wheels through **La Bicicleta Naranja** (☎11/4362-1104 ⊕www.labicicletanaranja.com.ar). You can rent a bicycle and gear to follow one of the routes on their excellent maps or go with a guide on general or theme trips. See Buenos Aires from the river on a 2½-hour sailboat tour with **Smile on Sea** (☎11/15-5018-8662 ⊕www.smileonsea.com). What better way to explore the waterways of the Tigre delta and Puerto Madero's docklands than from the water? **Puro Remo** (☎11/15-6397-3545 ⊕www.puroremo.com.ar) is a rowing club that offers guided kayaking and rowing tours (no experience needed).

Large onboard screens make the posh minibuses used by **Opción Sur** (☎11/4777-9029 ⊕www.opcionsur.com.ar) part transport and part cinema. Each stop on their city tour is introduced by relevant historical footage (e.g., Evita rallying the masses at Plaza de Mayo). You get serious insight into Buenos Aires' Jewish community on day tours run by Deb Miller's company, **Travel Jewish** (☎11/4106-0541 ⊕www.traveljewish.com).

Tick off the major sights and get the lay of the land on the basic three-hour bus tours run by **Travel Line** (☎11/4393-9000 ⊕www.travelline.com.ar). For tailor-made city tours contact **Wow! Argentina** (☎11/5239-3019 ⊕www.wowargentina.com.ar). Cintia Stella and her team can also arrange excursions all over Argentina.

When to Go

Remember that when it's summer in the United States, it's winter in Argentina, and vice versa. Winters (July–September) are chilly, though temperatures never drop below freezing. Summer's muggy heat (December–March) can be taxing at midday but makes for wonderful, warm nights. During these months (as well as in July for school holidays), Argentines crowd resorts along the Atlantic. Meanwhile traffic-free Buenos Aires has a host of city-sponsored concerts that bring people out into the sun and moonlight.

Spring (September–December) and autumn (April–June), with their mild temperatures—and blossoms or changing leaves—are ideal for urban trekking. It's usually warm enough for just a light jacket, and it's right before or after the peak (and expensive) season. The best time for trips to Iguazú Falls is August–October, when temperatures are lower, the falls are fuller, and the spring coloring is at its brightest.

Buenos Aires Temperatures

°F   BUENOS AIRES   °C

WHAT'S WHERE

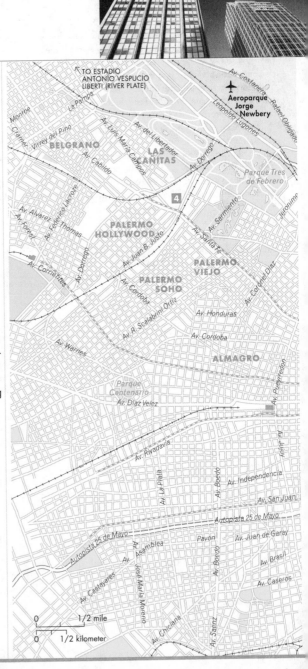

1 El Centro: Microcentro, Plaza de Mayo, Retiro & Puerto Madero. Locals use "El Centro" as an umbrella term for several action-packed downtown districts. The heart of the city's heart is the Microcentro, which bursts with banks, offices, theaters (including the Colón), bars, cafés, bookstores, and crowds. The area around Plaza and Avenida de Mayo is the hub of political life and home to some of the city's oldest buildings. Posh hotels, gleaming skyscrapers, and an elegant boardwalk make up Puerto Madero.

2 San Telmo & La Boca. The tango was born in these traditional southern barrios. Today, antiques and hip clothing compete for store space along San Telmo's dreamy cobbled streets—ideal for lazy wandering and relaxing at bars or cafés. Just to the south, La Boca was the city's first port and originally settled by immigrants from Italy. Today visitors come for a snapshot of the colorful but tacky Caminito, and locals come to scream for soccer idols in the Boca Juniors stadium.

3 Recoleta & Almagro.
Today's elite live, dine, and shop along Recoleta's gorgeous Paris-inspired streets. They're also often buried in the sumptuous mausoleums of its cemetery. Art galleries and museums—one major (the Museo Nacional de Bellas Artes) and a few minor—are also draws. Gritty, working-class Almagro is known for its fringe theater pickings and tango scene, and the large Abasto shopping mall.

4 Palermo, Belgrano, Costanera Norte & Las Cañitas. Large Palermo has many subdistricts. If it's cool and happening, chances are it's in Palermo Viejo: boutiques, bars, restaurants, clubs, galleries, and hotels line the streets surrounding Plaza Serrano (also known to locals as Plazoleta Cortázar). The area across Avenida Juan B. Justo took the name Palermo Hollywood for the film and TV studios that are based here. There are two excellent museums (the MALBA and Museo Evita) in Palermo Chico, the barrio's northern end, also home to parks and the zoo. Clubs and bars line nearby Costanera Norte, along the river, which comes alive after midnight. It's also home to a golf course and the Jorge Newbery airport (for domestic flights). Local models and TV stars adore the chichi shops, restaurants, and bars of the northern neighborhoods of Las Cañitas and Belgrano.

Río de La Plata

Darsena F
Darsena E
Darsena A

PALERMO CHICO
RECOLETA
RETIRO
Estación Terminal de Omnibus
Estación Retiro
Antepuerto
Dársena Norte
Av. Santa Fe
Av. Cordoba
CENTRO
Av. Corrientes
PUERTO MADERO
Tte. Gral. Juan Peron
Plaza del Congreso
Av. de Mayo
Av. Rivadavia
PLAZA DE MAYO
Av. Belgrano
Reserva Ecologica
SAN TELMO
Autopista 25 de Mayo
Estación Constitución F.C.G. Roca
LA BOCA
Brandsen
Brandsen

Av. Pres. Figueroa Alcorta
Av. del Libertador
Av. Callao
Av. 9 de Julio
Av. Leandro N. Alem
Av. Paseo Colón
Dársena Sur
Av. Pedro Mendoza
Av. Entre Ríos
Av. Amancio Alcorta
Av. 9 de Julio
Av. M. Montes de Oca
Av. Reg. de Patricios
Irala
Vélez Sarsfield
Dique 4
Dique 3
Dique 2
Dique 1
Av. Martín García
Defensa

TOP BUENOS AIRES ATTRACTIONS

Plaza de Mayo

(A) Since the city was founded, civic and political life has centered on this large, palm-shaded square in Centro. The favored stage of protesters and politicians alike, this was where Evita told a rally of thousands not to cry for her. During the 1976–1982 dictatorship, a group of mothers (now a nongovernmental organization called Madres de Plaza de Mayo) protested their children's disappearances here each week. The seat of the nation's government, a cathedral, the central bank, a colonial town hall, and the senate all flank the square.

Cementerio de la Recoleta

(B) The city's illustrious departed rest in mausoleums as sumptuous as their mansions. Heavily adorned with marble facades and dramatic statues, these second homes are arrayed along shaded avenues, forming an eerie but beautiful city of the dead. Residents include the must-see Evita, national heroes, sporting greats, writers, and several wandering ghosts—or so local legend goes.

Museo de Arte Latinoamericano de Buenos Aires (MALBA)

(C) Buenos Aires' first truly world-class museum is a luminous temple to the gods of 19th- and 20th-century Latin American art. A vigorous acquisitions program means you see the latest talents as well as Frida Kahlo, Diego Rivera, and Fernando Botero. The architecture, rooftop views over surrounding Palermo, and gift shop are excuses in themselves to stop by.

Museo Nacional de Bellas Artes

(D) Originally the city's waterworks, this russet-color columned building in Recoleta is your one-stop shop for Argentine painting and sculpture, especially modern and postmodern works. A surprisingly comprehensive collection of lesser

works by European and North American masters, spanning the 13th century to the present, are an added boon.

Caminito

(E) An entire postcard industry has been built on the Technicolor corrugated-iron constructions on this street in La Boca. A purpose-built tourist attraction, Caminito is unashamedly tacky and brash but is still an exuberant must-see (and must-snap) on your first visit to Buenos Aires.

Plaza Dorrego

(F) Sunday sees this quiet San Telmo square transformed into the Feria de San Pedro Telmo, Buenos Aires' biggest antiques market. Junk, memorabilia, and, occasionally, genuine antiques are all part of the cult of nostalgia celebrated here, in the shadow of century-old town houses. A beer or a coffee at a traditional bar are an essential part of the experience.

Museo Evita

(G) Forget Madonna: for the true scoop on Argentina's most iconic citizen, come to this well-curated museum. Evita's life, works, and, yes, wardrobe are celebrated through insightful displays and original video footage, all housed in a gorgeous turn-of-the-20th-century mansion she requisitioned as a home for single mothers.

Parque Tres de Febrero (Los Bosques de Palermo)

(H) Porteños desperate for some green relief love this 200-acre Palermo park, which includes wooded areas, lakes, a planetarium, and the Eduardo Sívori art museum. Slump in the sun with a picnic and/or a book, or make like sporty locals and go for a run or a bike ride around its trails.

BUENOS AIRES LIKE A LOCAL

Pamper Yourself Like a Porteño

It's not just good genes that keep porteños looking fab: the *peluquería* (beauty salon) is a home away from home. Most local women eschew expensive French potions and faux-zen decor of luxury for cheap, nondescript neighborhood salons where they can gossip and read trashy magazines. A normal Friday evening session would include *brushing* (blow-dry and styling, 20–30 pesos), usually with *planchita* (straightening irons), as most porteñas dislike curls.

A weekly *belleza de manos y pies* (manicure and pedicure, 20 or 30 pesos) is also standard. Local waxers are so good (and charge so little) that no porteño would dream of touching a razor. Most salons use the *sistema español,* involving thick, gloopy wax that's pulled off without fabric strips. Given the fierce rivalry between Argentina and its neighbor, all-out bikini waxing isn't called "a Brazilian." You can get the same effect by picking a combo of *cavado profundo* (regular bikini), *tira de pelvis* (a strip along the top, ideal for low-cut bikinis), and *tira de cola* (literally, "ass strip"—need we say more?).

Llongueras (⊕*www.llongueras.com*), **D'antuan** (⊕*www.dantuan.com*), and **Paulino Acosta** (⊕*www.paulinoacosta. com.ar*) have branches all over town, and you usually don't need an appointment. **Club Creativo** (⊠*Montevideo 1161, Barrio Norte, C1019ABW* ☎*11/4816–1016*) is one of the hippest salons, but staffers are as friendly, down-to-earth, and gossipy as any neighborhood beauty parlor.

Travel Like a Porteño

For many porteños, the run-down colectivos that rocket around in a cloud of exhaust are the only form of transport

UNDERCUTTING THE COMPETITION

People will often go to the ends of the earth to look good. The latest trend in special-interest tours to Buenos Aires is cosmetic surgery. Some visitors buy dedicated surgery packages (you know, flights, hotel, transfers, tummy tuck) while others combine treatments with a vacation.

Rock-bottom prices are the main attraction, but Argentina's cosmetic surgeons also have a good international reputation. It's not all liposuction and boob jobs, either: dental implants and whitening procedures are also popular

available. Hopping one of these buses can transport you from dolled-up tourist haunts to residential barrios in minutes. Complex winding routes and different routes on each leg of a journey make getting on a bus a leap into the unknown. If you're adventurous try the first bus that comes along and see where it takes you. If you're a control freak, go to a news kiosk and buy a *Guía T,* which lists routes numerically at the back. One route to try is that taken by Bus 60, which goes from Constitución through Congreso and Barrio Norte before branching into myriad subroutes, most through the northwest of Buenos Aires. Another good bet is Bus 126, which travels southwest from Plaza de Mayo through San Telmo, Boedo, Caballito, and Flores.

Exercise Like a Porteño

True, when it comes to sports, cheering on a soccer team is what locals love most. But porteños are also image-obsessed, so there are plenty of fitness options. Winding tracks through Parque 3 de Febrero (Los Bosques de Palermo) make it a mecca for runners and in-line skaters. Quiet streets and boardwalks in Puerto Madero also make great tracks. One of the most popular places to sweat and be seen (preferably in your best sportswear) is at a branch of the **Megatlón** (⊕*www. megatlon.com.ar*) chain. Membership of up to a month costs around 150 pesos for access to all 14 branches, each with cardio and weight machines, lots of classes, saunas, and sometimes pools. If you're on a lightning visit, sign on to their Web site for a one-day free trial pass.

Go Out Like a Porteño

Porteños never have trouble finding an excuse to get together with friends, and not just on Friday and Saturday night. Wondering how they manage to combine a nightlife scene that doesn't kick off until 3 AM with getting to work the next morning? We'll let you in on a secret: many don't. These days, it's much cooler to head to an "after-office," an extended happy hour found in most bars in the Microcentro between 6 and 9 PM. As well as cheap drinks, you can count on meeting lots of locals unwinding after a hard day at work. Older couples and groups of friends prefer to catch a show or a play along Avenida Corrientes—most go wild over the lame jokes and sequin-and-feather-bedecked dancers of the big reviews, but there's plenty of highbrow theater on offer, too.

Eat Fast Food Like a Porteño

Porteños have a cultish devotion to local fast food. One of the quickest lunches in town is a couple of slices standing at the bars of classic Microcentro pizzerias like Las Cuartetas and El Cuartito (⇨*also, Chapter 5, Where to Eat*). The classics are *muzzarella* (cheese and tomato) and *fugazzeta* (tomato-less onion and cheese). Expect a doughy crust and more greasy cheese than you'll know what to do with.

The truly porteño touch is to put a slice of *fainá* (baked garbanzo dough) on top of your pizza. For fast-fare alfresco sink your teeth into a *choripán* or *vaciopán* (an oozing sandwich of chorizo or beef, respectively) from the stands that line the Costanera Sur walkway along the river near Puerto Madero. There are tubs of spicy *chimichurri* sauce to spoon over your sandwich.

You might not be able to dial a dozen empanadas to your hotel room, but you could certainly do takeout: ubiquitous chain El Noble Repulgue (⊕*www.elno blerepulgue.com.ar*) is a porteño favorite. The idea is to eat them lukewarm straight from the paper wrapping, preferably washing them down with a beer or a Coke while watching bad TV programs in bed. There's only one dessert option: ice cream from chains like Freddo (⊕*www.freddo. com.ar*) or Un'Altra Volta (⊕*www.unal travolta.com.ar*).

CITY ITINERARIES

Iconic Buenos Aires

Buenos Aires has no Eiffel Tower or Empire State Building. But every time a magazine runs a piece on the city, a few sights are inevitably photographed. Here's how to take your own set of pics of the city's icons in half a day.

Start with Microcentro's butterscotch-frosted wedding-cakey **Teatro Colón**. Although the best-known facade is the one looking onto Avenida 9 de Julio (stand on the traffic island for a decent shot), this is the *back* of the building. Go right around to Libertad for the columned main entrance.

Gaze south down Avenida 9 de Julio at your next landmark: the **Obelisco**, routinely berated by porteños for being too pointless, too pretentious, or just too phallic. Only maintenance staff are allowed up the 202-rung ladder within it, so you'll have to snap away from below.

Walk five blocks south to Avenida de Mayo, and take a left. The avenue leads you into Plaza de Mayo with great aspects of the **Casa Rosada**, Argentina's salmon-pink answer to the White House, which lies at the end of the square. Behind it, on Paseo Colón, catch the 33, 64, or 152 buses south to La Boca.

The primary-color corrugated iron buildings along **Caminito** beg to be photographed almost as much as the tangoing street performers (carry loose change if you plan on capturing them). Supplement your shots with postcards from nearby souvenir shops. Traditional café **La Perla** is great for coffee breaks.

19th-Century Europe in Buenos Aires

Stretching between the Congress and the presidential seat in the Casa Rosada, **Ave-nida de Mayo** isn't just a thoroughfare. For porteños it's a symbolic path between the two powers and the classic route for protest marches. A stroll west along it takes an hour or two.

The avenue was created just over a century ago, when the whole right half of the **Cabildo** was lopped off to make room for it. "Time travel" takes on a literal meaning in the subway stations of **Line A**, which runs under Avenida de Mayo. The city's oldest line (built in 1913) has clanking wooden carriages and gloomy tiled stations that haven't changed much in the last 50 years.

Above ground be sure to look up at the ornate cupolas and rooftops. A perfect example is the Opera-Garnier-style **Casa de la Cultura**, at number 575, which is topped by a torch-bearing statue of Athena. Look closely for the newspaper under the bronze goddess's arm: the building was once headquarters of conservative newspaper *La Prensa*, but was requisitioned by Perón, fed up with their criticism of his government. It's now property of the city, which organizes regular classical concerts in its exquisite Versailles-inspired Salón Dorado, where writer Borges gave his first conference.

Forget mere statues: the *whole* of number 1370, neo-Gothic **Palacio Barolo**, pays architectural homage to Dante Alighieri. The palacio is 100 meters (328 feet) tall, 1 meter for each of the 100 cantos of the *Divine Comedy*. The floors are divided into hell, purgatory, and the cupola-ed heaven, which contains a 300,000-bulb beam once used to transmit the results of the Dempsey–Firpo boxing match to Uruguay. So Dante-obsessed was its architect

Mario Palanti that he considered trying to bring the poet's ashes from Italy.

The soaring, sweeping, art nouveau lines of **Palacio Vera** (number 769) and **Hotel Chile** (number 1297) are a welcome contrast to their solid, classic-looking neighbors. Equally graceful are the elongated, twin crimson-tiled cupolas of the **Edificio La Inmobiliaria,** at number 1402.

The Iberian influences near the Avenida de Mayo come in culinary form: parallel street Hipólito Irigoyen's intersection with Salta is an unofficial Spanish quarters. One of the corner restaurants, **El Imparcial,** got its name because of its owners' neutral stance during the Spanish Civil War, when talking politics was forbidden within. A famous, albeit fictional, Spaniard flings his arm out over Avenida de Mayo's intersection with Avenida 9 de Julio: a statue of Don Quijote.

Avendia de Mayo also carries strong literary associations, especially at the **Café Tortoni** (number 829), the favorite haunt of literary greats Jorge Luis Borges and Roberto Arlt. It dates from 1858, making it the town's oldest café. A low-lighted ornate interior—all old-world elegance—makes it the perfect place for a *café con leche con medialunas* (coffee and croissants). Several dusty antiquarian bookshops operate nearby.

Bargain-Hunter Buenos Aires

You came to Buenos Aires to shop, but inflation has pushed local designer prices ever closer to those abroad. If you still want to strut around town laden with bags, spend a day rifling the racks in Buenos Aires' less-well-known stores.

Start early at ultracheap Chilean department store **Falabella,** which gets going at 9 AM, an hour before most shops (and shoppers). There are three branches on Calle Florida: clothes and cosmetics are at number 202, housewares are at number 343, and sports and electronics are at number 665. There are plenty of nearby cafés where you can grab a *cortado* (espresso with a dash of milk) and *medialuna* (croissant). Check out shoe shops along Calle Florida's 300 and 400 blocks afterward.

Next stop: outlet central. Take Bus 109 west along **Avenida Córdoba** (the stop is just east of the intersection with Florida), and get off at the 3900 block, just before the bus turns. Between Pringles and Serrano (the 4200 and 4900 blocks), Córdoba is lined with hundreds of outlets selling discontinued lines and second selections, including Ona Sáez, Ayres, Portsaid, Levi's, Bensimon, Oldbridge, Legacy, and Wanama. Nearby outlets sell hip handbag and leather goods: Uma at Humboldt 1868 and Prüne at Gurruchaga 867.

Walk a few blocks north into **Palermo Viejo** for a quick café lunch (and to feel doubly satisfied when you see how high prices are in shops here). Take Bus 39 from the stop on Costa Rica at Armenia, and get off at the intersection of Avenida Santa Fe and Avenida Callao. A mix of small boutiques and regular branches of many of the outlets you visited line **Avenida Santa Fe**'s 1100–1700 blocks. Be sure to duck into two landmark *galerías* (arcades or minimalls): **Bond Street**, at Callao, for club- and streetwear, and **La Quinta Avenida**, at Talcahuano, for vintage duds. Now taxi your bags back to your hotel and get your new togs on for dinner.

WITH KIDS

Family is a big part of local life. Porteños definitely believe kids should be seen and heard, and local children keep pretty much the same schedule as their parents. It's completely normal for kids to sit through adult dinners until the small hours, and restaurants (and other diners) are fine with them dozing at the table.

Museums

Kids can go to the bank, shop at a supermarket, and play at adult jobs **Museo de los Niños** (Children's Museum) in Almagro. Although the museum is entirely in Spanish, activities like crawling through a large-scale plumbing system and operating a crane on a building site have international appeal.

The motto of Recoleta's **Museo Participativo de las Ciencias** (Participative Science Museum) says it all—*Prohibido no Tocar,* or "Not touching is Forbidden." The colorful interactive displays—which explain how music, light, and electricity work—are hands-on enough for most kids to enjoy them despite the Spanish-only explanations. Better yet, it's on the first floor of the Centro Cultural Recoleta, so you can squeeze in some adult museum time, too.

Some of the dusty displays at the **Planetario Galileo Galilei** in Palermo's Parque 3 de Febrero seem almost as vintage as the gloriously retro building itself. Still, the night sky projection room and the meteorite collection add up to a quick, fun outing. Cotton candy and popcorn machines near the duck ponds outside make for more-earthly post-museum treats.

The dinosaur skeletons at the **Museo Argentino de Ciencias Naturales** (Argentine Museum of Natural Science ⊠*Av. Angel Gallardo 470, Villa Crespo, C1405DJR*

☎*11/4982–0306* ⊕*www.macn.secyt.gov. ar* ☞*3 pesos* ⊙*Daily 2–7*) are probably old hat, but your kids might get a kick from the megafauna fossils (think 10-foot hamster bones). Some sections—like the mollusk collection—are housed in rooms so dark and dusty they're more likely to induce nightmares than curiosity.

Young'uns with arty inclinations love the exquisite marionettes and glove, shadow, and finger puppets at the **Museo Argentino del Títere** (Puppet Museum of Argentina ⊠*Piedras 905, San Telmo, C1070AAS* ☎*11/4304–4376* ⊕*www.museoargdelti tere.com.ar* ☞*Free* ⊙*Tues.–Fri. 10–noon and 3–6, weekends 3–7*). Time your visit to coincide with weekend puppet shows at 4 and 5:30 PM.

Outdoors

The best place for unbridled running and jumping is Palermo's **Parque Tres de Febrero.** There are acres and acres of well-maintained greenery, and you can rent bicycles of all sizes (including ones with child seats), in-line skates, and pedal boats. There are also hamburger stands, balloon sellers, and clowns.

The **Zoo de Buenos Aires** is home to pumas, tapirs, llamas, *aguarrá guazús* (a kind of wolf), and *yacarés* (caymans). And these are just some of the South American animals here that your kids might not have ever seen.

Adrenaline

The rides at **Parque de la Costa** (⊠*Vivanco 1509, Tigre, B1648DWE* ☎*11/4002– 6000* ⊕*www.parquedelacosta.com.ar* ☞*38 pesos* ⊙*Jan. and Feb., Tues.–Sun. 11–9; Mar.–Nov., Fri.–Sun. 11–7*), Buenos Aires' only theme park, are perfectly pitched for kids and tweens. The three most extreme roller coasters aren't the

world's scariest, but they can keep older adrenaline junkies occupied for a while, and relatively small lines mean you can keep going back for more.

You know you'll never be able to beat your kids on the Playstation. Go retro and give yourself a sporting chance with a Scalectrix championship at **Añe** (⊠*Scalabrini Ortíz 818, Palermo Viejo, C1414DNV* ☎*11/4775–5165* ⊕*www. anie-slot.com.ar* ⊙*Daily 10* AM*–midnight*), a video club with three large-scale electric miniature car racing tracks in a room behind it.

Getting Around

Your kids might not be into the city's crowded subways, but there are other fun forms of travel in Buenos Aires. Horse-drawn carriages (called *mateos*) line up outside the Zoo de Buenos Aires and take you on a ride around the Parque Tres de Febrero.

Trams once ran through most of the city. The **Asociación Amigos del Tranvía** (⊠*Emilio Mitre 500, at José Bonifacio, Caballito, C1424AYJ* ☎*11/4431–1073* ⊕*www.tranvia.org.ar* ⊙*Dec.–Feb., Sat. 5–8:30, Sun. 10–1 and 5–8:30; Mar.–Nov., Sat. 4–7:30, Sun. 10–1 and 4–7:30* Ⓜ*E to Emilio Mitre*) has saved some of the original carriages and operates free rides through the streets of the Caballito neighborhood on weekends.

For Treats

When it comes to rewarding—or bribing—their kids, porteño parents are unanimous: *helado* (ice cream) is the way to go. There are shops on nearly every street block, but classy chains Freddo, Un'Altra Volta, and Persicco do the creamiest scoops. Children's menus aren't common in Buenos Aires: local kids usually eat the

> ### MAFALDA WANTS WORLD PEACE, TOO
>
> Thanks to cable TV, most Argentine kids have pretty much the same cartoon diet as kids in America. But back when cartoons meant a strip in the newspaper, there were plenty of local heroes and heroines. The most famous is Mafalda, an idealistic little girl with a penchant for naïve but probing questions, world peace, and the Beatles. You can buy English-language translations of the strip, which was drawn by Quino, at bookshops and news kiosks.

same as adults, in smaller portions. The exception to the rule is Recursos Infantiles (⇨*Toys in Chapter 3, Shopping*), a toy shop with a small-scale restaurant that *only* does children's food.

Entertainment

You don't need Spanish-language skills to enjoy *circo* (circus), *títeres* (puppets), and *rock para chicos* (kiddie rock). For listings, check the "Chicos" section in the back of local papers or the online magazine *Revista Planetario* (⊕*www.revista planetario.com.ar*).

Street performers abound on squares and pedestrian malls, around outdoor markets, and even on the subway. The Abasto and Solar de la Abadía malls have supervised play rooms where you can leave little ones while you shop.

FREE (OR ALMOST FREE)

The devalued peso makes Buenos Aires a bargain. But if you really do need to save every centavo, there are plenty of ways to make cheap even cheaper.

Free Art

It costs absolutely nothing to visit what is arguably the best collection of Argentine art in the world: Recoleta's **Museo Nacional de Bellas Artes** is free all week. Entrance to most other state-run museums is less than a dollar or two, but serious penny-pinchers can schedule their trip around free days. Take in antique furnishings and neoclassical architecture in Recoleta at the **Museo Nacional de Arte Decorativo,** free on Tuesday.

Wednesday is good for the Argentine art and handicrafts of the **Museo de Artes Plásticas Eduardo Sívori**; it's in the middle of the Palermo Woods, so you can combine your visit with a picnic lunch. Check out colonial art downtown in Retiro free of charge on Thursday at the **Museo de Arte Hispanoamericano Isaac Fernández Blanco.** The one serious artistic saving you can make is at the **MALBA,** in Palermo, which waives its 14-peso entry fee on Wednesday—expect to compete for floor space, though.

Browsing the choice contemporary Argentine art displayed in galleries like **Galería Ruth Benzacar** in Microcentro, **Daniel Abate** and **Rubbers** in Recoleta, and **Braga Menéndez** in Palermo Hollywood is totally free, although you'd fork out thousands to buy any of it. Try Palermo Viejo's **Ernesto Catena Fotografía Contemporánea** for contemporary photography, gratis.

Free History

It costs thousands to spend an afterlife in the **Cementerio de la Recoleta** but nothing to spend an afternoon or morning there. San Telmo is the best barrio for a free local history lesson: churches and traditional houses (many now antiques shops) are some of the historic buildings open to the public. Public protests have made Plaza de Mayo a living history site. Nearby is **La Manzana de Las Luces,** a colonial Jesuit complex, where entrance is scandalously cheap. The two-hour historical walks run by tour group **Eternautas** in different parts of town only cost 7 pesos.

Cheap Entertainment

During January and February, there are free outdoor concerts and festivals in parks around the city, usually showcasing local rock, folk, and tango groups. Wednesday is half-price day at every cinema in town; many also do cut-price tickets Monday through Thursday and for the first screening of each day.

Instead of forking out hundreds at a fancy "for export" tango show, head to a low-key *milonga (⇨Tango in Chapter 4, After Dark).* The cover charge is usually only 10 or 15 pesos, drinks are cheap, dancing is excellent, and the experience is authentic. Tangoing street performers also abound on Calle Florida, in Plazas Dorrego and Serrano, and around the Caminito.

MASTER CLASS

Learn Spanish

Language tourism has boomed in Buenos Aires since the devaluation of the peso, and schools are popping up all over town. Many advertise online or in the *Buenos Aires Herald,* but be aware that not all employ qualified teachers. The city government tourism site (⊕*www.bue.gov.ar/servicios*) has listings of reliable schools, and below are some we recommend.

Two of the best-established Spanish schools are affiliated with the Universidad de Buenos Aires. Teaching levels at both are excellent and prices are reasonable, but be aware that you generally need to enroll in advance and to be available for level-testing several days before classes start. The **Centro Universitario de Idiomas** (⊕*www.cui.edu.ar/secretaria/espanol*) runs regular four-week (three hours per weekday) and intensive two-week (six hours per weekday) courses that start at the beginning of each month in several locations. They also organize homestays and cultural activities. The classes at the **Laboratorio de Idiomas** (⊕*www.idiomas.filo.uba.ar/extranjeros/ingles/extranjeros.htm*) are popular with exchange students, but less practical for short-term stays. Semester-long courses of four hours per week start in March and August; intensive four-week courses of 15 hours per week start every two months. They also run a Spanish certification program.

The approach at the nonprofit teaching organization **Asociación Argentina de Docentes de Español** (⊕*www.espanol.org.ar*) is ideal if you're interested in grammar as well as communicating. Private language school **Academia Buenos Aires** (⊕*www.academiabuenosaires.com*) stands out for the range and flexibility of its classes. They also offer combination Spanish and tango courses.

The lively four-day intro courses at **Español Andando** (⊕*www.espanol-andando.com.ar*) take place entirely on the streets of Buenos Aires: a lesson on transport culminates with getting real information from a ticket salesperson, for example. The level is pitched for beginners.

Via Hispana (⊕*www.viahispana.com*) is a friendly laid-back private school with branches in Buenos Aires, Mendoza, Salta, and Bariloche. They can tailor language packages around your trip. Tango, literature, and cinema classes are add-ons, and homestays can also be arranged.

Learn Food & Wine

A local chef runs Latin American cookery classes at **Try2Cook** (⊕*www.try2cook.com*), based in the southern suburb of Adrogué. Argentine options include making empanadas and doing a full-blown *asado* (local-style barbecue). **Maneras Argentinas** (⊕*www.manerasargentinas.com.ar*) runs food- and wine-related courses, including cookery classes, a *mate* appreciation class, and wine-tastings.

Award-winning sommeliers lead wine-tasting classes at the **Centro Argentino de Vinos y Espirituosas** (⊕*www.tryvino.com*). Classes last 1½ hours, and you can combine several into a short course. A friendly group of young sommeliers behind **Buenos Vinos** (⊕*www.buenos-vinos.com*) run weekly tastings in Las Cañitas and organizes tailor-made wine classes.

For information on Tango classes, see "The Dance of Buenos Aires" in Chapter 4, After Dark.

WHO ARE THESE PEOPLE?

Buenos Aires has some lively inhabitants. Here are a few things you can expect of them:

It's All in the Hands

Like their Italian ancestors, many porteños gesture, rather than speak, half of their conversation. Brushing your chin outward with your hand means "I have no idea." Bunching up your fingers is "What on earth are you talking about?" Pulling down the skin under one eye says "Watch out."

Getting Physical

Porteños greet each other with an effusive kiss on the cheek (always to the left) and look for other opportunities that allow displays of affection. Even men follow this pattern and laugh at foreign males who refuse to do so, saying that they're insecure in their masculinity.

Hey Good-Looking

Locals claim porteño women are the most beautiful in the world, and, in tribute, the men have perfected the *piropo* (catcall). Comments range from corny compliments to highly witty—and mildly offensive—wordplays. Follow local girls' cues and take it in stride.

Sweets for the Sweet

Even the tiniest espresso arrives with four packets of sugar (or sweetener), just one testament to the local sweet tooth. *Dulce de leche* (a gooey milk-caramel spread) is another. It's practically a food group. Not only does it come in many desserts, but porteños also spread it on toast and—in the privacy of their kitchens—eat spoonfuls straight from the jar.

A Different Language

Porteños speak a very local version of Spanish. Instead of *"tú"* for "you," the

> ### DID YOU KNOW?
>
> Roughly 85% of the Argentine population is of European origin. Indeed, Buenos Aires locals refer to themselves as *porteños* because many of their forebears arrived by ship to this *port* town.

archaic *"vos"* form is used, and "ll" and "y" are pronounced like "sh." A singsong accent owes a lot to Italian immigrants; indeed, an Italian-influenced slang—called *lunfardo*—is ever present.

Doggy Style

Porteños are big dog-lovers. Professional *paseaperros* (dog walkers) wander with packs of well-dressed hounds anchored to their waists. Most porteños seem to have excellent poop radar, too: though the streets are filled with dog mess, you rarely see anyone step in it.

Driving You Crazy

Crossing the street is an extreme sport: roads are packed, traffic rules are openly flaunted, drinking and driving is practically a norm, and porteños think seat belts are for sissies. Sadly, traffic accidents are the biggest cause of death in the city, but that hasn't caused local habits to change.

Rules are Made to Be Broken

Most porteños see laws, rules, and regulations as quaint concepts invented mainly to give them the satisfaction of finding a way around. Displaying *viveza criolla* (literally "native cunning" but really "rule-breaking ingenuity") is a matter of national pride.

ALL OF THE COW BUT THE MOO

Argentina is the world's capital of beef, and Buenos Aires the capital of Argentina. So does Buenos Aires have the world's best steak?

It's hard to say no after your first bite into a tender morsel of deeply flavored, grass-fed beef, carefully charred by an open fire. Indeed, aside from the *estancias* (ranches) on the pampas grasslands themselves, Buenos Aires is probably the best place to eat in a *parrilla* (steak house). That said, it can be difficult, upon a first glance at the bewildering menu of a parrilla, to know where to begin. Merely speaking Spanish isn't enough: entire books have been written attempting to pin down which cuts of meat in Argentina correspond to which ones in the United States and Europe. There's much disagreement. The juicy *bife de chorizo,* for example, the king of Argentine steaks, is translated by some as a bone-in sirloin, by others as a rump steak—and it's not as if "sirloin steak" is well defined to begin with.

Don't worry about definitions. If you order a *parrillada*—everything but the kitchen sink—a sizzling platter will be brought to you. Don't be timid about trying the more-unfamiliar pieces. The platter will usually include a salty, juicy link or two of *chorizo* (a large, spicy sausage), and a collection of *achuras* (innards), which some first-timers struggle with. King among them is the gently spicy and oozingly delicious *morcilla* (blood sausage—like the British black pudding or the French *boudin noir*); give it a chance. Even more challenging are the chewy *chinchulines* (coils of small intestine), which are best when crisped on the outside, and the strongly flavored *riñones* (kidneys). Although *mollejas* (sweetbreads) aren't usually part of a parrillada spread

(they're more expensive), don't miss their unforgettable taste and fatty, meltingly rich texture, like a meatier version of foie gras. You'll also want to try the rich *provoleta* (grilled provolone cheese sprinkled with olive oil and oregano) and garlic-soaked grilled red peppers.

You can also skip the ready-made parrillada and instead order à la carte, as the locals often do. You might try the *vacio* (flank steak, roughly translated), a common cut that is flavorful but can also be tough, especially if overcooked. You may instead be seduced by the *lomo* (tenderloin or filet mignon), the softest and priciest cut, and like the immortal *bife de chorizo,* always a safe bet. Both of those steaks are better when requested rare (*"vuelta y vuelta"*), or, at the least, medium-rare (*"jugoso"*).

But the true local favorite is the inimitable *asado de tira,* a rack of beef short ribs often cooked on a skewer over an open fire. Done properly, the asado brandishes the meatiest grass-fed flavor of all. As for accompaniments, the classics are a mix-and-match salad and/or french fries. And don't forget that delicious Argentine red wine; Malbecs and Cabernets both pair well with the deeply flavored meat. And though the first time you visit a parrilla the mountain of meat might seem mind-bogglingly high, chances are that by the time you leave, you'll be cleaning your plate and gnawing at the bones with the best of them.

–Robin Goldstein

TANGO

"Life is a *milonga* (dance hall)," says one famous tango. "Life is an absurd wound," goes another. "I'm dying, dying just to dance," cries a third. When it comes to tango, passions ride high. Whether you experience it through impassioned dancing or tortured lyrics, you'll find a mix of nostalgia, violence, and sensuality that reflects this city's spirit.

THE DANCE

At the turn of the 19th century, immigrants in Buenos Aires' La Boca neighborhood began sharing rhythms and dance steps from their homelands. There's no consensus on what elements of tango come from where, but many agree it's a fusion of African-Uruguayan candombe, Spanish-Cuban habanera, and polkas and mazurkas.

Tango's mood is said to be one of homesickness or nostalgia. Often, those who learn tango in a dance school before they come to Buenos Aires will be homesick for the moves they learned; here tango is all improvisation and subtlety and the rules are always changing.

There are plenty of English-speaking instructors and pre-milonga practice sessions to get you up to speed on tango Buenos Aires style. When you're ready, choose a milonga depending on the atmosphere you're looking for. For more, *see* "The Dance of Buenos Aires" feature, *and* Instruction *and* Milongas *under* Tango, *in* Chapter 4, After Dark.

THE SHOWS

For those who prefer a more-passive appreciation of this fanciest of footwork, fear not: there are options that won't require significant coordination. For many, the tango experience begins and ends with *cena-shows*. These include drinks and a three-course dinner, and are entirely aimed at tourists (the only locals are businesspeople entertaining clients). Some are flashy affairs known as *tango de fantasía* in expensive, purpose-built clubs; expect sequined costumes, gelled hairdos, and high-kicking moves. Others are relatively lower-key in older venues that once catered to porteños before tango tourism took off.

Best Bets for Shows

Not all shows are created equal; below are a few suggestions to guide you. For more details *see* Chapter 4, After Dark.

Atmospheric surroundings: Bar Sur for the worn checkered floor and old-world bar; **Maison Dandi Royal** for the Art Nouveau architecture.

Blowing the bank: Rojo Tango for the gorgeous surroundings—and tangoers; **Madero Tango** for varied, professional performances and first-rate food.

Least tacky: Querandí for classic café surroundings and polished shows; **El Viejo Almacén** for pedigree (founded by tango legend Edmundo Rivero) and high energy.

Shamelessly tacky: Señor Tango for fishnetted glitziness and over-the-top embracing of stereotypes.

THE MUSIC

The average porteño is much more likely to go see tango musicians than tango dancers. Offerings range from orchestras churning out tunes as was done in Carlos Gardel's day to sexy, bluesy vocals from divas like Adriana Varela to pared-down revisitings of the tango underworld by young groups like 34 Puñaladas or Dema

y su Orquesta Petitero. For tango that packs a punch, look out for the electronic fusion of groups like Gotan Project and Bajofondo Tango Club.

Best Bets for Music

The places below are reviewed fully in Chapter 4, After Dark.

Most laid back: Centro Cultural Torquato Tasso for a hip, clubby vibe; **Bar de Roberto,** for gin-guzzling old-timers and impromptu performances.

Most traditional: Café Homero for performances by classic orchestras and divas; **Teatro Bar Tuñón** for their sophisticated take on traditional dinner shows; **Gran Café Tortoni,** for the historic setting and consistently excellent performances.

Most modern: Ciudad Cultural Konex, for edgy young bands; **La Trastienda,** for the occasional electrotango show.

Tango Playlist

The tango never shook off its edgy origins: early lyrics ran the gamut from lewd to pornographic. Later songs are peppered with references to infidelity, crime, and cocaine. And there's tango's place in politics: some have encoded criticisms of governments, others are piercing social commentaries. For many, the richly metaphoric use of street slang elevates tango to a poetic form. Here's a selection to get you started. You can download most of them from iTunes.

Late 1800s–Early 1900s: *La Morocha*, Roberto Firpo y Su Quarteto Alma de Bohemio

1910s–20s: *La Cumparsita*, Juan D'Arienzo y Su Orquesta; *Caminito*, Agustín Magaldi

1930s (The Golden Age): *El día que me quieras*, *Por una Cabeza*, and *Volver*, Carlos Gardel; *Se dice de mí*, Tita Merello; *Cambalache*, Agustín Irusta

1940s–50s: *Naranjo en flor*, Floreal Ruiz; *La Última Curda*, Edmundo Rivero; *Que me van a hablar de amor*, Julio Sosa

1960s–80s: *Adiós Nonino*, Astor Piazzolla; *Balada para un Loco,* Roberto Goyeneche

Today: *Garganta con Arena*, Adriana Varela; *Santa María (del Buen Ayre)*, Gotan Project; *Canción Desesperada*, Orquesta Típica Fernández Fierro

CARLOS GARDEL

Carlos Gardel (1887 or 1890–1935)

Toting his trademark fedora, the face of Carlos Gardel oozes charm on walls and shop signs all over Buenos Aires, where he grew up and became a tango superstar. He repeatedly toured, hobnobbing with the likes of Charlie Chaplin and Josephine Baker. Gardel died tragically on June 24, 1935, at the height of his fame, when his plane crashed in Medellín, Colombia. Thousands followed his funeral cortege along Avenida Corrientes. Pay your respects at his grave in the Cementerio de Chacarita or at the Museo Casa Carlos Gardel (⇨ the listings *under* Recoleta & Almagro *in* Chapter 2, Neighborhoods).

GOOD MARKETING SKILLS

The array of open-air *ferias* (markets) in Buenos Aires testifies to the fact that locals enjoy stall-trawling as much as visitors. Argentina holds its craftspeople, both traditional and contemporary, in high esteem. The selections include not only crafts but also art, antiques, curios, clothing, jewelry, and housewares, and stalls are often attended by the artists themselves. Bargaining isn't the norm, although you may get a small discount for buying lots of items.

The **Feria de San Pedro Telmo** packs a small San Telmo square every Sunday. Elbow your way through the crowds to pick through antiques and curios of varying vintages as well as tango memorabilia, or watch dolled-up professional tango dancers perform on the surrounding cobbled streets. The unofficial "stalls" (often just a cloth on the ground) of young craftspeople stretch several blocks up Defensa, away from the market proper. As it gets dark, the square turns into a milonga, where quick-stepping locals show you how it's done. ✉*Plaza Dorrego, Humberto I y Defensa, San Telmo* ☎*11/4331–9855* ⊕*www.feria desantelmo.com* ☉*Sun. 10–dusk* Ⓜ*E to Independencia, then walk 9 blocks east along Independencia to Defensa. Alternatively, A to Plaza de Mayo, D to Catedral, E to Bolívar, then walk 8 blocks south on Bolívar.*

In the heart of colorful La Boca, **Feria de Artesanías de la Plaza Vuelta de Rocha (Caminito)** showcases local artists all week long. You can find attractive port scenes in watercolors as well as stylish photographs of the neighborhood's old houses, though don't expect any budding Picassos. The market expands on weekends with stalls selling handicrafts and tacky souvenirs. As shoppers here are almost exclusively tourists, prices tend to be overambitious—sometimes irritatingly so. ✉*Av. Pedro de Mendoza and Caminito, La Boca* ☉*Art market daily 10–6; craft market weekends 10–6.*

The sprawling **Feria Artesanal de la Recoleta** winds through several linked squares outside the Recoleta Cemetery. Artisans sell handmade clothes, jewelry, and housewares as well as traditional crafts. ✉*Avs. Libertador and Pueyrredón, La Recoleta* ☎*11/4343–0309* ☉*Weekends 10–dusk.*

The business conducted in hip Palermo Viejo's **Feria de Plaza Serrano** rivals that done in the neighborhood's trendy boutiques. In a small square—which is actually round—artisans sell wooden toys, ceramics, and funky jewelry made of stained glass or vintage buttons. This is also a great place to buy art: the railings around a playground here act as an open-air gallery for Palermo artists, and organizers control the quality of art on display. The feria continues unofficially at many nearby bars, which push their tables and chairs aside to make room for clothing and accessory designers: expect to find anything from cute cotton underwear and one-off T-shirts to clubbing dresses. Quality is often low, but so are prices. ✉*Plazoleta Cortázar (Plaza Serrano) at Honduras and Serrano, Palermo Viejo* ☉*Weekends 11–dusk.*

Far from the tourist trail, the sheltered **Mercado de las Pulgas** *(*Flea Market*)* is packed with furniture on its second (or third or fourth) time around. You won't come across any Louis XV in the warren of stalls, but original pieces from the 1940s, '50s, and '60s may turn out to be (relative) bargain investments. Lighting

up your life is also a cinch: choose from the many Venetian-glass chandeliers, or go for a chrome-and-acrylic mushroom lamp. If your taste is more rustic, there's also a sizable selection of hefty farmhouse-style tables and cabinets in oak and pine. Don't be deceived by the stalls' precarious-looking set-up: vendors are used to dealing with big-name local customers and can often arrange overseas shipping. At this writing, the market was operating from the nearby M2 warehouse at Conde and Dorrego while the city government overhauls the original premises. ⊠*Alvarez Thomas 000 block, between Dorrego and Concepción Arenales, Palermo Hollywood* ⊙*Daily 10–dusk.*

On weekends upscale craftspeople transform a posh Belgrano square into the **Feria de Artesanías de Belgrano.** German silver is a popular material here, for both jewelry and items like divided boxes for storing tea bags. You'll also find leather sandals and clogs, knitted ponchos, and wooden toys. Around Christmas this is a great place to buy nativity scenes and tree ornaments. ⊠*Juramento and Av. Cuba, Belgrano* ⊙*Weekends 10–dusk.*

One of the last surviving European-style indoor food markets in town, the **Feria Modelo de Belgrano** is a gourmet's dream. The building has stood more or less unchanged since 1891, and its 30 stalls are the ideal place to ogle top national produce like Patagonian trout and lamb, porcini mushrooms, and stuffed meats. The cheese stalls sell creamy ricotta by the kilo and chunky wheels of *queso Mar del Plata,* an eminently snackable Gouda-style cheese. ⊠*Juramento 2527, at Ciudad de la Paz, Belgrano* ⊙*Mon.–Sat. 8–1 and 5–8:30, Sun. 8–1.*

IN THE MARKET FOR SOME CULTURE

Jewelry and *mates* aren't the only things porteños stalk markets for: books and music, prohibitively expensive in Argentina, are also top finds. Kiosklike stalls on the traffic island of Avenida Santa Fe west of Plaza Italia (Ⓜ*D to Plaza Italia*) do a brisk trade in used and cut-price new books. You occasionally find gems amid the piles of scratched LPs on sale at Parque Rivadavia (Ⓜ*A to Acoyte*), but what locals really come for are the pirate CDs and DVDs for 6–10 pesos. (They browse innocent-looking folders, tell vendors the codes of what they want, and 10 minutes later are paying for an unassuming plastic bag of goodies.)

The best handicrafts in town and a vaguely authentic gaucho atmosphere make the trek west to the traditional **Feria de Mataderos** well worth it. Stalls sell great-value mates, *asado* knives, *boleadoras* (gaucho lassos), and leather goods, and there are usually traditional dance performances. Look out for real-life gauchos wearing woolen berets, scarves, and baggy pants wandering around with a horse or two in tow. Part of the experience is chomping through a *vaciopán* (dripping steak sandwich) from the immense barbecue; wash it down with a plastic beaker of *vino patero* (semi-sweet red wine). The subte doesn't go to Mataderos; take Bus 126 from outside the Retiro train station, or take a taxi (about 25 pesos from downtown). ⊠*Lisandro de la Torre at Av. de los Corrales, Mataderos* ⊙*Sun. 10–dusk.*

FASHION FORWARD

The stars of Argentine fashion have much in common with the country's top soccer players: they're as highly trained and technically proficient as their European counterparts, but there's a freshness and flair to their game that the weary old countries just don't have. And, of course, getting them into your wardrobe (or onto your team) is a relative bargain.

On the Runway

Technically speaking, **Buenos Aires Fashion Week** (⊕*www.bafweek.com*) is two fashion half-weeks. Fall–winter collections are presented in March, and spring–summer in September, at La Rural convention center. Entrance costs around 15 pesos, and there's a good chance of getting in to most shows. Plus, the clement exchange rate means you might actually be able to buy the creations you see.

Each year local trend spotters and international buyers descend hungrily on the **Feria Puro Diseño** (⊕*www.feriapurodiseno.com.ar*), an expo of works by up-and-coming local designers held at La Rural convention center. Clothing and accessories are the focus, but housewares, lighting, and textiles are also included.

Big in Buenos Aires

There's no question who makes the best little black dresses—and sharp black suits—in town. In fact just about every garment that comes off **Pablo Ramírez's** (⊕*www.pabloramirez.com.ar*) cutting table is black, but they're also exquisitely tailored, with waspish waists and structured draping that oozes '40s Hollywood glamour. He has designed costumes for several highbrow theater productions, and his clothes have been exhibited in three Buenos Aires museums.

Jessica Trosman (⊕*www.trosman.com*) has shown collections in Paris, been pronounced one of the 250 most influential people in the future of fashion by *i-D* magazine, and had her work featured in Taschen's *Fashion Now 2* and Phaidon's *Sample* books. Her signature fabric is richly colored cotton T-shirting, which she transforms into highly draped tops and dresses whose futuristic simplicity is both chic and slightly strange.

It's not just fabulous clothes **Martín Churba** creates, but also the textiles they're made of (his brand name, **Tramando** [⊕*www.tramando.com*], means both "weaving" and "plotting"). His pleats, floaty folds, and attention to detail recall the best Japanese designers, and indeed, Churba has opened three stores in Tokyo. Another in New York's Meatpacking District has sealed his stellar status.

Ask other top local designers whose work they admire, and **Vero Ivaldi**'s (⊕*www.veroivaldi.com*) name is sure to come up. Her perfect cuts scream high design, but they're also incredibly flattering, even on full figures. Full skirts and nipped-in waists hint of the 1950s in her prêt-à-porter, but take on a luxurious, grown-up Alice-in-Wonderful appeal in her couture. Best of all, her designs look very very expensive, but are surprisingly affordable.

Min Agostini (⊕*www.minagostini.com.ar*) "builds" her designs on mannequins, and the results are tunics, dresses, and wraps that look like a *Star Wars* wardrobe collision between Princess Amidala and the whole Jedi crew. Her clothes have been displayed in the windows of Harrods London.

THE SPORTING LIFE

Tens of thousands of ecstatic fans jump up and down in unison, roaring modified cumbia classics to the beat of carnival drums; crazed supporters sway atop 10-foot fences between the stands and the field as they drape the barbed wire with their team's flags; showers of confetti and sulfurous smoke from colorful flares fill the air. The occasion? Just another day's *fútbol* (soccer) match in Argentina—and all this before the game even begins.

For most Argentines soccer is a fervent passion. The national team is one of the world's best, and the World Cup can bring the country to a standstill as workers gather in cafés and bars to live out the nation's fate via satellite. Feelings also run high during the biannual local championships when rivalry between *hinchas* (fans) gets heated. In a country where people joke that if soccer great Diego Maradona were to run for president he'd win hands down, fútbol is the source of endless debate, fiery dispute, suicidal despair, love, and hate.

Matches are held year-round and are as exciting as they are dangerous. You're safest in the *platea* (preferred seating area), which costs anything from 20 to 150 pesos, depending on the importance of the match, rather than in the chaotic 14-peso *popular* (standing room) section. Be careful what you wear—fans carry their colors with pride, and not just on flags and team shirts. Expect to see painted faces, hundreds of tattoos, and even women's underwear with the colors of the best-known teams: Boca Juniors (blue and gold) and their archrivals River Plate (red and white), as well as Independiente (red), Racing (light blue and white), and San Lorenzo (red and blue).

The no-man's-land that separates each team's part of the stadium, the drum-banging antics of hooligan mafias known as the *barra brava*, and the heavy police presence at matches are a reminder of how seriously the game is taken.

You can buy tickets at long lines at the stadiums up to four days before matches or from the teams' official Web sites. Entrepreneuring tour company **Go Football** (☎11/4816–2681 ⊕*www.gofootball.com.ar*) takes the hassle out of catching a match. Their "tours" include transport, well-located platea seats, and an accompanied knowledgeable, soccer-loving guide.

Walls exploding with huge, vibrant murals of insurgent workers, famous inhabitants of La Boca, and fútbol greats splashed in blue and gold let you know that the **Estadio Boca Juniors** is at hand. The stadium that's also known as La Bombonera (meaning candy box, supposedly because the fans' singing reverberates as it would inside a candy tin) is the home of Argentina's most popular club. Boca Juniors' history is completely tied to the port neighborhood. The nickname, *xeneizes,* is a mangling of *genovés* (Genovese), reflecting the origins of most immigrants to the Boca area. Blue and gold decks the stadium's fiercely banked seating.

Inside the stadium is **El Museo de la Pasión Boquense** (The Museum of Boca Passion), a modern, two-floor space that chronicles Boca's rise from neighborhood club in 1905 to its current position as one of the world's best teams. Trophies, videos, shirts, match histories, and a hall of fame make up the rest of the circuit, together with a huge mural of Maradona, Boca's most beloved player. Everything you need to Boca up your life—from

THE SPORTING LIFE

team shirts to bed linen, school folders to G-strings—is available in the gift shop. You can buy cheaper copies in shops and stalls outside the stadium.

The extensive stadium tour is worth the extra money. Lighthearted guides take you all over the stands as well as to press boxes, locker rooms, underground tunnels, and the emerald grass of the field itself. ⊠*Brandsen 805, at del Valle Iberlucea, La Boca, C1161AAQ* ☏*11/4309–4700 stadium, 11/4362–1100 museum* ⊕*www.museoboquense.com.ar* ⊠*Museum: 14 pesos. Stadium: 14 pesos. Museum and stadium: 22 pesos* ⊘*Museum daily 10–6 except when Boca plays at home; stadium tours hourly 11–5; English usually available, call ahead.*

Horse Around

Combine the horsey inclinations of Argentina's landed elite with the country's general sporting prowess, and what do you get? All 12 of the world's best polo players. The game may be as posh as it gets, but most local sports fans take begrudging pride in the stunning athletic showmanship displayed by *polistas* like 10-goaler Adolfo Cambiaso or Ralph Lauren pinup Nacho Figueras.

Major polo tournaments take place at the **Campo Argentino de Polo** (*Argentine Polo Field* ⊠*Av. del Libertador 4000, at Dorrego, Palermo, C1426BWN*). Admission to autumn (March–May) and spring (September–December) matches is free. The much-heralded Campeonato Argentino Abierto (Argentine Open Championship) takes place in November; admission runs 15 to 200 pesos. You can buy tickets in advance by phone through **Ticketek** (☏*11/5237–7200* ⊕*www.ticketek.com.ar*) or at the polo field on the day

of the event. For polo match information contact the **Asociación Argentina de Polo** (☏*11/4331–4646* ⊕*www.aapolo.com*).

As well as polo players and polo ponies, Argentina also breeds swift racehorses, prized throughout the world.

Catch the Thoroughbreds in action at the **Hipódromo Argentino de Palermo** (⊠*Av. del Libertador 4101, Palermo, C1426BWC* ☏*11/4777–9009*). In Argentina's golden days the 100,000-capacity grandstand was always full and even now major races pull a crowd.

Tee Up

The 18-hole municipal course, **Campo de Golf de la Ciudad de Buenos Aires** (⊠*Tornquist 6397, Palermo* ☏*11/4772–7576*), is between Palermo and Belgrano. It's open Tuesday through Sunday from 7:30 to 5 for a 20-peso greens fee on weekdays, and a 30-peso fee on weekends.

If you want a range with a view, **Costa Salguero Golf** (⊠*Av. Costanera Rafael Obligado at Jerónimo Salguero, Palermo* ☏*11/4805–4734* ⊕*www.costasalguerogolf.com.ar*) is right on the river and includes a driving range (50 balls for 10 pesos), pitch 'n' putt (12 pesos for 18 holes) as well as club and ball hire. Access to the greens is free, and the course is open Monday from noon to 9:30, other weekdays from 8:30 to 9:30, and weekends from 8 to 8:30. For more information, contact the **Asociación Argentina de Golf** (*Argentine Golf Association* ☏*11/4394–2743* ⊕*www.aag.com.ar*).

A PASSIONATE HISTORY   by Victoria Patience

If there's one thing Argentines have learned from their history, it's that there's not a lot you can count on. Fierce—often violent—political, economic, and social instability have been the only constants in the story of a people who seem never to be able to escape that famous Chinese curse, "May you live in interesting times."

Although most accounts of Argentine history begin 500 years ago with the arrival of the conquistadors, humans have been living in what is now Argentina for around 13,000 years. They created the oldest recorded art in South America—a cave of handprints in Santa Cruz, Patagonia (c. 7500 ʙ#)—and eventually became part of the Inca Empire.

Spanish and Portuguese sailors came in the early 16th century, including Ferdinand Magellan, who sailed along the country's coast. The Spanish were forced out 300 years later by colony-sick locals hungry for independence. Internal conflict and civil war wracked the early republic, which swung constantly back and forth between democratic governments intent on modernizing the country and corrupt feudal systems.

Spanish and Italian immigrants arrived in the 20th century, changing Argentina's population profile forever. Unstable politics characterized the rest of the century, which saw the rise and fall of Juan Perón and a series of increasingly bloody military dictatorships. Over 25 years of uninterrupted democracy have passed since the last junta fell, an achievement Argentines value hugely.

(left) Ferdinand Magellan (c. 1480–1521)
(right) Stamp featuring Evita

TIMELINE

Magellan sails down
Argentinean coast

Juan de Garay
founds Buenos Aires

PRE-1500s | INCA INVASION | 1500 | 1600

(top left) Cave paintings, Cueva de las Manos, Santa Cruz; (top right) Río de la Plata aboriginals, pictured by Hendrick Ottsen; (bottom) Relief detail, San Ignacio Miní Mission, Misiones Province.

PRE–1500
PRE-CONQUEST/INCA

Argentina's original inhabitants were a diverse group of indigenous peoples. Their surroundings defined their lifestyles: nomadic hunter-gatherers lived in Patagonia and the Pampas, while the inhabitants of the northeast and northwest were largely farming communities. The first foreign power to invade the region was the Inca Empire, in the 15th century. Its roads and tribute systems extended over the entire northwest, reaching as far south as some parts of modern-day Mendoza.

1500–1809
BIRTH OF THE COLONY

European explorers first began to arrive at the River Plate area in the early 1500s, and in 1520 Ferdinand Magellan sailed right down the coast of what is now Argentina and on into the Pacific. Buenos Aires was founded twice: Pedro de Mendoza's 1536 attempt led to starving colonists turning to cannibalism before running for Asunción; Juan de Garay's attempt in 1580 was successful. Conquistadors from Peru, Chile, Paraguay, and of course Spain, founded other cities. The whole area was part of the Viceroyalty of Peru until 1776, when the Spanish king

Carlos III decreed present-day Argentina, Uruguay, Paraguay, and most of Bolivia to be the Viceroyalty of the Río de la Plata. Buenos Aires became the main port and the only legal exit point for silver from Potosí. Smuggling grew as fast as the city itself. In 1806–07 English forces tried twice to invade Argentina. Militia from Buenos Aires fought them off with no help from Spain, inciting ideas of independence among *criollos* (Argentine-born Spaniards, who had fewer rights than those born in Europe).

(left) Monument to General
San Martín; (right) Julio Roca

1810—1860s

BIRTH OF THE NATION: INDEPENDENCE AND THE CONSTITUTION

Early-19th-century proto-Argentines were getting itchy for independence. The United States and France had provided inspiration with their revolutions, and when Napoleon defeated Spain, the time seemed ripe. On the May 25th, 1810, Buenos Aires' leading citizens, armed only with umbrellas against the rain, ousted the last Spanish viceroy. A series of elected juntas and triumvirates followed while military heroes José de San Martín and Manuel Belgrano won battles that allowed the Provincias Unidas de América del Sur to declare independence in Tucumán on July 9, 1816. San Martín went on to liberate Chile and Peru.

Political infighting marked the republic's first 40 years. The 1819 constitution established a centralist state run from Buenos Aires, a position known as *unitario*, but landowners and warlords in the provinces wanted a federal state. The issue was settled when dictator Juan Manuel de Rosas came to power: from 1829 to 1852 he killed or exiled opposition, censored the press, and made red lapel ribbons obligatory (sky-blue and white were unitario colors).

1860—1942

RISE OF THE MODERN STATE

Argentina staggered back and forth between political extremes on its rocky road to modern statehood. Relatively liberal leaders alternated with corrupt warlord types. The most infamous of these is Julio Roca, who effectively stopped proper voting and undertook a military campaign that killed off most of Argentina's remaining indigenous population. He also started the immigration drive that brought millions of Europeans to Argentina between 1870 and 1930.

TIMELINE

Coup ends
privitization

Perón made
president

1930   1940   1950

(top left) Juan Perón and his wife Eva Duarte
attend Independence Day ceremonies, May
30th, 1951; (top right) Juan Perón addressing
the Congress. Buenos Aires, May 6th, 1949;
(bottom) Perón in discussion c. 1950

THE RISE AND FALL OF PERONISM

1942–1973

A 1943 coup ended a decade of privatization that had caused the gap between rich and poor to grow exponentially. One of the soldiers involved was a little-known general named Juan Domingo Perón. He rose through the ranks of the government as quickly as he had through those of the army. Uneasy about his growing popularity, other members of the military government imprisoned him, provoking a wave of uprisings that led to Perón's release and swept him to the presidency as head of the newly formed labor party in 1946. In the middle of his campaign, he quietly married the young B-movie actress he'd been living with, Eva Duarte, soon to be known universally as "Evita." Their idiosyncratic, his-'n'-hers politics were socialism and fascism, and hinged on a massive personality cult. While he was busy improving worker's rights and trying to industrialize Argentina, she set about press-ganging Argentina's landed elite into funding her social aid program. Their tireless efforts to close the gap between rich and poor earned them the slavish devotion of Argentina's poor and the passionate hatred of the rich. But everything began to go wrong when Evita died of uterine cancer in 1952. By 1955, a dwindling economy was grounds for Perón being ousted by another coup. For the next 18 years, both he and his party were illegal in Argentina—even mentioning his name could land you in prison.

(top) A British soldier and penguin on patrol in the Falkland Islands in 1983; (bottom) Argentina military junta during the Falkland's War: *(left to right)* Vice Admiral Jorge Anaya, President Leopoldo Galtieri, and Commander Basilio Lami Doso (June, 1982)

DICTATORSHIP, DIRTY WAR & THE FALKLANDS

1973–1982

The two civilian presidencies that followed both ended in fresh military coups until Perón was allowed to return in 1973. Despite turning his back on left-wing student and guerrilla groups who had campaigned for him in his absence, he still won another election by a landslide. However, one problematic year later, he died in office. His farcical successor was the vice-president, an ex-cabaret dancer known as Isabelita, who was also Perón's third wife. Her chaotic leadership was brought to an end in 1976 by yet another military coup. The succession of juntas that ruled the country called their bloody dictatorship a "process of national reorganization"; it would later become known as "the Dirty War." Much of the world seemingly ignored the actions of the Argentine government during its six-year reign of terror. Throughout the country, students, activists, and any other undesirable element were kidnapped and tortured in clandestine detention centers. Many victims' children were stolen and given up for adoption by pro-military families after their parents' bodies had been dumped in the River Plate. More than 30,000 people "disappeared" and thousands more went into exile. Government ministries were handed over to private businessmen. Massive corruption took external debt from $7 million to $66 million. In 1982, desperate for something to distract people with, the junta started war with Britain over the Islas Malvinas or Falkland Islands. The disastrous campaign lasted just four months and led to the downfall of the dictatorship.

TIMELINE

Falkland's War

Menem made president

State of Emergency declared

Cristina Kirchner made president

INFLATION REACHES 3,000% | 1990   ECONOMY IN TATTERS 2000   2010

(top) President Carlos Menem mobbed by the public; (top right) Riot police at protests about economic austerity measures in Córdoba, 2001; (bottom) Argentine riot police drag away a demonstrator near the Casa Rosada in Buenos Aires.

1982–1999

RETURN OF DEMOCRACY

Celebrations marked the return to democracy. The main players in the dictatorship went on trial, but received relatively small sentences. Inflation reached a terrifying 3,000% in 1988 and only stabilized when Carlos Menem became president the following year. Menem pegged the peso to the dollar, privatized services and resources, and even changed the constitution to extend his mandate. But despite an initial illusion of economic well-being, by the time Menem left office in 1999 poverty had skyrocketed, and the economy was in tatters.

2000—PRESENT

CRISIS & THE K YEARS

The longer-term results of Menem's policies came in December 2001, when the government tried to prevent a rush on funds by freezing all private savings accounts. Thousands of people took to the streets in protest; on December 20, the violent police response transformed the demonstrations into riots. President Fernando de la Rúa declared a state of emergency, then resigned, and was followed by four temporary presidents in almost as many days. When things finally settled, the peso had devaluated drastically, many people had lost their savings, and the future looked dark.

However, under the center-leftist government of Argentina's following president, Néstor Kirchner, the economy slowly reactivated. Unlike his predecessors, Kirchner openly expressed his abhorrence of the dictatorship and reopened trials of high-ranking military officials. In a rather bizarre turn of political affairs, he was succeeded by his wife, Cristina. Times may be better than a few years ago, but Argentines have lived through so many political ups and downs that they never take anything for granted.

MADE IN ARGENTINA

There's no doubt that Argentinians are an inventive lot. And we're not talking about their skill in arguing their way out of parking tickets: several things you might not be able to imagine life without started out in Argentina.

A bolígrafo (pen)

BALLPOINT PEN

Although Laszlo Josef Biro was born in Hungary and first patented the ballpoint pen in Paris, it wasn't until he launched his company in Argentina in 1943 that his invention began to attract attention. As such, Argentinians claim the world's most useful writing instrument as their own.

BLOOD TRANSFUSION

Before ER there was Luis Agote, an Argentinean doctor who, in 1914, was one of the first to perform a blood transfusion using stored blood (rather than doing a patient-to-patient transfusion). The innovation that made the process possible was adding sodium citrate, an anticoagulant, to the blood.

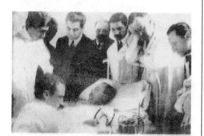

Luis Agote was one of the first to perform a nondirect blood transfusion, in Buenos Aires on November 9, 1914.

FINGERPRINTING

In 1891, Juan Vucetich, a Croatian-born officer of the Buenos Aires police force, came up with a system of classifying fingerprints. He went on to make the first-ever criminal arrest based on fingerprint evidence. Although his method has since been refined, it is still used throughout Latin America.

Puntos de los dedos (fingerprints)

- Other useful Argentinian claims to fame include the first working helicopter (1916); the first one-piece floor mop (1953); and the first one-use-only hypodermic syringe (1989).

Buenos Aires Neighborhoods

Recoleta Cemetery

WORD OF MOUTH

"We spent five days in Buenos Aires, which I thought was a good amount of time. We first thought we might take some day trips but soon realized there was more than enough in the city to occupy all our time. November was a perfect month to visit: the jacarandas were blooming, and the weather was sunny but not too hot. It was ideal for all the walking we did, exploring the different *barrios* (neighborhoods)."

—Lily3

By Victoria
Patience

INCREDIBLE FOOD, FRESH YOUNG DESIGNERS, and a thriving cultural scene—all these Buenos Aires has. Yet less-tangible things are at the heart of the city's sizzle—for one, the spirit of its inhabitants. Here, a flirtatious glance can be as passionate as a tango; a heated sports discussion as important as a world-class soccer match. It's this zest for life that's making Buenos Aires one of Latin America's hottest destinations.

Of course, the devalued peso is a draw, too. There have never been so many foreign visitors on the streets. New boutiques—and boutique hotels—seem to open daily. World-renowned architects are designing luxury housing projects aimed at international customers who visit and then decide to stay. Old houses, it seems, are coveted by arty expats in search of inspiration for that novel they want to write.

A booming tango revival means dance floors are alive again. And camera crews are now a common sight on street corners: low production costs and "Old World generic" architecture—hinting at many far-off cities but resembling none—are an appealing backdrop for European commercials. Women are taking more-prominent social roles, not least in the form of the first female president, Cristina Kirchner, elected in 2007. (She's technically the second female president, though she's the first woman *elected* to the position. When Perón died, his third wife, Isabelita, took over for a disastrous couple of years.) Recognized civil partnerships and a thriving scene make Buenos Aires a prime gay destination. And the country is finally seeking to bring the torturers of the Dirty War (as the 1976–82 dictatorship is often known) to justice.

Sadly, though the economic crisis of 2001 is in the past, there are increasing numbers of homeless people. Many *porteños* (as residents are called) seem to enjoy life to the fullest, but behind their warm welcomes and generosity is a deep-rooted pessimism at continuing financial instability.

Some things stay the same, though. Food, family, and *fútbol* (or fashion) are still the holy trinity for most porteños. Philosophical discussions and psychoanalysis—Buenos Aires has the largest number of psychoanalysts per capita of any city in the world—remain popular pastimes. And in the face of so much change, porteños still approach life with as much dramatic intensity as ever.

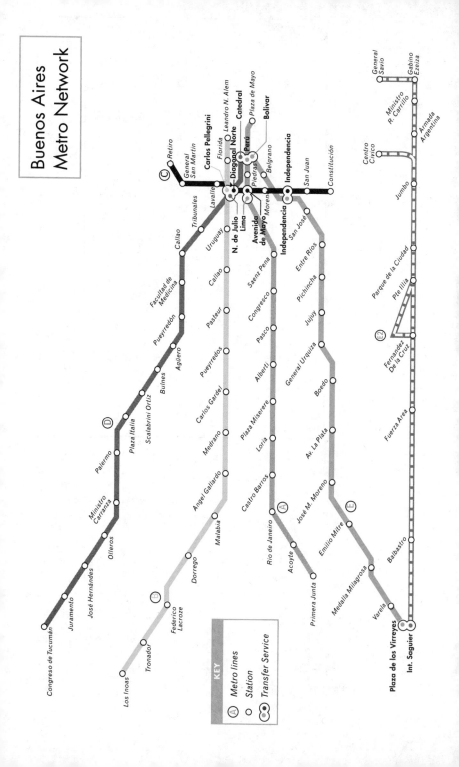

Buenos Aires Metro Network

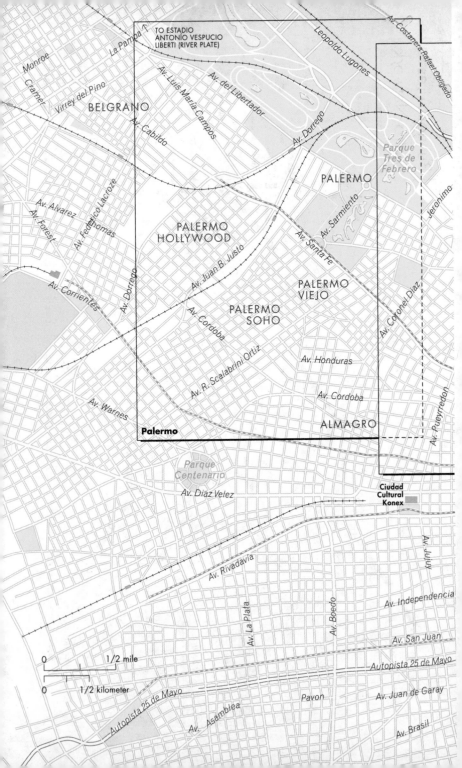

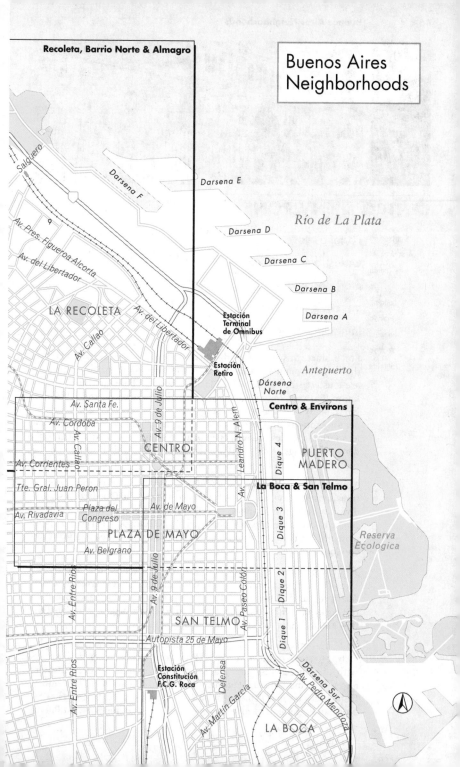

CENTRO & ENVIRONS

Sightseeing
★★★★★

Dining
★

Lodging
★★

Shopping
★★★

Nightlife
★

Porteños love to brag that Buenos Aires has the world's widest avenue (Avenida 9 de Julio), its best steak, and its most beautiful women. The place to decide if they're right is the city's heart, known simply as "El Centro," where many things merit superlatives.

For a start, this is one of the city's oldest areas. Plaza de Mayo is the original main square, and civic buildings both past and present are clustered between it and Plaza Congreso. Though you probably know Plaza de Mayo best from the balcony scene in the 1996 film *Evita*, many of Argentina's most historic events—including revolutions, demonstrations, and terrorist attacks—transpired around its axes. Bullet-marked facades, sidewalks embedded with plaques, and memorials where buildings once stood are reminders of all this history, and the protesters who fill the streets regularly are history in the making.

More-upbeat gatherings—open-air concerts, soccer victory celebrations, postelection reveling—take place around the Obelisco, a scaled-down Washington Monument look-alike that honors the founding of Buenos Aires. Inescapably phallic, it's the butt of local jokes about male insecurity in this oh-so-macho city. It's even dressed in a giant red condom each year on AIDS Awareness Day.

The town's most highbrow cultural events are hosted a few blocks away in the spectacular Teatro Colón, and the highest-grossing theatrical productions line Avenida Corrientes, whose sidewalks overflow on weekends with dolled-up locals. Argentina's biggest scandals center—the judicial district—is on nearby Tribunales.

Building buffs get their biggest kicks in this part of town, too. Architectural wonders of yesteryear—French-inspired domes and towers with Iberian accents—line grand avenues. Dreamy art deco theaters and severe, monumental Peronist constructions mark the 20th century. Contemporary masterpieces by such world-renowned architects as Sir Norman Foster and local boy César Pelli are fast filling adjacent Puerto

Madero. This onetime port area is now the city's swankiest district, with the most expensive real estate, hotels, and restaurants.

Office workers, shoppers, and sightseers fill Centro's streets each day. Traffic noise and driving tactics also reach superlative levels. Locals profess to hate the chaos; unrushed visitors get a buzz out of the bustle. Either way, Centro provokes extreme reactions.

TWO WAYS TO EXPLORE

A STREET THAT DEFINES A NEIGHBORHOOD

When porteños talk about **Florida** (pronounced flo-*ree*-da) they aren't referring to a vacation but rather a pedestrian street that crosses the Microcentro's heart. This downtown axis has fallen from grace and risen from its ashes at least as many times as Argentina's economy. Nothing sums up the chaotic Centro better than this riot of office workers, fast-food chains, boutiques, bookstores, and vendors selling (and haggling over) leather goods. You can wander it in an hour or so: start at the intersection with Diagonal Norte; a bench in shady Plaza San Martín will be your reward at the other end.

Like most of the banks that line the street, the **Bank Boston** building's 4-ton bronze doors are battered and paint-splattered—unhappy customers have been taking out their anger at *corralitos* (banks retaining their savings) since the economic crisis of 2001–02.

Witness Buenos Aires' careless attitude to building preservation on the corner of Florida and Avenida Corrientes, now home to Burger King. The sculpted Gothic windows above the signs are all that's left of the original facade. Buy a soda and drink it upstairs to check out the plaster molding and stained glass. Thankfully, a happier restoration process has left the soaring marble columns and stained-glass cupola of **Galería Güemes** gleaming. The tacky shops that fill the historic arcade do nothing to lessen the wow factor.

Milan's Galleria Vittorio Emanuele served as the model for **Galerías Pacífico,** designed during Buenos Aires' turn-of-the-20th-century golden age. Once the headquarters of the Buenos Aires–Pacific Railway, it's now a posh shopping mall and cultural center. Head to the central stairwell to see the allegorical murals painted by local greats Juan Carlos Castagnino, Antonio Berni, Cirilo Colmenio, Lino Spilimbergo, and Demetrio Urruchúa. The Centro Cultural Borges (⇨*also Art Galleries, below*), which hosts small international exhibitions and musical events, is on the mezzanine level. ⊠*Florida 753, Microcentro* ☎*11/5555–5100* ⊕*www.galeriaspacifico.com.ar* Ⓜ*B to Florida.*

PUERTO MADERO: A WORK IN PROGRESS

Nowhere in Buenos Aires is changing as fast as Puerto Madero. Before the 2001 economic crisis, this former port area was little more than abandoned warehouses and wasteland. Now it's home to some of Latin America's most expensive real estate and some of the most exciting buildings-to-be.

GETTING ORIENTED

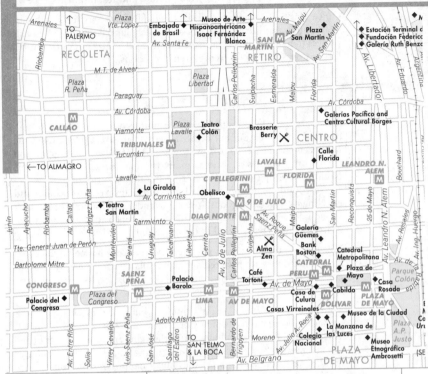

THE TERRITORY

The Microcentro (central business district) runs between Avenidas L.N. Alem and 9 de Julio and north of Avenida de Mayo. There are two axes: Avenida Corrientes (which runs east–west) and pedestrian-only shopping street Calle Florida (north–south). Florida's northern end leads into Plaza San Martín in Retiro. South of the Microcentro lies Plaza de Mayo. From here, Avenida de Mayo runs 12 blocks west to Plaza del Congreso. Puerto Madero borders Centro to the east. Both it and its main thoroughfare, Avenida Alicia M. de Justo, run parallel to the river.

TAKING IT IN

Crowds and traffic can make touring draining: try to do a few short visits rather than one long marathon. You can see most of the sights in the Plaza de Mayo area over the course of a leisurely afternoon; a late-morning wander and lunch in Puerto Madero is one good way to precede this.

Half a day in the Microcentro is enough to take in the sights and have your fill of risky street-crossing, though you could spend a lot more time caught up in shops. Avoid the Microcentro midweek between noon and 2, or sit it out in a restaurant. If you're planning on hard-core shopping, come on a weekend. The area is quiet at night.

SAFETY & PRECAUTIONS

Watch out for purse snatchers and pickpockets, and use ATMs only during bank hours (weekdays 10–3); thieves target them after hours. Stay alert on Lavalle, a pedestrian street peppered with adult entertainment. At night, wander with care.

Map labels:

◆ Museo de la Inmigración
inal de Omnibus,
lerico Jorge Klemm,
Benzacar

Antepuerto

Av. Antártida Argentina

Darsena Norte

Río de La Plata

Blvd. Cecilia Grierson

Dique 4

Av. Alicia M. de Justo

Juana Manuela Gorriti

Av. Costanera Carlos Noel

Av. De los Italianos

Juana Manso

Av. Costanera Tristán Achával Rodríguez

KEY
✕ Quick bites
Ⓜ Subte stops

Blvd. Macacha Guemes

Torre
Repsol YPF ◆
M. Sáenz
Parque de
◆ las Mujeres

**Reserva
Ecológica**
◆

Puente de
la Mujer ◆

**PUERTO
MADERO**

◆ Buque Museo Fragata
A.R.A. Pres. Sarmiento

Dique 3

Martha Lynch

Buque
Museo
Corbeta
Uruguay ◆

Azucena Villaflor

TO DIQUE 1 & 2
(SEE ALSO LA BOCA &
SANTELMO MAP) ↓

◆ Faena Hotel &
Universe Spa

0 ——— 1/2 mile
0 ——— 1/2 kilometer

GETTING AROUND

The quickest way into Centro is by subte. For the Microcentro, get off at Florida (Línea/Line B) or Lavalle (C). Retiro and Plaza San Martín have eponymous stations on Line C. Stations Avenida de Mayo (A), Catedral (D), and Bolívar (E) all serve Plaza de Mayo. Line A has stops along de Mayo, including at Congreso. Puerto Madero is fairly close to L.N. Alem on Line A. Lines B, C, and D intersect at Carlos Pellegrini/Diagonal Norte/9 de Julio, one big, badly connected station under the Obelisco. Only change lines here if you're going more than one stop. Otherwise, walking is quicker, especially during rush hour.

You can take a taxi or bus to the Microcentro, but, despite crowds and exhaust fumes, walking is the best way to move within it. Bus 17 connects Centro and Recoleta; so do Buses 59 and 93, which continue to the Palermo parks. Bus 130 connects these same areas with Puerto Madero. Buses 22 and 24 run between San Telmo and the Microcentro.

QUICK BITES

Give those cows (and your cholesterol count) a break with lunch at whole-food café **Alma Zen** (✉Perón 812, at Esmeralda, Plaza de Mayo, C1038AAR ☎11/4393–0003). Its light take on fast food includes whole-wheat tofu empanadas and salads.

Local businesspeople looking for a snappy but proper (i.e., three-course) lunch know that **Brasserie Berry** (✉Tucumán 775, at Diagonal Norte, Centro, C1049AAO ☎11/4394–5255) gives excellent value for your 25 pesos. Perfectly rare steak and roast pork or chicken are on the set-price menu; duck and rabbit are à la carte. The pains-au-chocolat and brioche are perfect for breakfast.

Beret-wearing intellectuals and perfumed theatergoers love café **La Giralda** (✉Av. Corrientes 1453, Centro ☎11/4371–3846). Don't let the small tables or surly waiters put you off; its signature *chocolate con churros* (hot chocolate with crisp cigar-shape donuts) are to die for. If it's savory you're after, try a *tostado mixto* (toasted ham-and-cheese sandwich).

Renovated redbrick warehouses fill the space between Avenida Alicia Moreau de Justo and Juana Manuela Gorriti, a promenade along the old docks with great views of the new developments across the water in Puerto Madero Este. They're also home to a string of chichi *parrillas* (steak houses), including the famed Cabaña las Lilas. Don't leave without playing on Puerto Madero's latest toy, a tramway that runs parallel to de Justo between Avenidas Córdoba and Independencia.

The biggest changes are taking place in Puerto Madero Este, on the other side of the docks. The most interesting way across is via Santiago Calatrava's **Puente de la Mujer**, a bridge whose sleek white curves were inspired by tango dancers.

The epicenter of Puerto Madero design is Dique 2, where the empire of local entrepreneur Alan Faena is taking shape. He calls it the Art District, and it hinges around his **Faena Hotel + Universe Spa**, a Philippe Starck–designed former grain silo at Marta Salotti and Juana Manso. The monumental redbrick exterior is pleasingly simple; check out the opulent interior over a cocktail or tea in the Library Lounge. Part of the building is given over to luxury apartments, as are the neighboring Porteña buildings, also designed by Starck.

Other Faena housing projects include **Los Molinos**, another immense ex–grain silo, this time made of creamy stone. But Faena's real baby is **El Aleph** residential complex, Norman Foster's first Latin American project and one named for Jorge Luis Borges's most-famous short-story collection. The long, low, curvaceous (and energy efficient) structure will line all of Dique 2's waterfront along Pierina Dealessi. The third-highest buildings in town are also slated to occupy Dique 2: twin residential **Torres Mulieris** on Aimé Painé.

Dique 3 is home to work by another big-name architect, Argentina's own César Pelli (of Petronas Towers fame). His mirrored **Torre Repsol YPF** is going up at Macacha Güemes and Juana Manso will have a mini-eucalyptus forest between the 26th and 31st stories. Look for another sterner-looking construction on Dique 4: the **Museo Fortabat**, which will eventually house the modern art collection of local cement heiress Amalia Fortabat (unsurprisingly, concrete is the main building material, topped by a curved steel-and-glass roof).

It's not all cranes and rubble, though. Dique 3 is punctuated by the landscaped **Parque de las Mujeres**, the ideal spot for a picnic lunch (stock up on goodies at the i Fresh Market deli at Azucena Villaflor and Olga Cossettini). For a bigger dose of green, head to the 856-acre **Reserva Ecológica**, east of Dique 2.

MAIN ATTRACTIONS

La Manzana de Las Luces *(The Block of Illumination)*. More history is packed into this single block of buildings southwest of Plaza de Mayo than in scores of other city blocks put together. Among other things, it was the enclave for higher learning: the metaphorical *luces* (lights) of its name refer to the "illuminated" scholars who worked within.

The block's earliest occupant was the controversial Jesuit order, which began construction here in 1661. The only survivor from this first stage is the galleried **Procuraduría** (✉*Corner of Alsina and Perú*)), the colonial administrative headquarters for the Jesuits' vast land holdings in northeastern Argentina and Paraguay (think: *The Mission*). Historic defense tunnels, still undergoing archaeological excavation, linked the Jesuit headquarters to churches in the area, the Cabildo, and the port. Visits here include a glimpse of a specially reinforced section.

After the Jesuits' expulsion from Argentina in 1767 (the Spanish crown saw them as a threat), the simple brick-and-mud structure housed first the city's first school of medicine and then the University of Buenos Aires. Fully restored, it's now home to a school of luthiers and a rather tacky crafts market.

The Jesuits honored their patron saint at the **Iglesia de San Ignacio de Loyola** *(Saint Ignatius of Loyola Church)* (✉*Corner of Alsina and Bolívar*). The first church on the site was built of adobe in 1675; within a few decades it was rebuilt in stone. Argentina's first congress convened within the **Casas Virreinales** *(Viceroyal Houses)* (✉*Corner of Moreno and Perú*): ironic, given that it was built to house colonial civil servants. The remaining historic building on the block is the neoclassical **Colegio Nacional**, a top-notch public school and a hotbed of political activism that replaced a Jesuit-built structure. The president attends graduation ceremonies, and Einstein gave a lecture here in 1925. The Iglesia de San Ignacio is open to the public, but you can only visit the rest of Manzana de las Luces on guided tours led by excellent professional historians. Regular departures are in Spanish; groups can call ahead to arrange English-language visits. ✉*Entrance and inquiries at Perú 272, Plaza de Mayo, C1067AAF* ☏*11/4342–6973* 💲*5 pesos* ⊙*Visits by guided tour only; Spanish-language tours leave daily at 3, 4:30, and 6* PM; *call to arrange tours in English* Ⓜ*A to Plaza de Mayo, D to Catedral, E to Bolívar.*

Museo Etnográfico Juan B. Ambrosetti *(Ethnographic Museum)*. Given that the 100-peso bill still honors General Roca, the man responsible for the massacre of most of Patagonia's indigenous population, it's unsurprising that information on Argentina's original inhabitants is sparse. This fascinating but little-visited museum is a welcome remedy.

Begun by local scientist Juan Bautista Ambrosetti in 1904, the collection originally focused on so-called exotic art and artifacts, such as the Australasian sculptures and Japanese temple altar showcased in the rust-color introductory room. The real highlights, however, are the Argentinean collections: this would be an eye-opening introduction to a visit to Argentina's far north or south.

The ground-floor galleries trace the history of human activity in Patagonia, with an emphasis on the tragic results of the European arrival. Dugout canoes, exquisite Mapuche silver jewelry, and scores of archive photos and illustrations are some of the main exhibits.

In the upstairs northwestern Argentina gallery, the focus is mainly archaeological. Displays briefly chronicle the evolution of Andean civilization, the heyday of the Inca Empire, and postcolonial life. Artifacts include ceramics, textiles, jewelry, farming tools, and even food: anyone for some 4,000-year-old corn?

The collection is now run by the liberal Philosophy and Letters Faculty of the University of Buenos Aires. Although their insightful labels and explanations are all in Spanish, you can ask for a photocopied sheet with English versions of the texts. It's a pleasure just to wander the quiet, light-filled 19th-century town house that houses both the collection and an anthropological library. The peaceful inner garden is the perfect place for some post-museum reflection when you're done. ⊠*Moreno 350, Plaza de Mayo, C1091AAH* ☎*11/4345–8196* ⊕*http:// museoetnografico.filo.uba.ar* ☜*2 pesos* ⊙*Tues.–Fri. 1–7, weekends 3– 7* Ⓜ*Line A, Plaza de Mayo; Line D, Catedral; Line E, Bolívar.*

★ **Plaza de Mayo.** Since its construction in 1580, this has been the focal point of Argentina's most politically turbulent moments, including the uprising against Spanish colonial rule on May 25, 1810—hence its name. The square was once divided in two by a *recova* (gallery), but this reminder of colonial times was demolished in 1883 and the square's central monument, the Pirámide de Mayo, was later moved to its place. The pyramid you see is actually a 1911 extension of the original, erected in 1811 on the anniversary of the Revolution of May, which is hidden inside. The bronze equestrian statue of General Manuel Belgrano, designer of Argentina's flag, dates from 1873 and stands at the east end of the plaza.

The plaza remains the traditional site for ceremonies as well as protests. Thousands cheered for Perón and Evita here; anti-Peronist planes bombed the gathered crowds a few years later; and there were bloody clashes in December 2001 (hence the heavy police presence and crowd-control barriers). The white head scarves painted around the Pirámide de Mayo represent the Madres de la Plaza de Mayo (Mothers of May Square) who have marched here every Thursday at 3:30 for more than two decades. Housewives and mothers–turned–militant activists, they demand justice for *los desaparecidos,* the people who were "disappeared" during the military government's reign from 1976 to 1983. Here, too, you can witness the changing of the Grenadier Regiment guards; it takes place weekdays every two hours from 9 until 7, Saturday at 9 and 11, and Sunday at 9, 11, and 1.

The eclectic Casa de Gobierno, better known as the **Casa Rosada** (✉*Hipólito Yrigoyen 219, Plaza de Mayo, C1086AAA* ☎*11/4344–3802* ⊕*www.museo.gov.ar* ✉*Free* ◷*Weekdays 10–6, Sun. 2–6*) or Pink House, is at the plaza's eastern end, with its back to the river. The building houses the government's executive branch—the president works here but lives elsewhere—and was built in the late 19th century over the foundations of an earlier customhouse and fortress. Swedish, Italian, and French architects have since modified the structure, which accounts for the odd mix of styles. Its curious hue dates from the presidency of Domingo Sarmiento, who ordered it painted pink as a symbol of unification between two warring political factions, the *federales* (whose color was red) and the *unitarios* (represented by white). Local legend has it that the original paint was made by mixing whitewash with bull's blood.

The balcony facing Plaza de Mayo is a presidential podium. From this lofty stage Evita rallied the *descamisados* (the shirtless—meaning the working class), Maradona sang along with soccer fans after winning one World Cup and coming second in another, and Madonna sang her filmed rendition of "Don't Cry for Me Argentina." Check for a small banner hoisted alongside the nation's flag, indicating "the president is in." Behind the structure are the brick-wall remains of the 1845 Taylor Customs House, discovered after being buried for almost a century. Enter the Casa Rosada through the basement of the Museo de la Casa Rosada, the only area open to the public, which exhibits often bizarre presidential memorabilia—*mates* (the national tea drink) and hats are two focuses—along with objects from the original customhouse and fortress.

The city council—now based in the ornate building over Avenida de Mayo—originally met in the **Cabildo** (✉*Bolívar 65, Plaza de Mayo, C1066AAA* ☎*11/4334–1782* ✉*3 pesos* ◷*Tues.–Fri. 10:30–5, weekends 11:30–6*). It dates from 1765 and is the only colonial building on Plaza de Mayo. The epicenter of the May Revolution of 1810, where patriotic citizens gathered to vote against Spanish rule, the hall is one of Argentina's national shrines. However, this hasn't stopped successive renovations to its detriment, including the demolition of the whole right end of the structure to make way for the new Avenida de Mayo in 1894. Inside, a small museum exhibits artifacts and documents pertaining to the events of the May Revolution as well as a jail cell. Thursday and Friday from 11 to 6, an artisan fair takes place on the Patio del Cabildo. Ⓜ*Line A, Plaza de Mayo; Line D, Catedral; Line E, Bolívar.*

Teatro Colón. Its magnitude, magnificent acoustics, and opulence (grander than Milan's La Scala) position the Teatro Colón (Colón Theater) among the world's top five operas. An ever-changing stream of imported talent bolsters the well-regarded local lyric and ballet companies. After an eventful 18-year building process involving the death of one architect and the murder of another, the ornate Italianate structure was finally inaugurated in 1908 with Verdi's Aida. It has hosted the likes of Maria Callas, Richard Strauss, Arturo Toscanini, Igor Stravinsky, Enrico Caruso, and Luciano Pavarotti, who said that the Colón has only one flaw: the acoustics are so good, every mistake can be heard.

The theater's sumptuous building materials—three kinds of Italian marble, French stained glass, and Venetian mosaics—were imported from Europe to create large-scale lavishness. The seven-tier main theater is breathtaking in size, and has a grand central chandelier with 700 lights to illuminate the 3,000 mere mortals in its red-velvet seats.

The theater is currently dark owing to restoration work that's slated to end in 2010. Until then, tours of the theater—once very popular—are suspended, and opera, ballet, and other performances normally held here are being held in other Buenos Aires theaters. ⊠*Main entrance: Libertad between Tucumán and Viamonte; Box office: Pasaje Toscanini 1180, Centro, C1053AAA* ☎*11/4378–7100 tickets, 11/4378–7132 tours* ⊕*www.teatrocolon.org.ar* Ⓜ*D to Tribunales.*

IF YOU HAVE TIME

Buque Museo Corbeta Uruguay (*Uruguay* Corvette Ship Museum). The oldest of the Argentine fleet, bought from England in 1874, the ship has been around the world several times and was used in the nation's Antarctic campaigns at the turn of the 20th century. You can see what the captain's cabin and officers' mess looked like at that time; there are also displays of items rescued from shipwrecks. A stroll around the decks affords views of the boat's structure and of Puerto Madero. ⊠*Dique 4, Alicia M. de Justo 1900 block, Puerto Madero, C1107AFL* ☎*11/4314–1090* ⊞*Free* ☉*Weekdays 2–7, weekends 10–7.*

Buque Museo Fragata A.R.A. Presidente Sarmiento (*President Sarmiento* Frigate Museum). The navy commissioned this frigate from England in 1898 to be used as an open-sea training vessel. The 280-foot boat used up to 33 sails and carried more than 300 crew members: the beautifully restored cabins afford a glimpse of what life onboard was like. Surprisingly luxurious officers' quarters include parquet floors, wood paneling, and leather armchairs; cadets had to make do with hammocks. ⊠*Dique 3, Alicia M. de Justo 900 block, Puerto Madero, C1107AAR* ☎*11/4334–9386* ⊞*2 pesos* ☉*Daily 9–8.*

Catedral Metropolitana. The Metropolitan Cathedral's columned neoclassical facade makes it seem more like a temple than a church, and its history follows the pattern of many structures in the Plaza de Mayo area. The first of six buildings on this site was a 16th-century adobe ranch house; the current structure dates from 1822 but has been added to several times. The embalmed remains of General José de San Martín, known as the Liberator of Argentina for his role in the War of Independence, rest here in a marble mausoleum lighted by an eternal flame. Soldiers of the Grenadier Regiment, an elite troop created and trained by San Martín in 1811, permanently guard the tomb. Group tours in English are available, but you need to call ahead. ⊠*San Martín 27,* *at Rivadavia, Plaza de Mayo, C1004AAA ☎11/4331–2845 ⊕www. catedralbuenosaires.org.ar ☞Free ⊙Weekdays 8–7, weekends 9–7:30 ⓂA to Plaza de Mayo, D to Catedral, E to Bolívar.*

Museo de Arte Hispanoamericano Isaac Fernández Blanco. The distinctive Peruvian neocolonial-style Palacio Noel serves as the perfect backdrop for the Isaac Fernández Blanco Hispanic-American Art Museum. It was built as the residence of architect Martín Noel in the late 18th century. He and museum founder Fernández Blanco donated most of the silver items, wood carvings, furnishings, and paintings from the Spanish colonial period that are on display. Guided tours in English can be arranged with prior notice. The museum is an easy five-block walk from Estación San Martí on Línea C: from there go west along Avenida Santa Fe and then turn right into Suipacha and continue four blocks. ✉*Suipacha 1422, at Av. Libertador, Retiro, C1011ACF ☎11/4327–0228 ⊕www. museos.buenosaires.gov.ar/mifb.htm ☞3 pesos, free Thurs. ⊙Tues.– Sun. 2–7 ⓂC to San Martín.*

Museo de la Ciudad. "Whimsical" is one way to describe the City Museum, which focuses on random aspects of domestic and public life in Buenos Aires in times past. "Eccentric" is probably closer to the mark for the permanent collection: an array of typical porteño doors. Historical toys, embroidery, religion in Buenos Aires, and garden gnomes (yes, really) are some of the focuses of temporary exhibitions. Still, the peaceful building is worth a 10-minute wander if you're in the neighborhood. Downstairs, the Farmacia La Estrella sells modern medicine and cosmetics from a perfectly preserved 19th-century shop. ✉*Alsina 412, Plaza de Mayo, C1087AAF ☎11/4331–9855 or 11/4343–2123 ⊕www.museos.buenosaires.gov.ar/ciudad.htm ☞1 peso; suggested donation 10 pesos ⊙Weekdays 11–7, Sun. 3–7 ⓂA to Plaza de Mayo, D to Catedral, E to Bolívar.*

Museo de la Inmigración. The Hotel de Inmigrantes that houses the modest Immigration Museum was the first stop for many of the millions of Europeans who arrived in Argentina between 1880 and 1930. Inside the imposing building, their lives and times are told through photos, personal effects, and film footage, with Spanish-only explanations. ✉*Antiguo Hotel de Inmigrantes, Av. Antárdida Argentina 1355, Retiro, C1104APA ☎11/4317–0285 ⊕www.mininterior.gov.ar/migraciones/ museo/index.html ☞1 peso suggested donation ⊙Weekdays 10–5, weekends 11–6.*

Puente de la Mujer. Tango dancers inspired the sweeping asymmetrical lines of Valencian architect Santiago Calatrava's design for the pedestrian-only Bridge of the Woman. Puerto Madero's street names pay homage to famous Argentine women, hence the bridge's name. (Ironically its most visible part—a soaring 128-foot arm—represents the man of a couple in mid-tango.) The $6-million structure was made in Spain and paid for by local businessmen Alberto L. González, one of the brains behind Puerto Madero's redevelopment; he also built the Hilton Hotel here. Twenty engines rotate the bridge to allow ships to pass through. ✉*Dique 3, C. Lorenzini, at Alicia M. de Justo, Puerto Madero.*

Reserva Ecológica. The 865-acre Ecological Reserve was built over a landfill and is home to more than 500 species of bird and a variety of flora and fauna. On weekends thousands of porteños vie for a spot on the grass, so come midweek if you want to bird-watch and sunbathe in peace or use the jogging and cycling tracks. A monthly guided "Walking under the Full Moon" tour begins at 8:30 PM; otherwise avoid the area at night. It's just a short walk across any bridge from Puerto Madero. ⊠*Av. Tristán Achával Rodríguez 1550, Puerto Madero, C1107ADZ* ☎*11/4315–1320, 11/4893–1588 tours* ☞*Free* ⊙*Apr.–Oct., Tues.–Sun. 8–6; Nov.–Mar., Tues.–Sun. 8–7; guided visits in Spanish weekends at 10:30 and 3:30.*

ART GALLERIES

Centro Cultural Borges. There's something very low key about this cultural center, despite its considerable size and prime location above the posh Galerías Pacífico mall. With a minimum of pomp and circumstance, it has hosted exhibitions of Warhol, Kahlo and Rivera, Man Ray, Miró, Picasso, and Dalí, among others. Occasional mass shows focus on new local artists and art students. There are also small, independent theater and dance performances. ⊠*Viamonte 525 at San Martín, Centro, C1053ABK* ☎*11/555–5359* ⊕*www.ccborges.org.ar* ⊙*Mon.–Sat. 10–9, Sun. noon–9.*

Fundación Federico Jorge Klemm. You'd never guess that this sober, tastefully curated space was founded by one of Argentina's true eccentrics. The late Federico Jorge Klemm used his significant family fortune to amass a fabulous collection of local and international art—on display here—and to start a prestigious local art prize, finalists of which are exhibited each year. Argentines remember Klemm best for his art-based TV program, which he presented dressed in exuberant outfits and wearing a trademark blond wig. ⊠*Marcelo T. de Alvear 626, Centro, C1058AAH* ☎*11/4312–4443* ⊕*www.fundacionfjklemm.org* ⊙*Weekdays 11–8.*

Galería Ruth Benzacar. This private gallery has set the standard for modern Argentine art for almost 50 years. As well as regularly changing exhibitions of established artists and promising newcomers, the gallery showcases a selection of unknown talents at the end of each year, known as Curriculum Cero. Serious buyers should ask to see the vast collection of paintings in the basement. ⊠*Florida 1000, Microcentro, C1005AAT* ☎*11/4313–8480* ⊕*www.ruthbenzacar.com* ⊙*Weekdays 11:30–8, Sat. 10:30–1:30* Ⓜ*C to San Martín.*

At a Glance

LANDMARKS & KEY STREETS
Av. Alicia M. de Justo
Av. Corrientes
Av. de Mayo
Calle Florida
Obelisco
Plaza Congreso
Plaza de Mayo
Plaza San Martín
Puente de la Mujer

SHOPPING ⇨ CH. 3
Department Store
Falabella
Malls
Galería Güemes
Galerías Pacífico

SIGHTS & EXPERIENCES ⇨ CHS. 1 & 2
Architecture—Historical
Cabildo
Casa Rosada
Catedral Metropolitana
La Manzana de Las Luces
Architecture—Modern
El Aleph
Bank Boston
Faena Hotel + Universe
Los Molinos
Museo Fortabat
Torre Repsol YPF
Torres Mulieris

Art Galleries
Centro Cultural Borges
Fundación Federico Jorge Klemm
Galería Ruth Benzacar
Museums
Buque Museo Corbeta Uruguay
Buque Museo Fragata A.R.A. Presidente Sarmiento
Museo de Arte Hispanoamericano Isaac Fernández
Museo de la Ciudad
Museo Etnográfico Juan B. Ambrosetti
Museo de la Inmigración
Parks
Parque de las Mujeres
Reserva Ecológica
Theater
Teatro Colón

WHERE TO EAT
Quick Bites (⇨ Getting Oriented)
Alma Zen
Brasserie Berry
La Giralda
Tea Connection
Restaurants–Budget (⇨ Ch. 5)
California Burrito Co., Mexican
Confitería La Ideal, Café
Las Cuartetas, Pizza

El Cuartito, Pizza
El Palacio de la Papa Frita, Argentine
Gran Café Tortoni, Café
La Parolaccia, Italian
Pippo, Argentine
Status, Congreso, Peruvian
Restaurants—Moderate (⇨ Ch. 5)
DaDá, Argentine
Filo, Pizza
El Imparcial, Monserrat, Spanish
Piola, Pizza
Restaurants—Expensive (⇨ Ch. 5)
La Caballeriza, Steak
El Globo, Monserrat, Spanish
Gran Bar Danzón, Eclectic
Matías, Irish
Restó, Argentine
Sabot, Argentine
Tancat, Spanish
Restaurants–Very Expensive (⇨ Ch. 5)
Bengal, Eclectic
Cabaña Las Lilas, Steak
Crystal Garden, Argentine
La Pérgola, Argentine
Plaza Grill, French
Le Sud, French
Tomo I, Argentine

LA BOCA & SAN TELMO

Sightseeing
★★★★
Dining
★★★
Lodging
★★★★
Shopping
★★★★
Nightlife
★★★

"The south also exists," quip residents of bohemian neighborhoods like San Telmo and La Boca, which historically played second fiddle to posher northern barrios. No more. The hottest designers have boutiques here, new restaurants are booked out, and property prices are soaring. The south is also the linchpin of the city's tango revival, appropriate given that the dance was born in these quarters.

San Telmo, Buenos Aires' first suburb, was originally inhabited by sailors and takes its name from their wandering patron saint. All the same, the mariners main preoccupations were clearly less than spiritual, and San Telmo became famous for its brothels.

That didn't stop the area's first experience of gentrification: wealthy Spaniards built ornate homes here in the early 19th century, but ran for Recoleta when a yellow-fever epidemic struck in 1871. Newly arrived immigrants crammed into their abandoned mansions, known as *conventillos* (tenement houses). Today these same houses are fought over by foreign buyers dying to ride the wave of urban renewal—the *reciclaje* (recycling), as porteños call it—that's sweeping the area and transforming San Telmo into Buenos Aires' hippest 'hood.

San Telmo has no sights per se; it's the barrio itself that's the attraction. A few hours gazing at its soaring Italianate town houses or writing in your travel journal over a drawn-out coffee is as much an insight into porteño life as any museum display. All those cobblestones aren't just picturesque; they're useful, too, as they force you to slow down and enjoy the barrio.

Although neighboring La Boca seems far touristier, it shares much of San Telmo's gritty history. La Boca sits on the fiercely polluted Riachuelo River, where rusting ships and warehouses remind you that this was once the city's main port. The immigrants who first settled here built their houses from corrugated metal and brightly colored paint left over from the shipyards. Today, imitations of these vibrant buildings form one of Buenos Aires' most emblematic sights, the Caminito. Two quite different colors have made La Boca famous: the blue and gold of the Boca Juniors soccer team, whose massive home stadium is the barrio's unofficial heart. Cafés, pubs, and general stores that once catered to passing sailors are now tourist traps dotting the partially renovated port. Whether your heart races over moves on the soccer field or the tango floor, over a fabulous building or a fabulous bargain, the south has plenty to spark your passions.

TWO WAYS TO EXPLORE

FROM COLONY TO REPUBLIC

Little remains of Buenos Aires' colonial past: buildings were typically made of short-lived adobe. Happily, San Telmo has a few exceptions.

Although a stretch of **Calle Balcarce** is known for its touristy tango spots, the 900 and 1000 blocks have some examples of Spanish colonial architecture, such as number 1016, the former home of painter Juan Carlos Castagnino, which dates from the late 18th century.Off Calle Balcarce, **Pasaje San Lorenzo** is a typical and charming colonial alley. At number 380 stand the ruins of Casa Minima, the city's thinnest building—about 8 feet wide. It once belonged to a freed slave.

The solid-looking **Viejo Almacén** (⊠*Balcarce 786, San Telmo* 🕾*11/ 4307–6689 or 11/4300–3388* ⊕*www.viejo-almacen.com.ar*) was built in 1798 as a general store. It then served as the British Hospital in the 1840s, and then as a customhouse. Tango artist Edmundo Rivero purchased it in 1969 and it's been a hot spot for tango ever since (it's only open for dinner and shows).

When Britain tried—unsuccessfully—to invade Buenos Aires in 1806--07, battles took place in San Telmo's streets. Patriotic residents assisted the improvised militia by throwing stones and boiling water at advancing limeys. Shoot-outs caused the pockmarks high on the left-hand tower of the **Convento de Santo Domingo** (⊠*Defensa 422, San Telmo, C1065AAH*). Displayed in the church are the only two British flags never recovered after a military surrender. The church looks onto Avenida Belgrano, named for Manuel Belgrano, creator of the Argentine flag, who was born and died in the next block.

La Casa de Esteban de Luca (⊠*Calle Defensa 1000* 🕾*11/4361–4338*) was once the home of a solider and distinguished poet who wrote the country's first national anthem and was a hero of the May Revolution of 1810. It's now a quaint, if somewhat touristy, restaurant.North of Plaza Dorrego, at Defensa 1066, is **La Galeria del Solar de French**, a neoclassical mansion built on the site where Domingo French, a hero of the War of Independence, once lived.

GETTING ORIENTED

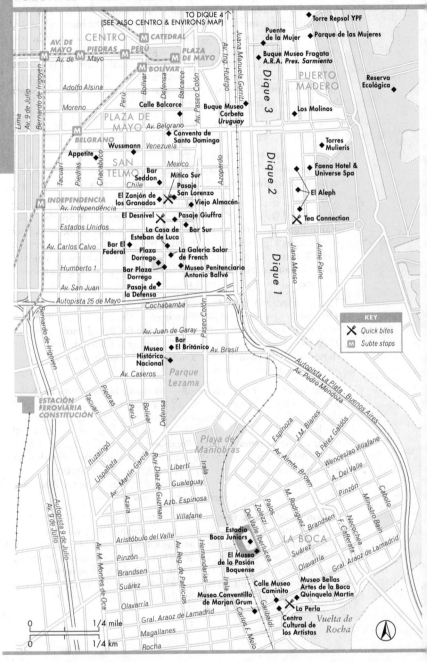

TO DIQUE 4 ↑
(SEE ALSO CENTRO & ENVIRONS MAP)

Torre Repsol YPF

Puente de la Mujer

Parque de las Mujeres

Buque Museo Fragata
A.R.A. *Pres. Sarmiento*

PUERTO MADERO

Reserva Ecológica

CENTRO

CATEDRAL

PIEDRAS

PERÚ

PLAZA DE MAYO

AV. DE MAYO

Av. de Mayo

BOLÍVAR

Adolfo Alsina

Moreno

Calle Balcarce

Buque Museo Corbeta Uruguay

Los Molinos

PLAZA DE MAYO

Av. Belgrano

BELGRANO

Wussmann

Convento de Santo Domingo

Venezuela

Torres Mulieris

Appetite

SAN TELMO

México

Faena Hotel & Universe Spa

Bar Seddon

Mítico Sur

Chile

Pasaje San Lorenzo

El Aleph

El Zanjón de los Granados

Viejo Almacén

INDEPENDENCIA

Av. Independencia

El Desnivel

Pasaje Giuffra

Tea Connection

Estados Unidos

La Casa de Esteban de Luca

Bar Sur

Av. Carlos Calvo

Bar El Federal

Plaza Dorrego

La Galería Solar de French

Humberto 1

Bar Plaza Dorrego

Museo Penitenciario Antonio Ballvé

Av. San Juan

Pasaje de la Defensa

Autopista 25 de Mayo

Cochabamba

Av. Juan de Garay

Bar El Británico

Museo Histórico Nacional

Av. Brasil

Av. Caseros

Parque Lezama

ESTACIÓN FEROVIARIA CONSTITUCIÓN

KEY

✕ Quick bites

Ⓜ Subte stops

Autopista La Plata - Buenos Aires

Av. Pedro Mendoza

Playa de Maniobras

Estadio Boca Juniors

El Museo de la Pasión Boquense

LA BOCA

Calle Museo Caminito

Museo Bellas Artes de la Boca Quinquela Martín

Museo Conventillo de Marjan Grum

La Perla

Centro Cultural de los Artistas

Vuelta de Rocha

0   1/4 mile

0   1/4 km

THE TERRITORY

San Telmo, south of the Centro, is bordered by Avenida Madero to the east, Avenidas Brasil and Caseros to the south, Piedras to the west, and—depending on whom you ask—Chile or Belgrano to the north. The main drag is cobbled, pedestrians-only, north–south Defensa.

South of Avenida Brasil lies La Boca, whose westernmost edge is Avenida Patricios. The Riachuelo River forms a curving, southwesterly border; Avenida Don Pedro de Mendoza runs alongside this.

GETTING AROUND

The subte takes you within nine blocks of San Telmo. The closest stations to the southern end are Independencia (Lines C or E) and San Juan (Line C). Be prepared to walk nine blocks east along Avenidas Independencia, Estados Unidos, or San Juan to get to Defensa, the main street. To approach San Telmo from the north, get off at Bolívar (Line E) or Catedral (Line D) and walk eight blocks south along Bolívar. Buses 22, 24, 26, and 28 connect San Telmo to Centro. The same route by taxi costs 8–10 pesos.

There's no subte to La Boca so taxi travel is a good bet, especially after dark: expect to pay 12–15 pesos to or from Centro. Bus 29 runs between La Boca and Centro; so do Buses 64 and 152, which continue to Palermo.

SAFETY & PRECAUTIONS

San Telmo's reputation as a dangerous neighborhood is changing: its popularity with visitors has led to increased police presence in the busiest areas (especially near Defensa). Instances of petty crime are still fairly common. Even George Bush's daughter Barbara had her bag snatched here, so keep your belongings close. After dark, stick to busy, well-lighted streets close to Defensa.

La Boca is far sketchier, and you'd do best not to stray from the Caminito area. Avoid the neighborhood after dark, and take radio taxis if you must visit then.

TAKING IT IN

San Telmo thrives on Sunday, thanks to the art and antiques market in Plaza Dorrego. During the week, a leisurely afternoon's visit is ideal. Start with lunch in a café at the northern or southern end of San Telmo, then spend an hour or two wandering the cobbled streets. You still have time for some shopping before winding up with a coffee or a drink. In La Boca, allow two or three hours to explore Caminito and do a museum or two. It's busy all week, but expect extra crowds on weekends.

QUICK BITES

El Desnivel ⊠*Defensa 855, San Telmo, C1065AAO* ☎*11/4300–9081.* , a classic parrilla, does great no-nonsense beef in a flash. Trimmings don't go beyond a mixed salad and fries, and surly waiters all but fling food at you. It's all part of the experience. So are the huge wedges of *flan* (crème caramel).

Mítico Sur ⊠*Pasaje San Lorenzo 389, San Telmo, C1064AFC* ☎*11/4362–4750* celebrates all things Patagonian. Handmade cheese, Parma ham, spicy salami, and even pickled deer might arrive on their *tablas de picadas* (snack boards).

The century-old **La Perla** ⊠*Av. Pedro de Mendoza 1899, La Boca, C1169AAC* ☎*11/4301–2985.* café is the spot for a *licuado* (milk shake), a *cortado* (coffee with a drop of milk), or the local take on the croque-monsieur, a *tostado mixto*.

BAR SAFARI

Get a taste of traditional San Telmo at the worn, wooden tables of its vintage bars. Most open from breakfast right through to the wee hours, so the liquid backbone of your safari could be coffee, or alcohol, or both. A city-government heritage scheme has named these other classic establishments *Bares Notables* (Bars of Note); find more information at the government Web site (*www.bue.gov.ar*).

The best-known bar is probably wood-paneled, dust-festooned **Bar Plaza Dorrego,** right on the square. Sip your *cafecito* (espresso) or icy beer from one of its window tables for some prime people-watching, all the while shelling your pile of peanuts.

Tango musicians often perform at **Bar Seddon,** on the corner of Chile and Defensa, an otherwise quiet bar with a beautiful checkered floor and old-fashioned cash register. You need to book to see the formal tango dinner-dance shows at **Bar Sur,** on the corner of Balcarce and Estados Unidos. Hong Kong art-house director Wong Kar-Wai set much of his film *Happy Together,* which won him best director at Cannes, here.

When your stomach starts to rumble, look for the ornate hand-painted sign of **Bar El Federal,** at Perú and Carlos Calvo. Veteran regulars assure that the *picadas* (snack board of cold cuts and bread) are some of the best in town, and you can linger over them for hours, no questions asked. In 2006, when they tried to shut down ultravintage **Bar El Británico,** on the northwest corner of Parque Lezama, the whole city rallied to its defense. Rub elbows with bohemian students and wizened old-timers as you perk up with a *cortado* (espresso "cut" with a dash of milk) or unwind with a *ginebra* (ginlike spirit).

MAIN ATTRACTIONS

Calle Museo Caminito.

See the highlighted listing in this chapter

Estadio Boca Juniors and Museo de la Pasión Boquense

See Get Your Kicks in the Sporting Life section of Chapter 1, Experience.

Pasaje de la Defensa. Wandering through this well-preserved house affords a glimpse of life in San Telmo's golden era. Behind its elegant but narrow stone facade, the house is built deep into the block around a series of internal courtyards. This type of long, narrow construction is typical of San Telmo and is known as a *casa chorizo* (sausage house). Once the home of the well-to-do Ezeiza family, it became a *conventillo* (tenement) but is now a picturesque spot for antiques and curio shopping. The stores here are open daily 10 to 6. ⊠*Defensa 1179, San Telmo, C1065AAU* ☎*No phone.*

★ **Plaza Dorrego.** During the week a handful of people and a few scruffy pigeons are the only ones enjoying the shade from the stately trees in the city's second-oldest square. Sunday couldn't be more different:

scores of stalls selling antiques, curios, and just plain old stuff move in to form the Feria de San Pedro Telmo (San Pedro Telmo Fair). Tango dancers take to the cobbles, as do hundreds of shoppers (mostly tourists) browsing the tango memorabilia, antique silver, brass, crystal, and Argentine curios. Note that prices are high at stalls on the square and astronomical in the shops surrounding it, and vendors are immune to bargaining. More-affordable offerings—mostly handicrafts and local artists' work—are on stalls along nearby streets like Defensa. ■TIP➡Be on the lookout for antique (or just plain old) glass soda siphons that once adorned every bar top in Buenos Aires. Classic colors are green or turquoise; prices start at around 20 pesos.

Be sure to look up as you wander Plaza Dorrego, as the surrounding architecture provides an overview of the influences—Spanish colonial, French classical, and ornate Italian masonry—that shaped the city in the 19th and 20th centuries.

★ **El Zanjón de Granados.** All 500 years of Buenos Aires' history are packed into this unusual house. The street it's on was once a small river—the *zanjón*, or gorge, of the property's name—where the first, unsuccessful attempt to found Buenos Aires took place in 1536. When the property's current owner decided to develop what was then a run-down conventillo, he began to discover all sorts of things beneath the house: pottery and cutlery, the foundations of past constructions, and, after almost 20 years of careful excavation, a 500-foot network of tunnels. These were once used to channel water, but like the street itself, they were sealed after San Telmo's yellow-fever outbreaks. With the help of historians and architects, they've now been restored. Excellent hour-long guided tours in English and Spanish take you through low-lighted sections of them, dotted with glass cases displaying the objects found within them. The history lesson continues above ground, where you can see the surviving wall of a construction from 1740, and rooms of the 19th-century conventillo built around it. If you want to spend even more time here, you can rent the whole place for functions. ✉*Defensa 755, San Telmo, C1065AAM* ☎*11/4361–3002* ⊕*www.elzanjon.com. ar* 🖳*Guided tours 20 pesos* ⊗*Tours weekdays 10–6 on the hr.*

IF YOU HAVE TIME

Museo de Bellas Artes de La Boca Quinquela Martín (*Quinquela Martín Fine Arts Museum of La Boca*). Vibrant port scenes were the trademark of artist and philanthropist Benito Quinquela Martín, the man who first put La Boca on the cultural map. His work and part of his studio are showcased on the third floor of this huge building, which he donated to the state to create a cultural center in 1936. Don't be surprised to have to jostle your way in through kids filing into class: downstairs is an elementary school, something that the galleries' bland institutional architecture doesn't let you forget. Quinquela Martín set out to fill the second floor with Argentine art—on the condition that works were figurative and didn't belong to any "ism." Badly lighted rooms and lack of any visible organization make it hard to enjoy the minor paint-

CALLE MUSEO CAMINITO

✉ Caminito between Av.
Pedro de Mendoza (La
Vuelta de Rocha prom-
enade) and Olivarría, La
Boca

💲 Free

🕐 Daily 10–6.

■ "Caminito" comes from
a 1926 tango by Juan de
Dios Filiberto, who is said
to have composed it while
thinking of a girl leaning from
the balcony of a ramshackle
house like those here. It was
chosen by local artists Benito
Quinquela Martín (⇨*also
Museo de Bellas Artes de La
Boca Quinquela Martín*), who
helped establish the street as
an open-air museum.

■ Expect to be canvassed
by rival restaurant owners
near the start of Caminito and
along every other side street.
Most are touting overpriced,
touristy menus: the best tactic
to get by them is to accept
their leaflets with a serene
smile and *"gracias."*

■ The Caminito concept
spills over into nearby streets
Garibaldi and Magallanes,
which form a triangle with
it. The strange, foot-high
sidewalks along streets like
Magallanes, designed to prevent flooding, show how the
river's proximity has shaped
the barrio.

Cobblestones, tango dancers, and haphazardly constructed, vividly painted conventillos have made Calle
Museo Caminito the darling of Buenos Aires' postcard
manufacturers since this pedestrian street and open-
air museum/art market opened in 1959. Artists fill the
block-long street with works depicting port life and
tango, which is said to have been born in La Boca. It's
all more commercial than cultural, but its embrace of
all things tacky make it a fun outing.

HIGHLIGHTS

Conventillos. Many of La Boca's tenements have been
recycled into souvenir shops. The plastic Che Guevaras
and dancing couples make the shops in the **Centro Cultural de los Artistas** (✉*Magallanes 861* 🕐*Mon.–Sat.
10:30–6*) as forgettable as all the others on the street,
but the uneven stairs and wrought-iron balcony hint at
what a conventillo interior was like. A sculptor artist
owns the turquoise-and-tomato-red **Museo Conventillo de Marjan Grum** (✉*Garibaldi 1429*). The opening hours of this gallery–cultural center are erratic, but
even the facade is worth a look.

Local Art. Painters, photographers, and sculptors peddle
their creations from stalls along Caminito. Quality varies considerably; if nothing tempts you, focus on the
small mosaics set into the walls, such as Luis Perlotti's
Santos Vega. Another local art form, the brightly colored scrollwork known as *fileteado*, adorns many shop
and restaurant fronts near Caminito.

Tangueros. Competition is fierce between the pairs of
sultry dancers dressed to the nines in split skirts and
fishnets. True, they spend more time trying to entice you
into photo ops than actually dancing, but linger long
enough (and throw a big enough contribution in the
fedora) and you'll see some fancy footwork.

ings by Berni, Sívori, Soldi, and other local masters. Outside is a huge sculpture terrace with great views of the river and old port buildings on one side; and the Boca Juniors stadium and low-rise downtown skyline on the other. ⊠*Av. Pedro de Mendoza 1835, La Boca, C1169AAC* ☎*11/4301–1080* ⊡*3 pesos* ⊙*Tues.–Sun. 11–5:30.*

Museo Histórico Nacional. What better place for the National History Museum than overlooking the spot where the city was supposedly founded? The beautiful chestnut-and-white Italianate mansion that houses the museum once belonged to entrepreneur and horticulturalist Gregorio Lezama. It became a quarantine station when cholera and yellow-fever epidemics raged in San Telmo, before opening as this museum in 1897. At this writing, the museum is closed for some much-needed renovations and improvements to its security system (there was a small robbery in 2007). It's due to reopen in mid-2008.

The National History Museum sits in the shade of enormous magnolia, palm, cedar, and elm trees on the sloping hillside of **Parque Lezama.** Bronze statues of Greek heroes, stone urns, and an imposing fountain shipped from Paris hint of former glory. Patchy grass, cracked paths, and unpainted benches are a nod to more-recent times. A monument in the northwestern corner celebrates conquistador Pedro de Mendoza, said to have founded Buenos Aires on this spot. Watching over the park are the onion-shape domes of the Catedral Santísima Trinidad Iglesia Ortodoxa Rusa (Holy Trinity Russian Orthodox Church) immortalized by Argentine writer Ernesto Sabato in his novel *Sobre Heroes y Tumbas* (*Of Heroes and Tombs*). ⊠*Calle Defensa 1600, San Telmo, C1143AAH* ☎*11/4307–4457* ⊡*2 pesos* ⊙*Feb.–Dec., Tues.–Sun. 11–6.*

Museo Penitenciario Antonio Ballvé (*Antonio Ballvé Penitentiary Museum*). Exhibiting artifacts from early-20th-century prison life, this modest museum, once a women's hospice, includes a genuine striped uniform and jail cell. Behind its large courtyard stands Nuestra Señora del Carmen chapel, named after the patron saint of the federal penitentiary service. The chapel dates from the Jesuit period. ⊠*Humberto Primero 378, San Telmo, C1103ACH* ☎*11/4362–0099* ⊡*1 peso* ⊙*Mar.–Dec., Tues.–Fri. 2–5, Sun. noon–6.*

ART GALLERIES

Appetite. Wild child Daniela Luna's edgy gallery celebrates all things trashy. Her trademark curatorial approach is to cram more paintings on each gallery wall than a teenager's bedroom has posters. And it's working: despite starting the space with no money in 2002, she has-opened up a branch in Brooklyn, New York, and even Francis Ford Coppola dropped by on a recent Argentina trip. Star exhibits have included Yamandú Rodríguez's soft-core porn photo montages and Nicanor Aráoz's eerie drawings and collages that include taxidermic cats. Painters Ana Vogelfang and Juliana Iriart offer marginally more-conventional work. ⊠*Chacabuco 551, San Telmo, C1069AAK* ☎*11/4331–5404* ⊕*www.appetite.com.ar* ⊙*Mon.–Sat. 2–7.*

Wussmann. It's hard to say which is more covetable at San Telmo's best-established gallery: the art or the building. A century-old house has been opened up into deep space, interrupted only by the original iron columns supporting the roof. The main exhibition space fronts the street; recent shows have included Roberto Plate's bold, semiabstract acrylics and beloved local illustrator Liniers. Up-and-coming artists and photographers exhibit in a smaller first-floor gallery. Exquisite leather-bound notebooks and handmade paper fill the back of the space. ⊠ *Venezuela 574, San Telmo, C1095AAL* ☎ *11/4343–4707* ⊕ *www.wussmann.com* ⊙ *Weekdays 10:30–8; Sat. 10:30–1.*

2

RECOLETA & ALMAGRO

Sightseeing
★★★★
Dining
★★★
Lodging
★★★★
Shopping
★★★★
Nightlife
★★

For the most-illustrious families, Recoleta's boundaries are the boundaries of the civilized world. The local equivalents of the Vanderbilts are baptized and married in the Basílica del Pilar, throw parties in the Alvear Palace Hotel, live in spacious 19th-century apartments, and wouldn't dream of shopping elsewhere. Ornate mausoleums in the Cementerio de la Recoleta promise an equally stylish after-life.

Recoleta wasn't always synonymous with elegance. Colonists, including city founder Juan de Garay, farmed here. So did the Franciscan Recoleto friars, whose 1700s settlement here inspired the district's name. Their church, the Basílica del Pilar, was almost on the riverbank then: tanneries grew up around it, and Recoleta became famous for its *pulperías* (taverns) and brothels. Everything changed with the 1871 outbreak of yellow fever in the south of the city.

The elite swarmed to Recoleta, building the *palacios* and stately Parisian-style apartment buildings that are now the neighborhood's trademark. They also laid the foundations for Recoleta's concentration of intellectual and cultural activity: the Biblioteca Nacional (National Library), a plethora of top-notch galleries, and three publicly run art museums are all based here. Combine Recoleta's art and architecture with its beautiful parks and squares—many filled with posh pooches and their walkers—and sightseeing here becomes a visual feast. And despite the luxury around you, many sights are free (and so is window-shopping). An unofficial subdistrict, Barrio Norte, is one step south of Recoleta proper and one step down the social ladder. Shopping is the draw: local chains, sportswear flagships, and mini-malls of vintage clothing and club wear line Avenida Santa Fe between 9 de Julio and Puerreydón.

Almagro lies southwest of Recoleta but is a world apart. Traditionally a gritty, working-class neighborhood, it spawned many tango greats,

GETTING ORIENTED

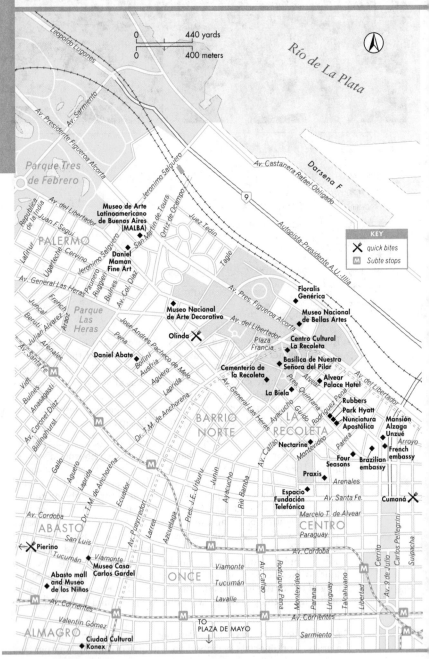

Río de La Plata

0   440 yards
0   400 meters

Leopoldo Lugones

Av. Presidente Figueroa Alcorta

Av. Sarmiento

Parque Tres de Febrero

Darsena F

Av. Castanera Rafael Obligado

Autopista Presidente A.U. Illia

9

PALERMO

Republica de la India

Av. del Libertador

Av. Juan F. Seguí

Lafinur

Ugarteche · Cervino

Jerónimo Salguero

Pasaraní

Bulnes

Av. Cnel. Díaz

Ruggieri

Av. General Las Heras

French

Juncal

Beruti

Arroz

Arenales

Julián Alvarez

Av. Santa Fe

Vidt

Bulnes

Anasagasti

Av. Coronel Díaz

Billinghurst

Gallo

Agüero

Laprida

Av. Córdoba

ABASTO

San Luis

Tucumán

Viamonte

Museo Casa Carlos Gardel

Abasto mall and Museo de los Niños

Av. Corrientes

Valentín Gómez

ALMAGRO

Ciudad Cultural Konex

Pierino

Museo de Arte Latinoamericano de Buenos Aires (MALBA)

San Martín de Tours

Ortiz de Ocampo

Juez Tedín

Tagle

Daniel Maman Fine Art

Jerónimo Salguero

Museo Nacional de Arte Decorativo

Parque Las Heras

Pena

José Andrés Pacheco de Melo

Olinda ✕

Daniel Abate

Bollini

Austria

Agüero

Laprida

Dr. T.M. de Anchorena

Cementerio de la Recoleta

BARRIO NORTE

Pres. J.E. Uriburu

Junín

Ayacucho

Río Bamba

Av. Callao

Azcuénaga

Larrea

Ecuador

Av. Pueyrredón

Dr. T.M. de Anchorena

Av. Pres. Figueroa Alcorta

Av. del Libertador

Plaza Francia

Av. General Las Heras

Guido

Pres. Quintana

Av. Callao

ONCE

Viamonte

Tucumán

Lavalle

TO PLAZA DE MAYO
↓

Sarmiento

Peña Zanjorigy

Rodríguez Peña

Montevideo

Paraná

Uruguay

CENTRO

Paraguay

Av. Córdoba

Av. Corrientes

Av. Santa Fe

Marcelo T. de Alvear

Talcahuano

Libertad

Cerrito

Av. 9 de Julio

Carlos Pellegrini

Suipacha

Floralis Genérica

Museo Nacional de Bellas Artes

Centro Cultural La Recoleta

Basílica de Nuestra Señora del Pilar

La Biela

Alvear Palace Hotel

Alvear

Av. del Libertador

Rubbers

Park Hyatt

Nunciatura Apostólica

Mansión Alzaga Unzué

Arroyo

French embassy

LA RECOLETA

Nectarine

Four Seasons

Brazilian embassy

Parera

Posadas

Praxis

Arenales

Espacio Fundación Telefónica

Cumaná ✕

THE TERRITORY

The River Plate borders Recoleta to the north. Uruguay and Montevideo join to form the eastern border; the jagged western edge is made up of Mario Bravo, Coronel Díaz, and Tagle. The area between Juncal and Córdoba—Recoleta's southern boundary—is known as Barrio Norte, whose main thoroughfare is Santa Fe. In Recoleta proper, Avenidas Alvear and Quintana are the key streets.

Almagro is officially bordered by Avenidas Córdoba and Estado de Israel to the north, Río de Janeiro to the west, Independencia to the south, and Sánchez de Bustamente and Gallo to the east. The Abasto subdistrict stretches a few blocks farther east into neighboring Balvanera.

GETTING AROUND

True to its elite roots, Recoleta has no subway, so taxis are the best option. Expect to pay around 10 pesos from downtown or Palermo. Buses are a cheaper option: Bus 17 runs from San Telmo and the Centro; the 92 connects Retiro and Recoleta, then continues to central Palermo and Almagro. Traffic can be slow within Recoleta and Barrio Norte—walking within the neighborhood is fast and pleasant.

Heavy traffic means Almagro is best reached by subte. Line B runs along Avenida Corrientes through Almagro; Carlos Gardel station leads right into the Abasto mall. Bus 24 connects Almagro with Centro and San Telmo; the 168 goes west to Palermo Viejo.

SAFETY & PRECAUTIONS

Recoleta and Barrio Norte are relatively safe in the day, but stick to well-lighted streets at night. Bag snatching is opportunist rather than systematic here: keep a firm grip on your purse in the crowded weekend market and in busy restaurants. Although Almagro is on the up, many streets near the Abasto mall are still run down, with many of the old houses functioning as squats. Wander with caution.

TAKING IT IN

You can blitz Recoleta's main sights in half a day, though you could easily spend a full morning or afternoon in the cemetery or cultural centers alone. Come midweek for quiet exploring, or on the weekend to do the cemetery and Plaza Francia crafts market in one fell swoop.

In Almagro, a couple of hours will suffice to see all things Carlos Gardel—tango's greatest hero—and get a feel for the district. The mall gets busier than most on weekends because of the Museo de los Niños (Children's Museum).

QUICK BITES

The stews and handmade empanadas at chaotic **Cumaná** (⊠*Rodríguez Peña 1149, Barrio Norte, C1020ADW* ☎*11/4893-9207*) are a far cry from Recoleta's posh European pretensions. Skip the desserts (nearby ice-creameries are better). Arrive early or late to avoid waiting.

Offerings like empanadas served with marinated pear, or goat cheese and Parma ham ravioli make for a perfect bistro lunch at **Olinda** (⊠*José León Pagano 2697, Recoleta, C1425AOA* ☎*11/4806-6343*). It's on a small side street several blocks north of the cemetery.

The exposed brick and the white tablecloths are clues that **Pierino** (⊠*Lavalle 3499, Almagro, C1190AAO* ☎*11/4864-5715*) is a homey trattoria. The owner-chef likes to suggest dishes; the pastas are usually excellent.

including the legendary Carlos Gardel. The Abasto subdistrict has long been the heart of the barrio: it centers on the massive art deco building (at Corrientes and Agüero) that was once the city's central market. The abandoned structure was completely overhauled and reopened in 1998 as a major mall, spearheading the redevelopment of the area, which now has several top hotels and an increasing number of restaurants and tango venues. More urban renewal is taking place a few blocks away at Sarmiento and Jean Jaurés, where the Konex Foundation has transformed an abandoned factory into a cutting-edge cultural venue.

TWO WAYS TO EXPLORE

WHISTLESTOP RECOLETA

Recoleta is perfect for whirlwind visits (after a meeting or before a flight, say): it's close to downtown and several major sights.

Museums open late midweek, so if you come in the morning, start at **Cementerio de la Recoleta.** To say "been there, done that," make a beeline for Evita. Walk straight from the entrance gate then take a left when you reach the small square. After about 400 yards turn right up a big "avenue," then take the third passage on your left: the Duarte family tomb is halfway down on the left-hand side. Five minutes is enough to take in the neighboring **Basílica del Pilar,** and you can get an overview of the cloister museum in 20–30 minutes. Vendors often sell sandwiches and soft drinks from carts outside.

Recoleta's poshest shops are concentrated on parallel **Avenida Quintana** and **Avenida Alvear:** wander down one as far as Rodríguez Peña then double back along the other. An espresso in the **Alvear Palace Hotel** lobby combines ogling with refueling.

Leave the **Museo Nacional de Bellas Artes** for last: it doesn't open until 12:30 and it takes almost as long to cross the busy avenues to reach it as to get around it. If you've got time to spare, do **Plaza Francia** (on the cemetery side of Avenida Figueroa Alcorta), then cross to Plaza Naciones Unidas for a photo of the **Floralis Genérica.** Back at Bellas Artes, play speed museum by heading straight upstairs to the Argentine collection. At the top, pre- and turn-of-the-20th-century work is in the galleries on the left, the 1930s to the present are on the right. Hail a cab on Avenida Figueroa Alcorta to get downtown quickly; hail one on Avenida del Libertador to go to Palermo.

IN THE LAP OF LUXURY

See how Buenos Aires' other half live with an hour or two strolling the environs of Avenida Alvear. The stiffly coiffed grandes dames of Recoleta have long favored **La Biela,** a café on the corner of Avenidas Quintana and R.M. Ortíz, for their morning coffee and people-watching (poodle parking is available). Be warned that a nondescript sandwich and coffee can add up to 40 pesos. For a Recoleta dinner, only French cuisine will do: **Nectarine** is perfect for a romantic night out.

Ralph Lauren, Louis Vuitton, and Armani all have shops of Avenida Alvear, but your peso packs more punch if you buy from local designers like Martín Churba. Jewelry genius Celedonio Lohihoy is one of the favored few to have a shop inside the Alvear Palace Hotel's shopping arcade. Parallel Avenida Quintana is home to rising local couture stars Evangelina Bomparola and Zitta Costura.

Gorgeous late-19th- and early-20th-century mansions line Alvear. Diplomatic missions occupy three of the most opulent: the Vatican's representatives work from the **Nunciatura Apostólica** (Number 1637); while the **French embassy** and the **Brazilian embassy** take up buildings inspired by French palaces near the intersection with Cerrito.

Two more former residences now rival the Alvear Palace Hotel as Alvear's most-luxurious digs. Creamy neoclassical stone columns front the **Park Hyatt,** once the Palacio Duhau, where lavish afternoon tea or Sunday brunch are the perfect excuse for a glimpse inside. Only the likes of Madonna are allowed to cross the threshold of the **Mansión Alzaga Unzué,** an annex to the Four Seasons. The corner of Alvear and Cerrito affords good views of its stylish redbrick-and-stone facade, inspired by Loire Valley castles (you'll just have to imagine the gold-plated faucets and Carrara marble staircases within).

MAIN ATTRACTIONS

Basílica de Nuestra Señora del Pilar. This basilica beside the famous Cementerio de la Recoleta on Junín is where Buenos Aires' elite families hold weddings and other ceremonies. It was built by the Recoleto friars in 1732 and is considered a national treasure for its six German Baroque–style altars. The central one is overlaid with Peruvian engraved silver; another contains relics and was sent by Spain's King Carlos III. In the cloisters, which date from 1716, is the **Museo de los Claustros del Pilar,** a small museum of religious artifacts as well as pictures and photographs documenting Recoleta's evolution. There are excellent views of the cemetery from upstairs windows.

Fodor'sChoice **Cementerio de la Recoleta.**
★
See the highlighted listing in this chapter.

Centro Cultural La Recoleta. Former cloister patios of the Franciscan monks have been converted into a cultural center with exhibits, performances, and workshops. Kids love the mini-museum inside it, whose motto, Prohibido No Tocar (Not Touching Is Forbidden), says it all. On weekends the area around the center and cemetery teems with shoppers and street performers in a large artisan fair: **La Feria de Plaza Francia.** At the end of a *veredita* (little sidewalk), you can find the Paseo del Pilar lined with expensive places to eat and the Buenos Aires Design Center, a mini-mall selling home wares and souvenirs. ⊠*Junín 1930, Recoleta, C1113AAT* ☎*11/4803–1040* ⊕*www.centroculturalrecoleta. org* ⊘*Tues.–Fri. 2–9, weekends 10–9.*

Fodor'sChoice **Museo Nacional de Bellas Artes.**
★
See the highlighted listing in this chapter.

IF YOU HAVE TIME

Cementerio de Chacarita. This cemetery is home to Carlos Gardel's tomb, which features a dapper, Brylcreemed statue and dozens of tribute plaques. Rather than a monument, it's treated more like a shrine by hordes of faithful followers who honor their idol by inserting lighted cigarettes in his statue's hand. On June 24, the anniversary of his death, aging tangueros in suits and fedoras gather here to weep and sing. Fellow tango legends Aníbal Troilo and Osvaldo Pugliese are also buried in this cemetery, which is about equidistant from Palermo and Almagro. If you're heading from Almagro, hop subte Line B at the Carlos Gardel Station for a 10- to 15-minute ride west to the Federico Lacroze stop. Depending on where you are in Palermo, a cab here will cost you 10 to 20 pesos. ⊠*Guzmán 680, at Corrientes, Chacarita C1427BOT* 📞*11/4553-9338* ⊕*www.cementeriochacarita.com.ar* 🎫 *Free* ⊘*Daily 7 AM–8 PM* Ⓜ *B to Federico Lacroze.*

Floralis Genérica. The gleaming steel and aluminum petals of this giant flower look very space age, perhaps because they were commissioned from the Lockheed airplane factory by architect Eduardo Catalano, who designed and paid for the monument. The 66-foot-high structure is supposed to open at dawn and close at dusk, when the setting sun turns its mirrored surfaces a glowing pink: the mechanism is often out of order, however. The flower stands in the Plaza Naciones Unidas (behind El Museo Nacional de Bellas Artes over Avenida Figueroa Alcorta), which was remodeled to accommodate it. ⊠*Plaza Naciones Unidas at Av. Figueroa Alcorta and J.A. Biblioni, Recoleta* ⊘*Dawn–dusk.*

Museo Casa Carlos Gardel. Hard-core tango fans shouldn't pass up a visit to the home of tango's greatest hero, Carlos Gardel. The crumbling *casa chorizo* (sausage house, that is a long, narrow house) has been restored with the aim of re-creating as closely as possible the way the house would have looked when Gardel and his mother lived here, right down to the placement of birdcages on the patio. Concise but informative Spanish texts talk you through the rooms and Gardel paraphernalia, and there are lots of tango souvenirs on offer in the shop. ⊠*Jean Jaurés 735, Almagro, C1215ACM* 📞*11/4516-0943* ⊕*www.museos. buenosaires.gov.ar/gardel* 🎫*3 pesos, Wed. free* ⊘*Mon. and Wed.–Fri. 11–6, weekends 10–7* Ⓜ*B to Carlos Gardel.*

☾ **Museo de los Niños.** The real world is scaled down to kiddie size at this museum in the Abasto shopping mall. Children can play at sending letters, going to a bank, acting in a mini-TV studio, or making a radio program. You need to speak Spanish to participate in most activities, but the play areas and giant pipes re-creating the city's water system are internationally comprehensible. ⊠*Abasto Shopping Center, Level 2, Av. Corrientes 3247, Almagro, C1193AAE* 📞*11/4861-2325* ⊕*www.museoabasto.org.ar* 🎫*9 pesos, 4-person family ticket 27 pesos* ⊘*Tues.–Sun. 1–8.*

Museo Nacional de Arte Decorativo. The harmonious, French neoclassical mansion that houses the National Museum of Decorative Art is as much a reason to visit as the period furnishings, porcelain, and silver within it. Ornate wooden paneling in the Regency ballroom, the imposing Louis XIV red-and-black marble dining room, and a lofty Renaissance-style great hall are some of the highlights of the only house of its kind open to the public in Buenos Aires. There are excellent English descriptions of each room, and they include gossipy details about the house's original inhabitants, the well-to-do Errazuriz family. The museum also contains some Chinese art. Guided tours include the Zubov collection of miniatures from Imperial Russia. ⊠*Av. del Libertador 1902, Recoleta, C1425AAS* ☎*11/4801–8248* ⊕*www.mnad. org* ⊠*2 pesos, free Tues.; guided tours 3 pesos* ⊙*Mar.–Dec., Tues.– Sun. 2–7; Jan. and Feb., Tues.–Sat. 2–7; closed last wk of Dec. and 1st wk of Jan.; guided tours in English Tues.–Sun. at 2:30.*

ART GALLERIES

★ **Daniel Abate.** Most of Abate's artists have yet to reach their 30th birthdays, yet they've got plenty of local prizes among them. Unusual media is a common denominator—look for Alita Olivari's Koons-like sculptures, Lila Siegrist's high-color photos of diminutive model landscapes, and outlandish installations by Eduardo Novarro and Oligatega Numeric. Abate alternates individual and collective shows. ⊠*Pasaje Bollini 2170, Recoleta, C1425ECB* ☎*11/4804–8247* ⊕*www.daniela bategaleria.com.ar* ⊙*Tues.–Sat. noon–7.*

Espacio Fundación Telefónica. Spanish-owned phone company Telefónica is behind this slick gallery, which they've strived to make as technological as possible. Video art and new media are showcased on the huge flat screens of the Espacio Plasma. There's a state-of-the-art media library, and audio guides come in the form of programmed cell phones—a nifty bit of marketing. ⊠*Arenales 1540, Barrio Norte, C1061AAR* ☎*11/4333–1300* ⊕*www.espacioft.org.ar* ⊙*Tues.–Sun. 2–8:30.*

Praxis. Choice contemporary Argentine painting and photography are the main emphases of this sparse gallery. Their discreet shows have attracted Argentine collectors for years—their branches in Miami and New York are now taking local work international. ⊠*Arenales 1311, Recoleta, C1061AAM* ☎*11/4813–8639* ⊕*www.praxis-art.com* ⊙*Weekdays 10:30–8, Sat. 10:30–2.*

Rubbers. The name may sound quirky, but this formidable gallery on Avenida Alvear is anything but. The list of artists it represents reads like a who's who of Argentine art, and includes grand masters Xul Solar, Berni, Spilimbergo, and Seguí; photographer Aldo Sessa; and abstract genius Luis Felipe Noé, who exhibits here each year. ⊠*Av. Alvear 1595, Recoleta, C1014AAC* ☎*11/4816–1864* ⊕*www.rubbers. com.ar* ⊙*Weekdays 11–8, Sat. 11–1:30.*

CEMENTERIO DE LA RECOLETA

✉ Junín 1760, Recoleta, C1113AAT

☎ 11/4803–1594

💲 Free

🕐 Daily 8–6.

The ominous gates, Doric-columned portico, and labyrinthine paths of the city's oldest cemetery (1822) may leave you with a sense of foreboding. The final resting place for the nation's most-illustrious figures covers 13.5 acres that are rumored to be the most expensive real estate in town. The cemetery has more than 6,400 elaborate vaulted tombs and majestic mausoleums, 70 of which have been declared historic monuments. The mausoleums resemble chapels, Greek temples, pyramids, and miniature mansions.

HIGHLIGHTS

Evita. The embalmed remains of Eva Perón, who made it (almost intact) here after 17 years of posthumous wandering, are in the Duarte family vault. Around July 26, the anniversary of her death, flowers pile up here.

Late Greats. If the tomb of brutal *caudillo* (dictator) Facundo Quiroga looks small, it's because he's buried standing—a sign of valor—at his request. Prominent landowner Dorrego Ortíz Basualdo resides in Recoleta's most monumental sepulcher, complete with chandelier. The names of many key players in Argentina's history are chiseled over other sumptuous mausoleums: Alvear, Quintana, Sáenz Peña, Lavalle, Sarmiento.

Spooky Stories. Rufina Cambaceres is known as the girl who died twice. She was thought dead after suffering a cataleptic attack and was entombed on her 19th birthday in 1902. Rufina awoke inside her casket and clawed the top open but died of a heart attack before she could be rescued. When Alfredo Gath heard of Rufina's story he was appalled and commissioned a special mechanical coffin with an opening device and alarm bell. Gath successfully tested the coffin in situ 12 times, but on the 13th the mechanism failed and he died inside.

Calle Azcuénaga

Cementerio de la Recoleta

Calle Pres. J. E. Uriburu

Calle Vicente López

Basílica del Pilar

Calle Junín

ENTRANCE

Luis Ángel Firpo

Roque Sáenz Peña

Juan Lavalle

Evita

Domingo Faustino Sarmiento

Rufina Cambaceres

Dorrego Ortíz Basualde

Facundo Quiroga

Carlos M. de Alvear

Office

Capilla

Administration

MUSEO NACIONAL DE BELLAS ARTES

✉ Av. del Libertador 1473, Recoleta, C1425AAA

☎ 11/4803–0802 tours (in Spanish)

🌐 www.mnba.org.ar

🎟 Free

🕐 Tues.–Fri. 12:30–7:30, weekends 9:30–7:30.

TIPS & TRIVIA

■ Head straight for the first-floor Argentine galleries while you're feeling fresh, and keep the European collection for later.

■ Information about most works is in Spanish only, as are the excellent theme guided tours. For English information, check out one of the MP3 audio guides (15 pesos) in the scant gift shop at the bottom of the stairs.

■ You wouldn't know it by looking at the museum's elegant columned front, but the building was once the city's waterworks.

■ Cándido López painted his panoramic battle scenes with his left hand after losing his right arm in the War of the Triple Alliance of the 1870s. His work spearheaded contemporary primitive painting. Local master Eduardo Sívori's tranquil landscapes portray less-turbulent times.

■ The large modern pavilion behind the museum hosts excellent temporary exhibitions, often showcasing top local artists little known outside Argentina.

The world's largest collection of Argentine art is displayed in this huge golden-color stone building. The 24 ground-floor galleries contain European art. Upstairs, the beautifully curated Argentine circuit starts in Room 102 with works from colonial times through the 19th century. Follow the galleries around to the right and through 20th-century art.

HIGHLIGHTS

The Rest of the River Plate. Uruguayan artists like Rafael Barradas and Joaquín Torres García are the focus of the hushed Colección María Luisa Bemberg, tucked away off the 19th-century Argentinean gallery.

Picturesque Portraits. Gauchos cut evocative figures in Cesáreo Bernaldo de Quirós's oil paintings. The highly colorful depictions of port laborers in *Elevadores a Pleno Sol* are typical of the work of Benito Quinquela Martín, La Boca's unofficial painter laureate.

At the Cutting Edge. The huge final gallery shows the involvement of Argentine artists in European avant-garde movements before adopting homegrown ideas. Emilio Pettorutti's *El Improvisador* (1937) combines cubist techniques with a Renaissance sense of space, while Lino Enea Spilimbergo's *Terracita* (1932) is an enigmatic urban landscape.

Movers and Shakers. Contemporary Argentine art exhibits include geometric sculptures and the so-called *informalismo* (informalism) of the '60s. Its innovative use of collage is best exemplified in works by Antonio Berni. Psychedelic paintings, op art, and kinetic works from '60s gurus like Jorge de la Vega and Antonio Seguí follow.

Museo Nacional de Bellas Artes

2

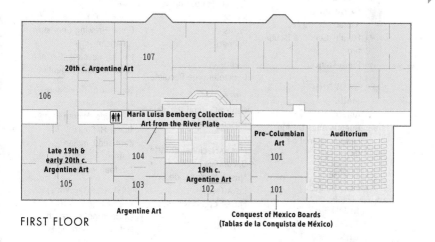

107
20th c. Argentine Art
106

♿ María Luisa Bemberg Collection: Art from the River Plate

Pre-Columbian Art
101

Auditorium

Late 19th & early 20th c. Argentine Art
105

104

19th c. Argentine Art
102

103

101

Argentine Art

Conquest of Mexico Boards
(Tablas de la Conquista de México)

FIRST FLOOR

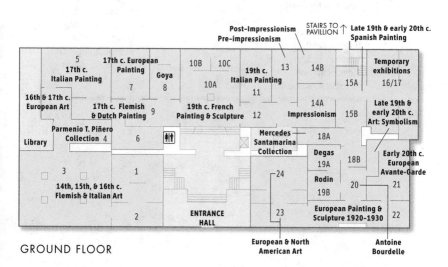

Post-Impressionism
Pre-impressionism

STAIRS TO PAVILLION ↑

Late 19th & early 20th c. Spanish Painting

5
17th c. Italian Painting

17th c. European Painting

Goya
8

10B   10C

10A

19th c. Italian Painting
11

13   14B

15A

Temporary exhibitions
16/17

16th & 17th c. European Art

7

17th c. Flemish & Dutch Painting
9

19th c. French Painting & Sculpture
12

14A

Impressionism

15B

Late 19th & early 20th c. Art: Symbolism

Library

Parmenio T. Piñero Collection 4

6

♿

Mercedes Santamarina Collection

18A

Degas
19A

18B

Early 20th c. European Avante-Garde

3

14th, 15th, & 16th c. Flemish & Italian Art

1

24

Rodin
19B

20   21

2

ENTRANCE HALL

23

European Painting & Sculpture 1920–1930

22

GROUND FLOOR

European & North American Art

Antoine Bourdelle

At a Glance

LANDMARKS & KEY STREETS
Av. Alvear
Av. Corrientes (2800–3900 blocks)
Av. Quintana
Avenida Santa Fe
Floralis Genérica (sculpture)
Plaza Francia

SHOPPING ⇨ CH. 3
Malls
Abasto
Buenos Aires Design
Feria Artesanal de Recoleta

Market
Patio Bullrich

SIGHTS & EXPERIENCES ⇨ CHS. 1 & 2
Architecture—Historical
Alvear Palace Hotel
Basílica del Pilar
Brazilian embassy
French embassy
Mansión Alzaga Unzué

Nunciatura Apostólica
Park Hyatt

Art Galleries
Daniel Abate
Espacio Fundación Telefónica
Praxis
Rubbers

Cemetery
Cementerio de Recoleta

Museums
Centro Cultural Recoleta
Museo Casa Carlos Gardel
Museo Nacional de Arte Decorativo
Museo Nacional de Bellas Artes
Museo de los Niños

WHERE TO EAT
Quick Bites (⇨ Getting Oriented)
Cumaná
Olinda
Pierino

Restaurants—Budget (⇨ Ch. 5)

La Biela, Café
La Maroma, Argentine
Modena Design Café, Café

Restaurants—Moderate (⇨ Ch. 5)
Buller Brewing Company, American
Munich Recoleta, German
El Sanjuanino, Argentine

Restaurants—Expensive (⇨ Ch. 5)
Club Sirio, Middle Eastern
Juana M, Steak
Katmandú, Indian
Malevo, Argentine
Tandoor, Indian

Restaurants—Very Expensive (⇨ Ch. 5)
La Bourgogne, French
Duhau Restaurante & Vinoteca, Eclectic
Le Mistral, Mediterranean
Nectarine, French
Oviedo, Spanish
Republica, Argentine
San Babila, Italian

2

PALERMO

Sightseeing
★★★★
Dining
★★★★★
Lodging
★★★★
Shopping
★★★★★
Nightlife
★★★

Trendy shops, bold restaurants, elegant embassies, acres of parks—Palermo really does have it all. Whether your idea of sightseeing is ticking off museums, flicking through clothing rails, licking your fingers after yet another long lunch, or kicking up a storm on the dance floor, Palermo can oblige. The city's largest barrio is subdivided into various unofficial districts, each with its own distinct flavor.

Luminous boutiques, minimal lofts, endless bars, and the most fun and daring restaurants in town have made Palermo Viejo (also known as Palermo Soho) the epicenter of Buenos Aires' design revolution. Many are contained in beautifully recycled town houses built in the late 19th century, when Palermo became a popular residential district. Most shops and eateries—not to mention desirable properties—in Palermo Viejo fill the cobbled streets around Plazoleta Cortázar.

In neighboring Palermo Hollywood, quiet barrio houses and the rambling flea market at Dorrego and Niceto Vega sit alongside sharp tapas bars filled with media types from the TV production centers that give the area its nickname.

Some say Palermo takes its name from the surname of a 16th-century Italian immigrant who bought lands in the area, others from the abbey honoring Saint Benedict of Palermo. Either way, the area was largely rural until mid-19th century, when dictator Juan Manuel de Rosas built an estate here. After his defeat, these grounds were turned into the huge patchwork of parks north of Avenida del Libertador. Their official name, Parque Tres de Febrero, is a reference to February 3, 1852, the day Rosas was defeated in battle. The park, which is more commonly known as Los Bosques de Palermo (the Palermo Woods), provides a peaceful escape from the rush of downtown. The zoo and botanical gardens are at its southern end.

GETTING ORIENTED

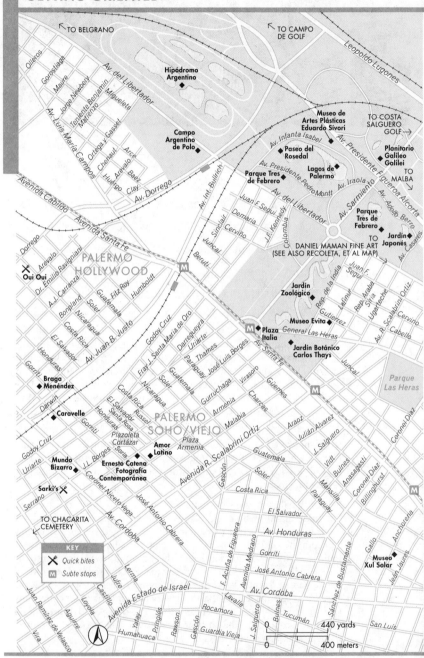

TO BELGRANO

TO CAMPO DE GOLF

Leopoldo Lugones

Olleros
Gorostiaga
Maure
Jorge Newbery
Teniente Benjamín Matienzo
Miguelets
Av. del Libertador
Av. Luis María Campos

Hipódromo Argentino

Campo Argentino de Polo

Museo de Artes Plásticas Eduardo Sívori

TO COSTA SALGUERO GOLF

Av. Infanta Isabel

Paseo del Rosedal

Planitario Galileo Galilei

Av. Presidente Figueroa Alcorta

TO MALBA

Ortega y Gasset
Arce
Arévalo
Báez
Huérgo
Clay
Chenaut
Arévalo

Parque Tres de Febrero

Lagos de Palermo

Av. Presidente Pedro Montt

Av. Iraola

Av. Sarmiento

Av. Adolfo Berro

Avenida Cabildo

Av. Dorrego

Juan F. Seguí
Demaría
Cerviño
Sinfial
Juncal
Beruti
J.F. Kennedy
Colombia

Av. del Libertador

Parque Tres de Febrero

Jardín Japonés

Av. Cáseres

Dorrego
Arévalo

Avenida Santa Fe

DANIEL MAMAN FINE ART
(SEE ALSO RECOLETA, ET AL MAP)

Juan F. Seguí

PALERMO HOLLYWOOD

Oui Oui

Dr. Emilio Ravignani
A.J. Carranza
Bonpland
Nicaragua
Costa Rica
El Salvador
Honduras
Gorriti
Soler
Guatemala
Fitz Roy
Humboldt
Av. Juan B. Justo

Godoy Cruz
Santa María de Oro
Darégueyra
Uriarte
Thames
Paraguay
José Luis Borges

Jardín Zoológico

Rep. de la India
Gutiérrez
Lafinur
Rep. Árabe Siria
Ugarteche
R. Scalabrini Ortiz
Cerviño
A.R. Cabello

Museo Evita

Braga Menéndez

Darwin

Caravelle

Fray J. Santa María de Oro

Virasoro
Guemes
Charcas

Plaza Italia

Jardín Botánico Carlos Thays

General Las Heras

Av. Santa Fe

Parque Las Heras

PALERMO SOHO/VIEJO

Costa Rica
Russel
El Salvador
Santa Rosa
Honduras
Plazoleta Cortázar
Soria
Nicaragua
Soler
Guatemala
Gurruchaga
Armenia
Malabia

Plaza Armenia

Amor Latino

Araoz
Julián Álvarez
J. Salguero
Vidt
Bulnes
Coronel Díaz

Godoy Cruz
Uriarte
Serrano

Mundo Bizarro

Ernesto Catena Fotografía Contemporánea

Sarki's

Avenida R. Scalabrini Ortiz

Guatemala
Soler
Costa Rica
El Salvador

Gascón
Mansilla
Paraguay
Anasagasti
Coronel Díaz
Billinghurst

TO CHACARITA CEMETERY

J.L. Borges
Coronel Niceto Vega
José Antonio Cabrera
Av. Córdoba

Av. Honduras
Gorriti
José Antonio Cabrera
Av. Córdoba

Gallo

Museo Xul Solar

Anchorena

Lerma
Juffe
Castillo

F. Acuña de Figueroa
Avenida Medrano
Lavalle
Rocamora
Gascón
Guardia Vieja

El Salvador

Sánchez de Bustamante
Jean Jaurés

Juan Ramírez de Velasco
Aguirre
Víal
Loyola
Yatay
Pringlés
Ravson

Avenida Estado de Israel
Humahuaca

J. Salguero
Bulnes
Tucumán

San Luis

KEY	
✕	Quick bites
Ⓜ	Subte stops

0 — 440 yards
0 — 400 meters

THE TERRITORY

The city's biggest barrio stretches from Avenida Costanera R. Obligado, along the river, to Avenida Córdoba in the south. Its other boundaries are jagged, but include Avenida Coronel Díaz to the east and La Pampa and Dorrego to the west. Avenida Santa Fe cuts the neighborhood roughly in half. Palermo's green spaces and Palermo Chico lie north of it. To the south are Palermo Viejo and Palermo Hollywood, east and west of Avenida Juan B. Justo, respectively.

GETTING AROUND

Subte Línea (Line) D runs along Avenida Santa Fe but only brings you within about 10 blocks of Palermo's attractions, so you may need to combine it with a taxi or some walking. Indeed, weekday traffic makes this combination a better idea than coming all the way from Centro by cab (which costs 15–20 pesos). Get off the subte at Bulnes or Scalabrini Ortíz for Palermo Chico; Plaza Italia for Palermo Viejo and the parks; and Ministro Carranza for Palermo Hollywood.

A more-scenic route to Palermo Viejo and Hollywood from Centro is Bus 39 (Route 3, usually with a windshield sign PALERMO VIEJO). It runs along Honduras on the way to Palermo and Gorriti on the way back, and it takes 30–60 minutes. Once you're in Palermo, walking is the best way to get around: much of the district is leafy and there's little traffic on its smaller streets.

SAFETY & PRECAUTIONS

Pickpocketing is the biggest threat, especially on crowded streets on weekends. Palermo Viejo's cobbled streets aren't well lighted at night, so avoid walking along any that look lonely. Although locals usually hail cabs on the street, it's safer to ask a restaurant or bar to call one for you. The usual caveats about parks apply to the Palermo woods: don't linger after dark, and avoid remote areas at any time if you're female and alone.

TAKING IT IN

Palermo is so big that it's best to tackle it in sections. An even-paced ramble through Parque Tres de Febrero should take no more than two hours, though you could easily spend an entire afternoon at the zoo, Japanese Garden, and Botanical Garden. Shoppers have been known to spend their whole trip in Palermo Viejo, but a couple of hours and a meal is enough to get a feel for it. In architectural and geographic terms, Palermo Chico and the MALBA tie in nicely with a visit to Recoleta: allow at least a couple of hours for such an experience.

QUICK BITES

French-cute is one way to describe the baby-pink tables and black-board filled with quirkily named dishes at **Oui Oui** (✉ *Nicaragua 6068, Palermo Hollywood* ☎ *11/4778–9614* ⊘ *Closed Mon.*). Chef Rocío García Orza achieves a rare thing: homemade breakfast, lunch, and tea that's so much better than anything you could make at home. By teatime the counter is crammed with baked goods.

The southern end of Palermo Viejo is Buenos Aires' Little Armenia, and no one does the old country's food better than **Sarkis** (✉ *Thames 1101, Palermo Viejo* ☎ *11/4771–4911*). A selection of classic mezes—hummus, tabouleh, baba ghanoush, kepeh, stuffed vine leaves—add up to a filling but great-value lunch. You'll want to leave room for some baklava, though.

Palermo has two mainstream shopping areas. The streets around the intersection of Avenidas Santa Fe and Coronel Díaz are home to the mid-range Alto Palermo mall and many cheap clothing stores. There are more-exclusive brands at El Solar de la Abadía mall and the nearby streets of Las Cañitas, Palermo's northwestern outpost. Its thriving, in-your-face bar-and-restaurant scene is the favorite of local models, TV starlets, and others dying to be seen. If a week away from your analyst is bringing on anxiety attacks, the quiet residential district around Plaza Güemes might bring some relief: it's nicknamed Villa Freud, for the high concentration of psychoanalysts who live and work here.

Plastic surgery and imported everything are the norm in Palermo Chico (between Avenidas Santa Fe and Libertador), whose Parisian-style mansions are shared out between embassies and rich local stars like diva Susana Giménez. The new kid on the block is the gleaming MALBA (Museo de Arte Latinoamericano de Buenos Aires or the Museum of Latin American Art of Buenos Aires), whose clean stone lines stand out on Avenida Figueroa Alcorta.

TWO WAYS TO EXPLORE

LADEN WITH SHOPPING BAGS

Ask any porteño which barrio is *fashion* (inventive local-speak for "trendy") and the answer will be Palermo Viejo. Home to all things hip since the economic crisis, the area blends boho style with truly hedonistic pleasures. Instead of museums and monuments, it's window- and people-watching that are top activities here. The outside tables at cafés **Plazoleta Cortázar** (better known as Plaza Serrano) and **Plaza Armenia,** Palermo Viejo's two centers of gravity, are a great place to watch alluring *palermitaños*—many arty rock- and film-stars live here—and see what's hot this season.

Shopping-mall staples have their Palermo outposts along parallel streets **Honduras** and **El Salvador,** between Malabia and J.L. Borges. Skip the familiar Nike and Levi's and focus on local chains like Paula Cahen D'Anvers, Bensimon, Complot, Rapsodia, Wanama, and Ayres. They're punctuated by pricier women's street wear and posh frock stops. For one-offs, hand-finishes, and more-unusual cuts, turn into the nearby blocks of the intersecting streets.

Boy-alley is **Gurruchaga,** home to metrosexual marketers and several dressy sneaker stores. The best shoes are south of Honduras, on parallel streets **Armenia, Malabia, Gurruchaga,** and **Fitzroy.** The Palermo stores of Argentina's more-exclusive designers are in satellite locations that you'll need to walk a few blocks from the main drags to reach.

ROSE PINK TO RED HOT

Palermo is perfect for a long, long afternoon of romance. Forget about a dozen red roses: at the **Paseo del Rosedal** (Rose Garden) you're surrounded by hundreds of blooms on thousands of bushes. The paths are perfect for wandering hand-in-hand. True, the pedal boats on the **Lagos de Palermo** (Palermo Lakes) aren't exactly Venetian gondolas, but there's plenty of tongue-in-cheek romancing to be had as you pedal in tandem. Worked up an appetite? Pink-painted tables, dried roses on the walls, and a dark dense chocolate cake that begs you to feed it to someone: French café **Oui Oui** will have you saying just that.

Window-shopping along Palermo Viejo's cobbled streets is romantic in itself, but you can dress the experience up with a visit to designer lingerie store **Amor Latino** on El Salvador (Number 4813). Add fuel to the fire with an industrial-strength cocktail at **Mundo Bizarro** (Serrano 1222): its red velour booths and Betty Page posters are naughty but oh-so-nice.

You can't say you've made love like a porteño until you've checked into a *telo*. These hourly hotels are where privacy-deprived local parents, teenagers, adulterers, and just plain lovers come for some time alone. They're clean, safe, and cheesy rather than sleazy—think mirrored ceilings, water beds, Muzak, and mood lighting. At **Caravelle**, on the corner of Niceto Vega and Darwin, you get a two-hour slot for 50–100 pesos (depending on the level of luxury); if you check in after midnight you can stay all night.

MAIN ATTRACTIONS

☾ **Jardín Japonés** (Japanese Garden). Like the bonsais in the nursery within it, this park is small but perfectly formed. A slow wander along its arched wooden bridges and walkways is guaranteed to calm frazzled sightseeing nerves during the week; crowds on the weekend make for a less-than-zen experience. A variety of shrubs and flowers frame the ponds, which brim with friendly koi carp that let you pet them should you feel inclined (kids often do). The traditional teahouse, where you can enjoy sushi, adzuki-bean sweets and tea, overlooks a zen garden. ⊠*Av. Casares at Av Adolfo Berro, Palermo* ☎*11/4804–4922* ⊕*www.jardinjapones.com.ar* ✉*Weekdays 3 pesos, weekends 4 pesos* ⊙*Daily 10–6.*

★ **Museo Evita.**

See the highlighted listing in this chapter.

Fodor'sChoice **Museo de Arte de Latinoamericano de Buenos Aires** (MALBA, Museum of
★ Latin American Art of Buenos Aires)

See the highlighted listing in this chapter.

☾ **Parque Tres de Febrero.** Known locally as Los Bosques de Palermo (Pal-
Fodor'sChoice ermo Woods), this 200-acre green space is really a crazy quilt of smaller
★ parks. Rich grass and shady trees make this an urban oasis, although the busy roads and horn-honking drivers that crisscross the park never quite let you forget what city you're in. South of Avenida Figueroa Alcorta you can take part in organized tai chi and exercise classes or impromptu soccer matches. You can also jog, bike, or in-line skate here, or take a boat out on the small lake.

MUSEO EVITA

✉ Lafinur 2988, 1 block north of Av. Las Heras, Palermo, C1425FAB

☎ 11/4807–9433

⊕ www.museoevita.org

🎫 10 pesos

🕘 Tues.–Sun. 1–7

Ⓜ D to Plaza Italia.

Eva Duarte de Perón, known universally as Evita, was the wife of populist president Juan Domingo Perón. She was both revered by her working-class followers and despised by the Anglophile oligarchy of the time. The Museo Evita shies from pop culture clichés and conveys facts about Evita's life and works, particularly the social aid programs she instituted and her role in getting women the vote. Knowledgeable staffers answer questions enthusiastically.

HIGHLIGHTS

Photographic Evidence. The route through the collection begins in a darkened room screening footage of thousands of mourners lining up to see Evita's body. Family photos and magazine covers document Evita's humble origins and time as a B-list actress. Upstairs there's English-subtitled footage of Evita's incendiary speeches to screaming crowds: her impassioned delivery beats Madonna hands down.

Death Becomes Her. The final rooms follow Evita's withdrawal from political life and her death from cancer at age 33. A video chronicles the fate of Evita's cadaver: embalmed by Perón, stolen by political opponents, and moved and hidden for 17 years before being returned to Argentina, where it now rests in the Recoleta Cemetery.

Fabulous Clothes. Evita's reputation as fashion plate is reflected in the many designer outfits on display, including her trademark working suits and some gorgeous ball gowns.

If you're looking for a sedate activity, try the **Museo de Artes Plásticas Eduardo Sívori** (*Eduardo Sívori Art Museum* ⊠*Av. Infanta Isabel 555, Palermo* ☎*11/4774–9452* ⊕*www.museosivori.org* ☑*1 peso, Wed. free* ⊙*Tues.–Fri. noon–8, weekends 10–8*). The focus of this 4,000-works-strong collection is 19th- and 20th-century Argentine art, including paintings by local masters like Lino Eneo Spilimbergo and the museum's namesake Sívori, and handmade textiles and weavings from all over the country. The shaded sculpture garden is the perfect combination of art and park.

Close to the Museo de Artes Plásticas Eduardo Sívori is the **Paseo del Rosedal** (*Rose Garden* ⊠*Avs. Infanta Isabel and Iraola* ☑*Free* ⊙*Apr.–Oct., daily 9–6; Nov.–Mar., daily 8–8*). About 15,000 rose-bushes (more than 1,000 different species) bloom seasonally in this rose garden. A stroll along the paths takes you through the Jardín de los Poetas (Poets' Garden), dotted with statues of literary figures, and to the enchanting Patio Andaluz (Andalusian Patio) whose majolica tiles and Spanish mosaics sit under a vine-covered pergola.

The **Planetario Galileo Galilei** (*Galileo Galilei Planetarium* ⊠*Avs. Sarmiento and Figueroa Alcorta, C1425FHA* ☎*11/4771–6629* ⊕*www.planetario.gov.ar* ☑*Free* ⊙*Weekdays 9–5, weekends 3–8*) is a great orb positioned on a massive concrete tripod. It looks like something out of *Close Encounters of the Third Kind*, and it seems as though small green men could descend from its central staircase at any moment. Content inside is flimsy, but the authentic 3,373-pound asteroid at the entrance is a highlight. The pond with swans, geese, and ducks is a favorite. The park gets crowded on sunny weekends, as this is where families come for strolls or picnics. If you'd like to picnic, take advantage of the street vendors who sell refreshments and *choripan* (chorizo sausage in a bread roll) within the park. There are also many posh cafés lining the Paseo de la Infanta (running from Libertador toward Sarmiento in the park). ⊠*Bounded by Avs. del Libertador, Sarmiento, Leopoldo Lugones, and Dorrego, Palermo* Ⓜ*D to Plaza Italia.*

IF YOU HAVE TIME

Jardín Botánico Carlos Thays. With 18 acres of gardens and 5,500 varieties of exotic and local flora, the Charles Thays Botanical Garden is an unexpected green haven wedged between three busy Palermo streets. Different sections re-create the environments of Asia, Africa, Oceania, Europe, and the Americas. Among the treasures is the Chinese "tree of gold," purportedly the only one of its kind. Winding paths lead to hidden statues, a brook, and past the resident cats and dragonflies. The central area contains a beautiful greenhouse, brought from France in 1900, and the exposed-brick botanical school and library. ⊠*Av. Santa Fe 3951, Palermo, C1425BHB* ☎*11/4832–1552* ☑*Free* ⊙*Sept.–Mar., daily 8–8; Apr.–Aug., daily 9–6.*

☾ **Jardín Zoológico.** You enter through the quasi-Roman triumphal arch into the architecturally eclectic, 45-acre city zoo. The pens, mews, statuary, and fountains themselves—many dating from the zoo's opening

MALBA

✉ Av. Presidente Figueroa
Alcorta 3415, Palermo,
C1425CLA

☎ 11/4808–6500

⊕ www.malba.org.ar

🎟 12 pesos, free Wed.

🕐 Thurs.–Mon. noon–8, Wed.
noon–9.

TIPS & TRIVIA

■ MALBA also has a great
art cinema showing restored
copies of classics, never-
released features, and silent
films with live music, as well
as local films of note.

■ Kids love hands-on
kinetic works like Julio Le
Parc's *Seven Unexpected
Movements,* a sculpture with
gleaming parts that move at
the press of a button.

■ Leave time to browse the
art books and funky design
objects of the museum's
excellent gift shop.

■ Young enthusiastic guides
give great tours in Spanish;
you can call ahead to arrange
group English-language tours.

■ Give your feet—and eyes—
a rest on the first-floor sculpture deck, with views over
Belgrano and Barrio Norte.

■ Córdoba-based studio AFT
Arquitectos' triangular construction in creamy stone and
steel is one of the museum's
draws. The main galleries run
along a four-story atrium,
flooded in natural light from a
wall of windows.

The fabulous Museum of Latin American Art of Buenos Aires (MALBA) is one of the cornerstones of the
city's cultural life. Its centerpiece is businessman and
founder Eduardo Constantini's collection of more than
220 works of 19th- and 20th-century Latin-American
art in the main first-floor gallery.

HIGHLIGHTS

Europe vs. Latin America. Early works in the permanent
collection reflect the European avant-garde experiences of painters like Diego Rivera, Xul Solar, Roberto
Matta, and Joaquín Torres García. Soon the Latin
American experience gave rise to works like *Abaporu*
(1928) by Tarsila do Amaral, a Brazilian involved in the
"cannibalistic" Movimento Antropofágico (rather than
eating white Europeans, proponents of the movement
proposed devouring European culture and digesting it
into something new). Geometric paintings and sculptures from the 1940s represent movements such as Arte
Concreto, Constructivism, and Arte Madí.

Argentine Art. Argentina's undisputed modern master is
Antonio Berni, represented by a poptastic collage called
The Great Temptation (1962) and the bizarre sculpture
Voracity or Ramona's Nightmare (1964), both featuring the eccentric prostitute Ramona, a character Berni
created in this series of works criticizing consumer society. Works by living local greats Liliana Porter, Marta
Minujín, Guillermo Kuitca, and Alejandro Kuropatwa
form the end of the permanent collection.

Temporary Exhibitions. World-class temporary exhibitions are held on the second floor two or three times
a year, and two small basement galleries show art by
cutting-edge locals.

2

in 1874—are well worth a look. Jorge Luis Borges said the recurring presence of tigers in his work was inspired by time spent here. Among the expected zoo community are a few surprises: a rare albino tiger; indigenous monkeys, known to perform lewd acts for their audiences; and llamas (watch out—they spit). Some smaller animals roam freely, and there are play areas for children, a petting farm, and a seal show. *Mateos* (traditional, decorated horse-drawn carriages) stand poised at the entrance to whisk you around the nearby parks. ⊠*Avs. General Las Heras and Sarmiento, Palermo* 📞*11/4806–7412* ⊕*www.zoobue nosaires.com.ar* 💲*13.50 pesos* ⊗*Tues.–Sun. 10–6:30.*

Museo Xul Solar. Avant-garde artist, linguist, esoteric philosopher, and close friend of Borges, Xul Solar is best known for his luminous, semi-abstract watercolors. They glow against the low-lighted concrete walls of this hushed museum. Solar's wacky but endearing beliefs in universalism led him to design a pan-language, pan-chess (a set is displayed here), and the Pan Klub, where these ideas were debated. One of its former members, architect Pablo Beitia, masterminded the transformation of the town house where Solar lived and worked. Open stairways crisscross the space, an homage to one of Solar's favorite motifs. ⊠*Laprida 1212, Palermo, C1425EKF* 📞*11/4824–3302* ⊕*www.xulsolar.org.ar* 💲*6 pesos* ⊗*Tues.–Fri. 12:30–7:30, Sat. noon–7.*

ART GALLERIES

★ **Braga Menéndez.** Florencia Braga Menéndez has created a space where a group of 30 artists is fast becoming popular with independent collectors. Curious browsers get a warm welcome, and serious buyers get professional guidance. Artists in her care include Warhol's buddy Marta Minujín and rising stars Juan Tessi and Max Gómez Canle. ⊠*Humboldt 1574, Palermo Hollywood, C1414CTN* 📞*11/4775–5577* ⊕*www.galeriabm.com* ⊗*Weekdays 11–8, Sat. 11–6.*

★ **Daniel Maman Fine Art.** This gallery space is stark, so try to let the art do the talking. Expect avant-garde artists like the Mondongo collective, whose wacky collages mix resin-encased *fiambres* (cold cuts) with textiles and X-rated photos. London's Tate Modern and New York's MoMA both snapped up a work for their permanent collections. ⊠*Av. del Libertador 2475, Palermo, C1425AAK* 📞*11/4804–3700* ⊕*www. danielmaman.com* ⊗*Weekdays 11–8, Sat. 11–7.*

Ernesto Catena Fotografía Contemporánea. Not content with bringing Argentina's best wines to the world, Ernesto Catena is determined to show off local photographic talent, too. In typical Palermo style, this clean white gallery is on the first floor of a recycled town house. Ultra-realist, high-color photography is a constant—think local answers to Nan Goldin, Martin Parr, and Rineke Dijkstra. ⊠*Honduras 4882, 1st fl., Palermo Viejo, C1414BMN* 📞*11/4833–9499* ⊕*www.ecfotografia contemporanea.com* ⊗*Tues.–Sat. noon–8.*

At a Glance

LANDMARKS & KEY STREETS
Av. Coronel Díaz
Av. Figueroa Alcorta
Av. del Libertador
Av. Santa Fe
Calle Honduras
Plaza Italia
Plazoleta Cortázar (Plaza Serrano)

SHOPPING
Malls
Alto Palermo
Paseo Alcorta
El Solar de la Abadía

Markets
Feria de Artesanías de Belgrano
Feria Modelo de Belgrano
Feria de Plaza Serrano
Mercado de las Pulgas

SIGHTS & EXPERIENCES
Art Galleries
Braga Menéndez
Daniel Maman Fine Art
Ernesto Catena Fotografía Contemporánea

Golf
Campo de Golf de la Ciudad de Buenos Aires
Costa Salguero Golf

Horse Racing
Hipódromo Argentino de Palermo

Polo
Campo Argentino de Polo

Museums
Museo de Arte de Latinoamericano de Buenos Aires
Museo Evita
Museo Xul Solar

Planetarium
Planetario Galileo Galilei

Parks & Gardens
Jardín Botánico Carlos Thays
Jardín Japonés
Jardín Zoológico
Parque Tres de Febrero/ Los Bosques de Palermo
Paseo del Rosedal

WHERE TO EAT
Quick Bites (⇨ Getting Oriented)
Oui Oui
Sarkis

Restaurants—Budget (⇨ Ch. 5)
Bangalore, Indian
Club Eros, Argentine
Mark's, American
Na Serapia, Argentine

Restaurants—Moderate (⇨ Ch. 5)
Don Julio, Steak
El Encanto, Steak
El Trapiche, Steak

Freud y Fahler, Argentine
Jardín Japonés, Japanese
Xalapa, Mexican

Restaurants—Expensive (⇨ Ch. 5)
Al Andalus, Spanish
La Baita, Italian
Barolo, Argentine
Bar 6, Argentine
Bar Uriarte, Argentine
Bella Italia, Italian
La Cabrera, Steak
El Estanciero, Steak
Kansas, American
Lelé de Troya, Eclectic
Malasaña, Argentine
María Félix, Mexican
Novecento, Argentine
Ølsen, Scandinavian
El Pobre Luis, Steak
Pura Tierra, Argentine
Rio Alba, Steak
Social Paraíso, Argentine
Sushi Club, Japanese

Restaurants—Very Expensive (⇨ Ch. 5)
Casa Cruz, Argentine
Desde El Alma, Argentine
Green Bamboo, Vietnamese
Lotus Neo Thai, Thai
Sifones & Dragones, Argentine
Sinclair, Spanish
Sucre, Argentine
Te Mataré, Ramírez, Eclectic

Saints, Sinners, & Prodigal Sons by Victoria Patience

One minute Argentines are cursing their country's shortcomings; the next they're waving a flag and screaming "Ar-gen-tina" as their soccer team chalks up a victory. But when it comes to their famous sons and daughters, most Argentinans are resolutely proud.

Were it not for the heroics of one man, José de San Martín, Argentina might not exist at all. Raised in Spain, he was a passionate believer in Latin American independence.

You could say that in modern Argentine politics, it takes two to tango. The original political double act was Juan Domingo Perón and his wife, Evita, who were revered and reviled in equal measure.

Indeed, passionate hatred of Perón and serious literary genius were among the few things shared by two great Argentine writers: erudite Anglophile Jorge Luis Borges and bearded bohemian Julio Cortázar.

Revolution was the passion of Ernesto Guevara, or rather, El Che. This middle-class med student was instrumental in the building of Castro's Cuba, and remains the figurehead of many left-wing student movements. You'll find Che's face tattooed on the arm of a different secular saint: Diego Armando Maradona, voted the 20th century's best soccer player by FIFA (International Football Association). The toughest local machos have been brought to tears by his goals.

POLITICAL FIGURES

AKA: El Libertador de America
BORN: February 25, 1778, in Yapeyú, Argentina
DIED: August 17, 1850, in Boulogne-sur-Mer, France
QUOTE: "Let us be free. Nothing else matters."
REMEMBERED: A national public holiday commemorates the anniversary of his death.

JOSÉ DE SAN MARTÍN

TOP 3 SAN MARTÍN SIGHTS

Plaza San Martín, named in his honor, contains a monument to the general, who looks dashing atop his horse.

Museo Histórico Nacional, which has recreated San Martín's bedroom at the time he died.

Catedral de Buenos Aires, home to his mausoleum.

BIO: Ironically, the man who freed Argentina from Spanish colonial shackles spent his formative years in Spain. But when news of Argentina's May 1810 revolution reached him, he abandoned an illustrious career in the Spanish army and rushed back to the country of his birth. His flamboyant military campaigns were instrumental in the independence of the Viceroyalty of the Río de la Plata (Argentina, Paraguay, Bolivia, and Uruguay). He then led his forces across the Andes to liberate Chile and Peru.

Today, San Martín's selfless idealism is universally lauded. However, he fell from favor in his lifetime by refusing to spill a fellow Argentine's blood and participate in Argentina's civil war. His military pension was never honored, and he died in France in severe financial straits, far from the country he'd fought so hard for.

POSTHUMOUS ADVENTURES: San Martín expressly requested in his will that his heart be buried in Buenos Aires. Political disagreements and red tape meant 30 years went by before his body was repatriated and he was finally laid to rest in a mausoleum in Buenos Aires Cathedral. The urn-like structure designed to contain his coffin was built too short, so he was placed in it on an angle (head down, local legend says) to fit.

(top) General José de San Martín engraving; (bottom) Monument to the Libertador General San Martín, by Frances Louis Joseph Daumes in Plaza San Martín, Buenos Aires, Argentina

2

AKA: El General; The Father of the Nation
BORN: October 8, 1895, in Lobos, Argentina
DIED: July 1, 1974, in Olivos, Argentina
QUOTE: "Better than saying is doing; better than promising, achieving."
REMEMBERED: Union members and fiercely loyal Peronists recreate the demonstrations in Plaza de Mayo that got Perón freed on October 17, 1945, the so-called Día de la Lealtad (Day of Loyalty).

POSTHUMOUS ADVENTURES: In 1987, thieves stole Perón's hands from his tomb in Buenos Aires' Chacarita Cemetery. Some say they demanded an $8 million ransom, others that they needed his finger prints to access a bank deposit box in Switzerland. When the body was moved to a special mausoleum in 2006, scuffles between police and Peronist demonstrators led to 40 injuries.

JUAN DOMINGO PERÓN

BIO: Fathoming the complexities of Perón and the Peronist movement is tricky. Inspired by Mussolini's brand of national socialism, Perón revolutionized worker's rights and nationalized Argentina's services, while his wife, Evita, instigated a huge social aid program. Despite this he loathed communism, and even secretly facilitated the entry of scores of Nazi war criminals into Argentina.

The General and Evita were the people's pin-ups, but things began to fall apart after her death. Ousted by a coup in 1955, Perón went into an 18-year exile, during which Peronism was made illegal in Argentina. He made a glorious comeback in 1973, but party in-fighting and his outright betrayal of young Peronist guerrilla groups soon soured things. He died in office in 1974 and was briefly and disastrously succeeded by the vice-president Isabel, his third wife, a former cabaret dancer. Argentina's most horrific dictatorship soon followed. Today, the Peronist party is riddled with contradictions and rival left- and right-wing factions, but Argentine politics still lives in its shadow.

(top) Juan Domingo Perón (1895-1974), president of Argentina, addressing the parliament, May, 1952; (bottom) Perón and Evita

SANTA EVITA

AKA: Evita, mother of the nation, Spiritual Leader of the Nation, Santa Evita (Saint Evita), *esa mujer* (that woman)

BORN: May 17, 1919, in Los Toldos, Argentina

DIED: July 26, 1952, in Buenos Aires

QUOTE: "I have only one thing that counts, and I carry it in my heart. It burns my soul, it aches in my flesh, and it stings my nerves, and that is my love for the people and for Perón. I never wanted anything for myself, nor do I want it now. My glory is and will always be Perón and the flag of my people."

REMEMBERED: Loyal Peronists cover Evita's tomb with flowers and hold candlelight vigils on the anniversary of her death.

EVA MARÍA DUARTE DE PERÓN

BIO: Evita was revered long before musicals and films made her internationally famous. Born in the provinces, she left home for Buenos Aires at 17, and soon became a B-movie actress. Her loyalties switched from showbiz to politics upon meeting Perón: when he became a political prisoner, she was instrumental in the uprising that got him released and eventually elected as president. Her campaign for female suffrage helped his re-election in 1951. Until her untimely death from cancer at the age of 33, Evita and Perón were a duo of unprecedented popularity. However, Evita is a contradictory figure: despite her designer frocks and perfect blonde chignon, her politics were radical, to the horror of the conservatives of the time. Her activism championed the working class as well as the poor and such marginalized groups as single mothers, and brought her millions of fanatical followers, who, more than 50 years on, still campaign for her to be made a saint.

POSTHUMOUS ADVENTURES: When a coup overthrew Perón in 1955, Evita's embalmed body was stolen by the opposition. The casket was stored in several army offices, hidden in an embassy garden in Bonn, buried under a false name in Italy, and put on display by Perón's third wife before it was finally laid in the family vault in Recoleta cemetery in 1977.

(top) 1950, Eva Peron being presented with an insignia by volunteer workers of the Institute for Work of Argentina

EVITA PILGRIMAGE

"¡Evita vive!" ("Evita lives"), her faithful followers never tire of saying. It's not just the national psyche she's left a lasting impression on: the city itself is full of places inextricably linked to her. Here's how to see them all during one day in Buenos Aires.

Start your pilgrimage in morbid Argentine style, at her tomb in **Recoleta Cemetery** (Junín 1760, Recoleta). If you come near the anniversary of her death, July 26, expect to be elbowed aside by weeping black-clad elderly women.

Intrigued? Catch a taxi or Buses 37, 59, or 60 north along nearby Avenida Las Heras to the 3900 block in Palermo to get the Evita 101 at the excellent **Museo Evita** (Lafinur 2988, 1 block north of Av. Las Heras, Palermo). The museum doesn't open until 1, which is a great excuse to make its classy restaurant (open all day) your first stop. You can also stock up on Evita goodies at the gift shop.

When you've had your fill of food and facts, catch the subte from nearby Plaza Italia to Catedral, which brings you up into the heart of **Plaza de Mayo**. Here, thousands of Perón's supporters protested his imprisonment in 1945 and were moved to tears by Evita's inflammatory speeches from the balcony of the **Casa Rosada**. Vendors on the square sell rosettes and lapel pins in Argentina's colors.

Six blocks south of Plaza de Mayo, along Paseo Colón, is the monumental **Facultad de Ingeniería** (Faculty of Engineering; Paseo Colón 850, San Telmo). A typical Peronist construction, this rather totalitarian-looking building was originally designed for the Fundación Eva Perón, Evita's aid organization. Before being stolen by anti-Peronists, Evita's embalmed body lay in state for three years at the **Edificio de la CGT** (Building of the General Confederation of Labor; Azopardo 802, San Telmo), just around the corner from the Facultad de Ingeniería.

You can pick up Evita-print packing tape and other kooky collectibles at **Materia Urbana** (Defensa 707, San Telmo), two blocks west of the Edificio de la CGT along Avenida Independencia. Now the only thing left to do is throw back your head and sing "Don't Cry for Me, Argentina."

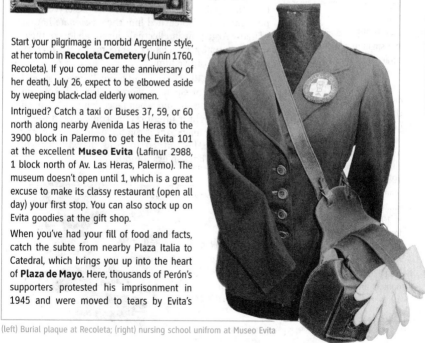

(left) Burial plaque at Recoleta; (right) nursing school unifrom at Museo Evita

LITERARY GIANTS

AKA: Georgie (his family nickname); H. Bustos Domecq (the pseudonym he and friend Adolfo Bioy Casares used for their collaborations).

BORN: August 24, 1899, in Buenos Aires

DIED: June 14, 1986, in Geneva, Switzerland

QUOTES: "To me it seems impossible that Buenos Aires once began / I judge her as eternal as the water and the air." "Reading . . . is an activity subsequent to writing: more resigned, more civil, more intellectual."

POLITICAL LEARNINGS: Extreme conservative, so much so that he initially praised the 1976 military coup, but ended up petitioning General Videla over disappearances.

DAY JOBS: Librarian; first in a small neighborhood library where his anti-Peronist sentiments got him fired; and eventually director of the National Library, courtesy of a military government he supported.

MARRIAGES: Two: Elsa Astete Millán, a one-time childhood sweetheart, in 1967. Borges described the marriage as "total incompatibility," and they divorced in 1970. María Kodama, a former student, 45 years his junior, shortly before his death in 1985. She had been his secretary, travel companion, and then partner for 10 years.

JORGE LUIS BORGES

BIO: Borges claimed all his life to belong far more to the 19th century than the 20th. A lifelong Anglophile, his conservative politics were probably what denied him the Nobel Prize many feel he deserved. His political ideas also earned him the passionate hatred of many Argentine intellectuals, although lots of them were eventually sufficiently overcome by his literary brilliance to forgive him.

LINGUISTIC TRIVIA: Legend has it Borges first read that greatest of Spanish works, *Don Quixote,* in English translation, and when faced with the Spanish original, thought it inferior. For, ironically, although Borges was a magician of the Spanish language, the first language he learned to read in was English, thanks to his English grandmother.

NOW READ ON: BORGES

- *The Aleph and Other Stories*
- *Fictions*
- *Brodie's Report*

Penguin

(top) Jorge Luis Borges, at home, Buenos Aires, 1983

2

AKA: Julio Denis, the pseudonym he published early work under.

BORN: August 26, 1914, in Argentine Embassy of Brussels, Belgium

DIED: February 12, 1984, in Paris, France

QUOTE: "Nothing is lost if we have the courage to admit that everything is lost and that we have to start again."

POLITICAL LEARNINGS: Very left-wing, he was a committed supporter of the Cuban revolution but was rejected by Castro when he protested the arrest of a Cuban poet for political reasons.

DAY JOBS: High-school teacher, but resigned when Perón came to power; translator for UNESCO; also translated Edgar Allan Poe and G.K. Chesterton, among others, into Spanish.

MARRIAGES: Three: Aurora Bernárdez, an Argentine translator, in 1955. Ugné Karvelis, a Lithuanian activist, whom he met in 1967. Carol Dunlop, a Canadian poet, in 1979.

JULIO CORTÁZAR

BIO: Cortázar's semi-surreal prose and flamboyant bohemian lifestyle have long made him the intellectual pin-up for idealistic students throughout Latin America. He began to publish in earnest after 1951, when a scholarship took him to Paris. He lived in that city for the rest of his life but always wrote in Spanish. His most famous works appeared in the 1960s, including the highly experimental *Hopscotch*, a story of Argentine beatniks afloat in Paris, the chapters of which can be read in any order. Stories from his several collections were published in English as *Blow-Up: And Other Stories*; Michelangelo Antonioni based his award-winning film on the title story. Jazz, boxing, and politics were also big passions, and he signed over the royalties of two books to Argentine political prisoners and the Sandinista movement in Nicaragua. Ironically for one who was also a brilliant translator, the English-language versions of his work have yet to gain him the respect he commands in Spanish.

NOW READ ON: CORTÁZAR

- *Hopscotch*
- *"Blow-Up": And Other Stories*
- *62: A Model Kit*

Pantheon

LINGUISTIC TRIVIA: His early childhood in Belgium left him incapable of pronouncing the Spanish "r."

(left) June 1967, Paris, France; (right) Mature Cortázar and cat

SOUL STIRRERS

AKA: Fuser (the nickname his rugby teammates gave him), El Che ("che" is a typically Argentinean interjection, an old-fashioned version of "man" or "dude" or just "hey." His constant use of the word caused coworkers to start calling him by it. It stuck.)

BORN: June 14, 1928, in Rosario, Argentina

DIED: October 9, 1967, in La Higuera, Bolivia

QUOTES: *"Hasta la victoria siempre"* (Always toward victory). "I am not a liberator. Liberators do not exist. The people liberate themselves."

SUPPORTED: Rugby: San Isidro Club, of which his father was one of the founders. Soccer: Rosario Central.

HEALTH PROBLEMS: Chronic asthma

ERNESTO "CHE" GUEVARA DE LA SERNA

BIO: Ironically, this socialist figurehead started life in an upper-middle class family and was a keen player of rugby, considered a posh sport. Soon, his horror at the plight of Latin American peasants and workers and a chance meeting with the young Fidel Castro in Mexico led to his well-known participation in the Cuban revolution, first as a guerrilla and eventually as President of the National Bank and Minister of Industries.

Darker allegations also surround this time in Che's life: some say the trials—and executions—of Batista followers he oversaw in La Cabaña prison in 1959 were unfair. Che soon realized that he was more suited to fighting oppression than to pushing paper at the ministry. He led guerrilla campaigns in the Congo and Bolivia, where he was executed by Bolivian soldiers on October 9, 1967. His ideals, ascetic lifestyle, and, more than anything, a lot of very dramatic photographs have transformed him into a pop icon.

DID YOU KNOW?

■ Mario Terán, the Bolivian army sergeant who fired the shots that killed Che, benefited greatly from the Cuban health system. Just shy of the 40th anniversary of Che's death, Teran had cataracts removed by Cuban doctors in Bolivia as part of Operation Milagro, a program offering eye surgery to Latin Americans in need of free treatment.

(top left) Argentinian revolutionary portrait; (top right) posters; (bottom) Che Guevara and Fidel Castro

AKA: El 10 (Number 10), El Diego de la Gente (The Diego of the People), La Mano de Dios (The Hand of God).

BORN: October 30, 1960, in Buenos Aires

QUOTE: "It was the hand of God!" in defense of his supposed hand-goal in the 1986 World Cup.

SUPPORTS: Boca Juniors

DEFINING MOMENT: 1986 soccer World Cup quarter-final against England, when he scored his goal after dribbling down half the field and dodging round five players and the goalkeeper. FIFA voted it the Goal of the Century.

HEALTH PROBLEMS Recurring cocaine addiction and obesity.

MARADONA SPOTTING

He might not be making the headlines, but you might see him...

■ ... cheering on Boca Juniors or the Argentine soccer team with his daughters from a special box. He's often in the crowds at international tennis and polo matches, too.

■ ... in TV interviews giving his opinion on everything from soccer coaching to Latin American politics (in 2007 he was a guest on Venezuelan president Hugo Chávez's show, *Aló Presidente*).

DIEGO ARMANDO MARADONA

BIO: Ask any local soccer fan what nationality God is, and their answer will be "Argentinian," in clear reference to Diego Armando Maradona, whose status as national sporting idol can't get any higher. A football prodigy, Maradona grew up in one of Buenos Aires' shantytowns, but started playing professionally at the age of 10. He shot to fame in the early '80s playing for Boca Juniors and then Italian team Napoli, before his 1986 goal against England won the World Cup for Argentina and immortality for Maradona. Too much time at the top took its toll, though: after retiring Maradona's cocaine addiction bloomed and his weight skyrocketed, and for a while it looked like Argentina's greatest hero was on his way out. However, in 2005 the nation wept tears of joy as he returned to Argentina slimmed-down and drug-free to host a TV show.

(top) World Cup, 1986;
(bottom) World Cup, 1990

Shopping

Mariano Toledo Boutique, Palermo Viejo

WORD OF MOUTH

"Yes, I bought a lot of handbags, so? and gifts. Beaded necklaces are very big in Buenos Aires. Big beads, long ropes of them. Not expensive and fun and great presents. Tango music CDs and things for the house, as well as cute clothes and shoes. So many shoes. Note to self . . . go back for more shoes. And then the ultimate shopping day. Real estate."

—Scarlett

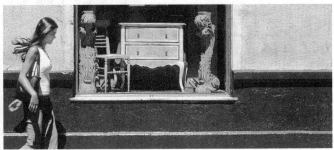

By Victoria
Patience

Whether you're looking for a unique handicraft, the latest boutique-vineyard Malbec, or jeans no one's got back home, you're sure to leave Buenos Aires with your bags full. An unstable economy's forced fashion-savvy *porteños* to abandon international brands and spend locally again. Couple this with bargain-hungry tourist hordes and you get an explosion of new design, a revival of classic brands, and a shopping scene that just keeps getting better.

If hustle and bustle are your thing, elbow your way to the stalls at the city's outdoor markets on weekends, or through the crowds of office workers that keep Centro buzzing on weekdays. In Recoleta, elegant old buildings that house hallowed brand names inspire a statelier pace (or maybe it's the price tags). Things are slower in Palermo and San Telmo, too: strolling their cobbled streets or people-watching in corner cafés are just as popular as buying.

Clothing bargains abound: local chains and new, young designers turn out the latest trends at distinctly postdevaluation prices. Quality varies, but it'll be out of fashion next year anyway, so who cares? From the kings and queens of local couture, you can expect world-class design with a porteño edge; although their price tags aren't particularly South American, you still get top-quality garments for less than you'd pay at home. A handful of these designers are beginning to export or open stores stateside; here's your chance to shop at the source.

Argentina is cow central, and leather goods—from shoes and jackets to polo saddles—are also excellent value. Buenos Aires' well-established antiques trade is thriving, but modern home ware shops are putting up some fierce competition. Many local wines still aren't exported, so this may be your only chance to try them.

Just because there's a favorable foreign-exchange rate doesn't mean you have to shop like a foreigner. Here's how to navigate the shopping scene with local savvy.

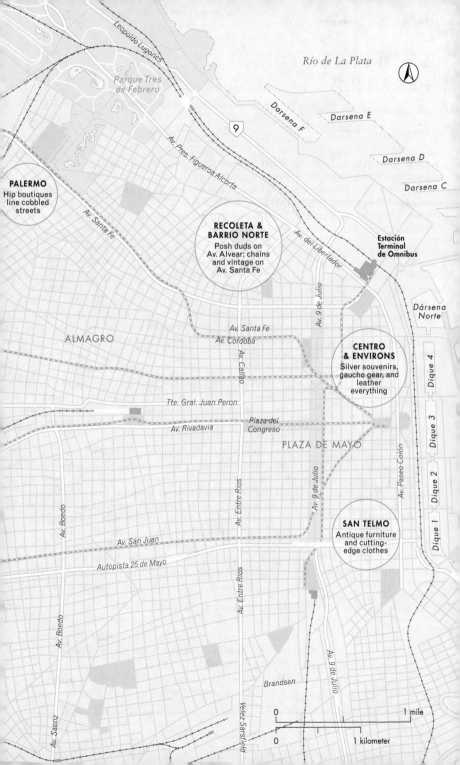

Río de La Plata

Darsena F

Darsena E

Darsena D

Darsena C

Leopoldo Lugones

Parque Tres de Febrero

9

Av. Pres. Figueroa Alcorta

PALERMO
Hip boutiques line cobbled streets

Av. Santa Fe

RECOLETA & BARRIO NORTE
Posh duds on Av. Alvear; chains and vintage on Av. Santa Fe

Av. del Libertador

Estación Terminal de Omnibus

ALMAGRO

Av. Santa Fe

Av. Córdoba

Av. Callao

Av. 9 de Julio

Dársena Norte

CENTRO & ENVIRONS
Silver souvenirs, gaucho gear, and leather everything

Dique 4

Tte. Gral. Juan Peron

Av. Rivadavia

Plaza del Congreso

PLAZA DE MAYO

Av. Paseo Colón

Dique 3

Dique 2

Av. Boedo

Av. San Juan

Av. Entre Rios

Av. 9 de Julio

SAN TELMO
Antique furniture and cutting-edge clothes

Dique 1

Autopista 25 de Mayo

Av. Boedo

Velez Sarsfield

Av. 9 de Julio

Brandsen

Av. Saenz

0   1 mile

0   1 kilometer

SHOPPING PLANNER

Doing Business

Some stores give you a discount on display prices for paying cash; others charge a premium for using credit cards. Carry both, and keep your options open.

Stores in tourist areas may try to charge you in dollars or euros what they charge Argentines in pesos. Always confirm which currency you're dealing with up front. Bargaining is accepted only in some leather-goods shops on Calle Florida. Elsewhere—even in markets—prices are fixed.

"Refund" is a dirty word in Argentina. No shop will give you back your money just because you change your mind about something. Even if a product is faulty, exchanges or credit notes are the norm. Many shops won't process exchanges or refunds on Saturday.

Keep your receipts: the 21% V.A.T. tax, included in the sales price, is entirely refundable for purchases exceeding $200 at stores displaying a duty-free sign. Leave time to visit the return desk at the airport to obtain your refund.

Sweet & Savory Souvenirs

What's the Beef? Can't kick your Argentine cow habit? Remind yourself of all those steaks with a traditional *asado* knife. Practical wood- or horn-handled knives are available at most markets from around 50 pesos; silver and alpaca decorate the hilt and sheath of the more elaborate (and more expensive) knives at silversmiths like Platería Parodi.

Sweet Stuff. It's brown, goopy, and sickly sweet but you know you want more *dulce de leche* (a spread made from sweetened condensed milk). All supermarkets stock popular brands like La Serenísima (5 pesos), or go to any Havanna coffee shop (they proliferate in the city like Starbucks branches in Seattle) for a posh glass jar (16 pesos). Havanna's *alfajores* (chocolate-covered dulce-de-leche–filled cookies) are also sure to earn you fans back home (20 pesos for 12).

Salud! Although award winners like Catena Zapata can be hundreds of dollars a bottle, excellent wines start at 30 pesos at Winery. For another 200 pesos, you can get a three-bottle leather carrying case. In traditional restaurants, wine is served in a *pingüino* (penguin-shape jug): get yours from Calma Chicha for 15 pesos.

Mate for Two. Yours truly might not love the drink, but its paraphernalia make unusual souvenirs. Juan Carlos Pallarols's ornate silver drinking vessels and straw go for hundreds of dollars; the kid-size sets at Recursos Infantiles go for 40 pesos, include a minikettle and thermos, and pack easily. The best boxy leather mate bags (for carrying thermos and vessel) sell at La Feria de Mataderos for 150 pesos and up, but at La Feria de la Recoleta, simple gourds start at 10 pesos. Supermarkets sell *yerba mate* (the tea itself); Rosamonte, one of many brands, costs 4 pesos.

Timing Is Everything

Shopping starts late here. Malls open at around 10 AM, but the designer boutiques in Palermo and San Telmo often don't get going until 11 or noon and close at around 8 PM. Don't plan much purchasing on Sundays: many shops close, and though malls don't, they're usually packed with locals.

What's the Buzz?

Locked shop doors are standard anti-theft practice. Don't be surprised (or intimidated) by having to ring a doorbell and be buzzed in. Furthermore, porteños take shopping seriously, and they dress for the occasion. You should, too: sloppily dressed customers usually get sloppy service. Ditch the sneakers and fanny pack, and look like you mean business.

Best Buys

The Beautiful Game. You've been to the fútbol stadium, you've sung the songs, you've screamed the goals—time to get the T-shirt. Stock Center's great range starts at 130 pesos. Alternately, get your hands—or thumbs, rather—on Maradona's greatest moment with the photo flipbook *El Gol del Siglo*. It shows his famous goal against England in the 1986 World Cup and is 25 pesos at the MALBA and Prometeo. Materia Urbana sell T-shirts showing the path of the same goal for 70 pesos.

Comic Relief. It may be unfamiliar to you, but the classic '60s cartoon strip Mafalda is close to the heart of all Argentines. The idealistic little girl it stars is an icon, and most downtown *kioscos de diarios* (newsstands) sell the flimsy Ediciones de la Flor collections of the strip for around 15 pesos. Other cartoonists who have Buenos Aires down to a T are Liniers, Rep, and Fontanarrosa. Prometeo stocks books by all of them.

Holy Cow. Give your house the gaucho look with a cowskin rug: at the leather wholesalers on Avenida Boedo's 1200 to 1400 blocks they start at about 300 pesos. Modern versions dyed in toxic-looking colors go for twice that at Calma Chicha. Beautifully designed cow-skin bags, wallets, and Birkenstock-style shoes from Humawaca start at 500 pesos. Large illustrated editions of *Martín Fierro,* the national gaucho epic, come bound in leather or cowhide at El Ateneo. You can even get *mates* made of polished cow hoof: most outdoor markets sell them for around 30 pesos.

Don't Cry for Me Argentina. The country's most famous first lady is quite the pop icon. Score a kitsch plastic bust of her for around 50 pesos at the Feria de San Pedro Telmo, which also sells packets of used stamps bearing her image. Stamps like these adorn the handmade Evita notebooks sold at Papelera Palermo for 60 pesos. Wrap your goodies up in Evita-print packing tape, 22 pesos from Materia Urbana.

Value for Money

Clothing in Buenos Aires can be very cheap. Just be mindful that the quality may match the price. Pay particular attention to seams and hems; stitching isn't always superlative. This is true even with international-brand items, which are nearly always locally made.

Local brands come at even lower prices in the discount outlets on Avenida Córdoba (4400 to 5000) in Palermo, and most chain stores have a shop here. End-of-season sales can work to your advantage, too—when summer is ending in Buenos Aires, it's just beginning in the United States and Europe.

Sizing Things Up

Porteños are, on average, smaller than Europeans and North Americans. Chic women's boutiques often don't have any clothes in sizes larger than a U.S. 8. It doesn't get any better for men: a porteño men's large will seem more like a small to many visitors, and trousers rarely come in different lengths.

ANTIQUES & CURIOS

La Candelaria. A Spanish-style house is the site of several choice shops. One is filled with enough miniature wooden furniture to fill several dollhouses; another sells golden-age Argentine cinema posters. Wind-up monkeys, brass fittings, and old leather suitcases are other finds. ⊠*Defensa 1170, San Telmo* ☎*No phone* Ⓜ*C to San Juan.*

★ **Gabriel del Campo.** Gabriel's good taste means 50-year-old Louis Vuitton trunks don't look out of place beside wooden church statues or scale-model ships with canvas sails. Ceramic rubber-glove molds, one of his specialties, are some of the more accessible conversation pieces. The flagship store takes up a sizable patch of Plaza Dorrego shop front; there are also branches on Defensa and in the northern suburbs. ⊠*Bethlem 427, on Plaza Dorrego, San Telmo* ☎*11/4307–6589* ⊠*Defensa 990, San Telmo* ☎*11/4361–2061* Ⓜ*C or E to Independencia.*

Gil Antigüedades. Sequined flapper dresses, dashing white-linen suits, and creamy lace wedding veils are some of the things you might find in this pink *casa chorizo* (similar to a railroad apartment). Period accessories include Castilian hair combs and lacy fans that beg you to bat your lashes from behind them. ⊠*Humberto I 412, San Telmo* ☎*11/4361–5019* ⊕*www.gilantiguedades.com.ar* Ⓜ*C to San Juan.*

★ **HB Anticuario.** White-leather trefoil chairs and gleaming walnut side tables with black-lacquer details are among the many heavenly art deco furniture items. Much more packable (though not cheap) are the Clarice Cliff dinner services. ⊠*Defensa 1016/18, San Telmo* ☎*11/4361–3325* ⊕*www.hbantiques.com.ar* Ⓜ*C or E to Independencia.*

Pasaje del 900. All that glitters in this small, darkened warehouse is not gold, but glass. Several small-scale dealers share the space and a passion for drinking vessels, decanters, chandeliers, and other fragile finds. ⊠*Defensa 961, San Telmo* ☎*No phone* Ⓜ*C or E to Independencia.*

★ **Silvia Petroccia.** Despite being crammed with furniture, this corner store looks extravagant rather than chaotic. It's probably due to the alluring collectibles, ranging from gilt-wood church candles to Louis XV–style chairs reupholstered in buttercup-yellow silk. ⊠*Defensa 1002, San Telmo* ☎*11/4362–0156.* Ⓜ*C or E to Independencia*

BEAUTY

Sabater Hermanos. Third-generation Spanish soap makers are behind this shop that sells nothing but—let's come clean about it—soap. Get into a lather over the trays of no-nonsense rectangles that come in heavenly sandalwood, chocolate, old lavender, and tea-rose, to name a few. You can also buy your soap in brightly colored petals. ⊠*Gurruchaga 1821, Palermo Viejo* ☎*11/4833–3004* ⊕*www.shnos.com.ar.*

Universo Garden Angels. Despite the rather new-age brand name, these cosmetics mix hard science with color- and aromatherapy. More and more porteñas are turning to home-grown goo like Patagonia Earth anti-age cream or the Malbec Wine-therapy body cream. Even if the promises don't hold up, the slick packaging makes these products a worthwhile gift for lotion-lovers. ⊠*Av. Santa Fe 917, Microcentro*

☎11/4325–0004 Ⓜ C to Gral. San Martín ✉El Salvador 4588, Palermo Viejo ☎11/4832–0680 ⊕www.universogardenangels.com.

BOOKS

Prometeo. It's a low-key corner store frequented by trendy design types and bearded literature students alike. Non–Spanish speakers need not despair: this is the place to pick up diminutive flipbooks by Cine de Dedo, which poke good-natured fun at Argentine culture. The larger *Gol del Siglo* flipbook depicts Maradona's celebrated goal against England in the 1986 World Cup. ✉Honduras 4912, Palermo Viejo ☎11/4832–0466 ⊕www.prometeolibros.com.ar.

★ **Walrus Books.** If only all bookshops could be like this. Quality used books in English overflow from the shelves and tables as jazz and folk promote leisurely browsing. When it comes to making decisions, American owner Geoff and his wife Josefina give helpful, friendly advice. Their selection is strong on contemporary literary fiction, though there are also bargain selections of more forgettable reads for whiling away time at airports. Walrus also has excellent English translations of local masters. ✉Estados Unidos 617, San Telmo ☎11/4300–7135.

CLOTHING

LINGERIE

Amor Latino. Amor Latino does stylish and oh-so-hot underwear and negligees—sexy rather than sturdy. There are even high-heeled slippers. Look for fun, tactile materials—whisper-light Lycra, gleaming satin, violet plush. The 1940s-inspired satin nightgowns are pure bedroom glamour. ✉ El Salvador 4813, Palermo Viejo ☎ 11/4831–6787 ✉Rodríguez Peña 1216, Recoleta ☎ 11/4815–7294 ⊕ www.amor-latino.com.ar .

Piel. The name means "skin," and pink and flesh tones are the backbone of each collection. Bras and panties come in cotton-Lycra, satin, and sometimes sheer fabrics. Although most bras are of the triangle-and-string variety, a few models have properly cut cups and reasonably supportive straps. The two-tone swimwear sells fast in summer. ✉Gorriti 4721, Palermo Viejo ☎11/4832–4092 ⊕www.pielargentina.com.

Victoria Cossy. Flaunting it is the order of the day at Victoria Cossy, whose lingerie comes only in sheer materials. Her white tulle *culottes,* edged with lace and sequins, are a cross between girly briefs and a sexy string. Printed mesh panties, bras, and crop tops are comfortable and playful. ✉Armenia 1499, Palermo Viejo ☎11/4831–5565.

CLOTHING: MEN'S & WOMEN'S

CASUAL & COOL

Antique Denim. Burberry meets Diesel at Antique Denim, where smart, dark jeans are worn with colorful tweed jackets with leather elbow patches. The denim cuts are sharp and tailored, made for cruising the town. ⊠*Gurruchaga 1692, Palermo Viejo* ☎*11/4834–6829.*

A.Y. Not Dead. Rainbow vinyl, fake snakeskin, truckloads of nylon: it's all very synthetic at A.Y. Not Dead. Seen anywhere other than under a strobe, the clothes may be hard to take, but to carve a space for yourself on a heaving club floor, shopping here's the way forward. ⊠*Soler 4193, Palermo Viejo* ☎*11/4866–4855* ⊕*www.aynotdead.com.ar.*

Fábrica de Bananas. The entrance is small, but inside there's a vast warehouse filled with clothes by scores of young designers. Street wear predominates, but there's space for accessories, hats, underwear, art books, and even sex toys. On weekend nights, the sofas in the middle of the store become Espacio Björk, a laid-back bar. Note that late nights mean the store doesn't open until 1 PM. ⊠*Arévalo 1445, Palermo Hollywood* ☎*11/4777–6541* ⊕*www.fabricadebananas.com.ar.*

Kosiuko. Branches of Kosiuko, the ultimate local teen brand, are always packed with trendy adolescents served by hip-wiggling staff not much older than they are. The girls come for the improbably small, low-cut pants, the guys for budding metrosexual-wear. Kosiuko's fragrances and deodorant are a favorite with the population's most perspiring age group. ⊠*Av. Santa Fe 1779, Barrio Norte* ⊠*Abasto Mall, Av., Corrientes 3247, Almagro* ☎*11/4707–4091* ⊕*www.kosiuko.com.ar.*

Un Lugar En El Mundo. San Telmo's hippest shop showcases young designers, whose men's and women's clothing is both wearable and affordable. Bolsas de Viaje's vinyl and canvas creations evoke the golden age of air travel, Mir's satchels and totes in heavily stitched chestnut leather make you want to go back to school, and Paz Portnoi's cowhide heels are perfect for dressing up. ⊠*Defensa 891, San Telmo* ☎*11/4362–3836* Ⓜ*C or E to Independencia.*

María Aversa. There's a touch of gypsy in María Aversa's colorful knitwear, and the two-story town house store gives you plenty of room to roam. In addition to large-gauge knits, look for more unusual offerings, such as a velvet jacket with crocheted sleeves. ⊠*El Salvador 4580, Palermo Viejo* ☎*11/4833–0073* ⊕*www.mariaaversa.com.ar.*

Ona Saez. The ultrafitted jeans at Ona Saez are designed to be worn with sky-high heels and slinky tops for a sexy night out. The menswear is equally slick, mixing dressed-down denim with cool cotton shirts and tees. ⊠*Florida 789, Centro* ☎*11/5555–5203* ⊠*Abasto Mall, Av. Corrientes 3247, Almagro* ☎*11/4959–3602* ☎*11/4775–1151* ⊕*www. onasaez.com.*

Refans A+. Footballers, soap-opera stars, clubbers: everyone seems to be wearing one of Refans's trademark T-shirts. They come in ultrabright colors, emblazoned with quirky Italian phrases like *siamo fuori* ("We are out," a reference to the World Cup). Lucas Castromán, a local football star himself, is behind the brand. Anoraks, hoodies, jeans, and messenger bags round up the offerings. ⊠*El Salvador 4577, Palermo Viejo* ☎*11/4777–7251* ⊠*Arévalo 2843, Las Cañitas* ⊕*www.refans.net.*

Tienda Porteña. Browsing the building is almost as fun as browsing the clothes here. This multibrand boutique takes up the whole of a traditional San Telmo casa chorizo. Each room opens onto another, all containing simple railings hung with different small designers. Belocca's tango-inspired shoes are one reason to come; the cheerful baubles that dangle above the original bathroom sink are another. At night, the back turns into a bar serving microbrewery beers. ⊠*Carlos Calvo 618, San Telmo* ☎*11/1362–3340* Ⓜ*C to San Juan; C or E to Independencia.*

HIGH DESIGN

Giesso. A classic gents' tailor for nearly a century, Giesso is now pulling a Thomas Pink by adding jewel-color ties and shirts to its range of timeless suits. A new women's-wear line includes gorgeous linen suits and cashmere overcoats. ⊠*Av. Alvear 1882, Recoleta* ☎*11/4804–8828* ⊠*Florida 997, Centro* ☎*11/4312–7606* ⊕*www.giesso.com.ar.*

Kostüme. It's all very space odyssey at Kostüme. Extra-brief dresses might be made of netting or bunched-up nylon, worn over drainpipe trousers. Many tops are asymmetrical, and pants come with saddlebag-like protrusions. Menswear includes unusual Jedi-esque hooded robe-jackets. ⊠*República de la India 3139, Palermo Botánico* ☎*11/4802–3136* ⊕*www.kostume.net* Ⓜ*D to Plaza Italia.*

Nadine Zlotogora. Bring your sense of humor to Nadine Zlotogora: her way-out designs are playful yet exquisitely put together. Sheer fabrics are embroidered with organic-looking designs, then worn alone or over thin cotton. Even the menswear gets the tulle treatment: military-look shirts come with a transparent top layer. ⊠*El Salvador 4638, Palermo Viejo* ☎*11/4831–4203* ⊕*www.nadinez.com.*

Fodor'sChoice
★ **Pablo Ramírez.** His tiny shop front is unadorned except for "Ramírez" printed on the glass over the door—when you're this big, why say more? Pablo's couture doesn't come cheap, but given the peso prices, his perfectly tailored numbers are a (relative) bargain. He favors black for both waspishly waisted women's wear and slick gent's suits, though a few other shades are beginning to creep in. ⊠*Perú 587, San Telmo* ☎*114342–7154* ⊕*www.pabloramirez.com.ar* Ⓜ*E to Belgrano.*

★ **Varanasi.** The structural perfection of Varanasi's clothes is a clue that the brains behind them trained as architects. Equally telling is the minimal, cavernous shop, fronted by plate glass. Inside, A-line dresses built from silk patchwork and unadorned bias cuts are some of the night-out joys that local celebs shop for—indeed, few others can afford to. ⊠*Costa Rica 4672, Palermo Viejo* ☎*11/4833–5147* ⊠*Libertad 1696, Recoleta* ☎*11/4815–4326* ⊕*www.varanasi-online.com.*

SPORTSWEAR

Adidas Originals. This is one of the few Adidas shops in the world to stock limited-edition items, though there may only ever be one in the shop at a time. If you're less fussy about other people being able to own the same clothes as you, Adidas's retro jogging jackets are still as cool as it comes. The "I heart" Buenos Aires T-shirt is a local gem. ⊠*Malabia 1720, Palermo Viejo* ☎*11/4831–0090*

Nike Soho. You may know Nike inside-out and backward, but here the recycled rooms of an old town house are the unlikely backdrop for the

SAN TELMO

"No es Palermo!" screams graffiti on a San Telmo shop front, a protest of the clothing boutiques muscling in on the barrio's traditional antiques trade. San Telmo is changing, but the quirky mix of age-old and brand-new is what makes this such an exciting place to shop.

It's entirely appropriate that the city's oldest neighborhood is *the* place to shop for timeless collectibles and curios. Along cobbled streets like Defensa, historical buildings house dozens of stores dealing entirely in antiques. But you're as likely to get a shirt as a chandelier: after decades as one of Buenos Aires' most marginal barrios, San Telmo suddenly looks set to be the next epicenter of *porteño* cool. Local fashion god Pablo Ramírez certainly thinks so: he has set up shop on Perú.

Young designers yet to reach the dizzying heights of his fame (and price tags) share several multi-brand spaces closer to Plaza Dorrego. This plaza is the heart of the open-air Feria de San Pedro Telmo, a Sunday market that fills San Telmo's streets with artisans, performers, and antiques stalls.

BEST TIME TO GO

The market is on Sunday afternoon; every other visitor in town will be there, so don't expect to be able to move much, let alone shop. For leisurely browsing and coffee stops, weekdays are a better bet. Start with antiques shops, which open around 10 AM, then move on to clothes.

BEST SOUVENIR FOR SOMEONE WHO HAS EVERYTHING

High ceilings, parquet floors, period fittings: what's not to like about San Telmo's beautiful apartments? **Reynolds Propiedades** or **Ojo Propiedades** (⇨Big Spenders box, below) can set you up with one.

al Colección

REFUELING

Slip away from the crowds to the quiet tables of **Territorio** (⊠*Estados Unidos 500* ☏*11/4307–0896*) where pick-me-ups come in many forms: homemade panini, moist cakes, local tea blends, or microbrewery beer.

Shopping can be hot work. The extra-creamy handmade ice creams at **Nonna Bianca** (⊠*Estados Unidos 407* ☏*11/4362–0604*) are a luxurious cool-off. If an ice-cold pint's more your thing, consider their beer sorbet (yes, really).

BEST FOR

SERIOUS ANTIQUES

Gabriel del Campo: something old, something new . . . the playful mix of decades is always in good taste.

HB Anticuario: art deco perfection in furniture and tableware.

FIVE-STAR ARGENTINE DESIGN

Pablo Ramírez: the king of local couture favors nipped-in waists, hobble skirts, and perfectly cut Buster Keaton suits.

Juan Carlos Pallarols Orfebre: his curlicued *mates* and steak-knife sets adorn the tables of kings and movie stars alike.

MULTIBRAND BOUTIQUES

Un Lugar en el Mundo: the pioneer of the San Telmo clothing scene has been dealing the hippest togs in the barrio for years.

Materia Urbana: high-quality souvenirs or affordable art objects? Either way, you're going to want them.

Ffioca: several Palermo designers under one San Telmo roof.

brand's more exclusive lines. Ultratech women's tees and flexible yoga shoes contrast with riotous floral wallpaper and mauve lace curtains. Paint-stripped walls and chicken wire offset swoosh wear for the boys. ⊠*Gurruchaga 1615, Palermo Viejo* ☎*11/4832–3555.*

Stock Center. The official pale-blue-and-white shirts worn by the Argentine soccer team, the Pumas (the national rugby team), and the Leonas (women's hockey team) are some of the best sellers as this sporting megastore. The Nike, Adidas, and Puma clothing is all made in Brazil, and so is relatively cheap. Über-trendy Gola sneakers are another reason to come. ⊠*Corrientes 590, Microcentro* ☎*11/4326–2131.*

Topper. Impossible as it may seem, the coolest footwear on Buenos Aires' dance floors in the '80s were yellow Wellington boots from this local sportswear brand. They're still selling them, together with the football shirts and bargain gym wear that's kept Topper popular despite competition from big international names. ⊠*Gurruchaga 1573, Palermo Viejo* ☎*11/4832–6667* ⊕*www.topper.com.ar.*

MEN ONLY

CASUAL & COOL

Bolivia. Porteño dandies know that Bolivia is *the* place for metrosexual fashion. Expect floral prints on shirts, leather belts, even Filofaxes. Aged denim, top-quality silk-screen T-shirts, vintage military jackets, and hand-knit slippers are among the items that fill this converted Palermo town house to bursting. ⊠*Gurruchaga 1581, Palermo Viejo* ☎*11/4832–6284* ⊕*www.boliviaonline.com.ar.*

Félix. Waxed floorboards, worn rugs, exposed brick, and aging cabinets are the backdrop to the shop's cool clothes. Beat-up denim, crisp shirts, and knits that look like a loving granny whipped them up are among the many delights. ⊠*Gurruchaga 1670, Palermo Viejo* ☎*11/4832–2994* ⊕*www.felixba.com.ar.*

★ **Hermanos Estebecorena.** The approach at this trendy street-wear store is 100% practical: All the flat-front shirts, pants, and rain jackets have pockets, seams, and buttons positioned for maximum utility. Everything looks good, too, and the product range, including footwear and underwear, makes this a one-stop guy shop. ⊠*El Salvador 5960, Palermo Viejo* ☎*11/4772–2145* ⊕*www.hermanosestebecorena.com.*

Kristobelga. Lovers of Carhartt-style utility wear will find plenty of heavy-duty clothing at Kristobelga. As well as khakis and grays, the store has carpenter trousers, tees in upbeat colors, and canvas anoraks. ⊠*Gurruchaga 1677, Palermo Viejo* ☎*11/4831–6677.*

Mercer. Wooden shelving and layers of Persian rugs make Mercer look part general store and part 1,001 nights. Levi's-style jeans are reasonably priced; match them with slick leather jackets, shirts, and screen-printed tees. ⊠*El Salvador 4677, Palermo Viejo* ☎*11/4831–4891.*

Tienda Rethink. Bored of drab utility-wear? Rethink has, well, rethought the issue. Grown-up skaters and sophisticated rockers love its well-made jeans, hoodies, and tees. They're simple in cut but come alive with lively, graffiti-inspired designs, which spill over onto the shop

THE CHAIN GANG: MEN ONLY

Airborn. The shirts and pants here can look cool when dressed down with a hoodie, but are date-worthy if you add a tailored jacket. Although Airborn's cuts are simple, they're made interesting with different textures: expect raw linen in summer and velvet in winter. Stripes are a favorite pattern. ⊕*www.airborn.com.ar.*

Bensimon. Ertswhile purveyors of exuberant floral shirts and other sensitive guywear, Bensimon has recently prepped up its act, kicked out the pink T-shirts, and even painted its turquoise stores white. Its new-look wares—striped sailor tees, well-cut chinos, and corduroy jackets—are selling as fast as ever, though. Thinned-down Scandinavian-look sweaters are tempting in winter, while the stripy socks and colorful boxers ache to be taken home all year round. ⊕*www.bensimon.com.ar.*

Cristóbal Colón. A heady mix of coconut and board wax fills the air in this surfwear store: they don't care that the beach is hundreds of miles away, so why should you? Brazilian-made Billabong and Quiksilver board shorts, baggy tees, and hoodies are cheaper than back home, and local surf brands like Y Tú Quique?

are also represented. ⊕*www.cristobalcolon.com.*

Kevingston. Local rugby players love this brand—indeed, Kevingston has a dedicated rugby line—one of few to stock sizes large enough to fit them. Rugby and polo jerseys are a welcome variation on soccer shirts as sporty souvenirs; T-shirts printed with rugby caricatures are a more humorous option. Less macho basics include good-quality shirts and polo shirts in a rainbow of pastels. The functional anoraks look almost too cool among classic khakis and V-necks. ⊕*www.kevingston.com.*

Legacy. This is Argentina's budget answer to Polo by Ralph Lauren: the logo is two crossed polo sticks, and yes, polo shirts are the best seller. But there are also well-made khakis, argyle sweaters, jackets and shirts, in preppy cuts and plain colors. Pink, light-blue, and sandy yellow are favorite tones. ⊕*www.legacy.com.ar.*

Old Bridge. Despite turning out jeans, retro-print tees, and hoodies fit to rival other local brands, Old Bridge has somehow never hit Buenos Aires' most-wanted list. All the better for you: the quality is as good as the competition but prices are much lower. ⊕*www.oldbridge.com.ar.*

walls. ⊠*Marcelo T. de Alvear 1187, Barrio Norte* ☎*11/4815–8916* ⊕*www.7rethink.com* Ⓜ*C to Gral. San Martín.*

Vintage Hombre. If you like your suits old but not moth-eaten, Vintage is the place to head. Its small but carefully selected range of secondhand gear looks—and costs—almost like new. ⊠*El Salvador 4635, Palermo Viejo* ☎*11/4833–5450.*

HIGH DESIGN

Balthazar. Everything a modern gent needs—and plenty he didn't know he wanted—lies in this discreet Palermo town house. Find top-notch shirts, suits, cuff links, and even driving gloves. Best sellers are the handwoven alpaca scarves. Balthazar imports English and Italian fabric for many of their shirts, which are correspondingly pricey, but you get a 20% discount if you pay cash. ✉*Gorriti 5131, Palermo Viejo* ☎*11/4834–6235* ✉*Defensa 1008, 1st fl., San Telmo* ☎*11/4300–6926* Ⓜ *C or E to Independencia* ⊕*www.balthazarshop.com.*

★ **La Dolfina Polo Lifestyle.** Being the world's best polo player wasn't enough for Adolfo Cambiaso—he founded his own team in 1995, and then started a clothing line for which he does the modeling. And if you think polo is all about knee-high boots and preppy chinos, think again: Cambiaso sells some of the best urban menswear in town. The Italian-cotton shirts, sharp leather jackets, and to-die-for totes from the After Polo collection are perfect for after just about anything. ✉*Av. Alvear 1315, Recoleta* ☎*11/4815–2698* ⊕*www.ladolfina.com.*

Mickey. You won't see any billboards around town for Mickey: reputation is a far better way of advertising. Generations of porteños have been coming here for top-quality shirts and suits at very reasonable prices. Young, energetic assistants are as happy to show you wide-collar shirts in niftily patterned Italian cotton as classic button-downs. ✉*Perón 917, Microcentro* ☎*11/4326–7195* ⊕*www.camisasmickey. com.ar* Ⓜ*C to Diagonal Norte; D to 9 de Julio.*

★ **Spina.** Traditional tailoring with lots of twists is one way to describe Spina's sharp menswear. Suit jackets might come with extra-cinched waists or with overlay work in different fabrics, and drainpipes are their favorite pant style. Add a lime-green shirt with pale-blue cuffs and a vermilion tie to really be seen. Embroidered T-shirts and less busy short-sleeved shirts are a casual alternative. ✉*Gorriti 5887, Palermo Hollywood* ☎*11/4774–3574* ⊕*www.grupospina.com.ar.*

SPORTSWEAR

Gola. Other brands recycle Palermo buildings, but über-cool British sportswear label Gola has left this cavernous warehouse pretty much as is. Rust- and damp-stained walls somehow form a fitting backdrop for their ultra-utilitarian polo shirts, sweaters, and loose-cut trousers, all laid out on industrial cable bobbins. More incongruous is a small selection of posh Etiqueta Negra clothing, the brand responsible for making Gola clothing locally. ✉*Pasaje Russel 4924, Palermo Viejo* ☎*11/4833–2474* ⊕*www.golaclassics.com.*

WOMEN ONLY

CASUAL & COOL

Adorhada Guillermina. Local cinema and graphic-design students love Adorhada Guillermina's '80s-feel clothes. Box-pleated denim skirts are edgy but practical. More unusual materials such as metallic plush are also on hand. Dress things up or down with one of a hundred tops in fine, bias-cut T-shirt fabric. ✉*Santa Fe 1615, Barrio Norte* ☎*11/4814–0053* ✉*La Pampa 2368, Belgrano* ☎*11/4706–3196* ⊕*www.adorha daguillermina.com.ar* Ⓜ*D to José Hernández.*

Claudia Giuliano. The chunky knit sweaters and cardigans rival Donna Karan's and at a fraction of the cost. The llama wool wraps or heavy woven ponchos come in colors like coffee and chocolate. The north-ern-Argentine *copla* music that plays lets you know where all this natu-

THE CHAIN GANG: WOMEN ONLY

Akiabara. Slick jeans, pants, and suits pull sharp twenty- and thirty-something women to Akiabara like metal to a magnet. The slinky tops and soft, asymmetrical knits come unadorned—no prints, no embroidery, just plain lines and good draping. ⊕www.akiabara.com.

Ayres. Fine, strappy tops in bold colors like cherry and tangerine tell you that women who shop at Ayres don't mind standing out at the bar. For sweeter wallflowers there are ultrasoft cache-coeurs (wraparound cardigans), suits in powder-blue drill, or ruffled cotton sundresses. Ayres jeans are moving to the top of the most-wanted list (if you're smaller than a size 6, that is). ⊕www.ayres.com.ar.

Complot. "Ready to Rock!" screams Complot's labels, and the clothes live up to the claim. Teenage rebels and older festivalgoers flock here for the signature long T-shirts with lyrics or photos of Bowie, Sid Vicious, Blondie, or the Beatles. There are skinny jeans, animal-print leggings, and denim microminis to (mis)match them with. The anoraks are a porteño fashion must in winter. ⊕www.complot.com.ar.

Paula Cahen d'Anvers. This store's founder hails from a local dynasty and her choice of logo—a little embroidered crown—lets you know that her clothes are for urban princesses. Her take on preppy is tongue-in-cheek, mixing blazers and straight-leg pants with puffed-sleeve shirts and ties, or stripy sailor tees. The candy-stripe onesies and bright corduroy dresses of the kids' line are enough to make even the biggest girls' hearts melt. ⊕www.paulacahendanvers.com.ar.

Portsaid. Professional women who want a feminine touch to their work clothes shop at Portsaid, where satin-ribbon ties and discreet beadwork soften otherwise practical garments. Simply cut suits and twin-sets come in colors like baby pink and aqua to make you stand out in a drab office; woolen winter coats are always a bargain both in terms of quality and style, be they classic cuts or fuller '60s-influenced designs. ⊕www.portsaid.com.ar.

Rapsodia. Some of the most-sought-after jeans in town come from Rapsodia—look for the ocher wing design on local girls' back pockets. The shop is also the temple of Buenos Aires' boho princesses, who can't get enough of owner and model Sol Acuña's floaty, embroidered Indian tops. ⊕www.rapsodia.com.ar.

ral goodness originates. ⊠*Ayacucho 1895, Recoleta* ☎*11/4804–2991* ⊕*www.claudiagiuliano.com.ar.*

Desiderata. The curving wooden deck outside this store is inviting, but get inside for light and airy shirts, dresses, and tees. The well-cut jeans are merciful on your wallet and your hips: unusually for Palermo, they go up to a size 12 (that's an Argentine 5). ⊠*Honduras 4733, Palermo Viejo* ☎*11/4833–3883* ⊕*www.desiderata.com.ar.*

Eufemia. The designers say their clothes are for women who dare to be different, and they're dead right. Flashdance meets Warhol is one way to describe the screen-printed leggings and leotards that—trust us—no one else at your gym will have. ⊠*El Salvador 4601, Palermo Viejo* ☎*11/4775–5570* ⊕*www.eufemiaba.com.ar.*

Lupe. The '80s are alive and well at Lupe, whose bright T-shirt dresses are all about draping and plunging necklines. Subtler options include sexy, semitransparent muslin. ⊠*El Salvador 4657, Palermo Viejo* ☎*11/4833–0730* ⊕*www.lupeba.com.ar.*

Mäda. This store hails from posh Uruguayan beach resort Punta del Este, so it's no surprise that bikinis (think flower appliqués and glitter) are the main attraction. Slinky tank tops and T-shirts round off the collection. ⊠*El Salvador 4865, Palermo Viejo* ☎*11/4833–9622* ⊕*www.madastore.com.ar.*

María Alló. Trashy but nice is the best way to describe María Allo's full-on designs. Skinny satin pants and studded layered tees get you ready to rock, but you could go glam or formal in her full-skirted, slightly Gothic ball gowns. ⊠*Armenia 1637, Palermo Viejo* ☎*11/4831–3733.*

María Cher. Let the yards of racks draw you into this lanky shop, where simple cuts and natural fabrics make urban working clothes feel just a tad Jedi-like. The earthy, deconstructed look is also due to details like unfinished hems or exposed seams. ⊠*El Salvador 4724, Palermo Viejo* ☎*11/4833–4736* ⊕*www.maria-cher.com.ar.*

Nann. Although the woolen clothes at this store are fit to hang on the wall, you'll have more fun wearing them. You can face winter in a full-length woven coat with unfinished hems or greet spring with an Edwardian-style shoulder cape. Super-soft llama-wool kiddie ponchos are enviable playground wear. ⊠*Serrano 1523, Palermo Viejo* ☎*11/4831–8835* ⊕*www.nannargentina.com.*

Objeto. Creative use of fabrics and quirky crafting make the everyday clothes here something special. Their feminine T-shirts are textile collages combining silk screening and appliqué techniques; skirts and jackets often mix new materials with original '60s off-cuts. Check out the waterproof jackets cut from gingham-print tablecloths complete with photos of food. ⊠*Gurruchaga 1649, Palermo Viejo* ☎*11/4834–6866.*

Pesqueira. Big girls and little girls can thrill together at the quirky but feminine silk-screen T-shirts that are Pesqueira's signature garments. Simple casual clothes in pastels—a blush-color denim sailor jacket, for instance—are here to combine with the tees. ⊠*Armenia 1493, Palermo Viejo* ☎*11/4833–7218.*

Salsipuedes. In this party-frock boutique, Aida Sirinian's geometrically embroidered turquoise satin with tulle underskirts and 1930s-style bias-cut velvet are worth organizing a ball for. Salsipuedes also sells hard-to-find Manto Abrigo coats—original handmade designs using wool from the north of Argentina. ⊠*Honduras 4814, Palermo Viejo* ☎*11/4831–8467* ⊠*Libertad 1634, Recoleta* ☎*011/4813–8528.*

Seco. Singing in the rain is encouraged at Seco, where all the clothes are designed to get wet. See-through plastic numbers come with matching rain hats worth risking a soaking for. ⊠*Armenia 1646, Palermo Viejo* ☎*11/4833–1166* ⊕*www.secorainwear.com.*

HIGH DESIGN

★ **Cecilia Gadea.** The simple, almost stark, cuts Gadea favors are the perfect canvas for riotously pretty texture work. One dress might be adorned with hundreds of hand-embroidered petals, another is made of an open, modern take on embroidery. Feast further on her skirts, suits, and well-cut cotton tops. High-heeled patent Mary Janes, designed specially for her by Belocca, are part-girly, part-sophisticated, like everything else here. ⊠*Ugarteche 3330, Palermo Botánico* ☏*11/4801–4163* ⊕*www.ceciliagadea.com.*

Evangelina Bomparola. In the center of this hushed boutique, a glass case containing a dress from Evangelina's latest collection lets you know how seriously she takes her clothes. It's easy to see why. Top-quality fabric and detailed attention to the way they hang means that though simple, her designs are far from boring. This is *the* place to come for a little (or long) black dress, but wilder items like a '60s-style funnel-neck coat in silver brocade are also available. ⊠*Quintana 20, Recoleta* ☏*11/4814–2553* ⊕*www.evangelinabomparola.com.*

★ **Ffioca.** Half of this spare store stocks designs by palermitaños Vicki Otero and DAPP, whose soft jersey tops might come in lilac, dove gray, or moss green. As for Ffioca's own creations: her asymmetrical tailoring and pleats might seem futuristic, but the dusky-rose and beige-and-black silk they come in hint of 1940s glamour. ⊠*Perú 559, San Telmo* ☏*11/4331–4585* ⊕*www.ffioca.com* Ⓜ*E to Belgrano.*

Marcelo Senra. Irregular natural linen, heavy hand-knit sweaters, cow-hair boots—it's all about texture at Marcelo Senra, a long-established local designer. Loose, flowing evening dresses might come in raw silk or satin, offset by bulky belts or chunky wooden jewelry. Handwoven accessories complement the clothes' earthy palette, and are a reason in themselves to visit Senra's Barrio Norte showroom. ⊠*Talcahuano 1133, Unit 3A, Barrio Norte* ☏*11/4813–2770* ⊕*www.marcelosenra.com.*

María Marta Facchinelli. The designs of this Palermo goddess are feminine without being girly. Shirts and jackets are close fitting but not vampish and come in pastels. From her great evening dresses, expect swoopy skirts, glamorous fabrics, and plenty of structure. ⊠*El Salvador 4741, Palermo Viejo* ☏*11/4831–8424* ⊕*www.facchinelli.com.*

Mariano Toledo. Draping is Mariano Toledo's forte: affordable party dresses hang in semi-sheer, togalike folds, accentuated by futuristic harness-style belts. Colors like electric blue and lime are arresting. ⊠*Armenia 1450, Palermo ViejoC1414DKF* ☏*11/4831–4861* ⊕*www.marianotoledo.com.ar.*

★ **Min Agostini.** Acres of skirts, structured wraps with oversize funnel necks, and loads of layers: yes, it's all very Yamamoto. These seriously original party clothes are the result of architect-turned-designer Jazmín Agostini "building" her garments on mannequins, rather than using patterns (her cutting table is the shop centerpiece). ⊠*Julián Álvarez 1419, Palermo Viejo* ☏*11/4833–7563* ⊕*www.minagostini.com.ar.*

★ **Tramando, Martín Churba.** This store's name means both "weaving" and "plotting": designer Martín Churba is doing plenty of both. Unique evening tops made of layers of pleated sheer fabric adorned with geometric slashes and circular beads look fit for an urban mermaid. Asym-

PALERMO

The hungry gazes of fashionistas on the prowl, the bloodthirsty competition for a town-house shop front, the sheer number of boutiques per cobbled block: there's no question that this is the heart of Buenos Aires' fashion scene.

Shops cluster around three hubs: Palermo Viejo, Palermo Hollywood, and el Botánico. Take your time—the whole point of Palermo is to wander and be seduced.

Long home to small designer shops, now local chains also vie for space in Palermo Viejo, southeast of Avenida Juan B. Justo. Honduras, El Salvador, Gurruchaga, and Malabia are the main drags. Head to Honduras for contemporary Argentine housewares designers, and former warehouses near Avenida Juan B. Justo for classic retro originals (and copies). Craftspeople sell on weekends from stalls on Plaza Serrano, and several dedicated covered spaces fronting the plaza operate week-round.

To the west is Palermo Hollywood; rents are sending smaller, quirkier boutiques here, while exclusivity-minded designers favor quiet Botánico, north of Santa Fe.

BEST TIME TO GO

You can do Plaza Serrano (Plazoleta Cortázar) and the shops in one very crowded go on Saturday. Shops keep odd hours Sunday and Monday; for wandering, go Tuesday through Friday—though half the shops don't open before midday.

BEST SOUVENIR FOR YOUR BABYSITTER

Which will your sitter need more—a massage, or a stiff drink? Combine the two with Malbec Winetherapy Shower Gel and Body Lotion from **Universo Garden Angels.** Mini-handmade soaps or bath petals come in funky boxes at **Sabater Hermanos.**

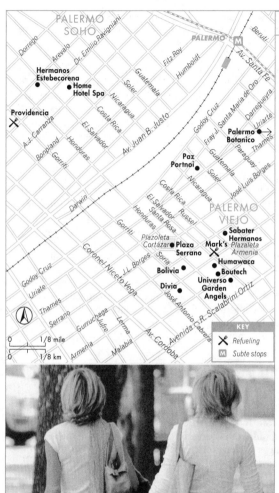

BEST FOR

HIP MENSWEAR

Hermanos Estebecorena: even the boxer shorts have been engineered at this stylish but ultra-pragmatic store.

Bolivia: the shirts are floral and the vintage jackets come with appliqués—wallflowers steer clear.

FOXY SHOES & SPACEY BAGS

Paz Portnoi: unusual materials like fish skin and hairy cowhide are transformed into teetering masterpieces for girls and slim lace-ups for guys.

Divia: there's something very retro about these limited-edition party shoes, which often combine metallic, stippled, and patent leathers.

Boutech: totally customizable cases for computers, cells, and MP3 players, in every hue of buttersoft Argentine leather imaginable.

Humawaca: from their cute round cowhide backpacks to stylish laptop totes, Humawaca's designs are edgier than anyone's in town.

REFUELING

Inspire yourself for your next purchase by checking out fellow shoppers' bags from a courtyard table at **Mark's** (⊠*El Salvador 4701* ☎*11/4832–6244*). Their hearty salads and sandwiches are served all day. Shake off the crowds behind the closed orange door of **Providencia** (⊠*Cabrera 5995* ☎*11/4772–8507*). Knock to be let in for the huge jugs of lemonade and earthy lunch combos.

Ayurvedic treatments and pick-me-up packages—some featuring local cures like wine grapes or Patagonian seaweed—are specialties at the ultracool **Home Hotel Spa** (⊠*Honduras 5860* ☎*11/4778–1008* ⊕*www.homebuenosaires.com*).

metrical shrugs, screen-printed tees, and even vases are some of the other woven wonders in the hushed town-house store. ✉*Rodríguez Peña 1973, Recoleta* ☎*11/4811–0465* ⊕*www.tramando.com.*

Trosman. Highly unusual beadwork is the only adornment on designer Jessica Trosman's simple clothes. There's nothing small and sparkling about it: her beads are smooth, inch-wide acrylic orbs that look futuristic yet organic. You might balk at the price tags, considering most of the clothes are made of T-shirting, but that hasn't stopped department stores worldwide from stocking her designs. The Palermo store carries jeans and more casual tops. ✉*Patio Bullrich Mall, Av. del Libertador 750, Recoleta* ☎*11/4814–7411* ✉*Armenia 1998, Palermo Viejo* ☎*11/4833–3085* ⊕*www.trosman.com.*

Vero Ivaldi. Unlike other heralded local designers, Vero Ivaldi sells gorgeous garments that flatter even less-than-perfect figures at scandalously accessible prices. Dresses and skirts come in bold tones like tomato red or ocher, and are often built of different-textured panels and strips. ✉*Gurruchaga 1585, Palermo Viejo* ☎*11/4832–6334* ⊕*www.veroivaldi.com.*

Zitta. It would be easy to pass by this unprepossessing Recoleta shop, but there's no way Fabián Zitta's evening dresses would slip by unnoticed. Local starlets love his bold designs, notable for their volume. Think balloon skirts, sheer layers, or organic-looking ruffled tubes snaking over bodices. Each collection includes black, white, and one other (usually blinding) color. ✉*Av. Quintana 10, Recoleta* ☎*11/4811–2094* ⊕*www.zittacostura.com.*

HANDICRAFTS, SILVER & SOUVENIRS

★ **Aire del Sur.** Alpaca, carved deer bone, onyx, and leather are some of the materials that might be combined into perfectly crafted trays, candelabras, or photo frames at Aire del Sur. The winning mix of these traditional materials with contemporary designs has won the hearts of stores like Barneys in New York and Paul Smith in London. Call ahead to arrange a visit to the Recoleta showroom. ✉*Arenales 1618, 9th fl., Recoleta* ☎*11/5811–3640* ⊕*www.airedelsur.com.*

★ **Fundacín Silataj.** This small handicraft shop is run by a nonprofit organization, which trades fairly with around 30 indigenous communities in Argentina. The shop smells like the aromatic palo santo wood used to make the trays, platters, cutting boards, and hair combs they carry. Other offerings include carnival masks, handwoven textiles, beaten tin ornaments, and alpaca jewelry. Prices, though higher than in markets, are reasonable, quality is excellent, and you know your money is going to the artisans. Note that the store closes for lunch. ✉*Vuelta de Obligado 1933, Belgrano* ☎*11/4785–8371* ⊕*www.fundacionsilataj. org.ar* Ⓜ*D to José Hernández.*

★ **Juan Carlos Pallarols Orfebre.** Argentina's legendary silversmith has made pieces for a mile-long list of celebrities that includes Frank Sinatra, Sharon Stone, Jacqueline Bisset, Bill Clinton, Nelson Mandela, the king and queen of Spain, and Princess Máxima Zorrequieta—Argentina's export to the Dutch royal family. A set of his ornate silver-handled steak knives is the perfect way to celebrate cow country, though you'll part with a few grand. ⊠*Defensa 1039, San Telmo* ☎*11/4362–0641* ⊕*www.pallarols.com.ar* Ⓜ*C or E to Independencia.*

Khori Wasi. Indigenous crafts from all over Latin America are chaotically arrayed in this vast, rust-color store. They're particularly strong on animal carnival masks and ceramics from Peru and Bolivia. There are also replicas of archaeological finds; cards next to each display explain the origins of the original. ⊠*Peru 863, San Telmo* ☎*11/4300–3784* ⊕*www.khori-wasi.com.ar* Ⓜ*C or E to Independencia.*

Lappas. The classic silver trays, cutlery sets, tea sets, and ice-buckets are favorites on porteño high-society wedding lists. Department stores worldwide stock Lappas silverware, but why pay export prices? ⊠*Florida 740, Microcentro* ☎*11/4325–9568* Ⓜ*B to Florida* ⊠*Santa Fe 1381, Barrio Norte* ☎*11/4811–6866* ⊕*www.lappas.com.*

★ **Materia Urbana.** The quirky, postmodern souvenirs this store specializes in are a welcome variation from all those mates and gaucho knives. The ubiquitous cow comes as a bright leather desk organizer here, while the national human icons Evita and Che adorn rolls of packing tape. Fridge-magnet poetry will help you remember your Spanish, and if you still can't manage more than "Hola," there's a hilarious illustrated dictionary of Argentine gestures to keep you going. Beautiful designer bags, jewelry, home ware, tango CDs, and prints by local artists are less ironic options. ⊠*Defensa 707, San Telmo* ☎*11/4361–5265* ⊠*Gorriti 4791, Palermo Viejo* ☎*11/4831–6317* ⊕*www.materiaurbana.com.*

Platería Parodi. This über-traditional store is chockablock with everything a gaucho about town needs to accessorize right, all in top-quality silver. There are belt buckles and knives for the boys, and the no-nonsense Pampa-style women's jewelry would go great with Gap and Ralph Lauren alike. ⊠*Av. de Mayo 720, Plaza de Mayo* ☎*11/4342–2207* Ⓜ*A to Piedras.*

★ **Tierra Adentro.** Beautiful indigenous crafts come with a clean conscience at Tierra Adentro, which insists on trading fairly with the native Argentine craftsmen whose work they stock. Fine weavings are the shop's hallmark, but wide silver bracelets and gobstopper-size turquoise beads are other tempting offers. ⊠*Arroyo 882, Retiro* ☎*11/4393–8552* ⊕*www.tierraadentro.info* Ⓜ*C to San Martín.*

HOME DECOR

★ **Arte Étnico Argentino.** Naturally dyed weavings and hand-hewn wooden basins are some of the things made by indigenous craftsmen at this shop-cum-gallery. Owner Ricardo Paz handpicks items like tables carved from a single tree trunk; exquisite woolen rugs are the most transportable of the shop's temptations. ⊠*El Salvador 4656, Palermo Viejo* ☎*11/4833–6661* ⊕*www.arteetnicoargentino.com.*

★ **Calma Chicha.** Calma Chicha's simple but fun approach to household items is flourishing in this warehouse-like shop. Signature pear-shape bean bags covered in denim, bright canvas, or leather are ideal for living-room chilling. Unusual gift items include a retro *pingüino* (penguin-shape wine jug). ⊠*Honduras 4925, Palermo Viejo* ☎*11/4831–1818*

⊠*Defensa 856, San Telmo* ☏*11/4300–6938* Ⓜ*C or E to Independencia* ⊕*www.calmachicha.com.*

Gropius 1920–2000. Always wanted furnishings by Mies van de Rohe, Charles and Ray Eames, or Pensi but never been able to afford them? Retro relief is on hand at Gropius, which sells near-perfect replicas of the 20th-century's greatest designers at relatively affordable prices. Its gravel-floor warehouse down the road has the real thing in mint condition; prices soar. ⊠*Honduras 5851, Palermo Hollywood* ☏*11/4774–1535* ⊠*Honduras 6027, Palermo Hollywood* ☏*11/4774–2094* ⊕*www.gropiusdesign-1920-2000.com.*

Newton. Fans of designers like Ray and Charles Eames or Le Corbusier will be in chair heaven at Newton. Gleaming white acrylic and chrome creations are piled to the ceiling, and although things here aren't cheap, it's still a bargain compared to what you'd find back home. They'll ship, too. ⊠*Honduras 5360, Palermo Viejo* ☏*11/4833–4007* ⊕*www.newtonba.com.ar.*

JEWELRY & ACCESSORIES

Abraxas. "Yes" is guaranteed if you propose with one of the period engagement rings that dazzle in the window of this antique jewelers. If you're not planning on an "I do" anytime soon, how about some art deco earrings with the tiniest of diamonds or a gossamer-fine bracelet? ⊠*Defensa 1092, San Telmo* ☏*11/4361–7512* Ⓜ*C to San Juan.*

Fodor'sChoice
★ **Celedonio.** Local boy Celedonio Lohidoy has designed pieces—often with frothy bunches of natural pearls—for Kenzo and Emanuel Ungaro; his work even appeared on Sarah Jessica Parker's neck on *Sex in the City.* He favors irregular semiprecious stones, set in asymmetrical, organic-looking designs. ⊠*Galería Promenade, Shop 39, Av. Alvear 1883* ☏*11/4809–0046* ⊕*www.celedonio.com.ar.*

Cousiño. Veined pinky-red rhodochrosite, Argentina's national stone, comes both in classic settings and as diminutive sculptures at this shop specializing in the unusual stone. Cousiño's sculptures of birds in flight are also exhibited in the National Museum of Decorative Arts. ⊠*Sheraton Buenos Aires Hotel, San Martín 1225, Retiro* ☏*11/4318–9000* ⊕*www.rodocrosita.com* Ⓜ*C to Retiro.*

Fahoma. This small boutique has enough accessories to make the rest of your outfit a mere formality. Berry-size beads go into chunky but affordable necklaces, and all manner of handbags line the back wall. ⊠*Libertad 1169, Recoleta* ☏*11/4813–5103* ⊕*www.fahoma.com.*

Homero. Shiny, colorful acrylic discs offset diamonds and white gold in Homero's innovative necklaces. Other rock-star pieces include cross-shape pendants and silver rings with acid-color stones. ⊠*Posadas 1399, Recoleta* ☏*11/4812–9881* ⊕*www.homero-joyas.com.ar.*

★ **Infinit.** Infinit's signature thick acrylic frames are favored by graphic designers and models alike. If the classic black rectangular versions are too severe for you, the same shape comes in a range of candy colors and two-tones. Pick up bug-eye shades while you're here, too. ⊠*Thames 1602, Palermo Viejo* ☏*11/4831–7070* ⊕*www.infinitnet.com.*

María Medici. Industrial-looking brushed silver rings and necklaces knitted from fine stainless-steel cables are some of the attractions at this tiny shop. María Medici also combines silver with primary-color resin to make solid, unusual-looking rings. ⊠*Niceto Vega 4619, Palermo Viejo* ☎*11/4773–2283* ⊕*www.mariamedici.com.ar.*

La Mercería. This sumptuous haberdashery is a shrine to luxury. Piles of floaty Indian scarves and fur-lined leather gloves beg to be touched. Even more hands-on are the reels of lace trims and sequined edging that line the walls. ⊠*Armenia 1609, Palermo Viejo* ☎*11/4831–8558.*

★ **Metalistería.** Seriously fun jewelry rules at this multidesigner boutique. As well as the silver, steel, and aluminum the store's name suggests, quirky pieces can include leather, wool, cotton, acrylic, laminated newspaper cuttings, or even colorful modeling clay. ⊠*Jorge Luis Borges 2021, Palermo Viejo* ☎*11/4833–7877* ⊕*www.metalisteria.com.ar.*

Midas Antigüedades. Everything a gentleman needs to accessorize like a lord is arrayed in the minimalist storefront. Watches are the specialty: a 1940s Longine with a snakeskin strap is one debonair option; jeweled tiepins, pocket watches, cuff links, and antique fountain pens round out the stock. ⊠*Defensa 1088, San Telmo* ☎*11/4300–6615* Ⓜ*C to San Juan.*

★ **Plata Nativa.** This tiny shop tucked away in an arcade is filled with delights for both boho chicks and collectors of singular ethnic jewelry. Complex, chunky necklaces with turquoise, amber, and malachite—all based on original Araucanian (ethnic Argentine) pieces—and Mapuche-style silver earrings and brooches are some of the offerings. Happy customers include Sharon Stone, Pedro Almodóvar, and the Textile Museum in Washington, D.C. ⊠*Galería del Sol, Unit 4, Florida 860* ☎*11/4312–1398* ⊕*www.platanativa.com* Ⓜ*C to San Martín.*

Santino. Delicate curlicued diamond rings are Santino's signature and a favorite accessory at top local fashion shoots. Contemporary art deco–style brooches share space in the small wine-red shop with the real antique McCoy. ⊠*Av. Callao 1702, Recoleta* ☎*11/4806–0120* ⊕*www.santinoba.com.*

LUGGAGE, LEATHER & HANDBAGS

★ **Arandú.** The estancia (ranch) crowd love the classic ranch wear that fills this three-story Recoleta house. Downstairs, the walls are lined with glass cabinets filled with asado knives, *mates,* and silver-and-textile jewelry. Racks of boots gleam temptingly at the back of the shop, and if you find the supple canvas and leather sports bags too conventional, check out such novelties as leather rifle cases. Price tags are sky high, but the quality is superlative. Pop upstairs for saddles and bridles; the downtown branch is smaller, but still well stocked. ⊠*Ayacucho 1924, Recoleta* ☎*11/4800–1575* ⊠*Paraguay 1259, Centro* ☎*11/4816–6191* Ⓜ*D to Tribunales* ⊕*www.tal-arandu.com.*

★ **Boutech.** Inside this sparse white store, colorful leather cases for just about every gadget on the market nestle like jewels in glass-topped drawers. Boutech has been selling their products online for years, but here you can get them from the source, postage-free. Basic designs

RECOLETA & BARRIO NORTE

Armani, Lauren, Hermès. Pristine century-old town houses. Darkened limos ferrying stars and royalty from shops to hotels. Paris? Rome? Berlin? Wait—you *are* still in Argentina. But Recoleta will do its utmost to convince you that you're not.

Argentina's high society has always looked to Europe for inspiration, nowhere more so than Recoleta—where the country's high society shops. Seriously big spenders needn't stray far from Avenida Alvear, where international designers rub shoulders with darlings of Argentine style like Martín Churba.

The linchpin of all this luxury is the Alvear Palace Hotel, home away from home for pop queens and real queens alike. Patio Bullrich shopping mall is as elegant as the rest of Recoleta, but its stylish local chains make less of a dent in your credit card. Even humbler yet no less desirable offerings are at the Feria Artesanal de Recoleta, a weekend arts-and-crafts market.

BEST TIME TO GO

Mirror the platinum-card brigade and shop weekdays between lunch and afternoon tea (at the Alvear Palace Hotel, of course). High prices keep streets uncrowded. To hit the market, come on weekends between 2 PM and dusk.

BEST SOUVENIR FOR YOUR IN-LAWS

The handmade chocolate truffles at **El Viejo Oso** are sure to sweeten even the sourest mother-in-law. Go for the *dulce de leche* fillings. If they prefer liquid sustenance, head to **Grand Cru**, where staff can recommend a bottle of yet-to-be-exported boutique-vineyard Malbec.

BEST FOR

HORSEY CHIC

La Dolfina Polo Lifestyle: an edgier, Argentine take on Ralph Lauren.

Arandú: exquisite leather hats, boots, saddles, and bridles—everything but the horse (though at these prices, you'll want a free one thrown in).

Cardon: the estancia look at high street prices.

AVANT-GARDE ARGENTINE DESIGN

Tramando, Martín Churba: Buenos Aires' answer to Issey Miyake weaves his wondrous, high-tech cloth into floaty masterpieces.

Evangelina Bomparola: the limited-edition suits, funnel-neck coats, and A-line party dresses pay tasteful homage to the 1960s.

Trosman: made chiefly of T-shirting, Trosman's unusually draped garments are comfortable and flattering (if you're below a size 6, that is).

Varanasi: exuberant fabrics built to structural perfection from architects-turned-designers.

REFUELING

Like the rest of Recoleta, the vibe is unashamedly French at **Sirop Folie** (✉*Vicente López 1661, Shop 12* ☎*11/4813–5900*). Lunchtime dishes, chalked on a blackboard, burst with fresh ingredients. The real stars here, however, are the painstakingly constructed patisseries. Laid-back yet just a block from posh Avenida Alvear, **El Sanjuanino** (✉*Posadas 1515* ☎*11/4804–2909*) is perfect for grabbing a traditional northern-Argentine empanada.

Water treatments play a big role in the express packages at **Aqua Vita Medical Spa** (✉*Arenales 1965* ☎*11/4812–5989* ⊕*www.aquavitamedicalspa.com*) which emphasizes health as well as beauty.

THE CHAIN GANG: HANDBAGS

Lázaro. Some are classic, some are ultrahip, but the handbags and purses here have in common simple lines, minimal adornment, and high-quality workmanship (which makes the prices especially reasonable). Their Jet line has fabulous futuristic totes, document holders, and bandolier bags in bright primary colors; plenty of inner divisions make them truly travel-worthy. Better yet, there are shoes and jackets to match. ⊕www.lazarocuero.com.ar.

Prüne. It's definitely favored by smart working chicks. Prüne does handbags that are chic but practical, with thoughtful compartments and enough room for all your bits 'n' bobs. Colors tend to be rich and dark and leathers are ultrasupple. Details like steel rings linking bags to straps lend urban touches. Leather jackets, belts, and shoes are also on offer. ⊕www.prune.com.ar.

come in a staggering range of colors, or you can design your own (including details like Swarowski crystals or a logo) and they'll make it in three days. Better still, design it online and it'll be waiting when you arrive. They receive advance copies of new Apple products, so as soon as the gizmos are out there, Boutech's got a case for them. ⊠*Malabia 1637, Palermo Viejo* ☎*11/4833–9469* ⊕*www.boutechstore.com.*

Carpincho. This shop specializes in the stippled leather of the carpincho (cabybara—the world's largest rodent, native to Argentina), which has supersoft skin. The real draw, though, are the gloves, which come in both carpincho and kidskin and in many colors, from classic chocolate brown to tangerine and lime. ⊠*Esmeralda 775, Centro* ☎*11/4322–9919* ⊕*www.carpinchonet.com.ar* Ⓜ*C to Lavalle.*

Cardon. Pine floors, pine walls, and pine cabinets—it's all very country down at Cardon. The estancia crowd comes here for reasonably priced, no-nonsense sheepskin jackets, cashmere sweaters, and riding boots. Items from the line of *talabartería* (traditional gaucho-style leather items), including cowboy hats, make great gifts. ⊠*Av. Alvear 1847, Recoleta* ☎*11/4804–8424* ⊠*Honduras 4755, Palermo Viejo* ☎*11/4832–5925* ⊕*www.cardon.com.ar.*

Casa López. Don't let Casa López's drab storefront put you off: you're as likely to find a trouser suit in flower-print suede as a handbag for grandma. It's a store in two parts: the right-hand shop (Number 658) has totes and soft-sided suitcases in chestnut- and chocolate-color leather that looks good enough to eat; there are also classic jackets. More unusual fare—fur sacks with natural wool fringes, black cowhide baguettes, aubergine leather clutches—are next door at Number 640. ⊠*Marcelo T. de Alvear 640 and 658, Centro* ☎*11/4311–3044* ⊕*www. casalopez.com.ar* Ⓜ*C to San Martín.*

Doma. The trendy leather jackets at Doma are hard-wearing *and* eye-catching. Military-style coats in olive-green suede will keep you snug in winter. Cooler summer options include collarless biker jackets—they might come in silver, hot pink, or electric blue. ⊠*El Salvador 4792, Palermo Viejo* ☎*11/4831–9003* ⊕*www.doma-leather.com.*

Fodor'sChoice
★ **Humawaca.** Their signature circular leather handbags and butterfly-shape backpacks are Buenos Aires design icons. The trendiest leather brand in town also makes stylish laptop totes and travel bags, which come with a handy magazine-carrying strap. Cowhide is a favorite here, as are lively combinations like chocolate-brown leather and moss-green suede, or electric-blue nobuk with a floral lining. Price tags on the bags may make you gulp, but there are wallets, clogs, and pencil cases, too. ⊠*El Salvador 4692, Palermo Viejo* ☎*11/4832–2662* ⊠*Posadas 1380, Recoleta* ☎*11/4811–5995* ⊕*www.humawaca.com.*

La Martina. With branches in Saratoga Springs and London, it's clear that the clothing line of polo team La Martina is targeted at the horsing jet set—and with prices to match. But it's not just about boots and jodhpurs; there are also corduroy pants and cashmere sweaters for lounging around your country house in style. To see what such a house could look like inside, head to the huge Belgrano branch. Screen-printed tees—including the Argentine national polo-team shirt—are somewhat cheaper options. ⊠*Paraguay 661, Microcentro* ☎*11/4311–5963* Ⓜ*C to San Martín* ⊠*Arribeños 2632, Belgrano* ☎*11/4576–0010* ⊕*www. lamartina.com.*

Qara. Sumptuously supple leather is crafted into stylish but totally practical bags at Qara. The Amanda line includes a big, practical tote, perfect for stashing everything but the kitchen sink. The big square courier bag and vertical leather map are stylish portage for girls and guys alike. The store is too dark to really appreciate colors like rich chestnut and olive green: ask the assistants (who are probably stalking you around the displays) if you can take bags outside to see them in daylight. ⊠*Gurruchaga 1548, Palermo Viejo* ☎*11/4834–6361* ⊕*www.qara.com.*

Rossi y Caruso. Top-quality workmanship and classic cuts are what bring distinguished customers like King Juan Carlos of Spain to Rossi y Caruso. The shop specializes in riding gear (think Marlborough foxhunt rather than Marlboro man) but also sells conservative handbags, leather jackets, and shoes. And should you need a saddle during your trip, those sold here are the best in town. ⊠*Posadas 1387, Recoleta* ☎*11/4811–1538* ⊕*www.rossicaruso.com.*

★ **Uma.** Light, butter-soft leather takes very modern forms here, with geometric stitching the only adornment on jackets and asymmetrical bags that might come in rich violet in winter and aqua-blue in summer. The top-quality footwear includes teetering heels and ultrasimple boots and sandals with, mercifully, next to no elevation. ⊠*Honduras 5225, Palermo Viejo* ☎*11/4832–2122* ⊕*www.umacuero.com.*

MALLS & DEPARTMENT STORES

Abasto. The soaring art deco architecture of what was once the city's central market is as much a reason to come as the three levels of shops. Although Abasto has many top local chains, it's not as exclusive as other malls, so you can find bargains at shops like Ver, Yagmour, and Markova. You can also dress up at Ayres, Paula Cahen d'Anvers, Akiabara, or the Spanish chain Zara, famous for its cut-price versions of catwalk looks. Levi's, Quiksilver, Puma, and Adidas are among the casual international offerings; for something smarter, there's Dior. Men can hit such trendy shops as Bensimon and Mancini or go for the *estanciero* (estate owner) look with Legacy chinos and polos. Take a break in the fourth-floor food court beneath the glass panes and steel supports of the building's original roof. The mall also has a cinema; if you prefer live entertainment, near the food court is a Ticketek booth. ⊠*Av. Corrientes 3247, Almagro* ☎*11/4959–3400* ⊕*www.abasto-shopping. com.ar* Ⓜ*B to Carlos Gardel.*

★ **Alto Palermo.** A prime Palermo location, choice shops, and a pushy marketing campaign have made Alto Palermo popular. Giggly teenage hordes are seduced by its long, winding layout. Ladies who lunch sip espresso in the cafés of its top-level food hall. The 154 shops are strong on local street-wear brands like Bensimon and Bowen for the boys and Akiabara, Ona Sáez, Las Pepas, and Rapsodia for the girls. Check out trendy local designers María Vázquez and Allo Martínez for way-out party frocks, and Claudia Larreta for more staid numbers. Paruolo, Sibyl Vane, and Lázaro are the best of many good shoe and handbag shops. Surf-and-skate store Cristobal Colón does board shorts and All-Stars; local versions of Puma and Adidas footwear disappear fast despite high price tags. Other international names include Levi's and Miss Sixty. ⊠*Av. Santa Fe 3251, at Av. Colonel Díaz, Palermo* ☎*11/5777–8000* ⊕*www.altopalermo.com.ar* Ⓜ*D to Bulnes.*

Buenos Aires Design. This fledgling mall alongside the Recoleta Cemetery mainly sells housewares—most of them imported and no less expensive than stuff back home. There are, however, a few noteworthy shops: two-level Morph does quirky colorful household items (think Philippe Starck on a budget), and rival OKKO does Indian appliqué and heavy rustic furniture. The must-see, though, is one-stop **Puro Diseño Argentino** (☎*11/5777–6104* ⊕*www.purodiseno.com.ar*), where Argentine designers show off their crafts, jewelry, clothing, accessories, furniture, and household items. This is one of the few places to pick up a one-of-a-kind Manto Abrigo coat, handwoven in luminous colors in the north of Argentina. The mall's open-air terrace has several cafés and restaurants with views of Avenida del Libertador. ⊠*Pueyrredón 2501, Recoleta* ☎*11/5777–6000* ⊕*www.designrecoleta.com.ar.*

Falabella. There's no love lost between Argentina and its neighbors, but when this Chilean department store opened, the seriously low prices soon had locals swallowing their pride. The ground floor of this busy corner store contains accessories and international perfumes and cosmetics, including the only local branch of MAC. Falabella has three own-brand clothing lines: Sybila does low-cost (and low-quality) street wear; University Club is preppier and harder-wearing; Basement includes better-quality casual and work clothes. A block away is the store's home-ware branch, **Falabella Hogar** (⊠*Florida 343, Microcentro*). It does a roaring trade in cheap but stylish crockery, kitchenware, and ornaments, mostly imported from China and India. The overworked staff at both stores don't give much guidance, but the low prices make up for it. Between noon and 2:30 the stores flood with office workers.

Life Before Malls

No shopping trip is complete without browsing one of the city's many galerías. These quirky shopping arcades are the precursors of malls and were mostly built in the 1960s and '70s. Their boxy architecture often includes gloriously kitsch touches, and the unpredictable retail offerings of their small stores could include designer gear, no-name brands, used books, sex toys, cigars and pipes, tattoos, imported vinyl records, and other wonders. Though many galerías have closed down, they're still thick on the ground along Avenida Santa Fe (800 to 1500) and Avenida Cabildo (1500 to 2200).

A favorite with teenagers and clubbers alike is **Galería Bond Street** (⊠ *Av. Santa Fe 1607, Barrio Norte* ☏ *No phone*). Downstairs stores sell club wear, punky T-shirts, and band pins. The top floor has the classier pickings of local designers who aren't big enough to move to Palermo yet.

Vintage vultures should swing by the **Galería Quinta Avenida** (⊠ *Av. Santa Fe 1270, Recoleta* ☏ *No phone*), which has a host of dusty boutiques ideal for a couple of hours of rack-roaming. There's a particularly good selection of leather jackets, as well as accessories like specs from the 1950s and '60s.

⊠ *Florida 202, at Sarmiento, Microcentro* ☏ *11/5950–5000* ⊕ *www. falabella.com.ar* Ⓜ *B to Florida; C to Lavalle; D to Catedral.*

Galerías Pacífico. Upscale shops line the three levels of this building, which was designed during the city's turn-of-the-20th-century golden age. Stores are organized along four glass-roofed passages, which branch out in a cross from the central stairwell; the cupola above it is decorated by Argentine greats like Antonio Berni. Top local menswear brands Etiqueta Negra and La Dolfina Polo Lifestyle have large stores here. Paula Cahen d'Anvers and Uma are some of the options for younger women, while Janet Wise and Claudia Larreta do more sophisticated looks. There are a basement food court, a cinema, and the Centro Cultural Borges, whose small international art exhibitions have featured Andy Warhol, Salvador Dalí, and Henri Cartier-Bresson. ⊠ *Calle Florida 753, at Av. Córdoba, Microcentro* ☏ *11/4319–5100* ⊕ *www.galeriaspacificos.com.ar* Ⓜ *B to Florida.*

★ **Paseo Alcorta.** If you're a serious shopper and only have time to visit one mall, make it this one. Local fashionistas favor it for its mix of high-end local chains and boutiques from some of the city's best designers, all under one roof. Trendsetters like Trosman, Jazmín Chebar, and María Vázquez do cool clothes for girls, while for more classic chic there's Claudia Larreta and Portsaid. The men can hold their own up at Hermanos Estebecorena and Etiqueta Negra. Ultrahip accessories come as handbags at Jet, or as glasses at EXE, and Mishka and Paruolo sell cute but dressy shoes. The international presence is strong, too, with stores from Armani Exchange, Hilfiger, Lacroix, and Cacharel, as well as the usual sports brands. A classy food hall and Wi-Fi round off the reasons to come. ⊠ *Jerónimo Salguero 3172, at Av. Figueroa Alcorta, Palermo* ☏ *11/5777–6500* ⊕ *www.paseoalcorta.com.ar.*

Patio Bullrich. The city's most upscale mall was once the headquarters for the Bullrich family's meat-auction house. Inside stone cow heads mounted on pillars still watch over the clientele. A colonnaded front, a domed-glass ceiling, and curlicued steel supports are other reminders of another age. Top local stores are relegated to the lowest level, making way for the likes of Lacroix, Cacharel, and Maxmara. Urban leather-ware brand Uma has a shop here, as does Palermo fashion princess Jessica Trosman, whose spare women's clothes are decorated with unusual heavy beadwork. The enfant terrible of Argentine footwear, Ricky Sarkany, sells dangerously pointed stilettos in colors that walk the line between exciting and kitsch. Edgy but elegant menswear line Etiqueta Negra has its first store outside the snooty northern suburbs here. When the gloriously huge bags these shops pack your purchases into begin to weigh you down, stop for a calorie-oozing cake at Nucha, on the Avenida del Libertador side of the building. ⊠*Enter at Posadas 1245, or Av. del Libertador 750, Recoleta* ☎*11/4815-3501* ⊕*www. shoppingbullrich.com.ar* Ⓜ*C to Retiro.*

MUSIC

Notorious. Intrigued by some of the sounds you've heard on your trip? Get some to take home with you from Notorious, which has a strong selection of local rock, folk, jazz, and (of course) tango. Friendly young staff will happily dig out your requests and make other suggestions. The shop is small, but there are plenty of listening stations so you can try before you buy. ⊠*Av. Callao 966, Barrio Norte* ☎*11/4813-6888* Ⓜ*D to Callao* ⊠*Estados Unidos 488, San Telmo* ☎*11/4361-6189* ⊕*www.notorious.com.ar.*

Oid Mortales. "Listen, mortals": so begins Argentina's national anthem, which this ultrahip store has taken as its name. You may be mortal, but the staff aren't. They subscribe to the High Fidelity school of service—unless you're Bob Dylan, expect to be abused. Avoid their sneers and turn to the unrivaled selection of local folk, rock, and indie, bursting with artists no one back home has even heard of, let alone heard. ⊠*Av. Corrientes 1145, Shop 17, Centro* ☎*11/4382-8839* ⊕*www.oid mortalesdiscos.com.ar* Ⓜ*B to Carlos Pellegrini.*

PAPER & STATIONERY

★ **Papelera Palermo.** Piles of handmade paper, leather-bound diaries, and vintage notebooks are arrayed on simple trestle tables. Writing implements range from old-world dipping pens to chunky pencils, and the soft leather artists' rolls are a luxurious way to carry them around. The store often showcases work by top engravers and graphic artists, who return the favor by designing the covers of sketchbooks. ⊠*Honduras 4945, Palermo Viejo* ☎*11/4833-3081* ⊠*Arenales 1170, Barrio Norte* ☎*11/4811-7698* ⊕*www.papelerapalermo.com.ar.*

SHOES

MEN'S & WOMEN'S

Guido. In Argentina, loafers means Guido, whose retro-looking logo has been the hallmark of quality footwear since 1952. Try on timeless handmade Oxfords and wing tips; there are also fun items like raspberry cow-skin handbags. ⊠*Av. Quintana 333, Recoleta* ☎*11/4811–4567* ⊕*www.guidomocasines.com.ar.*

★ **Paz Portnoi.** These unusual, sexy shoes are clearly meant for stepping on people's hearts. One half of the design team trained at Alexander McQueen in London, and it shows: the creations are wild but perfectly crafted. Fish skin is the material of choice (yes, really). It looks like scaly nubuck and comes as crimson or emerald heels for girls, or pointy, tapered numbers for boys. Dress trainers and cowboy boots are casual options. ⊠*Uriarte 1976, Palermo Viejo* ☎*11/4774–6961.*

28Sport. These leather bowling sneakers and boxing-style boots are the heart and, er, sole of retro. All the models are variations on a classic round-toed lace-up, but come with different-length legs. Plain black or chestnut uppers go with everything, but equally tempting are the two-tone numbers—in chocolate and orange, or black with curving white panels, for example. Even the store is a nod to the past, kitted out like a Buenos Aires living room from the 1950s. ⊠*Fitz Roy 1962, Palermo Viejo* ☎*11/4776–6007* ⊕*www.28sport.com.*

MEN ONLY

Agua Patagona. If these round-toe leather sneakers remind you of Camper, you're spot on—one of the designers also works for the Spanish brand. Agua Patagona also has a trademark rubber sole engraved with a map of Argentina. They mainly stock men's sizes, but can whip up custom-made versions of some designs in sizes 35–46 (U.S. sizes 3–11½): it takes five days, and costs the same as an off-the-shelf pair. ⊠*Gurruchaga 1479, Palermo Viejo* ☎*11/4833–6268* ⊕*www.agua patagona.com.*

WOMEN ONLY

de María. María Conorti was one of the first young designers to set up shop in the area, and she's going strong. Wedge heels, satin ankleties, and abundant use of patent leather are the trademark touches of her quirky designs. Head to the basement at the back of the store for discounted past seasons. ⊠*Libertad 1661, Recoleta* ☎*11/4815–5001* ⊕*www.zapatosdemaria.com.ar.*

★ **Divia.** Step out in a pair of limited-edition Divias, and it doesn't really matter what else you've got on. Designer Virginia Spagnuolo draws inspiration from travels to India, her own vintage shoe collection, and even her cat. The results are leather collages—suede, textured metallic, or patent leathers—in colors like teal, ruby, or plum. ⊠*Armenia 1489, Palermo Viejo* ☎*11/4831–9090* ⊕*www.diviashoes.com.*

CENTRO & ENVIRONS

"It's not what it used to be," porteños whine about downtown. But although pickings might not thrill locals, the excellent selection of crafts, leather, and silver are reason enough for visitors to brave the crowds of Centro.

On pedestrian-only Calle Florida, local chain stores and boutiques abound; score international duds at Spanish megabrand Zara and clothes and housewares at Chilean Falabella. Argentine soccer shirts are best sellers at the many sports shops; no-brand leather jackets are another draw, and armies of salesmen are positioned outside shops. At Florida's north end, established leather shops like Casa López and Prüne sell higher-quality bags and clothing.

Crowds of office workers, street artists, and tourists make walking up Florida slow progress. Pickpockets are common, so keep your valuables close. When the crowds and exhaust fumes start to cause retail burnout, browse through big-name local stores inside the Galerías Pacífico Mall at Avenida Córdoba. Calmer still: browse the free-entry art galleries on Calle Arroyo north of Avenida Santa Fe.

BEST TIME TO GO

Weekdays, but be warned that lunching office workers fill the streets between noon and 2:30. Things get sketchy at night, so don't linger after dark.

BEST SOUVENIR FOR CAFFEINE ADDICTS

Looking to wean a coffee junkie off the java (or hook them on another habit)? Gorgeous drinking sets for Argentina's national hot beverage, *mate*, come with silver trimmings at **Platería Parodi**. Leather specialists **Arandú** sell a variety of supple carrying cases for the gourd-and-thermos flask—they'd also make a stylish wine tote for picnics.

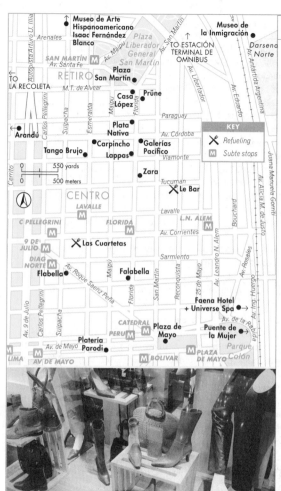

REFUELING

For an oh-so-porteño refuel, duck into classic pizzeria **Las Cuartetas** (✉*Av. Corrientes 838* ☎*11/4326–0171*). Stand at the bar for a slice in a trice, or get the whole pie at a Formica table. Forget about the chaos of the Centro and focus on the cool at **Le Bar** (✉*Tucumán 422* ☎*11/4307–0896*) A spacey interior, great lunch menus, and even better cocktails are sure to perk you up in no time.

Yoga classes, hammam, a range of massages, and La Prairie beauty treatments are available at the luxurious **Faena Hotel + Universe Spa** (✉*Marta Salotti 445* ☎*11/4010–9083* ⊕*www.faenahotelanduniverse.com*).

BEST FOR

SILVER

Platería Parodi: *mates*, belt buckles, knives—everything a gaucho needs, and more besides, in silver.

Lappas: why shop for their classic tea sets, trays, and cutlery at Barney's or Saks 5th Avenue when you can get them from the source?

Plata Nativa: chunky jewelry inspired by native Argentine designs, from single-piece silver earrings to strings of gobstopper-size coral beads.

CLASSIC LEATHER

Casa López: beautiful leather briefcases, baguettes, clutches, totes, suitcases, and sports bags—whatever the shape, it's in the bag.

Carpincho: a cornucopia of gloves; many made from stippled capybara leather.

TANGO

Flabella: high-quality shoes in a range of designs make this the *tanguero* footwear favorite.

Tango Brujo: clothing, shoes, music, DVDs . . . everything you need to tango but the dance floor.

TANGO TO GO

Need we remind you that Buenos Aires is the best place in the world to stock up on tango music, memorabilia, and serious dance wear? Some of the best tango shoes in town, including classic spats, 1920s T-bar designs, and glitzier numbers for men and women are all made to measure at **Flabella** (✉*Suipacha 263, Microcentro* ☎*11/4322–6036* ⊕*www.flabella.com*). For foxier-than-thou footwear that's kicking up storms on milonga floors worldwide, head to **Comme Il Faut** (✉*Arenales 1239, Apt. M, Barrio Norte* ☎*11/4815–5690* ⊕*www.commeil-faut.com.ar*); dedicated dancers love its combination of top-notch quality and gorgeous, show-stopping colors like teal or plum, usually with metallic trims. Animal-print suede, fake snakeskin, and glittering ruby take-me-home-to-Kansas numbers are some of the wilder options. **Tango Brujo** (✉*Esmeralda 754, Micro-centro* ☎*11/4326–8264* ⊕*www. tangobrujo.com*) is a one-stop tango shop selling shoes, clothes, and how-to videos. Recordings by every tango musician under the sun can be found at **Zivals** (✉*Av. Callao 395, Congreso* ☎*11/5128–7500* Ⓜ*B to Callao* ✉*Serrano 1445, Palermo Viejo* ☎*11/4833–7948* ⊕*www. tangostore.com*). They stock CDs of classics, modern performers, and electro-tango as well as DVDs, sheet music, books, and even T-shirts.

Josefina Ferroni. Thickly wedged heels and points that taper beyond reason and are some of Ferroni's trademarks. Also try the high heels in metallic leather with a contrasting trim or the slick black boots with a detail down the back that looks like leather ticker tape. ✉*Armenia 1471, Palermo Viejo* ☎*11/4831–4033* ⊕*www.josefinaferroni.com.ar.*

Lonte. There's something naughty-but-oh-so-nice about Lonte's shoes. Chunky gold peep-toe heels are a retro-queen's dream, and the outré animal-print numbers are a favorite of local diva Susana Giménez. For more discreet feet there are tweed boots or classic heels in straightforward colors. ✉*Av. Alvear 1814, Recoleta* ☎*11/4804–9270.*

Mishka. At this longtime Palermo favorite your feet can be sexy in high-heel lace-ups or brash in metallic pirate boots. The footwear comes in leather as well as in fabrics like brocade; most styles run narrow. ✉*El Salvador 4673, Palermo Viejo* ☎*11/4833–6566.*

TOYS

Calma Chicha Niños. Nostalgic for that Argentine childhood you never had? Outfit yourself (or your little ones) with the retro toys like wooden figurines and rubber soccer balls at the kiddie branch of Calma Chicha. More unusual are the life-size football-player dolls, decked out in Boca Juniors and River Plate colors. ✉*Gurruchaga 1580, Palermo Viejo* ☎*11/4832–1838* ⊕*www.calmachicha.com.*

★ **Recursos Infantiles.** Everything is designed with little ones in mind, right up to the small tables and kid-centered menu at the in-store café. Beautifully illustrated picture books delight even non–Spanish speakers, and a majority of toys are made of wood. The small-scale mate sets by

Big Spenders

If you're a shopper who just isn't satisfied by small-fry spending, why not splash out on something a little more extravagant, like, say . . . a house? Buenos Aires' latest shopping trend is led by a horde of foreigners who are acquiring porteño pied-à-terres as second homes or investments. Although tango-obsessed visitors spearheaded the tendency, more outsiders who simply love the Buenos Aires lifestyle are getting in on the action. Most look for a classic from the 1920s, '30s, or '40s, with 10-foot ceilings, crafted wooden doors and windows, and acres of gleaming floorboards. The most desirable districts are San Telmo, Palermo, and Recoleta, though there's been a surge in sales of apartments in Puerto Madero.

According to Reynolds Homes, a well-established real estate agency catering to foreigners, those who buy apartments over the Internet sightunseen tend to go for cheaper properties at around the $70,000 mark. Buyers who pound the pavement end up being tempted into spending more: $150,000 on average. Paying cash in

dollars can get you a hefty discount, though bringing cash into the country incurs a massive 1.5% levy. Although there are few restrictions imposed on non-Argentines buying property, the process can be a headache so it's best to deal with an agency that can smooth out all the bumps.

Years of experience have made **Reynolds Propiedades** a fail-safe option for foreign buyers. Reynolds works with other estate agents to increase the number of properties it can offer, and then guides you through the paperwork. Staffers can even help you furnish your house when you're done. ⊠*Junin 1655, 3rd fl., Recoleta* ☎*11/4801–9291* ⊕*www.argentin-ahomes.com.* If you feel guilty about taking the property out of the hands of locals, you can go easy on your conscience at **Ojo Propiedades,** where all profits go to the Red Cross. This hip outfit deals primarily with Palermo properties and has lots of foreign customers. ⊠*Serrano 1503, Palermo Viejo* ☎*11/4832–4040* ⊕*www.ojopropiedades.com.*

D'ak—complete with minikettle and thermos flask—come in a colorful bag. ⊠*J.L. Borges 1766, Palermo Viejo* ☎*11/4834–6177.*
Sopa de Príncipe. Sopa de Príncipe does funky fabric toys; heavy stitching on cotton and flannel gives their dolls an appealingly punky look. Crates are filled with an ark-worthy selection of calico animals— easy-to-pack gifts. ⊠*Thames 1719, Palermo Viejo* ☎*11/4831–8505* ⊕*www.sopadeprincipe.com.ar.*

WINE

Fodor'sChoice ★ **Grand Cru.** Don't let the small shop front put you off: as with all the best wine shops, the action is underground. Grand Cru's peerless selection includes wines from Patagonian vineyard Noemia, one of the country's best and exclusive to the shop. Incredibly savvy staffers will guide you, and they can FedEx up to 12 bottles anywhere in the world. ⊠*Av. Alvear 1718, Recoleta* ☎*11/4816–3975* ⊕*www.grandcru.com.ar.*

★ **La Finca.** Unusual wines from boutique vineyards are among the great finds here. Like their stock, the staff hails from Mendoza, capital of Argentine oenology, and they're a friendly, knowledgeable crew. Past the rustic shelving piled high with bottles are a few tables where you can sample wines like Carmelo Patti or Bramare, accompanied by a light *picada* (snack) of goat cheese and black olives, also from Mendoza. ⊠*Honduras 5147, Palermo Viejo* ☎*11/4832–3004.*

Ligier. Ligier has a string of shops across town and lots of experience guiding bewildered shoppers through their impressive selection. Although they stock some boutique-vineyard wines, they truly specialize in the big names like Rutini and Luigi Bosca. Their leather wine carrying cases make a great picnic accessory. ⊠*Av. Santa Fe 800, Retiro* ☎*11/4515–0126* Ⓜ*C to San Martín.*

Terroir. A wine-lovers heaven is tucked away in this white stone Palermo town house. Expert staffers are on hand to help you make sense of the massive selection of Argentine wine, which includes collector's gems like the 1999 Angélica Zapata Cabernet Sauvignon. Terroir ships all over the world. ⊠*Buschiazzo 3040, Palermo* ☎*11/4778–3443* ⊕*www.terroir.com.ar.*

After Dark

Bandonión player

WORD OF MOUTH

"There's nightlife everywhere, and it's easy to get around by taxi, which is very affordable and, late at night, a smart option."

—Scarlett

"I liked San Telmo better than Palermo—not as spread out and more restaurants and bars on each block. Palermo has pockets that are lively and other pockets that are residential only."

—globetrots

AFTER DARK PLANNER

What It Costs

Wines are generally very good value: wine lists in reputable bars start around the 30-peso mark, while beers and soft drinks approach 10 pesos. Cocktails, usually around 15–25 pesos, are starting to catch on more widely. Concert admission can be 80 pesos or more for established international acts. Nightclubs can charge a cover of around 20–30 pesos, which often includes a drink; fancier nightclubs charge more. Tips are roughly 10%–15% on top of the bill. A taxi ride from Palermo to Centro is around 15 pesos.

What to Wear

Stylish but rarely outlandish, porteños are conservative in their dress; even in summer, it's a safe bet that any men wearing shorts and open-toe shoes here are foreigners. As such, in all but the most snobbish places you won't find posted dress codes. But although they may let you into a club or bar with something less than flattering on, know that to Argentines, first impressions are everything and a too-casual look might signal not only "tourist" but also "poorly put together" in general.

Neighborhood Rundown

Centro, Palermo, and San Telmo are the three main areas for bars, though there's also a stretch of clubs along the Costanera Norte (the waterfront north of Palermo). Use common sense walking around at night in these places and you'll be fine; for getting between neighborhoods or through unlighted streets, take a taxi.

Centro & Environs: Downtown is chaotic on weekdays but can be deserted at night and on weekends. If you know where to look, there are some great bars and nightclubs.

San Telmo: Always an immigrant neighborhood, San Telmo is being revamped with establishments catering to the latest wave of visitors to the city—backpackers and tango hunters. Now with several trendy bars, the bohemian district is coming into its own again. La Boca to the south, on the other hand, is still best avoided at night.

Puerto Madero: A business district that's risen over the last decade from a nearly abandoned dock, Puerto Madero is centrally located and home to some of the city's most expensive hotels, restaurants, and bars; the scene here is poised to keep getting better.

Recoleta: Though upscale Recoleta isn't the nightlife spot Palermo and San Telmo are, there's still plenty here and just west in Barrio Norte to warrant exploration. You can find everything from swanky after-office spots to neighborhood watering holes—just avoid the seedier places near Recoleta Cemetery.

Palermo: Palermo Soho and Palermo Viejo—divided by the train tracks alongside Avenida Juan B. Justo—are the heart of porteño nightlife. Cool and diverse, the many bars that stay open all night are for socializing more than dancing, though some of the best clubs are here, too.

Las Cañitas: The cluster of bars and restaurants along Calle Báez, and a few more besides, has turned Las Cañitas from a nondescript residential neighborhood into a buzzing center of flirtation and food that keeps busy until dawn.

Costanera: Formerly the place to go for upscale dining, this stretch of riverfront found a new lease on life as home of the country's most famed and fabulous dance clubs. Most are within a mile of each other along the Río de la Plata, underneath the buzz of the nearby domestic airport.

What Are the Options?

Whatever your yen for the evening, start your planning with *What's Up Buenos Aires* (⊕ *www.whatsupbuenos aires.com*). This Web site, started in 2004 by two U.S. expats, is the go-to source for information about nightlife, theater, art exhibits, restaurants, and more.

Bars: Porteños may not be big drinkers, but they excel at everything else involved with spending time in bars—talking at length, seeing and being seen, and staying out all night. Expect a great variety of late-night bars and very little drunken behavior. And Argentina's wines may be big business these days, but its wine bars are still generally small, earnest spaces where wine is what matters.

Tango: The passion, drama, and nostalgia of tango is the most concise expression of the spirit of Buenos Aires—and a *milonga* (tango dance hall) should definitely be on every visitor's itinerary. Whether you eventually join in or not, spend some time at a floor-side table to appreciate the ritual. (⇨ *The Dance of Buenos Aires, below*)

Live Music: *Rock Nacional* (Argentine rock and roll) makes up the majority of live music; it's a unique sound, though not unlike metal. There's also the small but lively jazz scene, and—for those who need reminding they're in South America—folk *peñas* (meeting places), where guitars, pan pipes, and unpretentious singers conjure the spirit of the Andes.

Dancing the Night Away: An influx of foreigners is affecting the exclusivity of Buenos Aires' electronic music scene, but it's also supporting a more diverse range of club nights. There's plenty to please you here, especially if you like your house music progressive and your dress code smart.

Gay & Lesbian: Besides well-established cruising areas and a citywide gay-friendly attitude, Buenos Aires has a whole network of bars and clubs, meeting points, and milongas. There are many free gay guides, found in hotels and boutiques, to help you navigate the scene; GayBA (⊕ *www.gay-ba.com*) is available in bookshops and kiosks.

Safety

Buenos Aires is relatively trouble-free, but incidents do occur. At night, it's best to avoid La Boca, deserted areas of Montserrat and downtown, and parts of Abasto. Don't carry more money than you need; leave behind valuables that would be safer in your hotel. Take taxis: they're cheap, plentiful, and don't increase their fares at night.

Tips for a Good Night Out

Don't be afraid to stand in line outside. Lines are generally quick and painless, and if there isn't one, or those in line look average, the place might not be worth the wait.

Be prepared to buy a ticket or make a reservation. For concerts, shows, and club events, people often buy tickets in advance as many events do fill up or sell out.

Go late—really. Otherwise you'll miss on the atmosphere and find it a bit boring. If necessary, help smooth the adjustment with a *merienda* (a snack of coffee and croissants at around 6 PM) and a siesta.

Find out what's on and where. Scour flyers, Internet sites, ticket agencies, and magazine listings for up-to-date information. There's a lot more going on than you can find out from the billboards.

Look sharp. Porteños like to dress up, though they err on the conservative side and shy away from extravagant fashion statements. With the exception of one or two scruffy bars in San Telmo, you'll never feel overdressed.

Never imagine you've seen it all. Private parties and underground events are where it's at. Finding out about them isn't easy, but keep an ear out and tell people you're looking and you might luck out.

By Andy
Footner

Porteños *love* to party. Many don't think twice about dancing until 6 AM and heading to work at 8 AM. And alcohol doesn't play a vital role in whether people enjoy themselves or not; porteños could have fun at an insurance convention, provided the conversation and music were good and everyone looked marvelous. Indeed, for many, it's better to *look* good than to *feel* good.

Nightlife these days is starting earlier. Lately, in an effort to drum up business during the post-work/pre-dinner window, many downtown bars are promoting "after-office" drink specials; it's a happy hour that often lasts until 9 or 10 PM. This recent phenomenon aside, timing in Buenos Aires nightlife is an exercise in patience. Get there too early and the bar will be empty, and you'll be tired when the atmosphere finally builds. When families with kids in strollers don't turn up for dinner until nearly midnight, you know it will take a bit of work to be fashionably late.

Hours are very fluid here but there are some general guidelines: theater performances start around 9 or 9:30 PM, and the last movie begins after midnight. Bars get busy in the small hours, and clubs, which attract crowds in the 18–35 age range, don't begin to fill up until 3 or 4 AM. If in doubt, turn up later than you think is reasonable. That said, the subte closes around 11 PM, so going out means taking a taxi home or staying out until 5 AM when trains resume running.

First, our sections on theatrical performances and tango orient you to some of the more conventionally cultural options. Next, our listings take you on a chronological arch of a typical local's big night out—from after-office cocktails and live performances to late-night bars, dance clubs, and options for the morning after. Finally, a section on gay and lesbian options rounds out our listings, which really just scratch the surface of this city's constantly morphing, always intense nightlife.

PERFORMANCES

From living room get-togethers to stage spectaculars, shows are a big part of the city's cultural life. The problem is that there's no one central place to find out *every*thing that's going on. A great place to start is *What's Up Buenos Aires* (⇨ *What are the Options?, above*), but to get the full scope of events, keep an eye out for flyers and listings and ask around.

BROADWAY OF THE SOUTH

On Avenida Corrientes, performances of Shakespeare, Chekhov, and Pinter rub shoulders with revues starring dancing *vedettes* (scantily clad showgirls) wearing a few strategic sequins. Although Buenos Aires' answer to Broadway is nowhere near as glamorous as it once was, the crowds of porteños that fill the sidewalks each evening are testament to a thriving theater scene. If there aren't any shows that take your fancy, watch the theatergoers over an evening drink in one of the street's many cafés.

The **Teatro San Martín,** a three-stage complex, hosts a wide range of theater productions as well as contemporary dance performances, mime, and puppet shows. It's also the site of year-round classical music performances by top Argentine performers. Many concerts are free; tickets to others are available from the box office or from their Web site if you book 15 days in advance. ✉*Av. Corrientes 1530, Centro* ☎*11/4374–9680* ⊕*www.teatrosanmartin.com.ar* Ⓜ*B to Callao or Uruguay.*

All along Avenida Corrientes are exquisite art deco theaters like the **Gran Rex,** a favorite venue for rock, pop, and jazz musicians. Recent acts to have tested its great acoustics include Björk, Steve Vai, and Toto. Tickets are available through Ticketek's citywide network (⊕*www.ticketek.com.ar).* ✉*Corrientes 857, Centro* ☎*11/4322–8000* ☾*Box office daily 10–10* Ⓜ*B to Carlos Pellegrini.*

At the very end of Corrientes is **Luna Park,** a covered stadium that hosts boxing and other sporting events as well as rock concerts and ice-skating shows. Tickets normally need to be bought well in advance from the box office or from www.entradaplus.com.ar. ✉*Bouchard 465, Centro* ☎*11/5279–5279* ⊕*www.lunapark.com.ar* ☾*Box office Mon. –Sat. 10–10* Ⓜ*B to L. N. Alem.*

Many of these theaters have also been playing host to performances normally held in the opulent **Teatro Colón** (Colón Theater), which has been undergoing a massive renovation since November 2006. Though the theater was originally slotted to reopen in time for its centenary celebration in May 2008, new estimates have the place staying dark until the 2010 performance season.

TANGO

MILONGAS

Café Homero. "Tango not-for-export" could be the slogan of this well-established venue, where divas like Adriana Varela and Susana Rinaldi perform for an almost entirely local audience. Café Homero has all the hallmarks of a veteran tanguería: aging waiters, a checkered floor, and small, circular tables for holding your glass of wine and *picada* (small plate of finger food). ⊠ *Cabrera 4946, Palermo Viejo* ☏ *11/4775–6763* ⊕ *www.cafehomero.cancionero.net.*

La Catedral. Behind its unmarked doors is a hip club where the tango is somehow very rock. Casual milongas take place on Tuesday, Friday, and Saturday, and it's a cool night out even if you're not planning to dance. ⊠ *Sarmiento 4006, doorbell 5, Almagro* ☏ *11/15–5325–1630.*

FodorśChoice ★ **La Ideal.** Soaring columns and tarnished mirrors are part of La Ideal's crumbling old-world glamour. The classic tearoom hosts milongas organized by different groups in its first-floor dance hall every day of the week. Many include live orchestras. ⊠ *Suipacha 384, Plaza de Mayo* ☏ *11/4601–8234* ⊕ *www.confiteriaideal.com.*

La Marshall. A refreshing exception to the sometimes suffocatingly macho world of tango, this is *the* gay milonga, and it draws a cool set of guys and girls, both gay and straight, looking to break with the "he leads, she follows" doctrine. ⊠ *Maipú 444, Centro* ☏ *11/5406–9784* ⊕ *www.lamarshall.com.ar.*

Milonga Abierta en la Glorieta Barrancas de Belgrano. For tango alfresco, drop by the bandstand of this Belgrano park every Sunday evening year-round. Expect lots of old-timers dancing low-key steps. There are classes and a younger crowd on Monday and Wednesday. The milonga is canceled only during heavy rain; call ahead if you're unsure. ⊠ *11 de Septiembre at Echeverría, Belgrano* ☏ *11/4635–6894.*

La Nacional. The friendly Wednesday-night milonga here is a favorite with locals. The tables crammed around the dance floor fill up so fast that reserving is a good idea. ⊠ *Alsina 1465, Congreso* ☏ *11/4307–8796* ⊕ *www.la-nacional.com.ar.*

Niño Bien. This belle epoque–style milonga's vast wooden dance floor is the place to go late on Thursday night. The mix of older couples and younger dancers means you see very different styles in one place; all respect traditional *cabeceo* (nonverbal invitation to dance) and partnership rules. ⊠ *Humberto I 1462, Constitución* ☏ *11/4147–8687.*

FodorśChoice ★ **Salón Canning.** Several milongas call this large dance hall home. The coolest is Parakultural, which takes place Monday, Wednesday, and Friday. Originally an alternative, "underground" milonga, it now attracts large numbers of locals (including longtime expats). ⊠ *Av. Scalabrini Ortíz 1331, Palermo* ☏ *11/4832–6753* ⊕ *www.parakultural.com.ar.*

12 de Octubre *(El Bar de Roberto).* Cobweb- and dust-covered bottles line the walls of this tiny venue, with maybe the most authentic tango performances in town. Owner Roberto presides from behind the heavy wooden bar, dispatching *ginebra* (a local gin) to the old-timers and icy beer and cheap wine to the student crowd. When the singing gets going at 2 or 3 AM, it's usually so packed there's no room to breathe, but the guitar-and-voice duos manage gritty, emotional versions of tango classics all the same. ✉ *Bulnes 331, Almagro* ☎ *11/6327–4594* ⊘ *Thurs.–Sat. after midnight.*

La Viruta. Milongas Wednesday through Sunday make this the place for a very long weekend. The vibe on the floor is friendly and relaxed, and DJs mix tango with rock, salsa, and cumbia. ✉ *Armenia 1366, Palermo* ☎ *11/4774–6357* ⊕ *www. lavirutatango.com.*

THE ARTS AFTER DARK

Most galleries have opening nights worth casually sauntering into, and **MALBA** (✉ *Figueroa Alcorta 3415, Palermo* ☎ *11/ 4808–6500* ⊕ *www.malba.org. ar*) tends to have the biggest and best. Pick up a program for details on their free literary events and talks. **Ciudad Cultural Konex** (✉ *Sarmiento 3131, Almagro* ☎ *11/4864–3200* ⊕ *www.ciudad culturalkonex.org*)offers a mixed bag of rock and roll, film screenings, wild parties, and Pecha Kucha (sort of like a poetry slam but with performance art).

DINNER SHOWS

Bar Sur. Once a bohemian haunt, this bar went international after being a major location for Wong Kar-Wai's cult indie film, *Happy Together.* The move to the mainstream has led to glitzier dancing, worse food, and increasingly indifferent service. Still, the worn checkered floor and old-world bar make for a charming backdrop. ✉ *Estados Unidos 299, San Telmo* ☎ *11/4362–6086* ⊕ *www.bar-sur.com.ar.*

La Esquina de Homero Manzi. La Esquina was once a traditional café favored by the barrio's old men, but it's had the Disney-tango treatment and is now a kind of 1940s concept bar—though its checkered floor and original bar remain. Performances are showy but reasonably priced. ✉ *San Juan 3601, Boedo* ☎ *11/4957–8488* ⊕ *www.esquina homeromanzi.com.ar.*

Madero Tango. Local businesspeople looking to impress international clients invariably choose this showy concept restaurant. A night here may break the bank, but you get varied, highly professional performances, and food by local gastronome Martiniano Molina. Prices vary depending on how close you are to the stage. ✉ *Alicia Moreau de Justo at Brasil, Puerto Madero* ☎ *11/5239–3009* ⊕ *www.maderotango.com.*

Maison Dandi Royal. The unashamedly theatrical show at this tango concept hotel dances you through the history of tango. It's a fascinating look at how the dance evolved, and the hotel's art nouveau architecture is pretty fantastic, too. ✉ *Piedras 922, San Telmo* ☎ *11/4361–3537* ⊕ *www.maisondandiroyal.com.*

El Querandí. The polished shows at this classic café trace the history of the tango. The dancing and costumes are great, although the stagy interludes might make you wince. ✉ *Perú 302, at Moreno, San Telmo* ☎ *11/4342–1760* ⊕ *www.querandi.com.ar.*

Fodor'sChoice **Rojo Tango.** Five-star food, choreography, and glamour: you wouldn't ★ expect anything less from the Faena Hotel + Universe. Crimson velvet lines everything from the walls to the menu at the Cabaret, and tables often hold celebs both local and global. As well as classic tangos, the implausibly good-looking troupe does jazz-tango, semi-naked numbers, and even the tango version of Roxanne from *Moulin Rouge*. It's worth breaking the piggy bank for. ✉*Martha Salotti 445, Puerto Madero* ☎*11/5787–1536* ⊕*www.rojotango.com.*

Señor Tango. It doesn't get much glitzier—or much tackier. Performed daily, the unashamedly tourist-oriented shows are so eager to cash in on stereotypes that they even include a number from *Evita* (shock horror). Still, you can't fault the fishnetted dancers on their footwork. ✉*Vieytes 1655, Barracas* ☎*11/4303–0231* ⊕*www.senortango.com.ar.*

★ **El Viejo Almacén.** This place was founded by legendary tango singer Edmundo Rivero, but he wouldn't recognize the slick outfit his rootsy bar has become. Inside the colonial building lurks a tireless troupe of dancers and musicians who perform showy tango and folk numbers. ✉*Balcarce 786, at Independencia, San Telmo* ☎*11/4307–6689* ⊕*www.viejo-almacen.com.ar.*

MUSICIANS

Centro Cultural Torcuato Tasso. Here, classic trios and quartets share the stage with young musicians performing hip sets. There are also milongas on weekends. ✉*Defensa 1575, San Telmo* ☎*11/4307–6506.*

Gran Café Tortoni. Excellent local musicians put on low-key performances of tango classics in the downstairs salon. These daily shows are some of the best for listening to tango music. There's jazz sometimes on weekends, too. ✉*Av. de Mayo 829, Plaza de Mayo* ☎*11/4342–4328* ⊕*www.grancafetortoni.com.ar.*

ND Ateneo. This small, recycled theater has become a showcase for live music performances. Tango features heavily on the agenda. ✉*Paraguay 918, Centro* ☎*11/4328–2888* ⊕*www.ndateneo.com.ar.*

La Trastienda. Catch new tango groups like the Orquesta Típica Fernández Fierro showcasing their very rock take on tango. ✉*Balcarce 460, San Telmo* ☎*11/4342–7650* ⊕*www.latrastienda.com.*

COCKTAIL TIME

The late timing of porteño nightlife means even the busiest bars spend a good part of each evening empty. This has led to the rise of happy hours with half-price drink offers stretching for often three or four hours. This "after-office" trend is particularly noticeable in Centro. Most of the listings that follow offer some form of this; it's a good trend to take advantage of as you acclimatize to a more Argentine schedule.

CENTRO

★ **Le Bar.** Le Bar is a stylish addition to the Centro drinking scene. Up the stairs from the cocktail lounge is a clever sunken seating arrangement; farther still is a smokers' terrace. Office workers get the evening started; DJs start a bit later and play till 2 AM. ✉*Tucuman 422* ☎*11/5219–8580.*

Empire Thai. It's an "American bar" in a downtown Thai food restaurant that treats its cosmopolitan after-work crowd to an extended

Continued on page 149

The Dance of Buenos Aires

by Victoria Patience

"THE TANGO IS MACHO, THE TANGO IS STRONG. IT SMELLS OF WINE AND TASTES LIKE DEATH."

So goes the famous tango "Why I Sing Like This," whose mix of nostalgia, violence, and sensuality sum up what is truly the dance of Buenos Aires. From its beginnings, tango and its two-four beat marked and reflected the character of Buenos Aires. You may hear strains of tango on the radio while sipping coffee in a café, see high-kicking sequined dancers in a glitzy dinner show, or listen to musicians in a darkened cabaret. But one of the most memorable ways to experience the best of this broody, melancholic, impassioned art form is through dancing it yourself.

DANCING THE TANGO

Many milongas now kick off with group dance classes which usually last an hour or two and cost 10–15 pesos; some lessons are free, though chaotic. These classes are great for getting over nerves and getting you in the mood. However, most *milongueros* (people who dance at *milongas*, or tango dance halls) take tango very seriously and don't look kindly on left-footed beginners crowding the floor. We recommend you take a few private classes first—they can make a huge difference to your technique.

English-speaking private teachers abound in Buenos Aires; classes generally last 1½ hours and prices can range from $10 to $60 a class. Complete beginners should plan on at least three or four classes before hitting a milonga. Many private instructors organize milonga outings with groups of their students (usually for a separate fee). Others even offer a so-called "taxi dance service": you pay for them to dance with you all night. See the end of this feature for a run-down of some of the best options for lessons and milongas.

DANCE STYLES
Tango milonguero, the style danced at milongas and taught in most classes in Buenos Aires, is quite different from the so-called salon or ballroom tango danced in Hollywood movies and in competitions outside Argentina. Ballroom tango is all fixed steps and staccato movements, and dancers' backs arch away from each other in a stiff embrace. Tango milonguero is a highly improvised style built around a variety of typical movements, not fixed steps. Dancers embrace closely, their chests touching. There are other, historical tango styles, but it's less

common to see them on milonga floors. (Confusingly, "milonga" refers both to traditional tango dancehalls and to a style of music and dance that predates the tango; though similar to tango, it has a more syncopated beat and faster, simpler steps.)

AT THE MILONGA
Dancers of all ages sit at tables that edge the floor, and men invite women to dance through *cabeceo* (subtle eye contact and head-nodding), a hard art to master. Note that women sitting with male partners won't be asked to the floor by other men.

Dances come in sets of three, four, or five, broken by a *cortina* (obvious divider of non-tango music), and it's common to stay with the same partner for a set. Being discarded in the middle is a sign that your dancing's not up to scratch, but staying for more than two sets with the same partner could be interpreted as a come on.

To fit in seamlessly, move around the floor counterclockwise without zigzagging, sticking to the inside layers of dancers if you're a beginner. Respect other dancers' space by avoiding collisions and keeping your movements small on crowded floors. Don't spend a long time doing showy moves on the spot: it holds up traffic. Finally, take time to sit some out, catch your breath, and watch the experts.

TANGO TALK

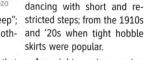

abrazo: the embrace or stance dancers use; in tango, this varies from hip-touching and loose shoulders to close chests and more fluid hips, depending on style.

abrazo

barrida

barrida: literally, "a sweep"; one partner sweeps the other's foot into a position.

caminada: a walking step that is the basis of the tango.

canyengue: style of tango dancing with short and restricted steps; from the 1910s and '20s when tight hobble skirts were popular.

ocho: eight; a criss-crossing walk.

parada: literally a "stop"; the lead dancer stops the other's foot with his own.

petitero: measured style of tango developed after the 1955 military coup, when large tango gatherings were banned and the dance relegated to small cafés.

caminada

MILONGA STYLE

parada

Wearing a fedora hat or fishnet stockings is as good as a neon sign reading "beginner." Forget what on-stage tango dancers wear and follow a few basic rules.

Go for comfortable clothes that allow you to move freely; a sure bet are breathable, natural fabrics with a bit of stretch. Be sure it's something that makes you feel sexy. If in doubt, wear black. Avoid showy outfits: it's your footwork that should stand out. It's also smart to steer clear of big buckles, studs, stones, or anything that might catch on your partner. Try not to wear skirts that are too long or too tight. Also a bad idea are jeans or gymwear.

A good example of what to wear for men would be black dress pants and a black shirt; for women, two of many options are a simple halter-neck dress with a loose, calf-length skirt or palazzo pants with a fitted top.

As for your feet: look for dance shoes with flexible leather or suede soles that allow you to glide and pivot. The fit should be snug but comfortable. Note that rubber-soled street shoes or sneakers mark the dance floor and are often forbidden. High-heels are a must for women; the most popular style is an open-toed sandal with an ankle-strap (which stops them coming off). Black lace-ups are the favorite among men, so leave your two-tone spats at home.

TANGO THROUGH TIME

The tango and modern Buenos Aires were born in the same place: the *conventillos* (tenement houses) of the port neighborhood of La Boca in the late 19th century, where River Plate culture collided with that of European immigrants. The dance eventually swept from the immigrant-quarter brothels and cabarets to the rest of the city; rich playboys took the tango to Paris on their grand tours, and by the 1920s the dance had become respectable enough to fill the salons

Carlos Gardel

and drawing rooms of the upper class in Argentina and abroad. In the 1930s, with the advent of singers like Carlos Gardel, tango music became popular in its own right. Accordingly, musical accompaniment started to come from larger bands known as *orquestas típicas*.

By the '40s and '50s, *porteños* (people from Buenos Aires) celebrated tango as the national music of the people, and tango artists lent Evita and Perón their support. The military coup that ousted Perón in 1955 forbade large tango dances, which it saw as potential political gatherings, and (bizarrely) encouraged rock 'n' roll instead. Young people listened, and tango fell out of popular favor.

The '90s saw a huge revival in both traditional *milongas* (dance halls) and a more improvised dance style. Musical offerings now include modern takes on classic tangos and electrotango or *tangofusión*. Even local rock stars are starting to include a tango or two in their repertory. And since 1998, thousands of people from around the world have attended the annual fort-night-long Festival de Tango in Buenos Aires (⊕www.festivaldetango.gov.ar), held late winter or spring.

Whether you decide to take in a show or take up dancing yourself, sit down for a classic concert or groove at an electrotango night, there are more ways to experience tango in Buenos Aires than anywhere else on earth.

4

THE DANCE OF BUENOS AIRES

DID YOU KNOW?

■ Tango so horrified Kaiser Wilhelm and Pope Pius X that they banned the dance.

■ In 1915, before he was famous, Carlos Gardel was injured in a bar room brawl with Ernesto Guevara Lynch, Che's father.

■ One of Gardel's most famous numbers, "Por Una Cabeza," is the tango featured in *Schindler's List*, *Scent of a Woman*, and *True Lies*.

■ The coup of 1930 prompted composers like Enrique Santos Discépolo to write protest tangos.

■ Finnish tango has been a distinct musical genre since at least mid-century and is still one of the most popular in Finland; there's even an annual *Tangomarkkinat* (tango festival) in Seinäjoki, complete with the crowning of a Tango King and Queen.

NEXT STEPS

TOURS & HOTELS

If you're serious about the dance of Buenos Aires, get in touch with the Web-based company **Argentina Tango** (⊕www.argentinatango.com). Run by a British devotee, it offers highly organized, tailor-made tango tours.

American ex-pat and professional dancer behind **Tanguera Tours** (⊕www.tangueratours.com) knows that some women find the world of tango intimidating. Her small, women-only tours include classes, shows, shoe-shopping, and loads of milonga action. And for the ultimate in eating, sleeping, and breathing tango, stay at a tango hotel like **Mansion Dandi Royal** (⇨see Where to Stay).

SHOPS WITH TANGO GEAR

Head to shoe shop **Comme Il Faut,** for colorful, handcrafted high heels so gorgeous they're worth taking up tango for. If you'd like high quality and classic designs, check out **Flabella.** At **Tango Brujo,** you'll find a variety of well-made footwear, clothing, how-to DVDs, and other tango merchandise. Your best bet for milonga-worthy duds is regular casual clothing stores. (For more information, ⇨see Shoes *and* Clothing *in* Shopping.)

SCHOOLS & INSTRUCTORS

Some schools we like are **La Escuela de Tango** (✉ San José 364, Constitución ☎ 11/4383–0466, infodetango@yahoo.com), **La Academia de Tango Milonguero** (✉ Riobamba 416, Centro, 11/4582–7050 ⊕ ww.susanamiller.com.ar), and **Estudio DNI Tango** (✉ Av. Corrientes 2140, Centro ☎ 11/4952–1688 ⊕ www.estudiodnitango.com.ar). Private instructors **Ana Schapira** (☎ 11/4962–7922 ⊕ www.anaschapira.com), **Claudia Bozzo** of La Escuela de Tango, and **Susana Miller** (⊕ www. susanamiller.tangoafficionado.com) of La Academia de Tango Milonguero are worth their salt.

MILONGAS

For a novice-friendly floor, try **La Ideal. La Nacional** and **Niño Bien** are popular with locals. The hippest tangueros flock to **La Catedral** and **Parakultural at Salón Canning.** For breaking the "he leads, she follows" rule, head to **La Marshall.** (For more information, ⇨see Milongas *in* After Dark.)

For the latest list of milongas, and instructors, look for the English-language publication **El Tangauta** and multilingual *Guía Trimestral—B.A. Tango* at newsstands; online, check out ⊕ www.todotango.com.ar or ⊕ www.tangodata.gov.ar. You can also contact the **Academia Nacional de Tango** (⊕ www.anacdeltango.org.ar).

happy hour till 9 PM weekdays and 11 PM weekends. The busiest nights are Thursday and Friday. ✉*Tres Sargentos 427* ☎*11/4312-5706* ⊕*www.empirethai.net* Ⓜ*A to Piedras.*

The Kilkenny. A popular pub that spawned a whole street of imitators, the Kilkenny serves surprisingly good Irish food and has Guinness on draft. Celtic or rock bands play every night, entertaining the after-work crowd from nearby government and commercial buildings who come for the 8 PM to 11 PM happy hour. ✉*Marcelo T. De Alvear 399* ☎*11/4312–7291* Ⓜ*C to San Martín.*

Palacio Alsina. On Saturday nights it fills to its capacity of almost 2,000 clubbers when it hosts The Big One, a giant dance party with big-name international DJs. It's strictly progressive house music without the pretensions of the Costenera clubs. It also has the city's biggest after-work party—Opera Town—every Wednesday, and a huge gay party on Friday. ✉*Alsina 940* ☎*11/4331–3231* Ⓜ*A to Piedras.*

RECOLETA

Gran Bar Danzon. If Carrie, Samantha, Charlotte, and Miranda lived in Buenos Aires, they'd probably frequent this first-floor hot spot where local business sharks and chic internationals sip wine and eat sushi by candlelight. It's extremely popular for happy hour, but people stick around for dinner and the occasional live jazz shows, too. The wine list and the appetizers are superb, as is the flirting. ✉*Libertad 1161* ☎*11/4811–1108* Ⓜ*C to Retiro.*

PALERMO

Bar 6. Somewhat of a Palermo Soho institution, Bar 6 suffers from the indifferent, sometimes rude waitstaff that such a reputation demands. If you can get past that, it's a convenient Palermo meeting point (it opens at 8 AM), a stylish bar, and a decent restaurant. A DJ often plays good music in the evenings. ✉*Armenia 1676* ☎*11/4833–6807* .

Cava Jufre. There aren't any wild nights at this wine bar, but gather around for plenty of earnest and good-natured appreciation of the output of lesser-known Argentinean bodegas. The decoration is simple and woody, and there's an impressive cellar downstairs. This is a good place to discover some new varietals—and do call ahead to see if there are any wine-tasting events planned. it's closed Sunday. ✉*Jufre 201, Palermo* ☎*11/4775–7501* ⊕*www.lacavajufre.com.ar* .

Club Museo. A privileged position next to the MALBA gallery and in one of the most expensive parts of town means this restaurant and bar attracts a well-heeled clientele. Regular sessions of live jazz (Saturday) and bossa nova (Thursday) and a first-rate sushi bar add to the atmosphere. ✉*Av. Figueroa Alcorta 3399, Palermo* ☎*11/4802–9626* ⊕*www.museorenault.com.ar* .

BEST HOTEL BARS

The recent boutique hotel boom has freshened up the city's rather grand hotel bar scene—but many remain exclusively for guests. Here's a selection of hotels with great bars that are open to everyone. (*For full hotel listings, see Chapter 6, Where to Stay.*)

Alvear Palace Hotel. At this grand hotel in Recoleta, Lobby Bar has old world charm to spare; it's the perfect vantage point for watching the comings and goings of high society.

Faena Hotel + Universe. These could easily be the most opulent hotel bar options; Philippe Starck–designed choices include poolside La Piscina, the racy tango show at El Cabaret, the decadent charm of the Library Lounge, or the Cellar—down a black granite staircase and purportedly with the largest wine selection in Argentina.

Home Hotel. Judged Best New Hotel of 2007 by Wallpaper magazine, this Palermo haunt's bar is best on Friday in summer when there's dance music in the garden until midnight.

Hotel Madero. Sofitel's "new generation" property doesn't want for drinking options; its Red Lounge, Blue Sky Bar, and superchic White Bar (in the lobby) are all great for a leisurely cocktail of any color.

Marriott. In Centro, the Mariott's Plaza Bar is old-school Argentina at its finest; it fills in the early evenings with a refined mix of locals and hotel guests.

Sofitel. The modern, classy Café Arroyo here transforms in the evenings into a venue for live jazz, soul, bossa nova, or gentle DJ music.

LAS CAÑITAS

Arguibel. You can sip Syrah and soak up the art—and the attitude—at this wine bar–cum–art gallery–slash–restaurant. Arguibel is porteño pretentiousness to the max. The service and food are fair, but the building is impressive: a three-story converted warehouse with an industrial, Chelsea-loft feel. ✉ *Arguibel 2826* ☎ *11/4899–0070.*

LIVE MUSIC

ROCK

After years of isolation, Buenos Aires is becoming part of a small South American tour circuit, and big international bands are visiting more frequently and playing to packed audiences. The biggest acts tend to play large festivals or stadium shows in **Club Ciudad de Buenos Aires** (Libertador 7501) or **Estadio River Plate** (Figueroa Alcorta 7597) and other big shows happen in the Gran Rex and Luna Park *(⇨ Performances, above)* or nightclubs such as Niceto and the Roxy *(⇨ Dance Clubs, below)*. Here's a selection of smaller venues.

CENTRO

Liberarte. Descend the steps to find one of the few spaces in Centro for local bands to perform showcase concerts; the standard is high. On weekends there's stand-up comedy in Spanish, but for local music at the source, pass by to check the program and pick a name that sounds good. ⊠*Av. Corrientes 1555* ☎*11/4375–2341* ⊕*www. liberarteteatro.com.ar.*

ND/Ateneo. This spacious theater and cultural space is given over mainly to mid-level local bands, showmen, and comedians. Get tickets from the box office each afternoon or from Ticketek. ⊠*Paraguay 918* ☎*11/4328–2888* ⊕*www.ndateneo.com.ar.*

SAN TELMO

Mitos Argentinos. A little rock bar with heroic ambitions, since the mid-1990s Mitos Argentinos has been celebrating rock nacional by providing space for bands to play covers and their own additions to the genre. Entry is cheap, inside it's cheerful, and if the band's no good, there's always another due on in a few songs' time. ⊠*Humberto 1489* ☎*11/4362–7601* Ⓜ*C to San Juan.*

La Trastienda. A San Telmo institution, La Trastienda brings in respected artists from all over to play its intimate stage. Some shows are seated affairs; others pack 1,000-plus into the small space to listen and dance to jazz, blues, tango, salsa, reggae, or rock. World-renowned musicians like Maceo Parker, Café Tacuba, Jorge Drexler, and Kevin Johansen have played here, but the club takes pains to promote local artists as well. ⊠*Balcarce 460* ☎*11/4342–7650* Ⓜ*A to Bolivar.*

JAZZ

CENTRO

Clásica y Moderna. Not just a jazz club but a restaurant and bookshop besides, an older, artsy crowd gathers here for dinner, drinks, philosophy, and live jazz. The program makes good use of their grand piano; singers take on bossa nova, tango, and bolero. ⊠*Callao 892* ☎*11/4812–8707* ⊕*www.clasicaymoderna.com* Ⓜ*D to Callao.*

★ **Notorious.** It's a jazz bar, restaurant, and record shop rolled into one. Some of the area's best jazz musicians, like Ricardo Cavalli and Adrian Iaies, play here often. You can also listen to the club's extensive music collection on the CD players at each table. ⊠*Av. Callao 966* ☎*11/4815–8473* ⊕*www.notorious.com.ar* Ⓜ*D to Callao.*

PALERMO

★ **Thelonious Bar.** The best porteño jazz bands (and occasional foreign imports) play at this intimate, upscale spot. Arrive early for a good seat as it's a long narrow bar and not all the tables have good views; on weekends there are usually two shows per night. ⊠*Salguero 1884* ☎*11/4829–1562.*

★ **Virasoro Bar.** A smallish space for local jazz musicians and appreciative audiences. The names on the program won't be familiar to anyone outside the local jazz circuit, but don't let that put you off—they draw from a deep well of talent and cover a lot of ground, from improv to standards to experimental. ✉*Guatemala 4328* ☎*11/4831–8918* ⊕*www.virasorobar.com.ar* Ⓜ*D to Scalabrini Ortiz.*

FOLK MUSIC

Argentine folk comes from the northwest of the country; is heavy on vocal harmonies, drums, and wind instruments; and is celebrated in *peñas folkloricas* (informal music halls specifically for folk music) set up by communities from the northwest. Most are far from the center and difficult to find, but Palermo now has a few of its own.

PALERMO

Los Cardones. Named after the tall cactus plants that typify the northwest, Los Cardones is where to go for a beer around a big table with strangers you'll get to know by the end of the night. Spontaneous dancing at this *peña folklorica* isn't unheard of; to prepare, ask ahead about their folk dancing classes. ✉*Jorge Luis Borges 2180, Palermo Soho* ☎*11/4777–1112* ⊕*www.cardones.com.ar.*

La Paila. A little piece of Catamarca transplanted to the middle of Palermo, this place has live folk music most nights from around 10:30. To get in the mood, have some of La Paila's great corn, llama, or potato-and-goat's cheese dishes, plus something from the long list of northwest wines. ✉*Costa Rica 4848, Palermo Soho* ☎*11/4833–3599* ⊕*www.lapaila-restaurante.com.ar.*

★ **La Peña del Colorado.** There's nothing pretentious about this place: laid-back groups gather to enjoy traditional Argentine folk music and hand-held foods like empanadas and tamales. The exposed-brick walls are adorned with rustic memorabilia, including guitars that you're welcome to play if so inspired. ✉*Guemes 3657* ☎*11/4822–1038* ⊕*www.delcolorado.com.ar.*

LATE-NIGHT BARS

These bars—while late-night by all rational standards—aren't to be confused with the *late* late-night bars known as "afters" *(*⇨ *When the Sun Comes Up, below).* Spending the wee hours at one (or several) of these places is sort of like the evening's main course, so be sure to save some energy for it.

CENTRO

La Cigale. Sip cocktails at a large turquoise bar while smooth sounds and hipsters young and old spin around you. Tuesday is French Soirée Night, and things get lively with techno and trance music straight from Paris. Other days DJs play reggae, rock, or electronica. ✉*25 de Mayo 722* ☎*11/4312–8275* Ⓜ*C to San Martín.*

★ **Milión.** At this beautiful mansion you can enjoy a cold Cosmopolitan or a nice Malbec at the upstairs bar while sophisticates chat around you. Be sure to explore all the hidden corners, including the back garden salon, which is lighted with candles and soft, colorful lights. ✉*Paraná 1048* ☎*11/4815–9925* Ⓜ*D to Callao.*

FOR THE SPORTS NUTS

Porteños love sports—and sports, for them, means fútbol (soccer). Although Argentine teams also excel at basketball, hockey, rugby, and polo, it's fútbol that evokes the most passion, with lots of people attending even the smallest scrimmages; most games play on wall-mounted TVs in regular cafés and restaurants. You can imagine, then, there are some decent options for catching big games, whatever the sport.

El Alamo Bar *(Shoeless Joe's).* More famous for bikini competitions and free beer promotions (ladies drink free until midnight every day) than for its solid program of sports, El Alamo's main level is nonetheless especially filled with expats when the Superbowl, World Series, or March Madness rolls around; upstairs has louder music and more porteños. ⊠ *Uruguay 1175* ☏ *11/4813-7324* ⊕ *www.elalamobar.com* 🎫 *Cover charge for big events* ⏲ *24 hrs.*

Locos x El Fútbol. Just try to count the number of televisions here and you'll realize the extent of their soccer madness—the x stands for *por,* which makes this place "crazy for soccer." Important games require a reservation but otherwise just turn up for big screens and big servings of burgers, fries, and beer. ⊠ *Vicente Lopez 2098* ☏ *11/4807-3777* ⊕ *www.locosxelfutbol.com* 🎫 *Minimum consumption for big matches* ⏲ *Sun.–Thurs. 9–2, Fri. and Sat. 9–4 or 5.*

Spell Café. A watering hole with a river view, Spell offers North American atmosphere with beer, burgers, and big screens. It also does stand-up nights, after-office and pre-dancing promotions, and sushi specials, and is a great spot to rest while wandering the neighborhood. ⊠ *Alicia Moreau de Justo 740, Puerto Madero* ☏ *11/4334-0512* ⊕ *www.spell-cafe.com.ar* 🎫 *Free* ⏲ *Mon.–Thurs. 8 AM–6 AM.*

SAN TELMO

Bar Britanico. This traditional corner bar opposite Parque Lezama spent most of 2006 in the news for the protests of its regulars in face of imminent closure. A few months later it was open again and continues to trade off its name and history. Day and night it's full of characters and passionate discussions. ⊠ *Brasil 399* ☏ *11/4361–2107.*

Bar Seddón. Relocated from Centro to one of the busiest corners in San Telmo where Chile Street is lined with pavement bars and cafés, Bar Seddón is a low-lighted bar with ancient wooden tables and live music on weekends. ⊠ *Defensa 695* ☏ *11/4342–3700.*

Gibraltar. A British boozer in the middle of San Telmo, Gibraltar has transformed from an expat refuge—lured by cheap beer in pint glasses—to a hip destination for locals. The result is one of the most happening places in the neighborhood; there's a pool table, too. ⊠ *Peru 895* ☏ *11/4362–5310.*

★ **La Puerta Roja.** Ring the bell at "The Red Door" and climb the stairs to a very cool-feeling bar free of the nostalgic trappings of much of the rest of San Telmo. The bar area is packed and serves cheap drinks, pool tables are in the back, and there's a sociable mix of locals and expats to get chatting with. ⊠*Chacabuco 733* ☏*11/4362–5649.*

Asia de Cuba. Once *the* spot to be seen sipping champagne and eating sushi, Asia de Cuba still draws local celebrities, though it's lost some of its white-hot luster. The candlelight and red-and-black Asian decor set the mood for an exotic evening—by local standards. Sometimes there's live music. ⊠*Pierina Dealesi 750* ☏*11/4894–1329.*

La Biela. Across from Recoleta Cemetery and on the corner of the most expensive shopping district in town, La Biela's been a neighborhood hub for the last half century. On sunny days when its outdoor seating is filled to bursting, there's almost always still a table to be found indoors; at night it stands out as a bastion of class among the young upstart bars and restaurants surrounding it. ⊠*Av. Quintana 600* ☏*11/4804–0432* ⊕*www.labiela.com.*

Los Porteños. A traditional Buenos Aires bar with plenty of *fileteado* (colorful, swirly graphic embellishments) and wooden tables, Los Porteños serves coffee and snacks all day and stays open late into the night; it doesn't shut at all on Saturday. It's one block from Recoleta Cemetery and a good option when the dives on Vicente Lopez get to be too much. ⊠*Av. Las Heras 2101* ☏*11/4809–3548.*

★ **Antares.** New Antares brews seven of its own ales—all of which you can taste-test in shot-size glasses—and attracts a cosmopolitan group of drinkers who keep the spacious bar open from after-office until the small hours. The service is friendly and efficient; the music's feel-good. ⊠*Armenia 1447, Palermo Soho* ☏*11/4833–9611* ⊕*www.cervezaantares.com.*

Bangalore. A pub and curry house in Buenos Aires? Well located, the Bangalore has it all—right down to a blazing log fire in winter. There's limited seating both at the bar and in the tiny restaurant upstairs, but somehow there's hardly ever a wait. Service is friendly and there's a wide range of draught beers. ⊠*Humboldt 1416, Palermo Hollywood* ☏*11/4779–2621.*

Carnal. Across from the Niceto club, Carnal and its open terrace have become quite the destination and remain busy all night long with crowds of young party people. The name fits, too; as the reggaeton blasts and the cocktails flow, many customers aren't shy about getting to know each other very well. ⊠*Niceto Vega 5511, Palermo Hollywood* ☏*11/4772–7582.*

★ **Congo.** A fashionable post-dinner, pre-club crowd—in faded fitted jeans, hipster sneakers, and leather jackets—frequents this hangout. The lines outside might seem a bit much, but it's all worthwhile once you get in. The back garden can get lively enough on warm nights to cause many would-be club goers to stick around for another gin and tonic. ⊠*Honduras 5329, Palermo Soho* ☏*11/4833–5857.*

878. Secret bars have been a big trend in porteño nightlife, a trend 878 was a part of until it went legit in 2007. It's still marked only by the group of smokers on the sidewalk outside, but it's become a great cocktail bar packed to the gills with determinedly up-to-date clientele. ✉*Thames 878, Palermo Viejo* ☎*11/4773–1098.*

Mundo Bizarro. They've been building their late-night crowd and perfecting their cocktails here since 1997, which is a long time in Palermo. Red lights, kitsch artwork, and rock and roll provide the backdrop; the rest gets improvised afresh every evening. ✉*Serrano 1222, Palermo Soho* ☎*11/4773–1967* ⊕*www.mundobizarrobar.com.*

Único. There's nothing really special about this corner bar-restaurant *except* for its location at the epicenter of Palermo Hollywood, close to TV studios and an array of great restaurants. A funky mix of rock, rap, and electronic music pumps up the hard-core clubbers who stop to whet their whistles on large Heineken drafts before a night of debauchery. ✉*Honduras 5604, Palermo Hollywood* ☎*11/4775–6693.*

LAS CAÑITAS

Beat House. Upstairs, it's the perfect spot to chill out in a bean bag and watch superchic porteños mingle at the eateries below. Cool trance and techno music fills the air; downstairs there's a small music boutique. ✉*Báez 211* ☎*11/4775–5616.*

Soul Café. One of the neighborhood's first nightspots has some of the city's sexiest female bartenders as well as its tastiest caipirinhas. A sleek red room lined with tables on one side leads to a large back room, where rock and hip-hop tunes fire up the crowd for a long night of partying. ✉*Báez 246* ☎*11/4778–3115.*

DANCE CLUBS

CENTRO

Fodor'sChoice ★ **Bahrein.** Sheik—er, chic and super-stylish, this party palace is in a 100-year-old former bank. Eat upstairs at Crizia, or head straight to the main floor's Funky Room, where beautiful, tightly clothed youth groove to pop, rock, and funk. The downstairs Excess Room has electronic beats and dizzying wall visuals. For 500 pesos, get locked in the vault and guzzle champagne all night with strangers—an entirely new kind of VIP experience. ✉*Lavalle 345* ☎*11/4315–2403* Ⓜ*B to Alem.*

Cocoliche. Cocoliche enjoys cultlike status in both the straight and gay communities. Upstairs is a diverse art gallery big on young locals; downstairs, house music drives on one of the city's darkest dance floors. ✉*Rivadavia 878* ☎*11/4331–6413* Ⓜ*A to Piedras.*

SAN TELMO

Rey Castro. Just because this Cuban restaurant-bar gets a little wild on weekends doesn't mean things get out of hand: the bouncers look like NFL players. It's a popular spot for birthday parties and great mojitos. After the nightly live dance show, DJs crank up the Cuban rhythms; you're likely to learn some sexy new moves. ✉*Perú 342* ☎*11/4342–9998* Ⓜ*C to San Juan.*

When the Sun Comes Up

Clubs starting so late means regular cafés are open for a hard-earned cortado and medialunas by the time you stumble out of clubs in the morning, but Buenos Aires does have a couple of alternative options for sunrise, too. The first is to head to the Costanera for a *choripan* (chorizo sausage and chimichurri sauce on a roll) from the 24-hour stands lining the river. If you're not already near the Costanera, sharing a taxi with friends to get there

is part of the fun. The more hard-core option is to keep dancing at one of the many "afters"—clubs that start at 9 AM and go until around 3 PM. The best-known is **Caix** (⊠ Centro Costa Salguero ☎11/4806–9749), but there are many others opening and closing all the time; any hardened clubber can take you through the options.

RECOLETA

The Basement. This rowdy nightspot downstairs at the Shamrock pub is owned by a couple of Irish guys and is popular with expats and young upwardly mobile porteño party people. Stop first for a Guinness at the bar upstairs, where you can yap away in English and easily forget you're in South America. Follow the techno beats to the downstairs dance club, where there's an enormous disco ball. ⊠ *Rodríguez Peña 1220* ☎11/4812–3584 Ⓜ *D to Callao.*

PALERMO

Club Aráoz. It may be intimate, but it attracts a serious party crowd. Thursday is block-rocking hip-hop night; Friday and Saturday see DJs spinning rock music and electronic dance music for a relatively laid-back bunch of Buenos Aires youth. ⊠ *Aráoz 2424* ☎11/4833–7775.

Honduras. Brave the queues at the big doors to enter this cavernous Palermo Hollywood bar. After 1:30 AM on weekends, the dinner tables get pushed aside and the place begins to fill for a party that goes on all night. With a sound track of "classic hits" it's not particularly cool—but it *is* wildly popular. ⊠ *Honduras 5535, Palermo Hollywood* ☎11/4899–0095 ⊕ *www.hondurasbar.com.ar.*

★ **Kika.** Right at the heart of Palermo and next door to the Congo bar, Kika is much bigger than you'd guess from the outside. Thanks to its funky musical orientation, though, its two dance floors fill up quickly. ⊠ *Honduras 5339, Palermo Hollywood* ☎11/4137–5311.

Fodor'sChoice **Niceto.** The former home of the outrageous Club 69 boasts one of the
★ city's most interesting lineups with everything from indie rock to minimal techno; it turns into one of the city's biggest cumbia venues every Wednesday at midnight with Club night Zizek. The larger main room with a balcony holds live shows and lots of dancing and there's usually something contrasting and chilled taking place in the back room, too. ⊠ *Cnel. Niceto Vega 5510, Palermo Hollywood* ☎11/4779–9396.

The Roxy. The Roxy is where the cream of the Argentine rock-and-roll scene hangs out—except Thursday when it's taken over by the glam queens, scenesters, and debauchery of Club 69. There are live shows, rock *nacional*, disco classics, and often scantily clad dancers. Order a Quilmes and take it all in. ⊠*Federico Lacroze at Alvarez Thomas* ☎*No phone* ⊕*www.theroxybsas.com.ar.*

COSTANERA

★ **Jet.** The speedboats, yachts, and pastel set such a "Miami Vice" tone at this riverfront club that it seems Crockett and Tubbs could walk through the door at any moment. Gangs of gorgeous people come here for sushi and cocktails before heading to Mint and Pachá. ⊠*Av. Costanera Rafael Obligado 4801* ☎*11/4782–5599.*

Mint. Pound Red Bull and champagne alongside trendy college kids and twentysomethings in what's essentially one cavernous room, with a dance floor surrounded by elevated VIP areas and an outside terrace. Stick around to watch the sun rise over the Río de la Plata, a porteño rite of passage. ⊠*Punta Carrasco, Av. Costanera Rafael Obligado at Av. Sarmiento* ☎*11/4806—8002* ⊕*www.mint-argentina.com.ar.*

★ **Pachá.** This pink, multilevel, riverbank behemoth, part of the eponymous global superclub brand, was the Buenos Aires dance-music scene mecca for many years and still pulls in big names and crowds. It can be hot and crowded, but total sensory overload is the point. ⊠*Av. Costanera Rafael Obligado at La Pampa* ☎*11/4788–4280* ⊕*www. pachabuenosaires.com.*

Rumi. Rumi gets packed with rich suburban socialites and the odd fashion model; all come for the less intense setting (compared to other Costanera clubs) and the electronica and pop. Two large bars surround the dance floor; elevated booths encourage that most Argentine of pastimes: checking people out. ⊠*Av. Figueroa Alcorta 6442* ☎*11/4782–1307* ⊕*www.rumiba.com.ar.*

Tequila. A magnificent mix of actors, models, and fashionistas comes here for cocktails; unconnected tourists might not make the cut. Make an early dinner reservation for one of the cushy booths and you'll not only avoid velvet-rope rejection, but you'll also get a bird's-eye view of porteño pick-up artists in action. ⊠*Av. Costanera Rafael Obligado at La Pampa* ☎*11/4781–6555.*

GAY & LESBIAN

CENTRO

Angels. Angels has several dance floors that play electronica, pop, and Latin music. It attracts a primarily gay male and transvestite clientele, but heterosexuals are welcome, too. ⊠*Viamonte 2168* ☎*No phone* ⊕*www.discoangels.com.ar* Ⓜ*D to Facultad de Medicina.*

Contramano. It's been around since 1984, when it was the city's most popular and pioneering gay disco; today it operates more as a laid-back bar with an older, male-only clientele. Occasionally there's live music and male strippers. ⊠*Rodríguez Peña 1082* ☎*No phone* ⊕*www.contramano.com* Ⓜ*D to Callao.*

Palacio. This massive downtown club attracts a mixed-age crowd of gays and lesbians on Friday and Sunday nights for electronic music and pop tunes. On Saturday the club goes straight and changes its name to Big One for a night of hard-core techno. ⊠*Alsina 940* ☎*11/4331–1277* ⊕*www.alsinabuenosaires.com* Ⓜ*A to Piedras.*

RECOLETA

★ **Glam.** Young, hip, and buff men come for smooth cruising in a classy setting: a fashionably restored home. Lesbians and straight women come for the festive atmosphere and raucous music. ⊠*Cabrera 3046* ☎*11/4963–2521* ⊕*www.glambsas.com.ar* Ⓜ*D to Pueyrredón.*

Zoom. A new club half a block from the very cruisey section of Santa Fe between Avenidas Callao and Coronel Díaz, Zoom has lots to offer, including a good bar, a maze, video cabins, and lots of dark corners. It's full on, but with good security and a good mix. ⊠*Uriburu 1018* ☎*11/4827–4828* ⊕*www.zoombuenosaires.com* Ⓜ*D to Pueyrredón.*

PALERMO

Amerika. This big gay disco club has three floors of high-energy action and shows. Thursday and Sunday are quieter with more emphasis on the music and cheaper drinks; Friday and Saturday are wild. ⊠*Gascon 1040* ☎*11/4865–4416* ⊕*www.ameri-k.com.ar.*

Bach. From the outside, it's a little unmarked bar on a quiet corner in Palermo Viejo; on the inside it's a very friendly and sociable gathering point for Buenos Aires' lesbians with occasional shows and even karaoke. ⊠*Cabrera 4390* ☎*11/4773–7521* ⊕*www.bach-bar.com.ar.*

Fodor'sChoice **Chueca.** Recently moved to the heart of Palermo Soho and with a new
★ bar in Puerto Madero, too, Chueca is good for dinner and cabaret shows or a drink at its well-appointed bar. Upstairs is another room and a terrace with DJs and a sushi bar. It's heterosexual-friendly; they also have a "pre-dance" for those headed to Palacio Alsina later on Friday and Sunday. ⊠*Guemes 4900, Palermo Soho* ☎*11/4773–7521* ⊕*www.chueca-restobar.com.ar.*

Kim y Novak Bar. On the edge of Palermo Soho, Kim y Novak is a kitschy cocktail bar that attracts both gay and straight lounge lizards. Upstairs, you can enjoy a mixed drink seated on vintage couches or in booths. Downstairs it's about predominantly gay men dancing to heavy electronic beats. ⊠*Guemes 4900, Palermo Soho* ☎*11/4773 7521.*

Where to Eat

Bar La Perla, La Boca district.

WORD OF MOUTH

"Good steaks are everywhere in Buenos Aires, so it is hard to go wrong. The quality is excellent in hoity-toity establishments as well as corner joints."

— drdawggy

"The best restaurant of our trip was El Trapiche in Palermo—the biggest, tastiest steaks of the trip. We told the waitstaff to bring what they recommended since our Spanish was limited. Best thing we did!'

–WisconsinJen

THE SCENE

By Brian
Byrnes

Buenos Aires isn't just the most cutting-edge food town in Argentina—it's the most cutting-edge food town in the southern hemisphere. Here, three things have come together to create a truly modern cuisine: diverse cultural influences, high culinary aspirations, and a relentless devotion to aesthetics, from plate garnishes to room decor.

And yet, at their core, even the most-modern international restaurants in Buenos Aires are fundamentally porteño, deeply informed by this city's aristocratic appreciation of the pleasure of a good bottle of wine, shared with friends and family, over a long and languid meal. People may eat dinner at 10 PM or 10:30 PM all over Argentina, but only in Buenos Aires are you likely to see a family, toddlers in tow, strolling into their local *parrilla* (steak house) at midnight.

Three areas—Palermo Soho, Palermo Hollywood, and Las Cañitas—have emerged as the epicenters of Argentina's modern food movement. In these neighborhoods, sushi is all the rage, and you can find Patagonian lamb, trout, and king crab rubbing elbows with Asian curries and northern Argentine *locros* (stews).

But much of the old guard still stands strong. Most porteños have Italian ancestry, which is evident in the proliferation of pizzerias all over the city, from the simple shops to the trendy pizza-and-champagne joints. But don't miss the chance to try the deeper-dish Argentine-style pizza, the most classic of which is the *muzzarella* (cheese and tomato pizza) and the immortal combination of *jamón* (ham), *morrón* (roasted red pepper), and *aceitunas* (olives).

Cafés are also a big part of Buenos Aires culture: open long hours, they constantly brim with locals knocking back a quick *cafecito* (espresso) or taking their time over a *café con leche* (coffee with milk). And finally, there are the delicious *heladerías* (ice-cream shops) to finish it all off.

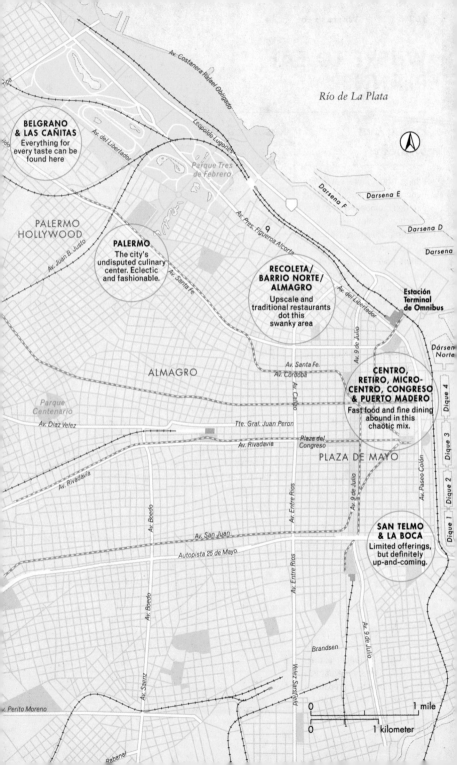

Río de La Plata

BELGRANO
& LAS CAÑITAS
Everything for
every taste can be
found here

Darsena F

Darsena E

Darsena D

Darsena

Parque Tres
de Febrero

PALERMO
HOLLYWOOD

PALERMO
The city's
undisputed culinary
center. Eclectic
and fashionable.

Av. Costanera Rafael Obligado

Leopoldo Lugones

Av. del Libertador

Av. Juan B. Justo

Av. Santa Fe

Av. Pres. Figueroa Alcorta

RECOLETA/
BARRIO NORTE/
ALMAGRO
Upscale and
traditional restaurants
dot this
swanky area

Av. del Libertador

Estación
Terminal
de Omnibus

Dársen
Norte

ALMAGRO

Av. Santa Fe.

Av. Córdoba

Av. Callao

Av. 9 de Julio

Dique 4

Dique 3

CENTRO,
RETIRO, MICRO-
CENTRO, CONGRESO
& PUERTO MADERO
Fast food and fine dining
abound in this
chaotic mix.

Parque
Centenario

Av. Diaz Velez

Tte. Graf. Juan Peron

Av. Rivadavia

Plaza del
Congreso

PLAZA DE MAYO

Av. Paseo Colón

Dique 2

Dique 1

Av. Rivadavia

Av. Boedo

Av. Entre Rios

Av. 9 de Julio

SAN TELMO
& LA BOCA
Limited offerings,
but definitely
up-and-coming.

Av. San Juan

Autopista 25 de Mayo

Av. Boedo

Av. Entre Rios

Vélez Sarsfield

Brandsen

Av. 9 de Julio

Av. Saenz

v. Perito Moreno

Rabanal

0   1 mile

0   1 kilometer

WHERE TO EAT PLANNER

Eating Out Strategy

Where should we eat? With hundreds of Buenos Aires eateries competing for your attention, it may seem like a daunting question. But fret not—our expert writers and editors have done most of the legwork. The selections here represent the best this city has to offer. Search "Best Bets" for top recommendations by price, cuisine, and experience. Sample local flavor in the neighborhood features. Or find a review quickly in the alphabetical listings. Dive in and enjoy!

In This Chapter

Smoking

Smoking is no longer allowed in Buenos Aires restaurants. If you're a smoker, be prepared to head outside for a cigarette.

Reservations

Getting a reservation in most Buenos Aires restaurants is easy. Most porteños make dinner reservations a day or two ahead of time, instead of weeks in advance.

What to Wear

Porteños dress to impress. Looking good is as important as feeling good in Buenos Aires. The finest restaurants in the city employ an "elegant sport" rule, but few require men to wear a tie and jacket. A sport coat and slacks will suffice. Jeans are fine just about anywhere, provided they are paired with a smart shirt or blouse.

Tipping

In most restaurants in Buenos Aires, a 10% tip is the norm. If the service was superb, 15% is always appreciated. In bars you can tip a peso or two per drink, but it's not expected. Bills for parties of six or more sometimes include the tip; look at the check. Many restaurants also charge a servicio de mesa (table service), which is usually around 3 to 5 pesos per person, and covers the cost of bread and butter. If a table charge exists, many locals tip less.

Prices

Credit cards are widely accepted, but some restaurants accept cash only. If you plan to use a card it's a good idea to check its acceptability when making reservations.

Some restaurants are marked with a price range ($$–$$$, for example). This indicates one of two things: either the average cost straddles two categories, or if you order strategically, you can get out for less than most diners spend.

WHAT IT COSTS IN ARGENTINE PESOS				
¢	$	$$	$$$	$$$$
under 12	12–18	18–24	25–34	over 35

Restaurant prices are for an average main course at dinner.

BEST BETS FOR B.A. DINING

With thousands of restaurants to choose from, how will you decide where to eat? Fodor's writers and editors have selected their favorite restaurants by price, cuisine, and experience in the Best Bets lists below. In the first column, Fodor's Choice properties represent the "best of the best" in every price category. You can also search by neighborhood for excellent eats—just peruse the following pages. Or find specific details about a restaurant in the full reviews, listed alphabetically in the chapter.

BEST JAPANESE

Jardin Japones $$
Sushi Club $$$
Yuki $$$

BEST SPANISH

El Globo $$
Oviedo $$$$
Sinclair $$$$

BEST STEAK

La Cabrera $$
El Estanciero $$
Rio Alba $$

Fodor'sChoice ★

Bangalore $
Bella Italia $$$
La Bourgogne $$$$
La Cabrera $$
Casa Cruz $$$$
Duhau Restaurante & Vinoteca $$$$
Patagonia Sur $$$
Pura Tierra $$$
Republica $$$
Rio Alba $$
Thymus $$$

Best By Price

¢

Bar Dorrego
Club Eros
El Cuartito

$

Bangalore
California Burrito Co.
Don Julio
El Encanto

$$

La Cabrera
El Estanciero
Filo
Juana M
El Pobre Luis
Rio Alba

$$$

La Baita
Bella Italia
Desde El Alma
Gran Bar Danzón
Patagonia Sur
Pura Tierra
Republica
Sifones y Dragones
Thymus

$$$$

La Bourgogne
Casa Cruz
Duhau Restaurante & Vinoteca
Nectarine
Oviedo

Sinclair

Best by Cuisine

BEST ARGENTINE

Bar 6 $$
Casa Cruz $$$$
Novecento $$$

BEST FRENCH

La Bourgogne $$$$
Brasserie Petanque $$$
Le Sud $$$$

BEST INDIAN

Bangalore $
Katmandú $$
Tandoor $$$

BEST ITALIAN

La Baita $$$
Bella Italia $$$
La Parolaccia $$

Best by Experience

BEST FOR ROMANCE

Desde El Alma $$$
Duhau Restaurante & Vinoteca $$$$
Republica $$$

BEST FOR MAKING THE SCENE

Casa Cruz $$$$
Novecento $$$
647 Dinner Club $$$$

BEST HOTEL DINING

La Bourgogne $$$$
Le Mistral $$$$
Tomo I $$$$

BEST FOR A COCKTAIL

Casa Cruz $$$$
Gran Bar Danzón $$$
Plaza Grill $$$$

5

CENTRO & ENVIRONS

This area offers a bit of everything: old-school porteño hangouts, fast-paced lunch spots, and modern tourist-friendly locales in Puerto Madero.

Centro is the political and financial heart of the city, and as most deals get sealed during the day, many of the restaurants in this area are more lunch-oriented and get packed with office workers at midday.

Puerto Madero is the exception, though. The fancy waterfront locales are jumping at night, with foreigners and bigwigs on expense accounts. Puerto Madero's proximity to downtown hotels, and its postcard-perfect location make it a convenient and charming area for dining tourists, but don't get trapped here; you'll be missing much of what Buenos Aires has to offer if you don't take the time to venture beyond the port.

Many Centro restaurants serve truly excellent food, but expect more-traditional fare, like parrilla and pastas, as opposed to the more-fusion-oriented cuisine you can find in neighborhoods like Palermo.

THE BURRITO KINGS OF BUENOS AIRES

Mexican cuisine has long been a favorite of porteños, but it was traditionally only available at family-style restaurants away from downtown. That's where three young American entrepreneurs saw their chance. In 2006 they opened the **California Burrito Co.** (Lavalle 441) on one of the busiest pedestrian streets in Centro. At lunchtime during the week, you'll find office workers and expats chowing down on massive beef, chicken, and pork burritos slathered with guacamole, beans, and spicy salsa.

CAFÉ LINGO 101

Coffee is taken seriously in Argentina. A 9 AM and 6 PM caffeine jolt is what gets many porteños through their long days and nights. Here's how to order it:

Café: Same as an American espresso.

Cortado: A café topped or "cut" with hot foamy milk.

Lagrima: Hot foamy milk with a "drop" of coffee.

Submarino: A tall glass of hot milk served with a chocolate bar submerged into the milk (aka hot chocolate).

Ristretto: A small, very strong shot of espresso.

Café con leche: Half coffee and half milk, served in a larger cup.

Unless you specify otherwise, your café will be served in a short espresso glass. If you want a larger coffee, order a jarrito, or medium. If you want an American-size coffee, order a doble, or double.

DOWNTOWN BA'S BEST CAFÉS

Centro is packed with cafés that are an integral part of Buenos Aires' past and present. Jump into café culture at these top spots:

Café Tortoni (✉Av. de Mayo 829) is the most famous Buenos Aires café of all, serving coffee to political, literary, and entertainment legends since 1858.

Florida Garden (✉Florida 899) offers a great respite from the chaos of the pedestrian shopping mall on Florida Street. Sit upstairs for great people-watching.

La Giralda (✉Av. Corrientes 1453) has been a favorite gathering spot for intellectuals since the 1970s and is famous throughout the city for its churros.

El Gato Negro (✉Av. Corrientes 1669) has an extensive offering of teas and coffees from around the world.

5

RESTAURANTS IN THIS AREA

Argentine
Crystal Garden, $$$
DaDá, $$
El Palacio de la Papa Frita, $
La Pérgola, $$$
Restó, $$$
Sabot, $$$
Tomo I, $$$$
Café
Confiteria La Ideal, ¢
Gran Café Tortoni, $
Eclectic
Bengal, $$$
Gran Bar Danzón, $$$
French
Plaza Grill, $$$$
Le Sud, $$$$
Irish
Matias, $$
Italian
La Parolaccia, $$
Japanese
Yuki, $$$
Mexican
California Burrito Co., $
Peruvian
Status, $$
Pizza
Las Cuartetas, ¢
El Cuartito, ¢
Filo, $$
Piola, $$
Spanish
El Globo, $$
El Imparcial, $$
Tancat, $$$
Steak
La Caballeriza, $$
Cabaña Las Lilas, $$$$

LA BOCA & SAN TELMO

The most historic neighborhoods in the city may not be prime culinary destinations, but they do offer a few gems that are well worth visiting.

La Boca and San Telmo are the neighborhoods where Buenos Aires originated. In the late 1800s, tens of thousands of European immigrants, mostly Italians, arrived off the boats in La Boca and quickly settled nearby.

Today the working class neighborhood still maintains a strong Italian feel, but oddly there aren't any restaurants here that offer fine Italian cuisine. Beware, as most of the eateries near the pedestrian-only El Caminito thoroughfare are cheesy tourist traps that offer basic pasta dishes for inflated prices.

In San Telmo the options are better and more varied. The area is currently experiencing a commercial revival, and there are new hotels, shops, and businesses opening every day, which should bring more dining options in the years to come.

DRINKING ON DEFENSA

Strolling the cobblestone streets of San Telmo is a rite of passage for all visitors to Buenos Aires. Hitting the countless antiques shops, art galleries, and fashion stores can be tiring work, so to relax hit one of many old-school bars for a cold Quilmes beer and some salty peanuts. Plaza Dorrego is considered the central point of the neighborhood and the main drag is Calle Defensa, which is lined with places that offer outdoor seating. Check out the historic **Bar Dorrego** (Defensa 1098) and the funky **Bar Fin del Mundo** (Defensa 700) for prime people-watching on the plaza.

TAPPING ARGENTINA'S TOP CULINARY TALENT

Francis Mallman
chef, restaurateur

Argentina's most famous chef and restaurateur runs a series of restaurants in the country, as well as in the United States and Uruguay. His latest Buenos Aires undertaking is **Patagonia Sur** (Rocha 803) in La Boca.

Q: **What's the current state of Argentine cuisine?**

A: Argentine food is behind Argentine wine because of how important Argentine wine has become worldwide during the past five years. It's very good for us, of course. Argentina is gaining a lot of attention because of its wine. Chefs, food writers, and the gastronomy media are all paying attention to us.

Q: **So what needs to improve for Argentine cuisine?**

A: It would be nice if some of the young and fashionable chefs took more interest in our local products and traditional cuisine. With all the fusion cooking and lab cooking these days, many of our young chefs are happier to emulate what's happening in the fashion world of cooking, instead of looking into their pantry to see what they have in hand. But it is improving.

Q: **What lessons do you try to teach the younger generation of Argentine chefs?**

A: I try to encourage young chefs to have at least one or two dishes on their menus

that represent our country, because foreigners come to our country to learn about us: our geography, how we live, and what we eat. I really think we have a lot to offer to diners, and I would like to see more of that on our menus.

Q: **Your menus always feature simple, understated plates. Why?**

A: I think simple is the most difficult. Because when you serve a plate that is swimming in sauce and has little towers and sticks hanging out, I don't think that is trustworthy, because you are hiding things. Food shouldn't be touched that much.

Q: **What's your favorite, most typical Argentine meal that you serve to friends?**

A: Grilled meat with chimichurri sauce, and potatoes, salad, and wine. It could be *ojo de bife* (rib eye), *cuadril* (tri-tip), or *entrana* (skirt steak). It represents our traditions, culture, and roots.

RESTAURANTS IN THIS AREA

Argentine
647 Dinner Club, $$$$
La Farmacia, $$
Patagonia Sur, $$$
Café
Bar Dorrego, ¢
French
Brasserie Petanque, $$$
Spanish
Burzako, $$
Taberna Baska, $$$
Steak
La Brigada, $$$
El Obrero, $

5

RECOLETA, BARRIO NORTE & ALMAGRO

Fantastic restaurants and cozy neighborhood spots populate this swanky, upscale neighborhood of grand boulevards, tree-lined streets, and world-class shopping.

Recoleta is the toniest neighborhood in Buenos Aires, and as such, is home to some of the city's top hotels and restaurants, like La Bourgogne and Duhau Restaurante & Vinoteca, both located in posh hotels on Avenida Alvear. But there are also quiet and hush-hush spots that offer fine food and romance for discreet diners.

If your budget is more modest, head to Avenida Santa Fe or RM Ortiz where there's an array of forgettable, but family-friendly restaurants that offer Argentine staples like meat, pasta, and fish at good prices. More and more ethnic places are popping up all over the neighborhood, with Indian, Syrian, and Peruvian cuisine now available.

RODI BAR

Just blocks away from the glitz of Avenida Alvear and the flashy lights of the Village Recoleta movie theater complex, sits **Rodi Bar** (⊠Vicente Lopez 1900), a throwback to a simpler era of Buenos Aires dining. Its decorations, clientele, waiters, and menu haven't changed much over the decades. They serve hearty, delicious porteño fare better than just about anyone else. At midday go for the old standby *milanesas con papas fritas* (breaded veal cutlet with fries). At night try the *lomo a la pimienta con papas a la crema* (steak in pepper sauce with creamed potatoes).

REFUELING SPOTS FOR SHOPPERS

Hit the world-famous Avenida Alvear for an afternoon of true culinary indulgence.

For the best lunch buffet in the city, the regal Alvear Palace Hotel's **L'Orangerie** (✉Av. Alvear 1891) restaurant is where you can dine with society socialites and finely tailored businesspeople who come here for the seafood and the scene. You can sip champagne, eat salmon, and indulge in mouthwatering desserts. Even at 100 pesos, it's a steal.

Walk off your lunch while shopping on the avenue, where you can visit Hermès, Louis Vuitton, Ralph Lauren, Armani, Escada, La Martina, and many more. Make your way to the stately new **Palacio Duhau** (✉Av. Alvear 1661) for their *Te de la Tarde* (afternoon tea) which is served daily from 4 to 7 PM. It features teas, coffees, cakes, tortes, scones, and more prepared by the hotel's French pastry chef, Ihame Guerrah.

After a long day of shopping, head around the corner to decadent **La Cabaña** (✉Rodriguez Peña 1967). This cathedral to beef is housed in a historic home outfitted with rich mahogany wood and rare works of Argentine art. They offer a gluttonous seven-course tasting menu, featuring the finest Argentine meats.

A TEMPLE TO WINE AND CHEESE

In addition to housing two great restaurants, the **Palacio Duhau** (✉Av. Alvear 1661) also has what must be the city's first Cheese Room, offering more than 45 Argentine cheeses produced in the provinces of Buenos Aires, Cordoba, and Santa Fe. You can try goat, blue, Reblochon, Brie, and other types, artfully paired with smoked meats and wine. The hotel's wine list offers more than 500 varieties and 3,500 bottles. Naturally, the selection is dominated by select smoky Malbecs and Cabernets from Argentina, but it also offers hard-to-find Italian, French, and American vintages.

RESTAURANTS IN THIS AREA

American
Buller Brewing Company, $
Argentine
Malevo, $$$
La Maroma, $$
Pippo, $$
Republica, $$$
El Sanjuanino, $
Cafés
La Biela, $
Modena Design Café, $
French
La Bourgogne, $$$$
Nectarine, $$$$
German
Munich Recoleta, $$
Indian
Tandoor, $$$
Italian
San Babila, $$$
Mediterranean
Le Mistral, $$$$
Middle Eastern
Club Sirio, $$
Modern Argentine
Duhau Restaurante & Vinoteca, $$$$
Spanish
Oviedo, $$$$

5

PALERMO

The city's largest neighborhood, Palermo offers something for every taste, style, and budget. It's the undisputed culinary hot spot of the city with enclaves that each have their own distinct style and vibe.

If you want the tastiest, most cutting-edge, most traditional, most ethnic, most daring, and most fashionable food in Buenos Aires, then you head to Palermo. It's that simple. The sprawling neighborhood is home to the hip areas of Palermo Soho and Hollywood as well as the quieter pockets of Palermo Botanico and Chico.

Soho's main landmark is the artsy Plaza Serrano. But steer clear of the restaurants that line the plaza; they uniformly serve bland and overpriced food. Instead, wander a few blocks in any direction, and you're bound to come across a worthwhile dining spot.

Across the train tracks and Avenida Juan B. Justo lies Palermo Hollywood, which does an admirable job of mixing old and new cuisines in a cool setting of TV production houses and studios.

PASS THE MATE, MAN

Mate is the unofficial national drink here. The bright green tea is packed into a gourd, infused with hot water, and then sucked through a metal straw. Its bitter flavor packs a punch, providing a jolt of energy. Drinking mate is a true ritual in Argentina. One person prepares the gourd, and then passes it to someone, who drinks all the tea in a series of sips. It's then returned to the pourer, who refills it and passes it on to someone else. The custom is a true social event, and is mostly consumed at home, but there are some places in the city like **La Pena del Colorado** (⊠Guemes 3657, Palermo) that offer it on their menu.

PALERMO PARRILLAS

The most cutting-edge cuisine can be found in Palermo, but it's also home to a high concentration of top-notch parrillas.

La Cabrera (✉Cabrera 5099) is always packed to the brim, and in addition to its fantastic cuts of beef, it's also well known for the cold and hot side salads they serve.

La Dorita (✉Humboldt and Costa Rica) is so popular that it occupies two corners of the same street. Actors, activists, musicians, and moms gather here; ask for a table outside to soak in the scene.

Miranda (✉Costa Rica 5602) is perhaps the most fashionable parrilla in all Palermo. It's brimming with beautiful people and the food is excellent, especially the ojo de bife.

COCKTAIL CRAZE

Buenos Aires is currently undergoing a cocktail craze. These days many porteños are no longer content drinking straight beer or booze, and are now demanding well-mixed libations for their nights out on the town.

In Palermo Soho, **Mundo Bizarro** (✉Serrano 1222) has been leading the charge, with scores of original concoctions. The place is decorated in kitschy florescent colors, yet it feels like a biker bar—but without the bikers.

Nearby, **Ocho7Ocho** (✉Thames 878) was once a hush-hush spot for a quiet cocktail among friends, but the secret's out now. Regardless, it's still worth a visit to take in its speakeasy atmosphere.

Casa Cruz (✉Uriarte 1658) is known for their cutting-edge cuisine, but they also have a small bar where the grande dame of the Argentine bartending scene, Inés de los Santos, mixes up delightful drinks, like the "Sol V. 2.0" (vodka, grappa, passion fruit, syrup, and Malbec).

RESTAURANTS IN THIS AREA

American
Kansas, $$$
Mark's, $
Argentine
Barolo, $$
Bar 6, $$
Bar Uriarte, $$$
Casa Cruz, $$$$
Club Eros, ¢
Desde El Alma, $$$
Freud y Falher, $$
Malasaña, $$
La Serapia, $
Social Paraíso, $$$
Thymus, $$$
Eclectic
Lelé de Troya, $$$
Te Mataré Ramirez, $$$
Indian
Bangalore, $
Italian
La Baita, $$$
Bella Italia, $$$
Japanese
Jardin Japonés, $$
Mexican
Maria Félix, $$$
Xalapa, $$
Middle Eastern
Sarkis, $$
Scandinavian
Ølsen, $$$
Spanish
Al Andalus, $$
Sinclair, $$$$
Steak
La Cabrera, $$
Don Julio, $$
El Encanto, $
Rio Alba, $$
El Trapiche, $$
Vietnamese
Green Bamboo, $$$

5

BELGRANO & LAS CAÑITAS

Belgrano is filled with family-friendly spots and a few gems, while über-cool Las Cañitas rocks seven nights a week with a vast array of culinary options.

Despite its reputation as a snooty upper-class neighborhood, Belgrano is in fact one of the city's most diverse food neighborhoods. Indeed, there are million-dollar mansions and embassies, but there are also enclaves filled with Asian immigrants, traditional English- and Irish-style homes and cafés, a big university, and a chaotic shopping street, Avenida Cabildo.

Although there are only a few restaurants that warrant a trip to Belgrano, there are many fun and fashionable places in Las Cañitas, the hastily defined pocket on the border between Palermo and Belgrano.

In Cañitas, as the locals call it, you can find everything from pizza to pasta, sushi to steak. You'll also see a few high-end spots that strive for contemporary porteño cuisine.

BARRIO CHINO

Buenos Aires' "Barrio Chino" is a mishmash of Chinese, Korean, and Japanese citizens and cultures. Compared to many other big cities, BA's Chinatown is relatively small and tame, occupying just a few blocks on and around Calle Arribenos, near the Belgrano C train station. There you can find a smattering of supermarkets, shops, and restaurants. Among the best are **Lai Lai** (✉Arribenos 2168), **Todo Contentos** (✉Arribenos 2177), and the fabulous **BuddhaBA** (✉Arribenos 2288), which serves excellent Asian fusion fare.

HEAVENLY HELADO

Buenos Aires has some of the best ice cream in the world. Porteños take their *helado* (ice cream) seriously, and shops can be found on nearly every other corner around the city. The neighborhood with the most *heladerías* is Belgrano, where fantastic mom-and-pop operations and chain shops abound. At many *heladerías*, you'll find an entire section of the menu devoted to caramel-y dulce de leche combinations. We recommend:

Cabaña Tuyu (⊠José Hernández 2275) for dozens of selections, including the buttery, wine-infused sabayon.

Freddo (⊠Av. Libertador 5200) for its juicy sorbets and refreshing fruit flavors (try banana).

Persicco (⊠Vuelta de Obligado 2092 and Migueletes 886), a local chain, for its delectable *dulce de leche* combinations.

Un Altra Volta (⊠Echeverria 2302) for its gorgeous chocolates and sculptural ice cream desserts, which taste as good as they look.

RESTAURANTS IN THIS AREA

Argentine
Novecento, $$$
Pura Tierra, $$$
Sifones y Dragones, $$$
Sucre, $$$
Japanese
Sushi Club, $$$
Steak
El Estanciero, $$
El Pobre Luis, $$
Thai
Lotus Neo Thai, $$$

5

TAKE A BREAK FROM STEAK

It may seem sacrilegious to stray from the red-blooded star of BA's culinary scene, but there is such a thing as a steak hangover. The antidote? A light sushi or seafood meal from one of Las Cañitas' many acclaimed restaurants. Our favorites include:

Azul Profundo (⊠Maure 1673) for its international seafood dishes like grilled salmon with wok-seared vegetables, and seafood risotto.

Bokoto (⊠Huergo 261), a sushi roll specialist, for its stylish, relaxed setting and creative presentations.

Moshi Moshi (⊠Ortega y Gasset 1707) for its swanky rooftop sake bar and stellar sushi. Try the Sake-Ebi Roll, with salmon, shrimp, and avocado, topped with caviar.

Sushi Club (⊠Báez 268, at Ortega y Gasset 1812), a local chain, for its reliable sushi and sashimi, and creative rolls, like the Buenos Aires roll.

ALPHABETICAL RESTAURANT LISTINGS

$$
SPANISH
Palermo

Al Andalus. At this Andalusian restaurant, you'll have trouble choosing between the lamb *tagine* (a rich, dark stew cooked with plums and almonds), the *Pastel Andalusí* (a sweet-and-sour phyllo packed with lamb and chicken), or the goat cheese, saffron, and wild mushroom risotto. The *torta antigua* (chocolate cake) is not to be missed. You can eat in a tented dining room under the ceramic lights of the quieter rust-red bar, or stretch out on sofas draped with Moroccan rugs beside a tiled fountain in the plant-filled courtyard. ⊠*Godoy Cruz 1823, Palermo* ☎*11/4832–9286* ⊟*AE, D, MC, V* ☉*Closed Sun.* ✛*1:B4*

$$$
ITALIAN
Palermo Soho

La Baita. In a city filled with first- and second-generation Italians, it's surprisingly hard to find a good Italian meal. Look no further than La Baita, a cozy corner spot in the heart of Palermo Soho that attracts highbrow porteños and Europeans looking for some Mediterranean cuisine. They do fantastic fresh pastas, and nice meats dishes, including rabbit and lamb. The main dining room is quaint, and some of the tables are too close together, but the romantic atmosphere, live music, and friendly service make up for it. ⊠*Thames 1603, Palermo Soho* ☎*11/4832–7234* ⊟*MC, V* ☉*No lunch Mon.* ✛*1:B4*

$
INDIAN
Palermo
Hollywood
Fodor'sChoice
★

Bangalore. This place does an admirable job of re-creating the atmosphere of a typical London pub, which probably explains its roaring popularity with Buenos Aires' booming expat population. Come here for fantastically spicy curries, microbrews, and the rowdy atmosphere. Seating is upstairs in a dark alcove. You won't be able to ignore the noise from the drinkers below, but who cares, you're not here for romance. This is a place for a quick Indian meal and jovial conversation. It's perfect for cheap food and a good beer before heading out to the many hot spots nearby. ⊠*Humboldt 1416, Palermo Hollywood* ☎*11/4779–2621* ⊟*No credit cards.* ✛*1:A4*

¢
CAFÉ
San Telmo

Bar Dorrego. Bar Dorrego probably hasn't changed much in the last 100 years or so. Dark wood and politely aloof waiters set the stage; good coffee, *tragos* (alcoholic drinks), sangria, and snacks complete the scene. When the weather is warm, sit at a table outside, order a cold Quilmes beer and some salty peanuts, and soak in the scene of San Telmo's busiest hub. ⊠*Defensa 1098, at Humberto I, on Plaza Dorrego, San Telmo* ☎*11/4361–0141* ⊟*No credit cards* Ⓜ*C or E to Independencia.* ✛*2:E6*

$$
ARGENTINE
Palermo
Hollywood

Barolo. Its opening in 1998 helped to spark Palermo Hollywood's emergence as a dining mecca, but the decade since has taken its toll and this is not the top spot it used to be. It's on a quiet street in an old town house done up in bright green and mauve. Dishes are well done, but the range is limited: meats, fish, pastas, and lamb, on occasion. Wines of the month are chalked up on a blackboard over the bar. ⊠*Bonpland 1612, Palermo Hollywood* ☎*11/4772–0841* ⊟*AE, V* ☉*Closed Sun. No lunch Sat.* ✛*1:A4*

$$ **Bar 6.** The seasonally changing menu is ambitious—sometimes too ambi-
ARGENTINE   tious—cycling through a universe of ingredients and preparations, from
Palermo Soho   Asian stir-fry to polenta to grilled seafood. Past highlights have included
marinated salmon with cilantro, and goat-cheese ice cream with candied
tomatoes. The waiters are usually too busy being beautiful to attend to
you in a hurry. Even if the service lags and the kitchen can be inconsis-
tent, it's worth stopping by to admire this dramatic stone, wood, and
glass space—simultaneously modern and down to earth. This place is
wildly popular for its well-priced lunch specials. There's an impressive
cocktail menu as well. ⊠*Armenia 1676, Palermo Soho* ☎*11/4833–
6807* ⊕*www.barseis.com* ⊟*AE, MC, V* ☾*Closed Sun.* ✛*1:C5*

$$$ **Bar Uriarte.** There is perhaps no place that better represents Palermo
ARGENTINE   Viejo's dining revolution than the bustling kitchen of Bar Uriarte,
Palermo Soho   which is enticingly set in the front of the restaurant, exposed to the
street. Inside lies a sophisticated bar with two intimate dining spaces.
You can even eat your meal while lounging on a sofa. Chef Julieta
Oriolo's dishes are as sleek as the surroundings, but some plates, like
the entrana (skirt steak) disappoint. The best items are the pizzas (lunch
only) and other dishes that come out of the prominent wood-fired mud
oven, like the ginger-and-lemon-marinated pork with sweet potatoes
and Dijon. Discrete live DJs warm things up on the weekend. Be sure to
check out the inspired local art at the gallery upstairs. ⊠*Uriarte 1572,
Palermo Soho* ☎*11/4834–6004* ⊕*www.baruriarte.com.ar* ⊟*AE, DC,
MC, V.* ✛*1:B4*

$$$ **Bella Italia.** This place serves the best veal chop in the city, sprinkled
ITALIAN   with rosemary and salty potatoes. It's enough to feed two people. The
Palermo   lemon ravioli with salmon is fantastic, too, as is the bruschetta. In addi-
Fodor's Choice   tion to the delicious food, Bella Italia wins points for its cozy, romantic
★   atmosphere; extensive wine list; and its friendly, although sometimes
overworked, servers. It's tucked into a quaint section of Palermo near
the zoo and close to good shopping. The owners also run a quaint Ital-
ian-style café a block away and a sister branch of the restaurant in Fort
Worth, Texas. ⊠*Republica Arabe Siria 3285, Palermo* ☎*11/4802–
4253* ⊕*www.bellaitalia-gourmet.com.ar* ⊟*AE, D, MC, V.* ✛*1:E3*

$$$ **Bengal.** Bengal serves a mixture of Italian and Indian fare in quiet
ECLECTIC   wood-paneled surroundings with dark colors. At midday it's popular
Retiro   with Foreign Ministry employees from next door, and at night upper-
crust local foodies fill the tables. If you're anxious for some heat, try
the *jhing masala* (prawn curry). Those with tender taste buds should
go for one of the delicious homemade pasta dishes. Their commitment
to wine is serious, with a detailed list, decanters, and artistic glasses.
⊠*Arenales 837, Retiro* ☎*11/4314–2926* ⊟*AE, MC, V* ☾*Closed Sun.
No lunch Sat.* Ⓜ*C to San Martín.* ✛*2:D2*

$ **La Biela.** Porteños linger at this quintessential sidewalk café opposite the
CAFÉ   Recoleta Cemetery, sipping espressos, discussing politics, and people-
Recoleta   watching—all of which are best done at a table beneath the shade of
an ancient rubber tree. Keep your eyes open for actor and tango enthu-

Staying Up with the Porteños

Buenos Aires is a 24-hour city, and you can find places that serve food around the clock, but most of these are downtown and tend to fall into the fast-food and pizza categories. Although much is made about porteños' late eating habits, the truth is the ideal and most popular dining time is 9–9:30 PM (though you can easily show up for dinner at midnight and no one will blink an eye). Most restaurants open at 8 PM for dinner and will serve until 1 or 2 AM. You can find more late-night *confiterias* (confectioneries) and cafés in the Centro area; most other neighborhoods have scarce late-night offerings.

You can find breakfast—coffee and pastries—anywhere, at any time. Lunch is served from noon to 4 PM, with 1–2 PM being the rush hour, especially downtown, which is packed with office workers.

---

siast Robert Duvall, who is a regular here. ✉*Quintana 600, at Junín, Recoleta* ☎*11/4804–0449* ▭*V.* ✛*2:B1*

$$$$
FRENCH
Recoleta
Fodor'sChoice
★

La Bourgogne. White tablecloths, fresh roses, and slick red leather chairs emphasize the restaurant's innate elegance. A sophisticated waitstaff brings you complimentary hors d'oeuvres as you choose from chef Jean-Paul Bondoux's creations, which include foie gras, rabbit, escargots, chateaubriand, *côte de veau* (veal steak), and wild boar cooked in cassis. The loquacious chef is known to stroll through the vast room and sit down for a chat with patrons. The fixed-price tasting menu is more affordable and more adventurous than à la carte selections and features a different wine with each plate. Ask to be seated in the mysterious wine cellar for a more-intimate experience. ✉*Alvear Palace Hotel, Ayacucho 2027, Recoleta* ☎*11/4805–3857 or 11/4808–2100* ✎*Reservations essential. Jacket and tie* ▭*AE, DC, MC, V* ⊘*Closed Sun. No lunch Sat.* ✛*2:B1*

$$$
FRENCH
San Telmo

Brasserie Petanque. Upon entering this classic French brasserie you're greeted by a long and imposing bar, bookended by white pillars and backed by shelf after enticing shelf of liquor and wine. This festive San Telmo locale has scores of small, white-linen tables where you can enjoy great onion soup and local interpretations of French classics, like steak tartare and beef bourguignonne. Surprisingly, the wine list is quite small, with only a few French wines, but they make up for it with an ample spirits selection, and friendly bartenders. Get a table by the window to check out the people cruising by outside. Reservations are recommended. ✉*Defensa 596, San Telmo* ☎*11/4342–7930* ⊕*www.brasseriepetanque.com* ▭*AE, D, MC, V* ⊘*Closed Mon. No lunch Sat.* ✛*2:D5*

$$$
STEAK
San Telmo

La Brigada. You'd be hard-pressed to find better Argentine steaks. Amid elaborate decor, including scores of soccer mementos, a courtly staff will treat you to unimpeachable *mollejas* (sweetbreads) and *chinchulines de chivito* (kid intestines), plus a brilliant array of grilled steaks. The baby beef is tender enough to cut with a spoon, which the waiters insist on doing, to much fanfare. This place is definitely on the tourist map, so be prepared pay a bit more and listen to several different languages at a time. Reservations are recommended. ⊠*Estados Unidos 465, between Bolívar and Defensa, San Telmo* ☏*11/4361– 5557* ⊟*AE, DC, MC, V* ⊗*Closed Mon.* Ⓜ*C or E to Independencia.* ✛*2:D6*

$
AMERICAN
Recoleta

Buller Brewing Company. The city's first microbrewery (the name is pronounced in the American way, not the Spanish double-L way) is more notable for its beer and its lively atmosphere than for its American-influenced brewpub food. But the brews really are impressive, and they're all made in a careful, German-inspired style. Don't miss the India Pale Ale or the unique honey beer. In Recoleta, which is full of cookie-cutter Irish pubs and sports bars, this is a nice break. ⊠*RM Ortiz 1827, Recoleta* ☏*11/4808–9061* ⊕*www.bullerpub.com* ⊟*AE, DC, MC, V.* ✛*2:B1*

$$
SPANISH
San Telmo

Burzako. Classic Basque dishes reinvented for a young Argentine public keep Burzako's tables busy. Dishes such as *rabo de buey* (a rich oxtail-and-wine stew) and seasonally changing fish use only the best and freshest local ingredients, and the huge portions leave you unable to move. Recover from the meal over another bottle from their savvy, well-priced wine list. Despite the rustic tavern furnishings, Burzako draws a funky crowd, and on weekends the basement becomes a bar where local bands often play. ⊠*México 345, San Telmo* ☏*11/4334– 0721* ⊟*AE, DC, MC, V* ⊗*Closed Sun. No dinner. Mon. and Tues.* ✛*2:D5*

$$
STEAK
Puerto Madero

La Caballeriza. People flock from all over the world to empty their wallets at touristy Cabaña Las Lilas next door, but locals in the know come instead to this big, lively, informal steak house, where you can pay much less for good, quality meat. Sip champagne at the friendly bar while you wait for a table. The parrilla is wood-fired, Uruguayan style, and the *asado de tira* (rack of beef short ribs) is a highlight, but you also can't go wrong with the classic *bife de chorizo* (bone-in sirloin or rump steak). There's another branch by the Recoleta mall next to the cemetery, but this one is superior. ⊠*A.M. de Justo 580, Puerto Madero* ☏*11/4514–4444* ⊕*www.lacaballerizapuertomadero.com* ⊟*AE, DC, MC, V* Ⓜ*B to L.N. Alem.* ✛*2:E4*

$$$$
STEAK
Puerto Madero

Cabaña Las Lilas. This place is a tourist trap, but a good one. It's probably the most famous steak house in all of Argentina, and as such has become wildly popular with foreigners. But although you'll definitely hear lots of English and German and French spoken here, if you look around, it's also populated with lots of locals, at least the ones who can afford it. Las Lilas is best known for its beef that comes directly from its own estancia in the Pampas. The best cuts are the (rib eye) and bife de lomo. Salads and desserts are fantastic, too. Bottom line: if you're pressed for time, and can't leave Centro, this is your place for steak. Otherwise, venture out to some better places outside downtown. ⊠*A.M. de Justo 515, Puerto Madero* ☎*11/4313–1336* ▤*AE, MC, V.* ✢*2:E3*

$$
STEAK
Palermo Soho
Fodor'sChoice
★

La Cabrera. Palermo's best parrilla is on the quiet corner of Cabrera and Thames. Fun, ancient paraphernalia hangs everywhere, giving the feel of an old grocery store. La Cabrera is particularly known for its excellent *provoleta de queso de cabra* (grilled goat cheese) and its *chinchulines de cordero* (small intestines of lamb). Try also the *cuadril vuelta y vuelta* (rare rump steak) and the mollejas (sweetbreads), which are also top-notch. The servings are abundant, as is the noise. What really sets it apart from other parrillas are the complimentary side dishes, like pumpkin purée, eggplant salad, and others—an amazing touch to accompany your steak. ⊠*Cabrera 5099, Palermo Soho* ☎*11/4831–7002* ▤*No credit cards* ⌁*Reservations essential* ☾*No lunch Mon.* ✢*1:B5*

$
MEXICAN
Centro
☾

California Burrito Co. This place changed the game for downtown lunch options by offering tasty Mexican food in an American fast-food-style environment. It's run with love by three twentysomething American guys who certainly know their Mexican food and offer huge burritos and tacos stuffed with tasty meat, fresh vegetables, and great side dishes. At midday, lines can run out the door with office workers, but at night it's more tame—a great place to take a break from steak and chill with a Corona in comfort. This place is also hugely popular with in-the-know expats and walk-in foreigners yearning for something spicy ⊠*Lavalle 441, Centro* ☎*11/4328–3057* ⊕*www.californiaburritoco.com* ▤*AE, D, MC, V* ☾*Closed weekends.* ✢*2:D2*

$$$$
ARGENTINE
Palermo Soho
Fodor'sChoice
★

Casa Cruz. Trendsetters come and go, but there are few whose food is truly sublime. With its unmarked entrance, dim lighting, expanses of mahogany, and cozy banquettes, you'd have to be a bumbling fool not to impress your date here. And yet it's chef Germán Martitegui's kitchen that will really blow your mind, working rabbit medallions into a state of melting tenderness, pairing delicately crisped *morcilla* (blood sausage) with jammy fruit. Is this the single best restaurant in Buenos Aires? Believe the hype. ⊠*Uriarte 1656, Palermo Soho* ☎*11/4833–1112* ⊕*www.casa-cruz.com* ⌁*Reservations essential* ▤*AE, DC, MC, V* ☾*Closed Sun. No lunch.* ✢*1:B4*

¢
ARGENTINE
Palermo Soho

Club Eros. A basic dining room attached to an old soccer club, Club Eros has developed a cult following for its downscale charm. The excellent fare at rock-bottom prices have begun to draw young Palermo trendies as well as older customers who have been loyal to the club for decades. There's no menu, but you can confidently order a crispy milanesa (breaded meat cutlet) or, if available, a bife de chorizo and fries. Pasta sauces fall flat, but the flan con dulce de leche is one of the best (and biggest) in town. ⊠*Uriarte 1609, Palermo Soho* ☎*11/4832–1313* ▤*No credit cards.* ✢*1:B4*

$$ **Club Sirio.** Walk up a curved double staircase to the lobby bar of this
MIDDLE breathtaking second-floor Syrian restaurant. Expect hummus, stuffed
EASTERN grape leaves, and lamb in the superb Middle Eastern buffet. Belly danc-
Recoleta ers entertain Wednesday through Saturday, and coffee-ground read-
ers predict fortunes. You can order a *narguilah* (large water-filtered
tobacco pipe) to finish things off in Syrian style. ☒*Pacheco de Melo
1902, Recoleta* ☎11/4806–5764 ⊟AE, V ☉Closed Sun. No lunch.
⊹2:B2

¢ **Confitería La Ideal.** Part of the charm of this spacious 1918 coffee shop–
CAFÉ milonga is its sense of nostalgia: think fleur-de-lis motifs, timeworn
Centro European furnishings, and stained glass. No wonder they chose to
film the 1998 movie *The Tango Lesson* here. La Ideal is famous for
its *palmeritas* (glazed cookies) and tea service and for the scores of
locals and foreigners who attend the milongas here. Tango lessons are
offered Monday through Saturday at varying times throughout the day
and night; evening concerts take place every night except Tuesday and
Thursday. Its informality is its best trait; just show up at any hour and
chances are you'll hear and see some great tango. ☒*Suipacha 384, at
Av. Corrientes, Centro* ☎11/5265–8069 ⊛*www.confiteriaideal.com*
⊟No credit cards Ⓜ*C to C. Pellegrini, D to 9 de Julio.* ⊹2:D4

$$$ **Crystal Garden.** There's one, and only one, reason to come to the over-
ARGENTINE priced restaurant of the Hotel Park Tower: to take in the evening views
Retiro across Retiro from the glass-covered dining room. Everybody needs
that gleaming-modern-city feeling now and then. The best time to come
is during the 7 PM–10 PM happy hour; drinks and appetizers are free for
hotel guests, but visitors, too, can crash the party, buy drinks, and par-
take in the extensive free buffet, which could easily become your dinner
if you don't watch out. (The real dinner menu, however, is overpriced.)
☒*Hotel Park Tower, Leandro N. Alem 1193, Retiro* ☎11/4318–9211
⊟AE, DC, MC, V Ⓜ*C to San Martín.* ⊹2:E2

¢ **Las Cuartetas.** The huge, flavor-packed deep-dish pizzas are a challenge
PIZZA to finish. If you want, you can walk up to the bar and order just a
Centro slice; the simplest version—*muzzarella*—is usually the freshest. They
☾ also do a good *fugazza* (onions, but no tomatoes). Las Cuartetas is
a good place for a quick solo lunch or a pretheater slice—among the
mobs at the Formica-top tables you'll see not just older men but also
women eating alone, a rarity in Buenos Aires. ☒*Corrientes 838, Centro* ☎11/4326–0171 ⊟No credit cards ☉No lunch Sun. Ⓜ*B to C.
Pellegrini, C to Diagonal Norte, D to Estación 9 de Julio.* ⊹2:D4

¢ **El Cuartito.** This porteño classic has been making pizza and empanadas
PIZZA since 1934, and the surroundings have changed little in the last 70
Centro years. The brusque waitstaff is part of the charm. Drop in for a slice
at the *mostrador* (counter) or make yourself comfortable under the
portraits of Argentine sporting greats for fantastic, no-nonsense food
and cold Quilmes beer. Try a slice of *fainá* (like a chickpea-flour flat
bread), one of the traditional Argentine variations on pizza, and don't
miss out on their flan with dulce de leche. ☒*Talcahuano 937, Centro*
☎11/4816–4331 ⊟No credit cards Ⓜ*D to Tribunales.* ⊹2:C3

5

$$
ARGENTINE
Retiro

DaDá. Eclectic porteño '60s pop culture characterizes one of the city's best-kept secrets, where murals inspired by Dalí, Miró, Lichtenstein, and Mondrian are splashed across the walls and jazz fills the small intimate space. Seasonal specials are chalked up behind the cluttered bar. The short but inventive menu showcases local produce, with relentlessly modern flavor combinations, and the bar is a scene at night. This place looks like a movie set. ⊠*San Martín 941, Retiro* ☎*11/4314–4787* ⊟*AE, MC, V* ◷*Closed Sun.* Ⓜ*C to San Martín.* ✛*2:D3*

$$$
ARGENTINE
Palermo Soho

Desde El Alma. It would be hard to create a cuter restaurant than this cozy little gem, which is nestled just to the Palermo Soho side of the train tracks. In front you can sit around an intimate fireplace, while the back room feels like an old Argentine family *comedor* (dining room). The menu is relatively short and simple; dishes like leek quiche and sesame-crusted salmon are tasty and thoughtful without overreaching. Reservations are recommended. ⊠*Honduras 5298, Palermo Soho* ☎*11/4831–5812* ⊟*No credit cards* ◷*Closed Sun. No lunch.* ✛*1:B4*

$
STEAK
Palermo Soho

Don Julio. In a neighborhood where it's becoming increasingly hard to find a parrilla, this is an aberration, and a good one. As a result, it's almost always packed with locals, who come to sample the work of the distinguished *parrillero,* who can be seen from the sidewalk, tending to the glowing embers. The room is simple and pleasant, with exposed brick walls, and the service is extremely polite. The creamy, spicy morcilla is a knockout. ⊠*Guatemala 4691, at Gurruchaga, Palermo Soho* ☎*11/4831–9564* ⊟*AE, MC, V.* ✛*1:C4*

$$$$
MODERN
ARGENTINE
Recoleta
Fodor'sChoice
★

Duhau Restaurante & Vinoteca. Just as the Palacio Duhau Hotel changed the game of luxury in Buenos Aires, so has its eponymous restaurant. This wonderful spot serves some of the best food in the city, complimented with impeccable and friendly service. The menu is French-inspired, but with proud touches of Argentine cuisine: sweetbreads with Patagonian berries, king prawns from Tierra del Fuego, and trout from Bariloche. The beef is all certified Black Angus from the province of Santa Fe. The wine list reads like a book; more than 500 varieties are available on what must be the biggest wine list in the city. After dinner, visit the Cheese Room, which offers 45 different cheeses made from an Argentine dairy. ⊠*Av. Alvear 1661, Recoleta* ☎*11/5171–1340* ⊕*www.buenosaires.park.hyatt.com* ⊟*AE, D, MC, V* ◷*No lunch weekends.* ✛*2:C1*

$
STEAK
Palermo
Hollywood

El Encanto. This unique spot is a Palermo Hollywood classic. It's a sports, cinema, and theater museum *and* a fantastic parrilla. Every inch of wall space is covered with sports and film memorabilia, and glass cases are packed with old trophies from soccer championships of years past. The food is fantastic, too. The bife de chorizo and ojo de bife are top-notch, as are the salads and desserts. Service is touch-and-go, but the chaos and eclectic crowd—from actors to former tennis pros to local hipsters—make for an unforgettable evening. ⊠*Bonpland 1690, Palermo Hollywood* ☎*11/15–5809–2240* ⊟*No credit cards.* ✛*1:A4*

$$ **El Estanciero.** It perfectly captures the vibrancy of Las Cañitas; even on
STEAK weekdays, you can see groups casually ambling in to dine as late as mid-
Las Cañitas night. They come for the juicy steaks and *achuras* (innards), all of which
are grilled over an open fire in full view of the restaurant. Grab one of the
tables on the open second floor and you'll get an even better view of the
parrilla and the action outside. Ask for your steak *vuelta y vuelta* (rare)
for best results. ⊠*Báez 202, at Argüibel, Las Cañitas* ☎*11/4899–0951*
☰*AE, DC, MC, V* Ⓜ*D to Ministro Carranza.* ✛*1:B2*

$$ **La Farmacia.** Mismatched tables and chairs, comfy leather sofas, and
ARGENTINE poptastic colors fill this cute, century-old corner house that used to
San Telmo be a traditional pharmacy. Generous breakfasts and afternoon teas
☺ are served on the cozy ground floor, lunch and dinner are served in
the first-floor dining room, and you can have late-night drinks on the
bright-yellow roof terrace. Arts and dance workshops are run upstairs,
and the building has two boutiques selling local designers' work. The
modern Argentine dishes are simple but well done, and the fixed-price
lunch and dinner menus get you a lot for a little. ⊠*Bolívar 898, San
Telmo* ☎*11/4300–6151* ☰*No credit cards* ☾*Closed Mon.* Ⓜ*C or E
to Independencia.* ✛*2:D6*

$$ **Filo.** Come here for the hip, lively atmosphere, but be prepared for
PIZZA crowds at all hours. The excellent individual-size pizzas are flat, in the
Retiro Italian style; the bubbly crust is wonderfully charred by the enormous
brick oven in the open kitchen. Toppings and sauce are remarkably
authentic—you can tell that the ownership is Italian. Embrace the city's
chic pizza-and-champagne aesthetic and wash your meal down with a
40-peso bottle of bubbly. Even the rock music is great; on your way to
the restroom, check out the art space in the basement. ⊠*San Martín
975, between Alvear and Paraguay, Retiro* ☎*11/4311–0312* ⊕*www.
filo-ristorante.com* ☰*AE, MC, V* Ⓜ*C to San Martín.* ✛*2:D3*

$$ **Freud y Fahler.** Red walls, colorful pane-glass screens, and vintage chan-
ARGENTINE deliers give warmth to this glassed-in corner restaurant along a peaceful
Palermo Soho cobblestone street. The menu is short but imaginative; try the braised
lamb, if available, perhaps followed by spiced white-chocolate cake
with plum ice cream and orange sauce. The young well-informed staff
gives friendly advice on food and wine. The lunch menus, which are
more vegetable-oriented, are an excellent value. It's also a popular stop
for an afternoon drink or a coffee. ⊠*Gurruchaga 1750, Palermo Soho*
☎*11/4833–2153* ☰*AE, V* ☾*Closed Sun.* ✛*1:C4*

$$ **El Globo.** Much like the neighborhood in which it resides, El Globo
SPANISH is touristy but good. Hearty *pucheros* (mixed boiled meat dinners),
Centro roast suckling pig, squid, and other Spanish-Argentine fare are served
in a large dining area, as they have been since the restaurant opened
in 1908. The *cazuela de mariscos* (seafood stew) is another specialty.
⊠*Hipólito Yrigoyen 1199, Centro* ☎*11/4381–3926* ☰*AE, DC, MC,
V* Ⓜ*C to Av. de Mayo, A to Lima.* ✛*2:C5*

$$$
ECLECTIC
Retiro

Gran Bar Danzón. Expansive wine lists have become all the rage in 21st-century Buenos Aires, but it will take more than just a rage to topple this king of wine bars from its lofty throne. The room is dark, loud, cramped, and filled with beautiful people; the menu is versatile, sometimes too much so—there's lamb raviolis with goat cheese and a pear sauce, steaks, and sushi. But skip the raw fish and focus on the

simple small plates that serve as good accompaniments to one of the thousands of excellent red wines on offer. ⊠*Libertad 1161, Retiro* ☏*11/4811–1108* ⊕*www.granbardanzon.com.ar* ♦*Reservations essential* ▭*AE, DC, MC, V* ⊘*No lunch* Ⓜ*C to San Martín.* ✛*2:C2*

$
CAFÉ
Centro

Gran Café Tortoni. In the city's first confitería, established in 1858, art nouveau decor and high ceilings transport you back in time. Carlos Gardel, one of Argentina's most famous tango stars; writer Jorge Luis Borges; local and visiting dignitaries; and intellectuals have all eaten and sipped coffee here. Don't miss the *chocolate con churros* (thick hot chocolate with baton-shape doughnuts for dipping). You must reserve ahead of time for the nightly tango shows, for which you'll pay a 50-peso cover. ⊠*Av. de Mayo 825, Centro* ☏*11/4342–4328* ⊕*www.cafetortoni.com.ar* ▭*AE, MC, V* Ⓜ*A to Perú.* ✛*2:D4*

$$$
VIETNAMESE
Palermo
Hollywood

Green Bamboo. At Buenos Aires' first Vietnamese restaurant, the walls are black, the waiters slick, and the olive-green vinyl chairs usually occupied by thirtysomething actors and producers. And those chairs are usually *all* occupied. The food is reasonably authentic; take your time over it and then move on to one of the fantastic *maracuyá* (passion fruit) daiquiris. Belgium-born bartender Peter Van Den Bossche mixes up some wildly creative creations. ⊠*Costa Rica 5802, Palermo Hollywood* ☏*11/4775–7050* ⊕*www.green-bamboo.com.ar* ▭*AE, MC, V* ⊘*No lunch.* ✛*1:A3*

$$
SPANISH
Centro

El Imparcial. Founded in 1860, the oldest restaurant in town owes its name (meaning impartial) to its neutrality in the face of the warring political factions of Buenos Aires' Spanish immigrants. Hand-painted tiles, heavy wooden furniture, and paintings of Spain are all strong reminders of the restaurant's origins, as are the polite, elderly waiters, many of whom are from the old country. Talking politics is no longer banned within, good news for today's Argentines, who keep coming to El Imparcial for the renowned puchero as well as seafood specialties like paella. ⊠*Hipólito Yrigoyen 1201, Centro* ☏*11/4383–2919* ⊕*www.elimparcial.com.ar* ▭*AE, DC, MC, V* Ⓜ*C to Av. de Mayo, A to Lima.* ✛*2:C5*

$$
JAPANESE
Palermo

Jardín Japonés. Easily the most impressive setting for sushi in Buenos Aires is inside the Japanese Garden on the northern edge of Palermo. Come for lunch, before or after touring the garden, or come for a romantic dinner. The sushi and sashimi are fresh, especially the salmon, but the hot dishes, such as pork with mushrooms, won't necessarily blow you away. ✉*Av. Casares 2966, Jardín Japonés, Bosques de Palermo* ☎*11/4800–1322* ⊟*No credit cards* ✲*Closed Tues.* ✢*1:D4*

$$
STEAK
Recoleta

Juana M. The minimalist chic decor of this hip basement restaurant stands in stark contrast to the menu: down-to-earth parrilla fare at good prices. Catch a glimpse of meats sizzling on the grill behind the bar, check out the impressive artwork on the walls, and then head to your table to devour your steak and *chorizo* (fat, spicy sausage). This place has the best salad bar in the city, hands down. The homemade pastas aren't bad, either. The staff is young and friendly. ✉*Carlos Pellegrini 1535, Recoleta* ☎*11/4326–0462* ⊟*AE, MC, V* ✲*No lunch Sat.* Ⓜ*C to San Martín.* ✢*2:D2*

$$$
AMERICAN
Palermo

Kansas. If you absolutely need to eat American cuisine during your time in Buenos Aires, Kansas is your spot. Boisterous groups come here for barbecued pork ribs, chicken, and burgers and beers. This place offers the best Caesar salad in town; even the fries and bread are great, too. Its sprawling open dining area has comfy booths and dim lighting, but the place is anything but romantic. It does offer a view of the horse track next door, though. Expect to get your food fast, and encouraged to eat quickly. The rowdy bar has good drinks and is popular with fortysomething singles on the prowl. ✉*Av. Libertador 4625, Palermo* ☎*11/4776–4100* ⊟*AE, D, MC, V.* ✢*1:B1*

$$
INDIAN
Almagro

Katmandú. The most popular Indian restaurant in the city, Katmandú fills up every night with locals and expats looking for some spice. Chefs create tasty vindaloos and curries in full view. Consider sharing the tandoori or Indian sampling platter for two; then indulge in creamy and milky desserts. The food is consistently good, but pricey by local standards. The waitstaff is always one step behind and the ambience is a bit dreary. Reservations are recommended. ✉*Córdoba 3547, Almagro* ☎*11/4963–1122* ⊕*www.katmandu.restaurant.com.ar* ⊟*AE, MC, V* ✲*Closed Sun. No lunch.* ✢*1:D6*

$$$
ECLECTIC
Palermo Soho

Lelé de Troya. This is one of the most spectacularly unusual spaces in the city. Each room of this converted old house is drenched in a different color—from the walls to the chairs to the plates—and the food is just as bold. The kitchen can be viewed from the vine-covered lemon-yellow patio, and you can watch as loaf after loaf of the restaurant's homemade bread is drawn from the clay oven. Follow dishes like salmon ravioli or mollejas in cognac with one of Lelé's many Middle Eastern and Italian desserts. The restaurant holds tango classes on Monday nights and has a changing art space. ✉*Costa Rica 4901, Palermo Soho* ☎*11/4832–2726* ⊟*AE, MC, V.* ✢*1:C4*

$$$
THAI
Las Cañitas

Lotus Neo Thai. Buenos Aires' first Thai restaurant has been packing them in since 1994 to a homey hippie-ish upstairs apartment. Enormous flower decorations and trippy music seem straight out of *Alice in Wonderland,* and if you want, you can dine sitting on pillows on the floor. Tropical frozen cocktails hit the spot. For the main courses, the curries are best. Although the Thai food doesn't excel by international standards, it's a spicy break from the city's norm, and a good choice for vegetarians. ⊠*Ortega y Gasset 1782, Las Cañitas* 🕾*11/4771–4449* ⊕*www.restaurantelotus.com.ar* ⊟*AE, DC, MC, V* ⊘*Closed Sun. No lunch* Ⓜ*D to Ministro Carranza.* ✛*1:B1*

$$ **Malasaña.** You'll feel like you're eating inside a gigantic wine cellar
ARGENTINE in this dizzying architectural jumble of glass, stone, and creative spot
Palermo Soho lighting. (Okay, maybe a wine cellar from *Star Trek.*) The menu is varied and ambitious, and often good (try the mushroom risotto with duck confit, if available). It's equally, if not more, worthwhile to come just for a cocktail or a bottle of wine and to experience the cutting edge of Palermo Soho. ⊠*Honduras 5298, Palermo Soho* 🕾*11/4831–5812* ⊟*No credit cards* ⊘*Closed Sun. No lunch.* ✛*1:C5*

$$$ **Malevo.** Named for the villain of the tango, Malevo was the first eat-
ARGENTINE ery to bring sleek modern dining to the city's classic tango district.
Almagro The old corner building has large plate-glass windows and an inti-
mate slate-and-aubergine interior where lights are low and white linen
abounds. The house's excellent wine selection is on display behind a
polished wooden bar—savor a bottle with your *Rebelión en la Granja*
(pork with braised fennel and tapenade) or homemade goat-cheese
ravioli with sun-dried tomatoes and almonds. ⊠*Mario Bravo 908, at
Tucumán, Almagro* 🕾*11/4861–1008* ⊟*AE, D, MC, V* ⊘*Closed Sun.
No lunch Sat.* Ⓜ*B to Carlos Gardel.* ✛*1:D6*

$$$ **María Félix.** Housed in a beautifully restored three-story home in Pal-
MEXICAN ermo Soho, Maria Felix serves some of the best Mexican food in the
Palermo Soho city. The rooms are decorated with Mexican artwork and artifacts;
venture all the way to the roof garden if you want to dine alfresco. The
large menu covers all the Mexican basics; the enchiladas and mole are
delicious, as are the quasi-authentic margaritas, about the best you're
gonna get in a city some 6,400 km (4,000 mi) from the Mexican border.
⊠*Guatemala 5200, Palermo Soho* 🕾*11/4775–0380* ⊕*www.mariafe-
lix.com.ar* ⊟*AE, D, MC, V.* ✛*1:C4*

$ **Mark's.** The first deli to arrive in Palermo Viejo, Mark's big sandwiches
AMERICAN and salads have been steadily drawing crowds for all-day munching
Palermo Soho (it's open 8:30 AM–9:30 PM). It's also become something of a scene
☺ for twentysomethings with New York fetishes—and perhaps unsurprisingly, also a top choice for brunch. Ingredients are top quality,
combinations inventive, and the large variety of breads—the house
specialty—is baked on premise. Tastefully mismatched tables, chairs,
and sofas are available if you want to eat in; there's also a small patio
if you want some sun. The cheesecake in itself is an excuse for a visit.
Be warned though: service is always slow. ⊠*El Salvador 4701, Palermo
Soho* 🕾*11/4832–6244* ⊟*No credit cards.* ✛*1:C5*

$$ **La Maroma.** The specials in this chaotic *bodegón* (tavern-style restau-
ARGENTINE rant) are erratically scrawled on bits of paper stuck on the walls under
Almagro hams hanging from the ceiling, strings of garlic, and demijohns of wine.
The homemade pastas are excellent, especially the lasagna, and so are
the *milanesas*. Portions are large—don't be surprised if you can't finish

your order. ⊠*Mario Bravo 598, at Humahuaca, Almagro* ☎*11/4862–9308* ▤*AE, V* Ⓜ*B to Carlos Gardel.* ✛*2:C6*

$$ | **Matías.** Wash down a savory lamb stew or a chicken potpie with a brew
IRISH | at this cheery Irish pub, one of many in this neighborhood. The steaks
Centro | are excellent—try the *lomo relleno* (wrapped in bacon and served with plums) or the *lomo al bosque* (in a wild mushroom sauce). At night the place becomes quite a scene, especially for foreigners, expats, and office workers looking to down a few Guinness and party. They have live rock bands several nights a week, which can definitely distract from your dining experience. ⊠*Reconquista 701, Centro* ☎*11/4311–0327* ⊕*www.matiaspub.com.ar* ▤*AE, DC, MC, V* ☾*Closed Sun.* Ⓜ*C to San Martín.* ✛*2:D3*

$$$$ | **Le Mistral.** The superb dining room at the Four Seasons is warm, invit-
MEDI- | ing, and, well, Mediterranean—without any of the bright, antiseptic,
TERRANEAN | or stuffy qualities of competing hotel restaurants. Lobster is treated
Recoleta | with loving care, and the flavors on the menu are as often refreshingly subtle and delicate as they are bold. The restaurant pays particular care to Middle Eastern and Spanish cuisine, offering marinated lamb kabobs and tapas, like fried crab with a green apple puree. Reservations are recommended. ⊠*Four Seasons Hotel, Posadas 1086, Recoleta* ☎*11/4321–1730* ▤*AE, DC, MC, V.* ✛*2:C1*

$ | **Modena Design Café.** This spacious Internet café has an ultramodern
CAFÉ | techno feel and showcases Ferraris—not surprisingly, it attracts porteño
Recoleta | trendsetters. Log on while snacking on sushi, or nurse a *lagrima* (milk with a teardrop of coffee) while you sit back in an oversize chair. It's behind the Museo Nacional de Bellas Artes. ⊠*Av. Figueroa Alcorta 2270, Recoleta* ☎*11/4809–0122* ▤*AE, V.* ✛*$:G4*

$$ | **Munich Recoleta.** Jam-packed Munich Recoleta has been a favorite gath-
GERMAN | ering spot for half a century, and the menu has barely changed since
Recoleta | its 1956 opening. Premium cuts of meat, milanesas, creamed spinach, shoestring potatoes, and *chucrut* (cabbage) are served quickly and in generous portions. The reasonably priced wine list is enormous but well chosen. The lively atmosphere attracts young and old alike, despite the often cantankerous waiters. Arrive early to avoid a wait. Reservations are not accepted after 9 PM. ⊠*R.M. Ortíz 1879, Recoleta* ☎*11/4804–3981* ▤*AE, V* ☾*Closed Tues.* ✛*2:B1*

$ | **Na Serapia.** Na Serapia, across from Parque Las Heras, is well known for
ARGENTINE | its hearty authentic northern Argentine food. Creamy steamed *humitas,*
Palermo | made from cornmeal and fresh corn, are excellent, as are cheese-and-onion empanadas. Carafes of wine, like everything else, are a bargain. This is strictly no-frills—it's nothing but a basic room with a few little tables—but the food is consistently good. Don't miss the quirky wall art, which includes a portrait of the owner stabbed in the heart. ⊠*Av. Las Heras 3357, Palermo* ☎*11/4801–5307* ▤*No credit cards.* ✛*1:D4*

$$$$ | **Nectarine.** This high-flying temple to nouvelle French cuisine has an
FRENCH | eight-course tasting menu costing (at last check) 260 pesos. Every dish
Recoleta | on the menu is delicious, though occasionally overambitious. The wine

list is extraordinary. Set aside an entire evening for this gustatory trip, but expect to pay dearly for the experience, at least by local standards. The feeling in the second-floor room is formal, except for the open kitchen—a concession, perhaps, to the trends of modern high-concept dining. Reservations are recommended. ⊠*Pasaje del Correo, Vicente López 1661, Recoleta* ☎*11/4813–6993* ☰*AE, DC, MC, V* ⊘*Closed Sun. No lunch Sat.* ✛*2:B2*

$$$
ARGENTINE
Las Cañitas

Novecento. This bistro, which has branches in New York, Miami Beach, and Punta del Este, is going for a *newyorquino* feel, and as such, it has become a magnet for young, highbrow porteños. Snug, candlelit tables offer intimacy. The menu is eclectic, but it drifts toward Italian, and has definitely lost its edge in recent years. Try the pyramid of green salad, steak, and fries, or shrimp with bacon. Crème brûlée and "Chocolate Delight" are tempting desserts. The Sunday brunch is notable, and in summer you can dine outdoors. Interestingly, all the names of the dishes are in English, but the waitstaff consistently has trouble remembering what they mean. ⊠*Báez 199, Las Cañitas* ☎*11/4778–1900* ⊕*www.bistronovecento.com* ☰*AE, D, MC, V* Ⓜ*D to Ministro Carranza.* ✛*1:B2*

$
STEAK
La Boca

El Obrero. When the rock band U2 played Buenos Aires and asked to be taken to a traditional Argentine restaurant, they were brought to this legendary hole-in-the-wall. For 50 years El Obrero has served juicy grilled steaks, sweetbreads, sausages, and chicken. The extensive blackboard menu includes *rabas* (fried calamari) and puchero. Try the *budín de pan* (Argentine version of bread pudding). This spot is popular with tourists and local workmen alike, so expect a short wait. La Boca is sketchy at night, so lunch is preferable; in any case, take a taxi. ⊠*Augustín R. Caffarena 64, La Boca* ☎*11/4363–9912* ☰*No credit cards* ⊘*Closed Sun.* ✛*2:F6*

$$$
SCANDINAVIAN
Palermo
Hollywood

Ølsen. Ølsen is a showcase for Nordic flavors *and* contemporary Scandinavian design. Past the walled sculpture garden and white lounge chairs is a cavern of exposed-brick walls. Lime-green furniture and cowhide barstools lend a '70s feel. Best are the *smørrebrød* (open sandwiches) with different vodka shots (the vodka selection is impressive here); other starters like gravlax and *rösti* (crispy sautéed potatoes) are better than the often dry and underseasoned meat entrées. This is *the* place for Sunday brunch, where expats flock for scrambled eggs and bagels. ⊠*Gorriti 5870, Palermo Hollywood* ☎*11/4776–7677* ☰*AE, MC, V* ⊘*Closed Mon.* ✛*1:A3*

$$$$
SPANISH
Recoleta

Oviedo. First and foremost is the dreamy ambience—dim lamps that illuminate the room like meditative orbs, walls lined with tantalizing wine bottles and cozy window-front tables. And then there's the Spanish food, which makes virtuoso use of luxurious ingredients in dishes like foie gras ravioli and tenderly seared sea scallops. The tortilla is delicious, but deceptively filling. Don't miss the house specialty cochinillo (suckling pig). The waiters are polite, yet they always seem to be busy doing absolutely nothing, which means you'll likely wait for your plate to be cleared or to see the dessert menu. Reservations are recommended.

✉*Beruti 2602, at Ecuador, Recoleta* ☎*11/4821–3741* ⊕*www.oviedoresto.com.ar* ▭*AE, DC, MC, V* Ⓜ*D to Pueyrredón.* ✛*2:A2*

$ **El Palacio de la Papa Frita.** This
ARGENTINE longtime standby is popular for its
Centro fanciful old-world atmosphere and
hearty traditional meals—steaks,
pastas, and salads. The *papas
soufflé* (inflated french fries) reign
supreme; try them *à la provençal*
(sprinkled with garlic and parsley)
along with the classic *bife a medio
caballo* (steak topped with a fried

egg). You don't come here strictly for the service or the food, you come
here to soak in the porteño lifestyle. ✉*Lavalle 735, Centro* ☎*11/4393–
5849* Ⓜ*C to Lavalle* ✉*Av. Corrientes 1612, Centro, 1042* ☎*11/4374–
8063* Ⓜ*B to Callao* ▭*AE, DC, MC, V.* ✛*2:B4, 2:D3*

$$ **La Parolaccia.** A polite waitstaff serves some of the city's better Italian
ITALIAN fare in a warm, relaxing environment. Lasagna and other pasta dishes
Centro are well executed, as are the desserts, like tiramisu. The real reason to
go, though, is for the amazing-value three-course set lunch—including
a complimentary lemon digestif—which will set you back 25 pesos.
The company runs additional, equally good restaurants in Belgrano,
Palermo, and Puerto Madero. ✉*Riobamba 146, Centro* ☎*11/4812–
1053* ⊕*www.laparolaccia.com* ▭*AE, MC, V* Ⓜ*C to Congreso, B to
Callao.* ✛*2:B4*

$$$ **Patagonia Sur.** Knowledgeable local foodies know to trust Argentina's
ARGENTINE most famous chef, even if he decided to put a restaurant in La Boca,
La Boca a culinary no-man's land. Francis Mallman, the purveyor of all things
Fodor'sChoice Argentine, has created another great space to enjoy typical Argentine
★ fare with a flair. The menu is fairly straightforward: beef, fish, and
poultry prepared with hearty local vegetables, but what makes them so
good is that Mallman always uses the best cuts and ingredients available. The crab salad starter and ojo de bife are particularly good here.
You'll feel as if you're eating at a friend's home: books and blankets are
strewn about; antique furniture and glassware abound. ✉*Rocha 803,
La Boca* ☎*11/4303–5917* ⊕*www.restaurantepatagoniasur.com* ▭*AE,
D, MC, V* ⊗*Closed Mon. –Wed. No dinner Sun.* ✛*2:F6*

$$$ **La Pérgola.** On the third floor of the Sheraton Libertador hotel, this
ARGENTINE weekday, lunch-only restaurant caters to a local business crowd, serving an all-you-can-eat appetizer buffet that includes dozens of salads,
and then a fairly standard Euro-Argentine menu of meats and fishes.
Ask for the daily specials. ✉*Sheraton Libertador, Av. Córdoba 690,
Centro* ☎*11/4321–0000* ▭*AE, DC, MC, V* ⊗*Closed weekends. No
dinner* Ⓜ*C to Lavalle.* ✛*2:D3*

5

$$ **Piola.** The first Piola opened in Treviso, Italy, in 1986; this outpost is
PIZZA   the second. Although there are now replicas in Brazil, Chile, Miami,
Retiro   and New York, this branch has become a well-loved landmark, and for
☾   good reason: beneath the trendy, funky veneer—modern art, modern
music, and a palm-shaded garden—the imposing oven turns out the
best pizza in town. Crusts are perfectly seared, and sauce and toppings
are judiciously applied for an uncanny replica of the real Italian thing.
Don't miss the pizza with *muzzarella di bufala* (buffalo-milk mozza-
rella), which must be the most authentic in South America. ⊠*Libertad
1078, Retiro* ☎*11/4812–0690* ⊟*AE, DC, MC, V* Ⓜ*C to San Martín*
☾*Closed Sun. No lunch Sat.* ✛*2:C2*

$$ **Pippo.** Historic Pippo, open since 1942, is a porteño classic known for
ARGENTINE   its simplicity and down-to-earth cooking. Pastas like *tallarines* and rav-
Centro, Recoleta   ioli are the most popular choices, but also try the *estofado* (beef stew),
or *lomo* (sirloin) with fries. For dessert, flan is topped off with cream
or dulce de leche. It's in the heart of the Corrientes theater district; as
such, don't expect particularly attentive service. ⊠*Paraná 356, Centro,
1017* ☎*11/4374–6365* Ⓜ*B to Uruguay* ⊠*Av. Callao 1077, Recoleta*
☎*11/4812–4323* ⊟*MC, V.* ✛*2:B4, 2:B2*

$$$$ **Plaza Grill.** Wrought-iron lamps and fans hang from the high ceilings,
FRENCH   and delft tiles decorate the walls at this favorite spot of executives and
Retiro   politicians. Visiting dignitaries and local playmakers have been dining here since the turn of the 20th century. The feeling, as you might
expect, is formal. The wine list is extensive, and the European-centric
menu includes excellent steak, salmon with basil and red wine, and
pheasant with foie gras. Reservations are recommended. ⊠*Marriott
Plaza Hotel, Florida 1005, Retiro* ☎*11/4318–3000* ⊟*AE, DC, MC,
V* Ⓜ*C to San Martín.* ✛*2:D2*

$$ **El Pobre Luis.** It's worth a visit to this Belgrano parrilla just to see the
STEAK   impressive collection of sports memorabilia, especially soccer jerseys
Belgrano   autographed by some of the sport's legends. Fortunately, the food is
fantastic, too. Jovial owner Luis Acuna ("Poor Luis") is from Uru-
guay, and serves some of that country's signature dishes, like pamplona:
grilled meat, vegetables, cheese, and spices rolled into a wrap. This
place packs 'em in with a raucous clientele, and the service suffers as a
result, but the good food and fun atmosphere make it well worth the
trip. ⊠*Arribenos 2393, Belgrano* ☎*11/4780–5847* ⊟*AE, D, MC, V*
☾*Closed Sun.* ✛*1:B1*

$$$ **Pura Tierra.** When it opened in 2005, Pura Tierra brought a much
ARGENTINE   needed touch of style to Belgrano's surprisingly limited restaurant
Belgrano   offerings. The name means "pure earth" and chef-owner Martin Mol-
Fodor'sChoice   teni effectively creates new and interesting flavors using simple recipes
★   that pay homage to the culinary traditions of northern Argentina and
southern Patagonia. Its standard offerings of beef, chicken, pork, and
salmon each have a distinct flavor. A highlight is the pork loin cooked
with honey and served with grilled apples and pears. The restaurant is
housed in an old Belgrano home, with high ceilings, tiled floors, and
an array of antiques and classic furniture. ⊠*3 de Febrero 1167, Bel-*

grano ☎*11/4899–2007* ⊕*www.puratierra.com.ar* ▭*AE, D, MC, V* ☽*Closed Mon.* ✛*1:A1*

$$$ **Republica.** This fabulous new upstairs restaurant opened in late 2007
ARGENTINE and is run by two young and up-and-coming chefs, Maria Jose Moretti
Recoleta and Javier Hourquebie, who also happen to be a couple. Romantic
Fodor'sChoice lighting, hip mood music, and table seating in small alcoves create
★ a dreamy atmosphere in which to try an impressive variety of fusion
dishes made from Argentine staples like meat, pork, and chicken. But
the real reason to visit this place is the costillar de ternera en dos coc-
ciones, a mind-blowingly flavorful rack of tender ribs that will literally
melt in your mouth and leave you smiling for hours. ⊠*Vicente Lopez
1661, Local 6, Recoleta* ☎*11/4816–7744* ▭*AE, D, MC, V.* ✛*2:B1*

$$$ **Restó.** After training with two of the world's most renowned chefs—
ARGENTINE Spain's Ferran Adriá and France's Michel Bras—chef-owner María Bar-
Centro rutia came back to Buenos Aires and made a very big splash in this very
small space, hidden deep inside the Society of Architects. Her menu is
short, sweet, and reasonably priced. Three set-price menus pair exotic
ingredients like *codorniz* (quail) with Argentina's more-traditional
foods like *zapallo* (squash). They're all honored with classic European
treatments, including expertly reduced sauces. The molten chocolate
cake, adapted from Bras, is unforgettable. ⊠*Montevideo 938, Centro*
☎*11/4816–6711* ⌨*Reservations essential* ▭*No credit cards* ☽*Closed
weekends. No dinner Mon.–Wed.* Ⓜ*D to Callao.* ✛*2:B3*

$$ **Rio Alba.** In terms of quality, price, and charm, this is the best parrilla
STEAK in Buenos Aires. Period. It consistently serves the tastiest and most
Palermo tender cuts of beef. The asado de tira is particularly good, as is the
Fodor'sChoice flavorful entrana. Ask for a minigrill at your table to keep your meat
★ warm; you're going to need time to finish the enormous servings. The
old-school waiters wear vests and bow ties and refuse to write anything
down, but they always get the order right. This place is packed every
night of the week, with businesspeople and families. If you arrive after
9:30 PM, expect to wait for a table. The front room is no-smoking;
the back room allows smoking. ⊠*Cervino 4499, Palermo* ☎*11/4773–
5748* ▭*AE, D, MC, V.* ✛*1:D3*

$$$ **Sabot.** You might consider Sabot a find if you're a tourist—but this
ARGENTINE dignified, timeless lunchroom is part of daily life to the scores of down-
Centro town businesspeople who have been coming here for ages. Since the
1970s, they've been doing the same things, day after (week)day. This
means absolutely impeccable service, fresh centolla (crab), and a puchero that gets at the very essence of what boiled meat is all about. ⊠*25
de Mayo 756, between Cordoba and Viamonte, Centro* ☎*11/4313–
6587* ⌨*Reservations essential* ▭*AE, DC, MC, V* ☽*Closed weekends.
No dinner* Ⓜ*B to L.N. Alem.* ✛*2:E3*

$$$ **San Babila.** This trattoria is known for its excellent handmade pas-
ITALIAN tas and classic Italian dishes, created from the century-old recipes of
Recoleta the chef's grandmother. *Cappelletti di formaggio* (cheese-filled round
pasta) and *risotto alla milanese* (risotto and veal cutlet) are good bets.
Prices are high, but there are fixed-price menus to choose from and a

friendly English-speaking staff. The outdoor terrace is a treat. ⊠*R.M. Ortíz 1815, Recoleta* 🕾*11/4804–1214* ⊕*www.sanbabilaristorante. com.ar* 🗖*AE, DC, MC, V* ☯*No lunch Mon.* ✦*2:B2*

$
ARGENTINE
Recoleta
☾

El Sanjuanino. Northern Argentine fare is served at this long-established, if touristy, spot. El Sanjuanino is known citywide for its tamales, *humitas* (steamed corn cakes wrapped in husks), and especially its empanadas, which crowds of people line up to take out for a picnic in the park (they're 20% cheaper to go). But they also make good *locro, pollo a la piedra* (chicken pressed flat by stones), venison, and antelope stew. Skip the boring, hamlike *lomito de cerdo* (pork steak). The decor in the cozy space borders on cheesy, with hanging hams and a stuffed deer head, but the vibe is still fun. ⊠*Posadas 1515, at Callao, Recoleta* 🕾*11/4804–2909* 🗖*AE, MC, V* ☯*Closed Mon.* ✦*2:C1*

$$
MIDDLE
EASTERN
Palermo
☾

Sarkis. Filled with cane tables and chairs, this chaotic family-style restaurant produces great Middle Eastern food. You could easily fill yourself up on several dishes from the large selection of mezes, which are the restaurant's best work. Be sure to leave room for baklava and other dripping, nut-filled pastries. The place is technically in Villa Crespo, but it's only about a block from Palermo Soho, across Avenida Córdoba. Most nights there are belly dancers and palm readers wandering through the restaurant. Arrive early or expect to wait for a table. ⊠*Thames 1101, at Jufré, Palermo* 🕾*11/4772–4911* 🗖*No credit cards.* ✦*1:A5*

$$$
ARGENTINE
Belgrano

Sifones y Dragones. This place proudly boasts that it's "not a restaurant, it's a kitchen with tables" and the motto rings true. Don't come here for the service or cushy atmosphere. The room is basically a personal experimental cooking space for couple Flavio La Vitola and Mariana de Rosa, who turn out delicious and different meals in full view of customers five nights a week. The one large room is fitted with kitschy decorations and mismatched tables and chairs and other knickknacks. Much of the cuisine is Asian inspired, and often vegetarian friendly. French über-designer Philippe Starck is a big fan. ⊠*Ciudad de la Paz 174, Belgrano* 🕾*11/15–4413–9871* ⊕*www.sifonesydragones.com.ar* 🗖*No credit cards* ☯*Closed Sun. and Mon.* ✦*1:A2*

$$$$
SPANISH
Palermo

Sinclair. Humility is not one of chef-owner Ramiro Rodriguez Pardo's traits—the enormous painting of him that hangs next to the entrance should make that clear—but his food certainly gives him a right to boast. He has been one of Argentina's most famous chefs since the 1980s. Sinclair is a bright and beautiful modern space in a quiet enclave called Palermo Nuevo. His Spanish cuisine is perhaps the tastiest—and priciest—in the city. The truly extensive and impressive menu includes cold and warm starters such as delectable Spanish hams and the city's only salmon-and-crab empanada. The main dishes include rack of lamb, venison, rabbit stew, tuna, and Spanish favorites like suckling pig and paella. This place is not to be missed. ⊠*Sinclair 3096, Palermo* 🕾*11/4899–0283* ⊕*www.sinclairresto.com.ar* 🗖*AE, D, MC, V* ☯*Closed Sun.* ✦*1:C2*

$$$$ **647 Dinner Club.** The 1930s-Shanghai-meets-1970s-Los-Angeles vibe is
ARGENTINE made possible by black walls, smoky mirrors, pink furnishings, crystal
San Telmo chandeliers, and photos of hot naked women. It's a really cool place
to have a cocktail (the drink menu is impressive), but unfortunately,
the food disappoints. It's not for lack of trying, though. The menu is
large and imaginative, but ultimately, uninspired and overpriced. There
are some highlights, though. The duck strudel appetizer is tasty, as are
the various fish plates, including swordfish and pacu from the rivers
of northern Argentina. ✉*Tacuari 647, San Telmo* ☎*11/4331–3026*
🌐*www.club647.com* 🖃*AE, D, MC, V* ⊘*Closed Sun.* ✦*2:D6*

$$$ **Social Paraíso.** Simple, airy, friendly, elegant—this Med-Argentine bis-
ARGENTINE tro has just the vibe for a lunch or dinner stop after a cheery round
Palermo Soho of shopping. Pastas such as ravioli are best. Vegetarians will also be
happy here, with inventive entrées that feature meaty vegetables like
eggplant. Social Paraíso has kept its prices low even as its fame has
grown, and the two-course lunch for (at last check) 24 pesos is a gift.
It gets crowded and loud in here, but that adds to the charm. You
can practically sit inside the kitchen and watch the young cooks work
their magic. A small open-air patio fits a few tables; if the weather and
mood is right, ask to sit outside. ✉*Honduras 5182, Palermo Soho*
☎*11/4831–4556* 🌐*www.socialparaiso.com.ar* 🖃*AE, MC, V* ⊘*Closed
Mon. No dinner Sun.* ✦*1:B4*

$$ **Status.** Status has some of the best Peruvian food in town, and the warm
PERUVIAN but simple dining room feels like home, but there is one thing: staffers
Congreso can be aloof, so you have to be assertive. Go for the *ceviche de pescado*
(raw marinated fish) rather than the mixed-seafood version; the fish is
impeccably fresh. Good, too, are the *criollo* rice dishes, and potatoes
any which way. ✉*Virrey Cevallos 178, Congreso* ☎*11/4382–8531*
🖃*AE, MC, V* Ⓜ*A to Sáenz Peña.* ✦*2:B5*

$$$ **Sucre.** Though it's in somewhat of a no-man's land at the northern tip of
ARGENTINE a neighborhood known as Belgrano Chico, Sucre has become synony-
Belgrano mous with high-concept dining. The visual impact is immediate, from
the open kitchen that stretches the length of the airy, warehouselike
space to a catwalk that's suspended next to the dramatic floor-to-ceiling
wall of illuminated liquors. The menu is original and inspired, drawing
in elements from Asia with dishes like a spectacular citrus-and-soy-
laced *tiradito de pescado* (like a fusion ceviche). Equally impressive are
the duck ravioli and the beautifully designed desserts. Be warned: the
tables are far too close together, service is sketchy at times, and the roar
from the crowds can be deafening. ✉*Sucre 676, Belgrano* ☎*11/4782–
9082* 🌐*www.sucrerestaurant.com.ar* 🖃*AE, MC, V.* ✦*1:A1*

$$$$ **Le Sud.** The Sofitel's flagship eatery blows away every other French
FRENCH restaurant in Buenos Aires—and that's really saying something. Chef
Retiro Thierry Pszonka, the recipient of numerous culinary accolades in his
native France, came over a few years ago to contribute his own brand
of nouvelle cuisine to the Argentine dining landscape in this careful
and elegant dining room. The results have been nothing less than spec-
tacular, from an *amuse-bouche* of soothing chicken liver mousse to a

dish of sensationally tender braised sweetbreads glazed with a silky brown sauce. ⊠*Hotel Sofitel, Arroyo 841–849, Retiro* ☎*11/4831–0131* ⌕*Reservations essential* ▤*AE, DC, MC, V* ⊗*Closed Sun.* Ⓜ*C to San Martín.* ✛*2:D2*

$$$
JAPANESE
Las Cañitas
Puerto Madero

Sushi Club. The restaurants in this mini-chain beat the competition with an ever-present atmosphere of young, cutting-edge luxury. If there's a wait for a table in the dim, lively room—and there often is—you can expect to be served an aperitif while you wait. Sushi menus don't vary much in this city, and these joints are no exception; choose from dozens of variations on salmon, which is what they do best. The two Las Cañitas branches are strangely right near each other; the third is in Puerto Madero. ⊠*Ortega y Gasset 1812, Las Cañitas* ☎*810/2227–8744* Ⓜ*D to Ministro Carranza* ⊠*Báez 268, Las Cañitas* ☎*810/2227–8744* Ⓜ*D to Ministro Carranza* ⊠*Alicia M. de Justo 286, Puerto Madero* ☎*810/2227–8744* Ⓜ*B to L.N. Alem* ▤*AE, DC, MC, V.* ✛*1:B1, 1: B2, 2:E3*

$$$
SPANISH
San Telmo

Taberna Baska. Old-world decor and efficient service are hallmarks of this busy, no-nonsense Spanish restaurant whose loyal clientele keeps coming back year after year. Try typical dishes such as *chiripones en su tinta* (a variety of squid in ink) or *fideua de chipirones* (a saffron dish with baby squid that's like a noodle version of paella). Meals come served with four different Basque sauces. ⊠*Chile 980, San Telmo* ☎*11/4334–0903* ▤*AE, DC, MC, V* ⊗*Closed Mon. No dinner Sun.* Ⓜ*C to Independencia* ✛*2:D6.*

$$$
SPANISH
Retiro

Tancat. Who would have thought that this unassuming Catalan tapas restaurant in a calm part of downtown could be such a showstopper? Tancat's romantic, warmly lighted room has a mellow vibe, just the right balance of bustle, music, and noise; here awkward moments just don't seem possible. The food couldn't be more authentic if this were Barcelona. Begin with *pan con tomate* (grilled bread rubbed with garlic, olive oil, and tomato) paired with buttery Spanish ham. A rich stew of *callos* (tripe) and *gambas al ajillo* (garlic shrimp) enjoy equal success. Even the price is right. ⊠*Paraguay 645, Retiro* ☎*11/4312–5442* ▤*AE, DC, MC, V* ⊗*Closed Sun.* Ⓜ*C to San Martín* ✛*2:D3*

$$$
INDIAN
Barrio Norte

Tandoor. An excellent new choice for Indian food in Barrio Norte, Tandoor occupies a corner space in a beautiful French-style building dating back to the early 19th century. The rich red walls, simple white linens, and big windows make for a relaxing dining experience, and the food is tops, too. A variety of meat, chicken, and vegetable kebabs (cooked in the tandoor) and curries are spiced to taste; the lamb plates are also highly recommended, as is the naan. It's somewhat pricey, but because of the lack of Indian offerings in Buenos Aires, they can get away with it. ⊠*Laprida 1293, Barrio Norte* ☎*11/4821–3676* ⊕*www.tandoor.com.ar* ▤*AE, D, MC, V* ⊗*Closed Sun.* ✛*1:E5*

$$$
ECLECTIC
Palermo Soho

Te Mataré, Ramírez. Te Mataré Ramírez, which translates as "I Will Kill You, Ramirez," is as unusual as it sounds. This self-styled "erotic restaurant" seduces with such dishes as "You Surrender to My Intimate Perversions" (roast lamb with fennel, celery, quinoa, and cream hummus) and desserts such as "Do What I'm Doing to You" (a four-layer alfajor, with cocoa, peanut butter, and red tart sauce). Tuesday through Thursday the temperature rises with a tastefully done "erotic theater" show and Monday night brings live jazz and bossa nova. From behind the red velvet bar comes all variety of cocktails to sip as you peruse the illustrated menu or gaze at the restaurant's erotic art collection. ☒*Gorriti 5054, Palermo Soho* ☏*11/4831–9156* ⊕*www.tematareramirez.com* Ⓜ*D to Plaza Italia* ☒*Primera Junta 702, San Isidro* ☏*11/4747–8618* ⊟*AE, DC, MC, V* ⊗*No lunch.* ✛*1:D4, 2:F6*

$$$
ARGENTINE
Palermo
FodorsChoice
★

Thymus. Just over the border of Palermo Viejo into Villa Crespo, Thymus (the name of the gland from which sweetbreads are derived) is one of the more-ambitious restaurants in this ambitious culinary neighborhood. Even if the minimalist decor with its sparse stone artwork cries out New York City 1992, the feel is soothing and upscale. One of the best features here is the tasting menu, which allows each guest to sample small portions of two starters, two mains, and two desserts for around 80 pesos. Not everything on the ultramodern fusion menu works, but it's always interesting, and they have a particular way with duck breast. ☒*Lerma 525, at Malabia, Palermo* ☏*11/4772–1936* ⊟*AE, DC, MC, V* ⊗*Closed Sun. and Mon. No lunch.* ✛*1:B5*

$$$$
ARGENTINE
Centro

Tomo I. The famed Concaro sisters have made this restaurant, on the mezzanine of the Hotel Panamericano, a household name. The French-inspired menu has excellent fried, breaded calf brains, and a chocolate tart that oozes warm, dark ganache. White linen–covered tables are set far apart in the romantic red room, making quiet conversation easy, although the place does lack vibe. Service is arguably tops in the city. Reservations are recommended. ☒*Carlos Pellegrini 521, Centro* ☏*11/4326–6698* ⊕*www.tomo1.com.ar* ⊟*AE, DC, MC, V* ⊗*Closed Sun. No lunch Sat.* Ⓜ*B to Carlos Pellegrini, D to 9 de Julio.* ✛*2:C3*

$$
STEAK
Palermo
Hollywood

El Trapiche. The enormous *matambre de cerdo,* a thin grilled pork steak, is the juicy highlight at this busy parrilla. High ceilings hung with hams and walls stacked with wine contain a pleasant racket. Share a selection of barbecued meats, as most do, or have the *sorrentinos de calabaza al scarparo* (squash-filled fresh pasta in a spicy cream sauce) all to yourself. If you have room, finish with a fruit-filled crepe, flambéed at your table. The wine list is great. ☒*Paraguay 5099, Palermo Hollywood* ☏*11/4772–7343* ⊟*AE, DC, MC, V* Ⓜ*D to Estación Palermo.* ✛*1:B3*

$$
MEXICAN
Palermo Soho

Xalapa. Don't come here for the regional Mexican cuisine, but by all means come when you get a margarita craving. This tangerine-color restaurant serves up mostly Tex-Mex versions of tacos, burritos, and enchiladas, as well as ambitious dishes such as chicken *con mole* (a spicy, chocolaty sauce), all at reasonable prices, which appeal to the youthful crowd that floods the place on weekends. Dishes can be spiced up on request. ⊠*El Salvador 4800, Palermo Soho* ☎11/4833–6102 ═*No credit cards* ☉*No lunch weekdays.* ✢1:C5

$$$
JAPANESE
Centro

Yuki. Find your way through the unmarked door and you'll notice the Japanese clientele—no Palermo hipsters here. This is where foodies go to get great sushi. Even more impressive is the fresh fish, which includes interesting local white fishes like *lisi, reza,* and *pejerrey.* The fried fish is great, too. The *teishoku* dinners are interesting prix-fixe tasting menus, but if you just want raw fish, stick to a sushi combination platter or order à la carte. ⊠ *Pasco 740, between Independencia and Chile, Centro* ☎11/4942–7510 ═*AE, MC, V* Ⓜ*E to Pichincha.* ✢2:A5

Buenos Aires Dining & Lodging Atlas

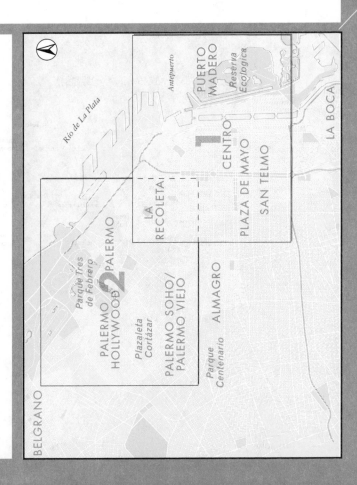

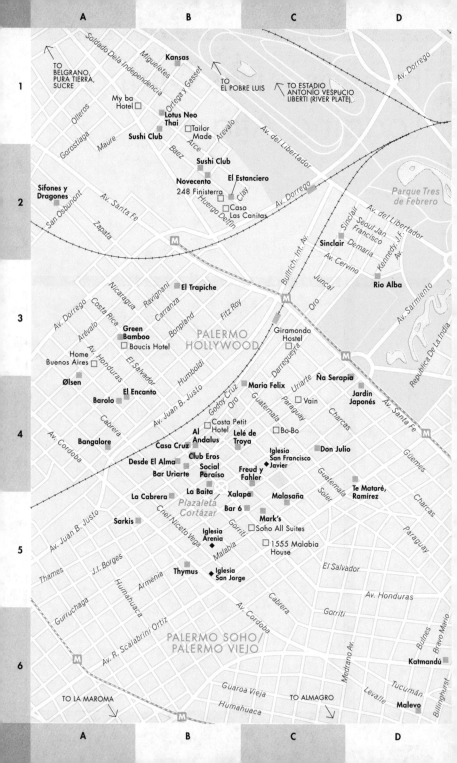

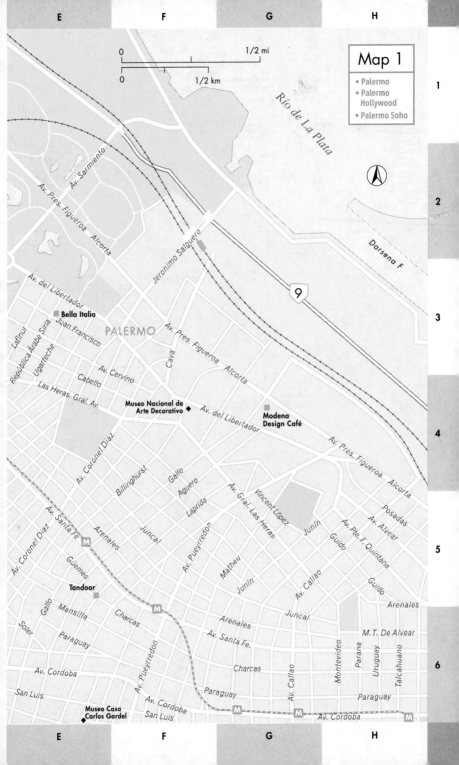

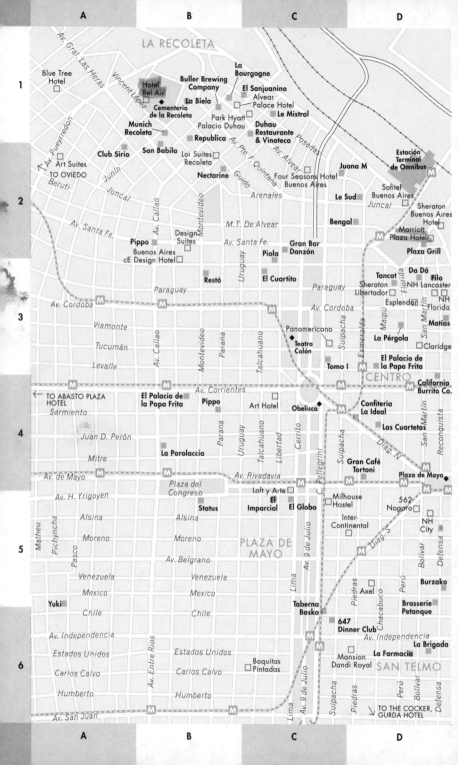

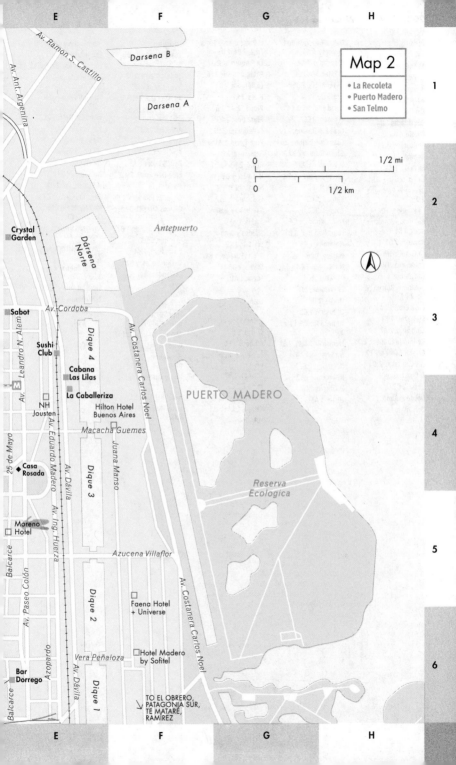

Dining

647 Dinner Club, 2:D6
Al Andalus, 1:B4
La Baita, 1:B4
Bangalore, 1:A4
Bar 6, 1:C5
Bar Dorrego, 2:E6
Bar Uriarte, 1:B4
Barolo, 1:A4
Bella Italia, 1:E3
Bengal, 2:D2
La Biela, 2:B1
La Bourgogne, 2:B1
Brasserie Petanque, 2:D5
La Brigada, 2:D6
Buller Brewing Company, 2:B1
Burzako, 2:D5
La Caballeriza, 2:E4
Cabaña Las Lilas, 2:E3
La Cabrera, 1:B5
California Burrito Co, 2:D4
Casa Cruz, 1:B4
Club Eros, 1:B4
Club Sirio, 2:B2
Confitería La Ideal, 2:D4
Crystal Garden, 2:E2
Las Cuartetas, 2:D4
El Cuartito, 2:C3
DaDá, 2:D3
Desde El Alma, 1:B4
Don Julio, 1:C4

Duhau Restaurante & Vinoteca, 2:C1
El Encanto, 1:A4
El Estanciero, 1:B2
La Farmacia, 2:D6
Filo, 2:D3
Freud y Fahler, 1:C4
El Globo, 2:C5
Gran Bar Danzón, 2:C2
Gran Café Tortoni, 2:D4
Green Bamboo, 1:A3
El Imparcial, 2:C5
Jardín Japonés, 1:D4
Juana M, 2:D2
Kansas, 1:B1
Katmandú, 1:D6
Lelé de Troya, 1:C4
Lotus Neo Thai, 1:B1
Malasaña, 1:C5
Malevo, 1:D6
María Félix, 1:C4
Mark's, 1:C5
La Maroma, 2:C6
Matías, 2:D3
Le Mistral, 2:C1
Modena Design Café, 1:G4
Munich Recoleta, 2:B1
Ña Serapia, 1:D4
Nectarine, 2:B2
Novecento, 1:B2
El Obrero, 2:F6
Ølsen, 1:A3
Oviedo, 2:A2

El Palacio de la Papa Frita, 2:B4, 2:D3
La Parolaccia, 2:B4
Patagonia Sur, 2:F6
La Pérgola, 2:D3
Piola, 2:C2
Pippo , 2:B4, 2:B2
Plaza Grill, 2:D2
El Pobre Luis, 1:B1
Pura Tierra, 1:A1
Republica, 2:B1
Restó, 2:B3
Rio Alba, 1:D3
Sabot, 2:E3
El Sanjuanino, 2:C1
San Babila, 2:B2
Sarkis, 1:A5
Sifones y Dragones, 1:A2
Sinclair, 1:C2
Social Paraíso, 1:B4
Status, 2:B5
Sucre, 1:A1
Le Sud, 2:D2
Sushi Club , 1:B2, 2: E3, 1:B1
Taberna Baska, 2:D6
Tancat, 2:D3
Tandoor, 1:E5
Te Mataré, Ramírez, 1: D4, 2:F6
Thymus, 1:B5
Tomo I, 2:C3
El Trapiche, 1:B3
Xalapa, 1:C5
Yuki, 2:A5

Lodging

1555 Malabia House, 1:C5
248 Finisterra, 1:B2
562 Nogaro, 2:D5
Abasto Plaza Hotel, 2:A4
Alvear Palace Hotel, 2:B1
Art Hotel, 2:C4
Art Suites, 2:A2
Axel, 2:D5
Baucis Hotel, 1:A3
Blue Tree Hotel, 2:A1
Bo-Bo, 1:C4
Boquitas Pintadas, 2:C6
Buenos Aires cE Design Hotel, 2:B2
Casa Las Canitas, 1:B2
Claridge, 2:D3
Costa Petit, 1:B4
Design Suites, 2:B2
Esplendor Buenos Aires, 2:D3
Faena Hotel + Universe, 2:F5
Four Seasons Hotel Buenos Aires, 2:C2
Giramondo Hostel, 1:C3
Gurda Hotel, 2:D6
Hilton Hotel Buenos Aires, 2:F4
Home Buenos Aires, 1:A3
Hotel Bel Air, 2:B1
Hotel Madero by Sofitel, 2:F6

InterContinental, 2:D5
Loft & Arte, 2:C4
Loi Suites Recoleta, 2:B2
Mansion Dandi Royal, 2:D6
Marriott Plaza Hotel, 2:D2
Milhouse Hostel, 2:C5
Moreno Hotel, 2:E5
My ba Hotel, 1:B1
NH City & Tower, 2:D5
NH Florida, 2:D3
NH Jousten, 2:E4
NH Lancaster, 2:D3
Panamericano, 2:C3
Park Hyatt Palacio Duhau, 2:C1
Sheraton Buenos Aires Hotel, 2:D2
Sheraton Libertador, 2:D3
Sofitel Buenos Aires, 2:D2
Soho All Suites, 1:C5
Tailor Made, 1:B1
The Cocker, 2:D6
Vain, 1:C4

Where to Stay

Home Hotel Buenos Aires

WORD OF MOUTH

"Is it me, or does Buenos Aires (especially Palermo and San Telmo) have an abundance of really cool-looking boutique hotels/B&Bs? We travel a lot and don't get too excited about vacations anymore, but this one has us totally hyped."

—mjz kc

THE SCENE

By Brian
Byrnes

Buenos Aires is experiencing a tourism boom unlike any in its history. The cheap peso has made it one of the most affordable big cities, and dollar- and euro-wielding visitors are arriving in record numbers. How is this good news in terms of where to stay? There are many new hotels, and existing ones have been renovated, so you have more choices than ever.

The real buzz these days is about boutique hotels, which have been popping up all over the city, but especially in the hot spots of San Telmo and Palermo. Most of them combine a minimalist vibe to contrast the renovated spaces in which they're housed. Most are outfitted with sleek furniture, wood-paneled walls and floors, quaint outdoor gardens with reclining lounge chairs, bamboo and plants, and the requisite pool or *parrilla* (steak house). It's a style that has been perfected in Buenos Aires in recent years, and one the city can call all its own.

In San Telmo, hotels are primarily grand old mansions with soaring ceilings and impressive wooden doors. Tango is big in this neighborhood, and some hotels here cater to tango tourists.

Centro and Puerto Madero are teeming with international hotel chains, and most of them are well located. But as is the case in any Sheraton or Hilton or Marriott around the globe, once you close your door, it's easy to forget where you are.

Across town in Palermo, it's a hipper, more-urbane feel. These places are so new they haven't had time to develop their own character yet, but just like the city itself, this constant cyclical reinvention is what makes everything so enchanting here.

WHERE SHOULD I STAY?

	NEIGHBORHOOD VIBE	PROS	CONS
CENTRO + ENVIRONS	The center of it all; you have a little bit of everything here from history (Retiro and Congreso) to modernity (Puerto Madero). It buzzes by day, but is quiet at night.	Close to all major city sights; good transportation options to other parts of the city. If you're only in town briefly, this is your place.	Certain areas are loud, chaotic, dirty, and deserted at night, which can make them dangerous. Don't walk around alone.
LA BOCA + SAN TELMO	The oldest barrios in the city, you can get a real feel of how Buenos Aires has operated for the past 100-plus years.	Old-world charm: cobblestone streets, corner cafés, tango music fills the air. You're sure to meet some interesting characters in this area.	Streets are dark and not well policed. Limited public transportation options. Locals have been known to prey on tourists.
RECOLETA/ BARRIO NORTE/AL- MAGRO	The most upscale area of the city, home to Argentina's high society. Certain enclaves will make you think you're in Paris.	International and local designers have shops here. It's safe, friendly, and chic. Great eating options and art galleries abound.	Prices are sometimes inflated for foreigners. Streets and sights are often crowded with tourists; you're likely to hear more English and Portuguese being spoken than Spanish.
PALERMO	The biggest neighborhood in the city; it's a mix of old family homes, soaring new towers, and renovated warehouses.	It's the undisputed hot spot of Buenos Aires' gastronomic scene. The city's biggest park, polo field, horse track, and casino are also here.	The über-cool attitude of some of the local hipsters can be a turnoff. Some quality-of-life issues like clean sidewalks and quiet streets have been sacrificed by the recent lightning-fast property developments.
BELGRANO/ LAS CAÑITAS	Quiet, leafy, upscale family neighborhoods that are home to embassies, schools, and universities. A strong British influence can be felt in the architecture and attitude of many of its inhabitants.	Fantastic restaurants and bars in Las Cañitas. Stately, unique homes in Belgrano. In certain areas it's easy to forget you're in a mega-metropolis.	In other areas, the main thoroughfares are packed with noisy city buses and reckless messengers on motorcycles. You're far from the downtown action.

6

WHERE TO STAY PLANNER

Strategy

Where should we stay? With hundreds of hotels to choose from, it may seem like a daunting question. But fret not—our expert writers and editors have done most of the legwork. The selections here represent the best lodging this city has to offer—from budget motels to luxury hotels. Scan Best Bets on the following pages for top recommendations by price and experience. Or locate a specific review in the listings. They're organized alphabetically within each neighborhood. Happy hunting!

What to Expect

Buenos Aires has chain hotels, boutique hotels, apart-hotels (short-term rental apartments), bed-and-breakfasts, hostels—you name it. World-class facilities include the majestic Alvear Palace Hotel, the ultra-hip Faena Hotel + Universe, and the luxurious Four Seasons—all celebrity favorites. High season includes the summer months of mid-December through February and the winter holidays that fall in July. Most hotels try to have at least one English-speaking employee on call at a given time.

Reservations

Due to Buenos Aires' increasing popularity, it's not just the high season that sees full capacity; spring and fall months can also be quite busy. It's always best to make a reservation with as early as possible. Most hotels in the city have Web sites where they accept online reservations. Some require a credit card.

Services

In general, hotels have bidets (a nod to the Continent) and high-speed Internet, but not, say, ice makers or vending machines (a nod to the fact that South Americans have different ideas about creature comforts from their neighbors to the north). Although Internet access is available in nearly every hotel in the city, the kind of access varies. Surprisingly, many of the international chains have not yet made Wi-Fi available in all rooms, and some of those that do provide it charge a fee. Most boutique hotels have Wi-Fi throughout and don't charge extra for the service. Cable television coverage is in constant flux in Argentina, so your hotel may or may not have English-language news channels, like CNN or BBC.

Check-in/out

As a rule, check-in is after 3 PM, check-out before noon; smaller hotels tend to be more flexible.

Parking

Driving in Buenos Aires is more trouble than it's worth for a tourist. The city streets are clogged and chaotic, and parking is scarce. So renting a car during your stay really isn't a good idea; public transportation and taxis can get you anywhere you want to go. If you do have a car, some hotels do provide parking, but it may be off-site, and they will likely charge a fee, likely a minimum of 50 pesos a day.

Family Travel

International chain hotels are always the most family-friendly, often providing booster seats, changing tables, roll-away beds, or other kids necessities. The smaller boutique hotels that are all the rage in Buenos Aires these days generally don't cater to families with children. Although none has a "no-kids" policy, it's best to ask ahead about exactly what your stay may be like with children in tow.

Prices

Though some small Argentine-owned hotels advertise their rates in pesos, most places cite them in dollars. That said, always confirm which currency is being quoted. If a hotel staffer tries to take a peso room rate and slap a dollar or euro sign on it, politely remind him or her that price gouging is a no-no and ask to speak to a manager. Unless there's a clearly advertised special for Argentine citizens, prices are the same for all visitors, regardless of nationality. The lodging tax is 21%; this may or may not be included in a rate, so always ask about it up front. Most prices include breakfast, although with the exception of the most expensive hotels, this always means continental, usually pastries, fruit, meats, and cheese. Be sure to ask when making a reservation. As a rule, Argentines don't eat big breakfasts.

WHAT IT COSTS IN ARGENTINE PESOS

¢	$	$$	$$$	$$$$
under 200	201–450	451–700	701—1000	over 1000

Hotel prices are for two people in a standard double room in high season.

6

BEST BETS

Fodor's offers a selective listing of quality lodging experiences at every price range, from the city's best budget motel to its most-sophisticated luxury hotel. Here we've compiled our top recommendations by price and experience. The very best properties—in other words, those that provide a particularly remarkable experience in their price range—are designated in the listings with the Fodor's Choice logo.

FODOR'S CHOICE ★

Alvear Palace Hotel, p. 216

The Cocker, p. 215

Faena Hotel + Universe, p. 208

Four Seasons Hotel Buenos Aires, p. 218

Gurda Hotel, p. 215

Marriott Plaza Hotel, p. 210

Moreno Hotel, p. 216

NH City + Tower, p. 211

Park Hyatt Palacio Duhau, p. 219

Tailor Made, p. 222

BY PRICE

¢

Boquitas Pintadas, p. 214

Giramondo Hostel, p. 220

Milhouse Hostel, p. 210

$

Art Suites, p. 217

The Cocker, p. 215

Gurda Hotel, p. 215

Hotel Bel Air, p. 218

$$

Home Buenos Aires, p. 221

Mansion Dandi Royal, p. 215

Marriott Plaza Hotel, p. 210

Moreno Hotel, p. 216

Tailor Made, p. 222

$$$

Axel Hotel Buenos Aires, p. 214

Hotel Madero by Sofitel, p. 209

InterContinental, p. 209

NH City & Tower, p. 211

Panamericano, p. 212

$$$$

Alvear Palace Hotel, p. 216

Faena Hotel + Universe, p. 208

Four Seasons Hotel Buenos Aires, p. 218

Park Hyatt Palacio Duhau, p. 219

Sofitel Buenos Aires, p. 214

BY EXPERIENCE

BEST RESTAURANT

Alvear Palace Hotel, p. 216

Bo-Bo, p. 219

Sofitel Buenos Aires, p. 214

BEST COCKTAILS

Claridge Hotel, p. 207

Home Buenos Aires, p. 221

Marriott Plaza Hotel, p. 210

BEST VIEWS

NH City & Tower, p. 211

Soho All Suites, p. 221

Panamericano, p. 212

BEST TO FEEL LIKE A LOCAL

Art Hotel, p. 217

My ba Hotel, p. 222

248 Finisterra, p. 223

BEST TO SEE AND BE SEEN

Faena Hotel + Universe, p. 208

Home Buenos Aires, p. 221

Hotel Madero by Sofitel, p. 209

BEST PLACE FOR TANGO JUNKIES

Abasto Plaza, p. 216

Gurda Hotel, p. 215

Mansion Dandi Royal, p. 215

BEST DESIGN

Axel Hotel Buenos Aires, p. 214

The Cocker, p. 215

Moreno Hotel, p. 216

BEST CONCIERGE

BoBo, p. 219

Buenos Aires cE Design Hotel, p. 207

Faena Hotel + Universe, p. 208

BEST FOR BUSINESS

Hilton Hotel, p. 208

Sheraton Buenos Aires Hotel, p. 212

Sheraton Libertador, p. 212

BEST FOR ROMANCE

Alvear Palace Hotel, p. 216

Four Seasons Hotel Buenos Aires, p. 218

Park Hyatt Palacio Duhau, p. 219

CENTRO & ENVIRONS

$$ **Buenos Aires cE Design Hotel.** This hotel drips with coolness. The lobby's glass floor looks down to a small pool, just one example of the transparency theme that runs throughout. Floor-to-ceiling windows afford amazing views, and mirrors are placed for maximum effect. Rooms feel like pimped-out Tribeca lofts, with rotating flat-screen TVs that let you watch from bed or from one of the leather recliners. Mattresses are high and mighty and covered in shades of brown and orange. Kudos go to the architect, Ernesto Goransky, who also did the Design Suites next door. **Pros:** Supermodern and spacious suites; great location. **Con:** The basement lounge feels like, well, a basement. ⊠*Marcelo T. Alvear 1695, Centro, 1060* ☎*11/5237–3100* ⊕*www.designce.com* ⊅*21 rooms, 7 suites* ♿*In-room: safe, kitchen, Ethernet, Wi-Fi. In-hotel: bar, pool, gym, laundry service, public Wi-Fi* ☐*AE, DC, MC, V* Ⓜ*D to Callao.*

$$ **Claridge.** Long white columns front the entrance, beyond which is the high-ceiling lobby and a traditional British café and piano bar. The red-brick building dates from 1946 and was built with an Anglo-Argentine clientele in mind; that feeling lingers in the spacious, elegant rooms with their bright floral patterns and wood paneling. The pool and spa are ideal for chilling out after a long porteño night. **Pros:** Just blocks from shopping on Florida Street; lobby bar serves up superb, stiff cocktails. **Cons:** Clientele is homogeneous—almost all retirement-age; bathrooms are small. ⊠*Tucumán 535, Centro, 1049* ☎*11/4314–7700, 800/223–5652 in U.S.* ⊕*www.claridge.com.ar* ⊅*152 rooms, 6 suites* ♿*In-room: safe, refrigerator, Ethernet, Wi-Fi. In-hotel: restaurant, room service, bar, pool, gym, spa, concierge, laundry service, airport shuttle, no-smoking rooms* ☐*AE, DC, MC, V* ⦿❘*BP* Ⓜ*C to San Martín.*

$$ **Design Suites.** A well-located, modern, minimalist hotel that's also reasonably priced is not an easy thing to find in Buenos Aires. This is it. The futuristic lobby cranks chilled-out electronic music and has a slim little swimming pool that's often used for photo shoots with even slimmer models. Sleek rooms have wooden floors, chrome furniture, and kitchenettes with espresso machines. The cheerful staff are tops at giving you a local's perspective on the best sites to visit. You're close to excellent shopping on Avenida Santa Fe and the stately Palacio Pizzurno. **Pros:** Cool, clean, and classy; a lobby art gallery showcases works by up-and-coming local painters. **Cons:** The gym is several blocks away; loud city buses linger out front during rush hour. ⊠*M.T. de Alvear 1683, Centro, 1060* ☎*11/4814–8700* ⊕*www.designsuites. com* ⊅*58 rooms* ♿*In-room: safe, kitchen (some), Ethernet, dial-up, Wi-Fi. In-hotel: restaurant, room service, bar, pool, laundry service* ☐*AE, DC, MC, V* Ⓜ*D to Callao.*

$$ **Esplendor Buenos Aires.** This iconic building is home to downtown's brashest new hotel. The Esplendor calls upon Argentine icons—Eva Perón, Che Guevara, Jorge Luis Borges, among others—to remind you just where you are; their enormous portraits line the walls of the lobby and art gallery. The rooms are high-ceilinged and large and are decorated in muted grays and whites. Splashes of color are found in the funky throw rugs, meshlike headboards, sparkly pillows, and abstract paintings. This is one of the few downtown hotels that makes a bold modernist statement, all the while gazing fondly back at Argentina's storied past. **Pros:** The suites have in-room Jacuzzis and comfy chaise lounges. **Con:** The open-air hallways have a corporate feel. ⊠*San Martin 780, Centro, 1004* ☎*11/5256–8800* ⊕*www.esplendorbuenosaires. com* ⌐*23 rooms, 28 suites* ⌂*In-room: safe, Ethernet, Wi-Fi. In-hotel: restaurant, bar, concierge, laundry service, parking (fee), no-smoking rooms* ⊟*AE, DC, MC, V* Ⓜ*C to San Martin.*

$$$$ **Faena Hotel + Universe.** Argentine fashion impresario Alan Faena and
Fodor's Choice famed French architect Philippe Starck set out to create a "universe"
★ unto itself, and they have succeeded in spades. Entering the long, tall hall transforms you to another place and time; it's a space so truly unique, it's almost as if the air is different inside. Rooms are feng shui perfect with rich reds and crisp whites. Velvet curtains and Venetian blinds open electronically to river and city views; marble floors fill expansive baths; velvet couches, leather armchairs, flat-screen TVs, and surround-sound stereos lend more luxury. The "Experience Managers" are basically personal assistants, making reservations and tending to every whim. Other highlights are two excellent restaurants and an elaborate spa with a Turkish bath. In El Cabaret, a blood-red music box dotted with red leather couches, you can swig champagne and watch sensual tango shows. Next door in the Library Lounge you never know who might show up: Coldplay and local rock legend Charly Garcia once held an impromptu jam session around the piano, playing Beatles songs until the wee hours. **Pro:** Quite simply, one of the most exhilarating hotels on the planet. **Con:** An "are you cool enough?" vibe is ever-present. ⊠*Martha Salotti 445, Puerto Madero, 1107* ☎*11/4010–9000* ⊕*www.faenahotelanduniverse.com* ⌐*110 rooms, 16 suites* ⌂*In-room: safe, DVD, Ethernet, dial-up, Wi-Fi. In-hotel: 2 restaurants, room service, bars, pool, gym, concierge, laundry service, parking (fee), no-smoking rooms* ⊟*AE, DC, MC, V.*

$$ **562 Nogaro.** The gigantic red neon sign outside may need a face-lift, but the rest of this downtown hotel—open since 1936—is in decent shape. The Nogaro attracts a diverse crowd from around the world, including Irish backpackers, Asian businessmen, and provincial Argentines. Although the rooms are nothing special and a bit tired, they are clean, bright, and have huge wooden closets and original parquet floors. Ask for a room on the avenue-side of the building, which is fronted by pretty jacaranda trees and has direct views of the imposing Buenos Aires City legislature building. **Pro:** Breakfast includes an omelet bar, a rarity in Buenos Aires. **Con:** The rooms and bathrooms are small by modern standards. ⊠*Av. Julio A. Roca 562, Centro, 1067* ☎*11/4331–0091* ⊕*www.562nogaro.com* ⌐*120 rooms, 16 suites* ⌂*In-room: safe, Wi-Fi. In-hotel: room service, bar, gym, concierge, laundry service, parking (fee), no-smoking rooms* ⊟*AE, DC, MC, V* Ⓜ*E to Bolivar.*

$$ **Hilton Hotel Buenos Aires.** This massive glass-and-steel structure puts you
☽ close to downtown *and* the restaurants and fresh air of Puerto Madero. In the atrium lobby, exposed glass elevators and wraparound hallways

are unique and dizzying at times. Rooms have big beds, walk-in closets, and large desks with stationery and magazines. Turndown service always includes delicious little chocolates. The rooftop pool is a great place to sip a fruit smoothie, stare at the skyline, and chat with the many flight attendants and businessmen who stay here. **Pros:** It's well priced, well run, and well located. **Con:** It's popular with conventioneers and cruise ship groups, which often means lots of people try to check in and out at the same time. ⊠*Macacha Guemes 351, Puerto Madero, 1106* ☎*11/4891–0000, 800/774–1500 in U.S.* ⊕*www. hilton.com* ⌨*418 rooms, 13 suites* ⌂*In-room: safe, Ethernet (fee), dial-up. In-hotel: restaurant, room service, bars, pool, gym, concierge, laundry service, public Wi-Fi, parking (fee), no-smoking rooms* ⊟*AE, DC, MC, V* ⍾*BP.*

$$$ **Hotel Madero by Sofitel.** This slick hotel is within walking distance of downtown as well as the riverside ecological reserve, and is a favorite for visiting British rock stars and fashion photographers. The big, bright, modern rooms have wood accents and white color schemes. Many rooms also have fantastic views of the docks and city skyline. The restaurant, Red, serves great Argentine–French fusion cuisine in an intimate setting. The breakfast buffet features exotic fresh fruits and Argentine baked goods. The lobby bar attracts a cool after-office crowd and has some of the most original cocktails in the city. **Pro:** They offer afternoon dance classes, where you can learn salsa, samba, and tango. **Con:** The gym and pool are in cramped quarters. ⊠*Rosario Vera Penaloza 360, Dique 2, Puerto Madero, 1007* ☎*11/5776–7777* ⊕*www. hotelmadero.com* ⌨*165 rooms, 28 suites* ⌂*In-room: safe, Ethernet, dial-up. In-hotel: restaurant, room service, bar, pool, gym, laundry service, public Wi-Fi* ⊟*AE, DC, MC, V.*

$$$ **InterContinental.** The hotel is lovely, but the location is lousy. After the office workers head home, the area is desolate; it's also on the fringe of some sketchy streets where it's ill advised to venture at night. Taxis are the way to go. By day, though, you can readily explore the quaint antiques shops, restaurants, and tango halls of nearby San Telmo. Rooms are modern, spacious, and equipped with sleeper chairs. The lobby bar is a great place for a drink; if the weather's right, sit in the courtyard, where you can forget you're in a concrete jungle. **Pro:** Smart staff knows how to handle expectations of foreign visitors. **Cons:** Lower floors have limited views; surrounding area can be dangerous at night. ⊠*Moreno 809, Centro, 1091* ☎*11/4340–7100* ⊕*www.ichotels group.com* ⌨*309 rooms, 8 suites* ⌂*In-room: safe, Ethernet, dial-up. In-hotel: 2 restaurants, room service, bar, pool, gym, concierge, laun-*

dry service, public Wi-Fi, parking (fee), no-smoking rooms ⊟*AE, DC, MC, V* ⦿*BP* Ⓜ*E to Belgrano.*

$ **Loft & Arte.** This family-run property is home to 25 suites in a building that dates back to 1890. It's a block from the Paris-esque Avenida de Mayo and surrounded by fantastic Spanish restaurants. The rooms—lofts, duplexes, and triplexes—are a hodgepodge of styles and designs, all featuring artwork (for sale) by local artists. There's a cute orange-color breakfast room and a quiet outside garden patio with a fountain and goldfish. It's a perfect spot for art lovers and tourists who revel in unique and unusual lodgings. This mazelike building will keep you guessing what's around every corner. **Pros:** Good price and good downtown location; the property also offers long-term rentals. **Con:** Many of the furnishings and bedding have seen better days and could stand to be replaced. ⊠*Hipolito Yrigoyen 1194, Centro, 1086* ☎*11/4381–3229* ⊕*www.loftyarte.com.ar* ⌑*25 rooms* ⌂*In-room: safe, kitchen, refrigerator, dial-up, Wi-Fi . In-hotel: concierge, laundry service, parking (fee)* ⊟*AE, DC, MC, V* Ⓜ*A to Lima.*

$$ ~~**Marriott Plaza Hotel.**~~ This Buenos Aires landmark brims with old-school style. Built in 1909 and renovated in 2003, the hotel sits at the top of pedestrian-only Florida Street and overlooks the leafy Plaza San Martín. The elegant lobby, crystal chandeliers, and swanky cigar bar evoke Argentina's opulent, if distant, past. Rooms are comfortable and clean, if not particularly spacious. The hotel is next to both the Kavanagh Building, a 1930s art deco masterpiece that was once South America's tallest, and the Basilica Santísimo Sacramento, where renowned Argentines of all stripes, like Diego Maradona, have tied the knot. Exploring the myriad nooks and crannies of this grand old hotel is part of its timeless appeal. **Pros:** Great prices; every area of the building offers a unique and fascinating view of the city. **Cons:** The main lobby is small and often gets crowded; check-in can be a lengthy process. ⊠*Florida 1005, Centro, 1005* ☎*11/4318–3000, 800/228–9290 in U.S.* ⊕*www.marriott.com* ⌑*313 rooms, 12 suites* ⌂*In-room: safe, Ethernet (fee). In-hotel: 2 restaurants, room service, bar, pool, gym, concierge, laundry service, public Wi-Fi* ⊟*AE, DC, MC, V* ⦿*BP* Ⓜ*C to San Martín.*

Fodor'sChoice
★

¢ **Milhouse Hostel.** This lovely and lively hostel goes the extra mile to make backpackers feel welcome with pool tables, televisions, and concierge services. The house, which dates from the late 1800s, has been tricked out with funky artwork and accessories. Its three floors overlook a beautiful tiled patio and all lead out to a sunny terrace, which the hostel skillfully uses to entertain guests, regardless of their interests. Morning yoga classes may well be followed by rowdy beer-swilling *asados* (barbecues). The dorm rooms are clean and big, and most have private bathrooms. At night, the surrounding streets can be dodgy, so take precautions. **Pros:** Fun and funky place; it's ideal for hooking up with travelers from around the world; close to all of San Telmo's nighttime offerings. **Cons:** It's a hostel; hygiene standards are sometimes below par. ⊠*Hipólito Irigoyen 959, Centro, 1086* ☎*11/4345–9604 or 11/4343–5038* ⊕*www.milhousehostel.com* ⌑*13 private rooms, 150 beds total* ⌂*In-room: no a/c, no phone, no TV, Ethernet, Wi-Fi. In-*

hotel: restaurant, bar, laundry facilities, parking (fee) ⊟*No credit cards* ⏼⏽*CP* Ⓜ*A to Piedras, C to Av. de Mayo.*

$$$ **NH City & Tower.** This enormous art deco hotel is a throwback to an
FodorsChoice earlier era. It would be the perfect image for a cover of Ayn Rand's *The*
★ *Fountainhead.* Inside, molded pillars support a stained-glass ceiling, which filters sunlight onto white marble floors. Upstairs, the contemporary rooms have dark-wood floors and color schemes that include bold oranges, reds, and black. The rooftop pool and patio are beloved by TV-commercial producers, thanks to the view of the cupolas in nearby San Telmo. A new tower opened in 2006 and added 69 luxury rooms to the complex. **Pros:** Old-school feel brings you back to another period in Buenos Aires's history; amazing views from the roof. **Cons:** Despite its downtown location, feels isolated from other attractions; area can be sketchy at night. ⊠*Bolívar 160, Centro, 1066* ☎*11/4121–6464* ⊕*www.nh-hotels.com* ⇆*327 rooms, 42 suites* ⏁*In-room: safe, refrigerator, Ethernet, dial-up, Wi-Fi (fee). In-hotel: restaurant, room service, bar, pool, gym, concierge, laundry service, public Wi-Fi* ⊟*AE, DC, MC, V* ⏼⏽*BP* Ⓜ*A to Perú, E to Bolívar.*

$$ **NH Florida.** Shiny parquet wood floors, extra fluffy pillows, and smiling young staffers are among the reasons to stay here. The hotel sits in the shadow of the massive Harrod's Building; the famed British department store was once *the* place for porteños to shop, but it has been sitting dark and abandoned on Florida Street for years. **Pros:** A block from busy Florida street; well priced. **Cons:** Room views are lacking; the surrounding area is dead on weekends. ⊠*San Martín 839, Centro, 1004* ☎*11/4321–9850* ⊕*www.nh-hoteles.com* ⇆*139 rooms, 21 suites* ⏁*In-room: safe, Ethernet, dial-up, Wi-Fi (fee). In-hotel: restaurant, bar, laundry service, parking (no fee)* ⊟*AE, DC, MC, V* ⏼⏽*BP* Ⓜ*C to San Martín.*

$$ **NH Jousten.** The historic Jousten Building on crazy Avenida Corrientes has some of the most luxurious rooms in the NH chain and has hosted the likes of Evita Perón over the years. Rooms have big, bouncy beds and handsome wood desks; the small bathrooms disappoint, though. The lobby café sits a half story above the sidewalk and offers grand views of the chaos below. Suites have private terraces overlooking the city and the River Plate. **Pro:** Classic charm and service make this a great choice for history buffs. **Con:** The building dates back a century and some of the spaces are sized to another era. ⊠*Corrientes 280, Centro, 1043* ☎*11/4321–6750* ⊕*www.nh-hoteles.com* ⇆*80 rooms, 5 suites* ⏁*In-room: safe, Ethernet, dial-up, Wi-Fi (fee). In-hotel: restaurant, room service, bar, concierge, laundry service, public Wi-Fi* ⊟*AE, DC, MC, V* ⏼⏽*BP* Ⓜ*B to L.N. Alem.*

$$ **NH Lancaster.** This historic hotel got a face-lift recently when it was purchased and rehabbed by Spanish group NH Hotels. Rooms are now clean and modern, but still respect the Lancaster's history. Rumor has it that many shady political deals were sealed over pints inside the White Rose, an adjoining British pub popular with the after-work crowd. **Pros:** Ideal for business visitors for its meeting rooms and services, as

well as its proximity to the financial district. **Con:** Avenida Cordoba is crowded and loud 24/7. ⊠*Av. Córdoba 405, Centro, 1054* ☎*11/4131–6464* ⊕*www.nh-hotels.com* ☞*72 rooms, 18 suites* &*In-room: safe, dial-up, Wi-Fi. In-hotel: restaurant, room service, bar, concierge, laundry service* ⊟*AE, DC, MC, V* ⊠⦶*CP* Ⓜ*C to San Martín.*

$$$ **Panamericano.** The popular, upscale Panamericano is near the famed ☾   Teatro Colón and the landmark Obelisco. The lobby's checked-marble floors lead to large salons, a snazzy café, and an Irish pub. Rooms are spacious and elegant, with dark-wood headboards and smart furnishings. The top-floor pool and spa afford amazing views. Visit in the late afternoon to watch the soft pastels of a smoggy sunset give way to the neon glow on the world's widest avenue, Avenida 9 de Julio. **Pros:** In the heart of the downtown action; amazing views of the city. **Cons:** Located on a busy, noisy avenue; at night, sketchy characters frequent nearby bars. ⊠*Carlos Pellegrini 551, Centro, 1009* ☎*11/4348–5000* ⊕*www.panamericanobuenosaires.com* ☞*267 rooms, 95 suites* &*In-room: safe, refrigerator, Ethernet, Wi-Fi. In-hotel: 3 restaurants, room service, bar, pool, gym, concierge, laundry service, parking (fee), public Wi-Fi* ⊟*AE, DC, MC, V* Ⓜ*B to C. Pellegrini.*

$$$ **Sheraton Buenos Aires Hotel.** What it lacks in charm, it makes up for ☾   in practicality, professionalism, and energy. There's always something happening here: a visiting dignitary, an international conference. Rooms are standard, clean, and well equipped, all of which explain the hotel's popularity among American businesspeople. When Latin heartthrobs like Luis Miguel or Ricky Martin are in town, they stay in the penthouse suite; scores of ecstatic Argentine females can usually be found holding vigils outside. **Pros:** Provides all the creature comforts you expect at hotel's at home; well located; well priced. **Cons:** It's a bit tired; rooms could use a sprucing up. ⊠*San Martín 1225, Centro, 1104* ☎*11/4318–9000, 800/325–3535 in U.S.* ⊕*www.sheraton.com* ☞*713 rooms, 29 suites* &*In-room: safe, Ethernet, dial-up. In-hotel: 2 restaurants, room service, bar, tennis courts, pools, gym, concierge, laundry service, public Wi-Fi, parking (fee), no-smoking rooms* ⊟*AE, DC, MC, V* ⊠⦶*BP* Ⓜ*C to Retiro.*

$$ **Sheraton Libertador.** It's on chaotic Avenida Córdoba, so you're better off choosing it if you're here in town on business or if you're looking for American-style service and nothing more. Rooms are clean, comfortable, and look like any other chain-hotel rooms in the world; for a little peace, request one facing away from the avenue. The street-level lobby café is one of the best places in the city to gawk inconspicuously at gorgeous Argentine passersby. **Pros:** Professional, no-nonsense staff; centrally located. **Cons:** On a noisy avenue; lacks charm. ⊠*Av. Córdoba 690, Centro, 1054* ☎*11/4321–0000* ⊕*www.sheraton.com* ☞*193 rooms, 6 suites* &*In-room: safe, kitchen (some), Ethernet, dial-up. In-hotel: restaurant, room service, bar, pool, gym, concierge, laundry service, public Wi-Fi, no-smoking rooms* ⊟*AE, DC, MC, V* ⊠⦶*BP* Ⓜ*C to Lavalle.*

CLOSE UP

Homes Away From Home

Buenos Aires is blessed with a wide array of hotels options, most of which are remarkably affordable compared with other international capitals. But if you are looking to save even more money, or if you just want the creature comforts of a real home, consider renting an apartment during your stay.

The options for renting in Buenos Aires run the gamut from cheap, simple, and sparsely decorated apartments to enormous, modern, and luxurious flats.

The city is a mishmash of architectural styles, so it's not unusual to see a 150-year-old home next to a gleaming 25-story apartment complex that was finished on Tuesday. As a result, some amenities or services are available in some properties, but not in others. Make sure you ask in advance whether the price includes utilities, telephone, and Internet fees.

AGENCIES

There are many apartment rental agencies in the city, and all of them have Web sites where you can view photos, see a list of each apartment's amenities, and make a reservation. Many of these agencies also provide concierge service, and will help you arrange an airport pickup.

We recommend the following apartment rental agencies: *www.apartmentsba.com; www.bytargentina.com; www.whatsupbuenosaires.com/tourism; www.buenosaireshousing.com; www.alojargentina.com; www.buenosaireshabitat.com; www.waytobaway.com.*

LOCATION, LOCATION

Deciding which neighborhood to rent in should be determined by the types of activities you plan to do during your stay in Buenos Aires.

In Centro, there are fewer options because much of the downtown area is a commercial district that houses offices and government buildings. However, many one- and two-bedroom apartments around Plaza San Martin in Retiro are good options if you want to be close to downtown.

In San Telmo and La Boca, the past is the present. With a few exceptions, most apartments in this area are two- or three-story homes that lack modern conveniences. If you're a tango junkie and looking to soak in the flavor of BA's yesteryears, then this is the barrio for you.

In Recoleta, the options are varied. This is likely the most-expensive neighborhood to rent in, because of its good location, security, and upper-crust residents.

In Palermo, fancy new apartment towers abound, matched with private homes and lofts that have been rehabbed in undyingly cool ways. Because Palermo is the largest barrio in the city, and home to the best restaurants and shopping, it is an ideal location for those who want to try to steer clear of tourists traps downtown.

Belgrano and Las Canitas offer much of the same as Palermo, but at cheaper rates. Many stately homes dot this area, and some are available for short- and long-term rentals.

6

$$$$ **Sofitel Buenos Aires.** Built in 1929 by a Yugoslavian shipping magnate, the tower was the tallest building in the city for some years. Left to disrepair, it was restored and renovated by Sofitel in 2003 and is now one of the classiest hotels in Buenos Aires, known for its understated elegance with French flair. Upper-level rooms are large and bright, offering amazing, panoramic views of Buenos Aires and the Rio de la Plata. All the hotel's beds are triple-layered, with down featherbeds and comforters. Soft carpets, dark wood furnishing, and modern bathrooms add to the allure. One of the city's nicest cafés, Café Arroyo, and restaurants, Le Sud, are on-site. **Pro:** Located on a quiet swanky street lined with art galleries. **Con:** The lobby can get crowded and noisy during receptions and art gallery exhibition openings. ⊠*Arroyo 841, Centro, 1007* ☎*11/4131–0000* ⊕*www.sofitelbuenosaires.com.ar* ⇆*115 rooms, 28 suites* &*In-room: safe, Ethernet, dial-up. In-hotel: restaurant, room service, bar, gym, concierge, laundry service, parking (fee), no-smoking rooms* ⊟*AE, MC, V* Ⓜ*C to San Martin.*

SAN TELMO

$$$ **Axel Hotel Buenos Aires.** Billed as Latin America's first gay hotel, the Axel Hotel Buenos Aires is modeled after the successful original hotel in Barcelona. The new building combines glass, wood, and water to an impressive effect, with lots of open spaces and fresh air. The floors of the common areas are lined with colorful mosaic tiling, a nod to the rainbow pride flag and Mac computers. The rooms are slick, modern, and bright, and equipped with hydro-massage tubs and leather-lined closets. The Axel also has what must be Buenos Aires' first transparent elevated pool, located on the top floor, and visible from all points below. Although the clientele and staff are predominantly homosexual men, the hotel vehemently promotes itself as "Hetero-friendly." **Pro:** The gigantic outside pool, bar, and deck area offer an upbeat and festive environment, a respite from the chaotic city streets. **Cons:** Rooms are small and very close together; the doors and balconies practically sit on top of each other, therefore privacy is at a minimum; pricey. ⊠*Venezuela 649, 1095* ☎*11/4136–9393* ⊕*www.axelhotels.com* ⇆*48 rooms* &*In-room: safe, Wi-Fi. In-hotel: restaurant, room service, bar, pools, gym, concierge, laundry service, parking (fee), no-smoking rooms* ⊟*AE, DC, MC, V* Ⓜ*E to Belgrano.*

¢ **Boquitas Pintadas.** The whimsically named "Little Painted Mouths" (a tribute to Manuel Puig's novel of the same name) is a self-proclaimed "pop hotel," and the German owner, Heike Thelen, goes out of her way to keep things weird and wild. World-famous "nude" photographer Spencer Tunick staged a shoot here and ended up spending the night, and other celebs have passed through over the years. Local artists, inspired by an array of provocative themes, redecorate and rename the five rooms every few months with names like "The Betrayal of Rita Hayworth." The restaurant serves dishes not found often in the city, including goulash. The hotel also hosts ever-changing art exhibitions, and theme parties for an eclectic crowd. The hotel is in the Constitución neighborhood, west of San Telmo, across Avenida 9 de Julio. **Pro:** It's a delightfully different place that makes for an unforgettable stay. **Con:** Use caution at night: the surrounding area is dodgy. ✉*Estados Unidos 1393, Constitución, 1101* ☎*11/4381–6064* ⊕*www.boquitas-pintadas.com.ar* 🛏*5 rooms* ⚹*In-room: Wi-Fi. In-hotel: restaurant, room service, bar, no elevator, laundry service* ▤*No credit cards* Ⓜ*E to San José.*

$ **The Cocker.** Run with love by two
Fodor'sChoice young British guys, the Cocker
★ (named after their pet spaniel, Rocco) is in an art nouveau mansion on a bustling avenue in San Telmo. Behind the wrought-iron doors and up the marble staircase, you can find a beautifully restored 19th-century home, with wooden floors, French windows, and decoration that smartly blends the past with the present. Each of the five rooms is truly unique and take full advantage of every inch of the property. Suite 19–03 has a four-post bed, a glass-encased bathroom, and a private garden. **Pro:** A rooftop garden offers a wonderful cityscape and is filled with plants and flowers; hummingbirds and butterflies stop by often. **Con:** The metal spiral staircase connecting the rooms with the common areas can cause vertigo for the faint of heart. ✉*Av. Juan de Garay 458, 1153* ☎*11/4362–8451* ⊕*www.thecocker.com* 🛏*5 rooms* ⚹*In-room: Wi-Fi. In-hotel: no elevator, no-smoking rooms* ▤*No credit cards* Ⓜ*C to San Juan.*

$ **Gurda Hotel.** Located in the heart of San Telmo, the Gurda will give you
Fodor'sChoice glimpse into what life was like at the turn of the 19th century. Seven
★ rooms line the long, open-air hallway with exposed brick, green plants, and bamboo sticks. Each room is named after something or someone decidedly Argentine—Jorge Luis Borges, Malbec, Patagonia—and are complete with decorations to match the title. (In the Borges room you can find volumes of his work and a colorful portrait of the literary legend.) The rooms are rustic and basic, but extremely charming. **Pros:** The young friendly staff can organize wine tastings with local sommeliers, and tango lessons. **Cons:** The entrance is right on a busy street full of buses; the restaurant and bar are noisy. ✉*Defensa 1521, 1413* ☎*11/4307–0646* ⊕*www.gurdahotel.com* 🛏*7 rooms* ⚹*In-room: safe, Wi-Fi. In-hotel: restaurant, room service, bar, concierge, laundry service, parking (fee), no-smoking rooms* ▤*AE, DC, MC, V* Ⓜ*C to Constitucion.*

$$ **Mansion Dandi Royal.** For a glimpse into early-20th-century high society, look no further than this hotel. Owner and tango legend Hector Villalba painstakingly transformed this 100-year-old mansion into both a hotel and a tango academy. The 20 exquisite rooms are decorated with classic wood furnishings and period murals. A stunning chandelier, sweeping staircase, and original artwork lend more authenticity. Tango lessons take place daily in the gorgeous dance hall, and every

evening the staff accompanies dancers to milongas, all-night tango parties that take place all over town. **Pro:** It's a tango junkie's heaven. **Con:** The surrounding streets are often populated with unsavory characters. ⊠*Piedras 922, 1070* 🕾*11/4307–7623* ⊕*www.mansiondandiroyal. com* ⟲*20 rooms* ⚲*In-room: safe, Ethernet, Wi-Fi. In-hotel: room service, bar, pool, gym, spa, laundry service, airport shuttle, parking (fee)* ⊟*AE, DC, MC, V* Ⓜ*C to San Juan.*

$$ **Moreno Hotel.** A gorgeous art deco building dating back to 1929, the

Fodor'sChoice Moreno's architects were posed with the challenge of restoring the 80-

★ year-old site without disturbing its original elements, like mosaic tiling and stained-glassed windows. The seven-floor hotel has spacious and sexy rooms, each decorated in a color motif complete with chaise lounges, Argentine cowhide rugs, and big fluffy beds. The "J-Loft" is feng shui–ed to the max, and has a big Jacuzzi inside. The top-floor terrace is armed with an outdoor fireplace, big wooden recliners, and amazing city views, including the enormous San Francisco Basilica directly across the street. **Pros:** There's a top-notch restaurant and 130-seat theater on-site. **Con:** Some rooms are just steps away from the main lobby and elevator. ⊠*Moreno 376, 1091* 🕾*11/6091–2000* ⊕*www.morenobuenosaires.com* ⟲*39 rooms* ⚲*In-room: safe, refrigerator, Ethernet, dial-up, Wi-Fi. In-hotel: restaurant, room service, bar, gym, concierge, parking (fee), no-smoking rooms* ⊟*AE, MC, V* Ⓜ*A to Plaza de Mayo.*

RECOLETA, BARRIO NORTE & ALMAGRO

$$ **Abasto Plaza Hotel.** This place is *all* about the tango. Photos and paintings of famous musicians line the walls that surround the checked-marble dance floor, which is next to a boutique where you can buy sequined skirts, stilettos, and fishnet stockings. Suites each have their own dance floor for private lessons, or you can join other guests for nightly tango lessons and a live show. Rooms are large and elegant with—surprise, surprise—a tango theme. The hotel is two blocks from an alleyway and theater dedicated to the godfather of tango, Carlos Gardel. The enormous Abasto Shopping Center is across the street. **Pro:** If you're in Buenos Aires to tango, this is your place. **Cons:** Tango overload is a very real possibility; the furnishings and bedding are a bit tired. ⊠*Av. Corrientes 3190, Almagro, 1193* 🕾*11/6311–4466* ⊕*www.abasto plaza.com* ⟲*120 rooms, 6 suites* ⚲*In-room: Ethernet, dial-up, Wi-Fi. In-hotel: restaurant, room service, bar, pool, gym* ⊟*AE, DC, MC, V* ⦿❙*BP* Ⓜ*B to Carlos Gardel.*

$$$$ **Alvear Palace Hotel.** If James Bond were in town, this is where he'd hang

Fodor'sChoice his hat. In fact, Sean Connery *has* stayed here, because when it comes

★ to sophistication, the Alvear Palace is the best bet in Buenos Aires. It has hosted scores of dignitaries since opening its doors in 1932, and although new and more-affordable hotels are making it something of a gray ghost, the Alvear is still stately and swanky. It's all about world-class service and thoughtful touches: butler service, fresh flowers, featherbeds with Egyptian-cotton linens. **Pros:** The lunch buffet is out of this world, and the superchic French restaurant, La Bourgogne, is one of the city's best. **Cons:** You'll pay dearly for the privilege of staying here; it's one of the country's most-expensive hotels. ⊠*Av. Alvear 1891, Recoleta, 1129* ☎*11/4808–2100 or 11/4804–7777, 800/448–8355 in U.S.* ⊕*www.alvearpalace.com* ⇆*100 rooms, 100 suites* ⑁*In-room: safe, Ethernet, dial-up, Wi-Fi. In-hotel: 2 restaurants, room service, bar, pool, gym, concierge, laundry service, no-smoking rooms* ⊟*AE, DC, MC, V* ⍟*BP.*

$ **Art Hotel.** The aptly named Art Hotel has an impressive ground-floor gallery where exhibits of paintings, photographs, and sculptures by acclaimed Argentine artists change monthly. You might even run into some fabulous art aficionados sipping Chardonnay and admiring the creations. Rooms are classified as "small and cozy," "queen," or "king" and many have wrought-iron bed frames with white canopies. The building's 100-year-old elevator will take you to the rooftop patio, where there's a hot tub and plenty of room to soak up some sun. **Pro:** Its bohemian vibe will make you feel like you've joined an artists colony. **Con:** Rooms are dark and somewhat antiquated. ⊠*Azcuenaga 1268, Recoleta, 1115* ☎*11/4821–4744* ⊕*www.arthotel.com.ar* ⇆*36 rooms* ⑁*In-room: safe, Ethernet. In-hotel: bar, laundry service, public Wi-Fi.* ⊟*AE, MC, V* Ⓜ*D to Pueyrredón.*

$ **Art Suites.** Perfect for businessmen on extended stay or couples looking for some stretching room, the 15 suites are bright, roomy, and pleasant. They all have shiny wooden floors, simple modern furnishings, balconies, kitchens, and contemporary artwork. Visit the first-floor office which doubles as a tourist resource library; you'll find dozens of magazines and guidebooks to Argentina, including Fodor's. It's on a quiet street in Recoleta, close to shopping and restaurants. It's not to be confused with the Art Hotel two blocks away; they have different owners and an entirely different vibe. **Pros:** Fantastic price; friendly service. **Con:** Wi-Fi only on the first and second floors. ⊠*Azcuenaga 1465, Recoleta, 1115* ☎*11/4821–6800* ⊕*www.artsuites.com.ar* ⇆*15 suites* ⑁*In-room: safe, refrigerator, Ethernet, dial-up. In-hotel: concierge, laundry service, parking, no-smoking rooms* ⊟*AE, DC, MC, V* Ⓜ*D to Pueyrredon.*

$$ **Blue Tree Hotel.** This Brazilian-owned hotel's name is misleading because nearly everything inside is black: black walls, black carpet, black-and-white photographs, black-tile bathrooms, and black bedding. If that doesn't turn you off, then this is a good choice if you want to be in the middle of the city in tony Recoleta. The rooms are tricked out with flat-screen TVs and Wi-Fi, and the beds are big and inviting. But be warned: a nearby elementary school means lots of screaming kids in the

6

morning and afternoon. **Pro:** The lobby café (decorated in purple) is a great place to whip out your laptop and sip an espresso. **Cons:** No pool, gym, or restaurant. ⊠*Laprida 1910, Recoleta, 1425* ☎*11/5199–8399* ⊕*www.bluetree.com.br* ⊷*42 rooms, 3 suites* ⋔*In-room: safe, Ethernet, Wi-Fi. In-hotel: room service, bar, concierge, laundry service, parking (fee), no-smoking rooms* ⊟*AE, MC, V* Ⓜ*D to Pueyrredon.*

$$$$ **Four Seasons Hotel Buenos Aires.** This exquisite hotel envelops you in a
Fodor's Choice pampering atmosphere that screams turn-of-the-19th-century Paris. In
★ fact, the gorgeous French embassy is just up the block. The hotel's 13-floor marble tower has an impressive art collection and large, luxurious rooms. The neighboring hotel mansion draws some of the world's most famous folks: Madonna (who stayed here while filming *Evita*), the Rolling Stones, and Robbie Williams, to name a few. Argentine soccer legend Diego Maradona and Bono partied together here after U2's 2006 shows in Buenos Aires. **Pros:** Classic elegance; good location. **Con:** Pandemonium breaks out when rock stars stay here. ⊠*Posadas 1086, Recoleta, 1011* ☎*11/4321–1200* ⊕*www.fourseasons.com/buenosaires* ⊷*138 rooms, 27 suites* ⋔*In-room: safe, Ethernet, dial-up, Wi-Fi. In-hotel: restaurant, room service, bar, pool, gym, concierge, laundry service, airport shuttle, parking (fee), no-smoking rooms* ⊟*AE, DC, MC, V* ⋔⊚*BP.*

$ **Hotel Bel Air.** Given the fancy French-style facade, you could mistake the Bel Air for a neighborhood hotel somewhere in Paris. Inside, a more-modern feel takes over, with a round wood-panel lobby bar and a snazzy café that looks onto exclusive Arenales Street, dotted with art galleries, fashion boutiques, and furniture stores. Rooms have handsome wooden floors and simple but stylish desks and couches in an array of earth-tone colors. **Pros:** Great price and great location on one of the city's poshest streets. **Cons:** The staff is easily distracted; hallways and common areas are cramped. ⊠*Arenales 1462, Recoleta, 1062* ☎*11/4021–4000* ⊕*www.hotelbelair.com.ar* ⊷*77 rooms* ⋔*In-room: safe, dial-up, Wi-Fi (fee). In-hotel: restaurant, room service, bar, gym, laundry service, airport shuttle, no-smoking rooms* ⊟*AE, DC, MC, V* Ⓜ*D to Tribunales.* ⋔⊚*BP.*

$$$ **Loi Suites Recoleta.** A white marble lobby leads to a garden area where you can enjoy a poolside breakfast or an afternoon drink. Sleek guest rooms have white-and-gray color schemes complemented by black-and-white photos on the walls. Executive suites have whirlpool baths and amazing views of a place that high-society Argentines have been dying to get into for years: Recoleta Cemetery. Loi Suites also operate two smaller apart-hotels downtown. **Pro:** In the heart of swanky Recoleta, you are close to historic sites, museums, art fairs and restaurants. **Con:** Despite its clean, white appearance, the place seems dated and lacks charm. ⊠*Vicente López 1955, Recoleta, 1128* ☎*11/5777–8950* ⊕*www.loisuites.com.ar* ⊷*88 rooms, 24 suites* ⋔*In-room: safe, Ethernet, dial-up. In-hotel: restaurant, room service, bar, pool, gym, laundry service, public Wi-Fi, parking (fee)* ⊟*AE, DC, MC, V* ⋔⊚*CP.*

$$$$
★
Park Hyatt Palacio Duhau. This gorgeous new hotel has upped the ante for elegance in Buenos Aires. Its two buildings, a restored 1930s-era mansion and a 17-story tower, are connected by an underground art gallery and a leafy garden. The rooms are decorated in rich hues of wood, marble, and Argentine leather. Ask to stay in the mansion where the rooms are larger and infinitely more charming. Be sure to sip a whiskey at the Oak Bar, constructed from 17th-century oak

> **WORD OF MOUTH**
>
> "On our first trip we stayed in Recoleta and enjoyed the area for dining and nightlife. On weekends there is a great outdoor market and you are also close to the Eva Perón cemetery. For anything further (like Palermo) we used taxis which were very reasonable."
>
> –kacollier

carvings from Normandy Castle, and visit the Ahin Spa (named after a Mapuche Indian welcoming ritual) which has five suites offering holistic and beauty treatments, next to the city's largest indoor pool. **Pros:** Understated elegance; great restaurant; the 3,500 bottle Wine Library and "Cheese Room" are unique attractions. **Cons:** A long walk from one side of the hotel to the other; although elegantly decorated, some of the common areas lack warmth. ⊠*Av. Alvear 1661, Recoleta, 1014* ☎*11/5171–1234* ⊕*www.buenosaires.park.hyatt.com* 126 rooms, *39 suites In-room: safe, Ethernet, dial-up, Wi-Fi, DVD. In-hotel: 2 restaurants, room service, bar, pool, gym, spa, concierge, laundry service* ⊟*AE, MC, V.*

6

PALERMO

$ **Baucis Hotel.** More bohemian than the other local boutiques, this new property is built in a restored family home close to all the fabulous action in Palermo Hollywood. The rooms—all of which were formerly the bedrooms of the previous occupants—are spacious with high ceilings and comfy beds. Decorating flourishes like sparkly pillows contrast well with the exposed brick walls and the colorful paintings by local artists that cover them. The outdoor patio that fronts all the rooms could definitely use some attention, though. It needs a good scrub and some new furnishings. **Pro:** An old-world feel reminds you that Palermo Hollywood was formerly a quiet family neighborhood. **Con:** Staff is indifferent and sometimes unhelpful. ⊠*Angel Carranza 1612, Palermo Hollywood, 1414* ☎*11/4772–2192* ⊕*www.baucis hotel.com* 10 rooms *In-room: safe, Wi-Fi. In-hotel: bar, no elevator, laundry service, public Wi-Fi, no-smoking rooms* ⊟*AE, DC, MC, V* Ⓜ*D to Ministro Carranza.*

$$ **Bo-Bo.** Quaint, quirky Bo-Bo shrewdly combines the bourgeois with the bohemian. In fact the hotel's name is a play on David Brooks's 2000 book, *Bobos in Paradise,* which you can find in the lobby library. Each room has a different motif—art deco, minimalist, techno. The largest and most luxurious, the Argentina Suite, is decorated in bright colors and has a small outdoor patio and hot tub. All rooms have such creature comforts as soft robes and such technological comforts as Wi-Fi access and DVD players. The downstairs restaurant-café is a nice place to relax after pounding Palermo's pavement all day. **Pro:** First-rate and friendly staff go out of their way to help you out. **Con:** Some of the rooms are on the small side. ✉*Guatemala 4882, Palermo Soho, 1425* 🕾*11/4774–0505* ⊕*www.bobohotel.com* ◊*7 rooms* ⌂*In-room: safe, Ethernet, Wi-Fi. In-hotel: restaurant, room service, bar, laundry service, parking (fee)* ▤*AE, MC, V* Ⓜ*D to Plaza Italia.*

$$ **Costa Petit.** This place is steps away from the slick modern feel of many of Palermo's smaller hotels, and goes for a rustic and rootsy charm. Suites are decorated with old wooden furniture—antique desks, chairs and beds—and the walls are lined with black-and-white photographs of gauchos and tango dancers, all meant to highlight the country's proud traditions. An array of authentic Argentine artifacts are found throughout the property and truly lend a farm feeling to what could only be considered an urban oasis. **Pro:** Upscale and cozy, you'll feel right at home looking out to the garden and pool. **Con:** The staff can be snobby and scarce. ✉*Costa Rica 5141, 1425* 🕾*11/4776–8296* ⊕*www.costapetithotel.com* ◊*4 suites* ⌂*In-room: safe, Ethernet, Wi-Fi. In-hotel: pool, concierge, parking (fee), no-smoking rooms* ▤*AE, DC, MC, V* Ⓜ*D to Palermo.*

$$ **1555 Malabia House.** Behind the unassuming white facade of this 100-year-old Palermo Soho town house is what the proprietors have dubbed Argentina's "first designer B&B." Common areas have bold colorful paintings and fanciful sculptures. Rooms, only some of which have en suite baths, are all about pale-wood floors and furnishings and simple white bedding and curtains. Both sides of the narrow hallways are lined with rooms, eliminating any sense of privacy, but the bustling Palermo location is hard to beat. The young staff can steer you toward the neighborhood's newest restaurants and nightspots. **Pro:** You can walk home from daytime shopping and nighttime carousing. **Cons:** It can be noisy; at the end of the day, it's still a house that was built more than a century ago. ✉*Malabia 1555, Palermo Soho, 1414* 🕾*11/4832–3345 or 11/4833–2410* ⊕*www.malabiahouse.com.ar* ◊*11 rooms, 4 suites* ⌂*In-room: safe, Wi-Fi. In-hotel: room service, bar, no elevator, concierge, laundry service, airport shuttle, parking (fee)* ▤*AE, DC, MC, V* ⍟*CP* Ⓜ*D to Scalabrini Ortiz.*

¢ **Giramondo Hostel.** The funky Giramondo has all that a hostel needs: plenty of beds and bathrooms, a kitchen, a TV and computer lounge, and a patio, where backpackers from around the world grill up slabs of Argentine beef. The dark, dank underground bar serves up cheap drinks; it also has a small wine cellar. Giramondo is two blocks from buses and the subte on Avenida Santa Fe—an ideal locale for taking part in Palermo's pulsing nightlife while also being close to downtown. There's now a sister location with suites just down the street at Oro 2472. **Pros:** They have the budget traveler in mind, and cater to short-term and long-term travelers. **Cons:** The surrounding streets are chaotic; loud buses buzz by all hours of the night. ✉*Guemes 4802, Palermo Soho, 1425* 🕾*11/4772–6740* ⊕*www.hostelgiramondo.com. ar* ⌂*In-room: no a/c, no phone, kitchen, no TV, Ethernet. In-hotel: bar,* *no elevator, laundry facilities* ⊟*No credit cards* Ⓜ*D to Palermo.*

$$ Home Buenos Aires. It's run by Argentine Patricia O'Shea and her British husband, Tom Rixton, a well-known music producer, and it oozes coolness and class. Each room is decorated with vintage French wallpaper and has a stereo, a laptop-friendly safe, and either a bathtub or a wet room. On-site there's a vast garden; a barbecue area; an infinity pool; a holistic spa; and a funky lounge bar where you

can sip a cocktail and listen to mood music created especially for the hotel by famed record producer Flood (U2, Smashing Pumpkins, Nine Inch Nails), one of the hotel's investors. **Pros:** Impossibly hip and fun; always interesting people staying here. **Con:** Lots of nonguests come here to hang out, reducing the intimacy factor. ⊠*Honduras 5860, Palermo Hollywood, 1414* ☎*11/4778–1008* ⊕*www.homebuenosaires. com* ↩*14 rooms, 4 suites* ⌂*In-room: safe, Ethernet, Wi-Fi. In-hotel: restaurant, room service, bar, pool, spa* ⊟*AE, MC, V* Ⓜ*D to Ministro Carranza.*

$$ Soho All Suites. In the heart of Palermo Soho, this smart hotel offers ♻ sneak peaks into the backyards of the neighborhood's many private homes, where some of Argentina's coolest artists reside. The big lobby area is great for informal business meetings and is chock-full of flyers and brochures that will help you seek out Soho's latest offerings. The amazing balconies in the front and back of the property are favored for local photo shoots and television commercials. The rooms all have kitchens but the faux gray marble table tops and cheap porcelain toilets definitely take away from the charm. **Pro:** Massage parlor on-site for those urgent post-shopping sores. **Con:** Not well-maintained: walls need painting and wood floors need polishing. ⊠*Honduras 4762, Palermo Soho, 1425* ☎*11/4832–3000* ⊕*www.sohoallsuites.com* ↩*21 suites* ⌂*In-room: safe, Wi-Fi. In-hotel: public Wi-Fi, parking (fee), nosmoking rooms* ⊟*AE, DC, MC, V* Ⓜ*D to Plaza Italia.*

$$ Vain. This Palermo Soho spot encourages guests to "unleash" their vanity and indulge in their offerings of modern luxury and minimalist design. Built in a restored century-old house, the rooms have high ceilings, big beds, and hardwood floors. The bathrooms have funky stand-up sinks, hydro-massage bathtubs, and are decorated in colorful ceramics. Upstairs, classical music plays in a large living area where you can work on your laptop or lounge on a sofa and catch up on your reading. It's well located just blocks from the subway, zoo, and parks, as well as scores of fantastic restaurants. **Pro:** The upstairs terrace is a great place for morning breakfast, which can be made-to-order. **Con:** It can be noisy: buses pass right in front and a nearby school means the sounds of screaming kids every afternoon. ⊠*Thames 2226, Palermo*

6

Soho, 1425 ☎*11/4776–8246* ⊕*www.vainuniverse.com* ⚲*9 rooms, 6 suites* &*In-room: safe, Ethernet, Wi-Fi. In-hotel: bar, concierge, laundry service, public Wi-Fi, parking (fee), no-smoking rooms* ▭*AE, DC, MC, V* Ⓜ*D to Plaza Italia.*

BELGRANO & LAS CAÑITAS

$$ Casa Las Cañitas. As its name suggests, this place feels like a home. A small library, leafy garden, and covered quincho (barbecue area) with parrilla are perfect for lounging around on steamy summer afternoons. Rooms are big, bright, and decorated in lively colors with modern furnishings. Some of them have private terraces that are well worth the extra cash. Bathrooms have big sinks and have soft robes and slippers. The friendly staff organizes gatherings in the garden and can make reservations for you at the neighborhood's best restaurants. **Pros:** Good rates; breakfast served until 3 PM, perfect for those who partake in the famous "Noche Porteno." **Con:** The common area is small and a bit disheveled. ⊠*Huergo 283, Las Canitas, 1426* ☎*11/4771–3878* ⊕*www.casalascanitas.com* ⚲*9 rooms* &*In-room: safe, Wi-Fi. In-hotel: bar, no elevator, laundry service, public Wi-Fi, parking (fee), no-smoking rooms* ▭*AE, DC, MC, V* Ⓜ*D to Ministro Carranza.*

$$ My ba Hotel. This unassuming boutique hotel sits on a quiet tree-lined street near the Universidad de Belgrano and several embassies, including the Australian Embassy. The hotel is decorated in an early 1960s motif with vintage swingers-era furniture splashed with dashes of rich purples and blues that liven up the rooms. Guest rooms are large and have eclectic designs with textured wallpaper, and colorful pillows and bedspreads. The one suite has access to a private garden that's really not very private at all, but charming all the same. **Pro:** It's one of the few hotels in Belgrano, and well worth a stay if you want to explore the upper-crust neighborhood. **Con:** It's far from major tourist sites. ⊠*Zabala 1925, Belgrano, 1426* ☎*11/4787–5765* ⊕*www.mybahotel. com* ⚲*9 rooms, 1 suite* &*In-room: safe, Ethernet, Wi-Fi. In-hotel: restaurant, bar, concierge, laundry service, public Wi-Fi, parking (fee), no-smoking rooms* ▭*AE, DC, MC, V* Ⓜ*D to J. Hernandez.*

$$ Tailor Made. This small and fashionable boutique hotel is steps away
Fodor's Choice   from the world-famous Argentine Polo Fields and caters to its guests'
★   most detailed preferences. Every room is equipped with a Mac Mini and flat-screen TV. If you give them a heads up, the staff will download your favorite music and movies before you arrive. The rooms are large and sparsely decorated in white with random touches of bold primary colors. The large suite has a outdoor terrace and Jacuzzi, perfect for sipping champagne. The property is located in a quieter enclave of Las Canitas and offers a nice break from the often chaotic main strip, Baez Street. **Pros:** Free VoIP calls to 35 countries worldwide; 24-hour concierge service. **Cons:** The breakfast room is small and located next to a large window overlooking the street; privacy is nil. ⊠*Arce 385, Las Canitas, 1426* ☎*11/4774–9620* ⊕*www.tailormadehotels.com* ⚲*5 rooms* &*In-room: safe, Ethernet, Wi-Fi. In-hotel: room service, con-*

cierge, laundry service, parking (fee), no-smoking rooms ⊟*AE, DC, MC, V* Ⓜ*D to Ministro Carranza.*

$$ **248 Finisterra.** A mix of modern and vintage designs dominate this boutique hotel located on the main drag of trendy Las Cañitas where gastronomic and fashion offerings continue to grow by leaps and bounds. The long entranceway hall leads to a comfy common area equipped with a TV and lots of books and glossy magazines. Outside there's a small garden with the requisite parrilla, which guests can use. The rooms are small, and the bedding and linen should definitely be replaced. The second-floor back terrace has lounge chairs and a Jacuzzi, perfect for late-afternoon dipping and dozing. **Pro:** Within spitting distance of a dozen restaurants and bars. **Cons:** Tiny bathrooms and even tinier showers. ⊠*Baez 248, Las Canitas, 1426* ☎*11/4773–0901* ⊕*www.248finisterra. com* ↩*10 rooms, 1 suite* ⚿*In-room: safe, Ethernet, dial-up. In-hotel: bar, no elevator, public Wi-Fi, parking (fee), no-smoking rooms* ⊟*AE, DC, MC, V* Ⓜ*D to Ministro Carranza.*

6

Side Trips

Iguazú Falls

WORD OF MOUTH

"Another day trip we enjoyed was visiting San Antonio de Areco, a historic gaucho town, which also included a trip to an estancia. Yeah, it was a little touristy, but hey, we *were* tourists. We loved it."

—sweet_polly

EXCURSIONS FROM BUENOS AIRES

TOP REASONS TO GO

★ **The Wall of Water:** Nothing can prepare you for the roaring, thunderous Cataratas del Iguazú (Iguazú Falls). We think you'll agree.

★ **Cowboy Culture:** No visit to the *pampas* (grasslands) is complete without a stay at an *estancia,* a stately ranch house. Sleep in an old-fashioned bedroom and share meals with the owners for a true taste of the lifestyle.

★ **Wetland Wonders:** The Esteros del Iberá, an immense wetland reserve in Corrientes Province, is home to a bewildering variety of plants and animals, including howler monkeys and capybaras (a quirky supersize rodent).

★ **Delta Dreaming:** Speeding through the Paraná River delta's thousands of kilometers of rivers and streams, we'll forgive you for humming "Ride of the Valkyries"—it does feel very Mekong.

★ **Colonial Days:** Gorgeous 18th- and 19th-century stone buildings line Colonia del Sacramento's cobbled streets. Many now contain the stylish bed-and-breakfasts favored by *porteños* looking to escape the big city.

3 The Atlantic Coast. Rolling dunes and coastal pine woods make windy Atlantic beaches peaceful places for some sea air in the low season; in summer, though, they're among Argentina's top party spots. Although they're a good escape from the city stifle, don't expect sugary sand or crystal-clear waters.

4 Los Esteros del Iberá. Few people have heard of these vast wetlands, halfway between Buenos Aires and Iguazú. Thousands of acres of still lakes, hordes of unusual animals—which you see up close—and a huge variety of birds are the attractions.

5 Iguazú Falls. The grandeur of this vast sheet of white water cascading in constant cymbal-banging cacophony makes Niagara Falls and Victoria Falls seem sedate. Allow at least two full days to take in this magnificent sight, and be sure to see it from both the Argentine and Brazilian sides.

1 Colonia del Sacramento, Uruguay. It's hard not to fall in love with Colonia. The picturesque town has a six-by-six-block old city with wonderfully preserved architecture, rough cobblestone streets, and an easy grace. Tranquillity reigns here—bicycles and golf carts outnumber cars.

2 Buenos Aires Province. An hour's drive from Buenos Aires leads to varied sights. The semitropical delta of the Paraná River lies to the north, near the town of Tigre. Elegant architecture and a quirky dinosaur museum stand out to the south in La Plata, the provincial capital. Northwest lies the gaucho town of San Antonio de Areco.

GETTING ORIENTED

Argentina's famous pampas begin in Buenos Aires Province—an unending sea of crops and cattle-studded grass that occupies nearly one-quarter of the country's landscapes. Here are the region's most-traditional towns, including San Antonio de Areco. In southern Buenos Aires Province, the pampas stretch to the Atlantic coast, which is dotted with resort towns that spring to life in summer. From Buenos Aires ferries cross the massive River Plate estuary to the small Uruguayan town of Colonia del Sacramento. Suburban trains connect Buenos Aires to Tigre, close to the labyrinthine waterways of the Paraná delta, explorable only by boat. The delta feeds the Esteros del Iberá, an immense wetland reserve hundreds of kilometers north, in Corrientes Province. On Argentina's northeastern tip, readily accessible by plane, are the jaw-dropping Cataratas del Iguazú.

7

SIDE TRIPS PLANNER

When to Go

Province temperatures rarely reach extremes, but some hotels and restaurants *only* open on weekends outside of peak season—this coincides with school holidays in summer (January and February), winter (July), and the Easter weekend. You'll get great discounts at those that open midweek in winter.

November's a good time to visit San Antonio de Areco, which holds its annual gaucho festival then. Like Buenos Aires, it feels curiously empty in January, when everyone decamps to the coast. December through March is peak season, and beach town establishments can be booked, so be sure to make advance reservations. Beaches get cold and windy in winter (June–September).

Visit the Esteros del Iberá and Iguazú Falls April through October to avoid the heat and humidity. Argentineans usually go in July, when hotels book up (and prices soar). Though the falls are thrilling year-round, seasonal rainfall and upstream Brazilian barrages (minidams) can affect the falls' water volume. If you visit between November and March, booking a hotel with air-conditioning and a swimming pool is as essential as taking mosquito repellent.

Border Crossings

U.S., Canadian, and British citizens need only a valid passport for stays of up to 90 days in Uruguay. Crossing into Brazil at Iguazú is a thorny issue. In theory, *all* U.S. citizens need a visa to enter Brazil. Visas are issued in about three hours from the Brazilian consulate in Puerto Iguazú (as opposed to the three days they take in Buenos Aires), and cost approximately 430 pesos. The Buenos Aires consulate also has a reputation for refusing visas to travelers who don't have onward tickets from Brazil.

If you stay in Foz do Iguaçu, travel on to other Brazilian cities, or do a day trip to Brazil by public bus or through an Argentinean company, you'll need a visa. There have been reports of getting around this by using a Brazilian travel agent or by using local taxis (both Argentine and Brazilian) that have "arrangements" with border control. Though the practice is well established (most hotels and travel agents in Puerto Iguazú have deals with Brazilian companies and can arrange a visa-less visit), it *is* illegal. Reinforcement of the law is generally lax but sudden crackdowns and on-the-spot fines of hundreds of dollars have been reported.

Brazilian Consulates

In Buenos Aires ✉ *Carlos Pellegrini 1363, 5th fl., Buenos Aires* ☏ *11/4515–6500* ⊕ *www.conbrasil.org.ar.*

In Puerto Iguazú ✉ *Av. Córdoba 264, Puerto Iguazú* ☏ *3757/421–348.*

Money Matters

Argentine money is accepted everywhere in Colonia, Uruguay—have a rough idea of the exchange rate to avoid overcharging. Not changing money? Use Argentine pesos for small transactions; hotels give better rates for dollars. Avoid exchanging at the ferry terminal, where the commission's often high.

Uruguayan bills come in denominations of 20, 50, 100, 200, 500, 1,000, and 2,000 pesos uruguayos. Coins are available in 50 centésimo pieces (half a peso), $1, $2, $5, and $10. $5- and $10-peso coins have recently replaced banknotes of the same value, which are no longer used. At this writing, there were 6.6 Uruguayan pesos to the Argentine peso, and 21 Uruguayan pesos to the U.S. dollar.

Brazil's currency is the real (R$; plural: *reais* or *reals*). One real is 100 centavos. There are 1, 5, 10, 20, 50, and 100 real notes and 1, 5, 10, 25, and 50 centavo and 1 real coins. At this writing, there were 0.53 reais to the Argentine peso, and 1.7 reais to the U.S. dollar.

Hotel & Restaurant Costs

Hotels and restaurants in Colonia list prices in U.S. dollars.

WHAT IT COSTS IN DOLLARS				
	¢	$	$$	$$$	$$$$
Dining	under $5	$5–$8	$8–$12	$12–$16	over $16
Hotels	under $50	$50–$80	$80–$130	$130–$200	over $200
WHAT IT COSTS IN BRAZILIAN REAIS				
Dining	under 15 reais	15–25 reais	25–38 reais	38–50 reais	over 50 reais
Hotels	under 100 reais	100–150 reais	150–220 reais	220–350 reais	over 350 reais
WHAT IT COSTS IN ARGENTINA PESOS				
Dining	under 15 pesos	15–25 pesos	25–38 pesos	38–50 pesos	over 50 pesos
Hotels	under 150 pesos	150–280 pesos	280-400 pesos	400–600 pesos	over 600 pesos

Restaurant prices are based on the median main course price at dinner. Hotel prices are for two people in a standard double room in high season.

Safety

Provincial towns like Tigre, San Antonio de Areco, and Colonia de Sacramento in Uruguay are usually extremely safe, and the areas visited by tourists are well patrolled.

Puerto Iguazú is fairly quiet in itself, but mugging and theft are common in nearby Foz do Iguaçu in Brazil, especially at night, when its streets are deserted. Worse yet is neighboring Ciudad del Este in Paraguay, where gun crime is a problem. Avoid the area near the border.

Taxi drivers are usually very honest, and are less likely to rip you off than the transport services arranged by top hotels. All the same, locals recommend unaccompanied women phone for taxis late at night, rather than hailing them on the street. The police in the provinces have an iffy reputation: at worst, horribly corrupt, and at best, rather inefficient. Don't count on support, sympathy, or much else from them if you're the victim of a crime.

Argentina Emergency Services: **Ambulance** (☎107). **Fire** (☎100). **Police** (☎101).

Brazil Emergency Services: **Ambulance** (☎192). **Fire** (☎193). **Police** (☎194). **Police Rodoviaria Federal** (☎191).

Uruguay Emergency Services: **General Emergencies** (☎911).**Ambulance** (☎105). **Fire** (☎104). **Police** (☎109). **Policía Caminera (Highway Patrol)** (☎108).

7

SIDE TRIPS PLANNER

Phone Home

To call Uruguay from Argentina, you dial the international access code 00, the country code of 598, the area code without the initial zero, and the local number. To call locally, dial the digits (Colonia's numbers have five digits) without any prefix (the prefix in Colonia is 052).

Uruguay had planned to change its phone number system in July 2008, but at this writing the change had been postponed until 2010. In the new system, area codes will be eradicated and all regular numbers will have eight digits. Montevideo's seven-digit numbers will be prefixed by a 2, so 6040386 will become 2604–0386. Numbers in the rest of the country will be prefixed by a 4, followed by the former area code minus its initial zero, and the former five-digit number. For example, Colonia's area code is 052, so local number 24897 will become 4522–4897. To call Brazil from Argentina, dial the international access code 00, the country code of 55, the area code without the initial zero, and the eight-digit local number. To call locally, dial the eight-digit numbers without any prefix. The area code for Foz do Iguaçu is 45.

Head Out on the Highway

Driving is the most convenient—though rarely cheap—option for getting around the province. Avis, Dollar, and Hertz have branches in many large towns and cities. At this writing, gas—known as *nafta*—costs around 2.20 pesos a liter, and if you plan to drive extensively, it's worth looking into renting a vehicle running on diesel, which will reduce fuel costs significantly. There are plenty of gas stations in cities and on major highways, but they can be few and far between on rural roads. A useful Web site when planning road trips is ⊕*www.ruta0.com*, which calculates distances and tolls between two places and offers several route options.

Be careful. Argentina has one of the world's worst records for traffic accidents, and the busy highways of Buenos Aires Province are often where they happen. January and February are the worst times, when drivers anxious to get to and from their holiday destination speed, tailgate, and exercise illegal maneuvers even more alarmingly than usual. If you're driving, do so very defensively and avoid traveling on Friday and Sunday, when traffic is worst.

Expressways and interprovincial routes tend to be atrociously signposted, so take a map, and privately owned, which means frequent tolls. There are sometimes alternative roads to use, but they're generally smaller, slower, and in poor condition. On main roads the speed limit is 80 kph (50 mph), while on highways it's 130 kph (80 mph), though Argentinean drivers rarely pay heed to this.

Cabbing It

If you're in a major city, take a taxi. Generally inexpensive (the fare is based on the number of blocks traveled), they can be hailed just about anywhere, though it's generally easier to get your hotel or restaurant to call you one. In smaller towns, numerous minicab firms (*remises*) replace taxis. These can be hailed on the street or called. In many touristy towns, you can book remises to ferry you around for several days. With a group of three or four, you may find this a more-economical and convenient way to get around.

Updated
by Victoria
Patience

TO HEAR *PORTEÑOS* (INHABITANTS OF BUENOS AIRES) talk of their city, you'd think Argentina stops where Buenos Aires ends. Not far beyond it, however, the skies open up and the pampas—Argentina's huge flat grasslands—begin. Pampean traditions are alive and well in farming communities that still dot the plains that make up Buenos Aires Province. The best known is San Antonio de Areco, a well-preserved provincial town that's making a name for itself as gaucho central.

Ranchland gives way to watery wonders. The quiet suburban town of Tigre is the gateway to the network of rivers and tributaries that form the delta of the Paraná River, lined with luscious tropical vegetation. One of Argentina's least-visited natural wonders, the Esteros del Iberá, an immense wetland reserve in Corrientes Province, is home to thousands of native plant and animal species, including *yacarés* (Argentine alligators) and hordes of capybara, a huge water-loving rodent. If you like your natural wonders supersized, head northeast of Buenos Aires to the Iguazú Falls. Here, on the border between Argentina and Brazil, two natural parks contain and protect hundreds of roaring falls and a delicate jungle ecosystem.

The sand and sea of the Atlantic coast begin just a few hours south from the capital. It might not be the Caribbean, but there's something charmingly retro about resorts like Mar del Plata and Pinamar. In the summer months, when temperatures in Buenos Aires soar, hordes of porteños seek relief here, and the capital's music and theater scene decamps with them, making these *the* places to see and be seen.

One of South America's most-beautiful towns, Colonia del Sacramento, Uruguay, juts out on a small peninsula into the Río de la Plata and is only an hour away from Buenos Aires. Here, sleepy cobbled streets and colonial buildings are a reminder of days gone by.

COLONIA DEL SACRAMENTO

The peaceful cobbled streets of Colonia are just over the River Plate from Buenos Aires, but they seem a world away. Founded in 1680, the city was subject to a long series of wars and pacts between Spain and Portugal, which eventually gave up its claim. Its many small museums are dedicated to the story of its tumultuous history.

The best sightseeing activity in Colonia, however, is simply walking through its *Barrio Histórico* (Old Town). Porteños come to Colonia for romantic getaways or a break from the city. It makes sense to follow their example: you don't get enough time here on a day trip to really relax or see the city at its own pace. A night in one of its many colonial-style bed-and-breakfasts offsets travel costs and time and makes a visit here far more rewarding.

GETTING HERE & AROUND
Hydrofoils and ferries cross the Río de la Plata between Buenos Aires and Uruguay several times a day. Boats often sell out, particularly on summer weekends, so book tickets at least a few days in advance.

Buquebus provides two kinds of service for passengers and cars between Buenos Aires and Colonia: the quickest crossing takes an hour on the hydrofoils or catamarans (111 pesos), the slower ferry takes around three hours (83 pesos). The Buquebus terminal is at the northern end of Puerto Madero, accessible by taxi or by walking seven blocks from Leandro N. Alem subte station along Trinidad Guevara and Avenida Alicia M. de Justo to the intersection with Bulevar Cecilia Grierson.

Colonia Express, a new company, operates the cheapest and fastest services to Colonia. The 50-minute catamaran trip costs 108 pesos one-way, or 178 pesos for a same-day return. Note that ferries leave from a different terminal to Buquebus, which you can reach by taxi or by walking five blocks from Retiro subte station along Avenida Ramos Mejía and its continuation Avenida de los Inmigrantes. The badly sign-posted terminal is at the intersection with Avenida Castillo.

Colonia's ferry port is undergoing renovation work until 2010, and is currently rather chaotic. The shortest way to the Barrio Histórico is to turn left out of the port car park into Florida—it's a six-block walk. Walking is the perfect way to get around this part of town; equally practical—and lots of fun—are golf carts and sand buggies, which you can rent from Thrifty.

ESSENTIALS

Bank Banco República (⊠*Av. Gral. Flores 151*).

Ferry Contacts Buquebus (⊠*Av. Antartida Argentina 821, Puerto Madero* ⊠*Patio Bullrich Shopping Mall, Av. Libertador 750, Recoleta* ☎*11/4316–6500* ⊕*www. buquebus.com*). **Colonia Express** (⊠*Av. de los Inmigrantes at Av. Castillo, Retiro* ⊠*Av. Córdoba 753, Microcentro* ☎*11/4313–5100 in Buenos Aires, 52/29676 in Colonia* ⊕*www.coloniaexpress.com*).

Medical Assistance Hospital de Colonia (⊠*18 de Julio and Rivera* ☎*52/20762*).

Rental Cars Thrifty (⊠*Av. Gral. Flores 172, 70000* ☎*52/22939* ⊕*www.thrifty. com.uy*).

Taxi Taxis Colonia (☎*52/22920*).

Visitor Info Colonia del Sacramento Tourist Board (⊠*General Flores and Rivera* ⊠*Manuel Lobo between Ituzaingó and Paseo San Antonio* ☎*52/23700* ⊕*www. colonia.gub.uy* ⊗*Daily 8* AM–7 PM).

EXPLORING

Begin your tour of the town at the reconstructed Portón de Campo or city gate, where remnants of the old bastion walls lead to the river. A block farther is Calle de los Suspiros, the aptly named Street of Sighs, a cobblestone stretch of one-story colonial homes that can rival any street in Latin America for sheer romantic effect. It runs between a lookout point on the river, called the Bastión de San Miguel, and the Plaza Mayor, a lovely square filled with Spanish moss, palm, and spiky, flowering *palo borracho* trees. The many cafés around the square are

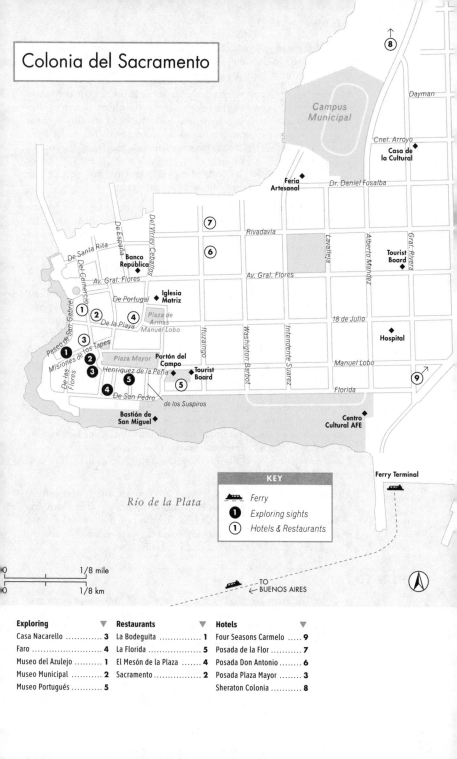

Colonia del Sacramento

Río de la Plata

Campus Municipal

Dayman

Cnel. Arroyo

Casa de la Cultural

Feria Artesanal

Dr. Daniel Fosalba

Rivadavia

Lavalleja

Alberto Mandez

Gral. Rivera

Tourist Board

De Santa Rita

De España

Del Virrey Ceballos

Banco República

Av. Gral. Flores

Av. Gral. Flores

Del Comercio

De Portugal

Iglesia Matriz

Plaza de Armas

Manuel Lobo

18 de Julio

Hospital

Paseo de San Gabriel

De la Playa

Misiones de los Tapes

Plaza Mayor

Portón del Campo

Tourist Board

Manuel Lobo

De las Flores

Henriquez de la Peña

Ituzaingo

Washington Barbot

Intendente Suarez

Florida

De San Pedro

de los Suspiros

Bastión de San Miguel

Centro Cultural AFE

Ferry Terminal

KEY

🚢 *Ferry*

❶ *Exploring sights*

① *Hotels & Restaurants*

TO ← BUENOS AIRES

1/8 mile
1/8 km

an ideal place to take it all in. Clusters of bougainvillea flow over the walls here and in the other quiet streets of the Barrio Histórico, many of which are lined with art galleries and antiques shops.

Another great place to watch daily life is the Plaza de Armas Manoel Lobo, where you can find the Iglesia Matriz, the oldest church in Uruguay. The square itself is crisscrossed with wooden catwalks over the ruins of a house dating to the founding of the town. The tables from the square's small eateries spill from the sidewalk right onto the cobblestones: they're all rather touristy, but give you an excellent view of the drum-toting *candombe* (a style of music from Uruguay) squads that beat their way around the old town each afternoon.

You can visit all of Colonia's museums with the same ticket, which you buy from the Museo Portugués or the Museo Municipal for $2.50. Most take only a few minutes to visit, but you can use the ticket on two consecutive days.

The one that's most worth a visit is the ❺ **Museo Portugués** (⊠*Plaza Mayor between Calle de los Suspiros and De Solís* ☯*Daily 11:15–4:45*), which documents the city's ties to Portugal. It's most notable for its collection of old map reproductions based on Portuguese naval expeditions. A small selection of period furnishings, clothes, and jewelry from Colonia's days as a Portuguese colony complete the offerings. Exhibits are well labeled, but in Spanish only.

A colonial Portuguese residence has been lovingly re-created inside the 17th-century ❸ **Casa Nacarello** (⊠*Plaza Mayor at Henríquez de la Peña* ☯*Daily 11:15–4:45*). A sundry collection of objects related to the city's history is housed in the ❷ **Museo Municipal** (⊠*Plaza Mayor at Misiones de los Tapies* ☯*11:15–4:45*). A small collection of the beautiful handmade French tiles that adorn fountains all over Colonia are on display at the ❶ **Museo del Azulejo** (⊠*Misiones de los Tapies at Paseo San Gabriel* ☯*Daily 11:15–4:45*), housed in a small 18th-century building near the river.

Also near the plaza are the San Francisco convent ruins, dating from 1683 but destroyed by Spanish bombardment not long after. Towering above the Plaza Mayor is the ❹ **Faro** (lighthouse), built in 1857. Your reward for climbing it are great views over the Barrio Histórico and the River Plate. ⊠*Plaza Mayor* ☜*$1.25* ☯*Daily 11–4*.

WHERE TO EAT

In Colonia, prices are displayed in dollars at all hotels and many restaurants. Uruguayan food is as beef-based as Argentinean fare, and also has a notable Italian influence. The standout national dish is *chivito*, a well-stuffed steak sandwich that typically contains bacon, fried egg, cheese, onion, salad, olives and anything else you care to throw into it, heavily laced with ketchup and mayonnaise.

¢–$ ✕**La Bodeguita.** Each night, this hip restaurant serves incredibly delicious, crispy pizza, sliced into bite-size rectangles. The backyard tables overlook the river, and inside is cozy, with rust- and ocher-color walls. ⊠*Calle del Comercio 167, 70000* ☎*52/25329* ⊟*No credit cards* ⊙*No lunch*.

$$$ ✕**La Florida.** The black-and-white photos, lace tablecloths, and quaint knickknacks that clutter this long, low house belie the fact that it was once a brothel. It still has private rooms, but it's dining that politicians and the occasional celeb rent them for these days. You, too, can ask to be seated in one, but consider the airy back dining room, which has views over the river. It's hard to say if it's the flamboyant French-Argentine owner's tall tales that keep regulars returning, or his excellent cooking. Specialties include kingfish, sole, and salmon cooked to order: you can suggest sauces of your own or go with house suggestions like orange-infused cream. ⊠*Florida 215, 70000* ☎*94/293–036* ⊟*AE, MC, V*.

$$–$$$ ✕**El Mesón de la Plaza.** Simple dishes—many steak-based—made with good-quality ingredients have made this traditional restaurant a favorite with porteño visitors to Colonia. The comprehensive wine list showcases Uruguayan vineyards hard to sample anywhere outside the country. Try to get one of the outside tables that sit right on the peaceful Plaza de Armas. ⊠*Vasconcellos 153, 70000* ☎*52/24807* ⊟*MC, V*.

$$ ✕**Sacramento.** It's in the heart of the Barrio Histórico, but chef Nico-
★ lás Díaz Ibarguren's fresh take on local ingredients is very now. Here the fish of the day comes in a cashew crust and chili sauce, and the minty, garlicky lamb—arguably Uruguay's best meat—is served with fried polenta chips. Set on a quiet corner, the renovated old house is light and breezy during the day, and its modern, dark wooden tables are candlelighted at night. ⊠*Calle del Comercio at De la Playa, 70000* ☎*52/29245* ⊟*AE, MC, V* ⊙*Closed Wed*.

WHERE TO STAY

$$$$ ⊞**Four Seasons Carmelo.** Serenity pervades this harmoniously decorated
★ resort an hour west of Colonia del Sacramento, reachable by car, boat, or a 25-minute flight from Buenos Aires. Everything is done in a fusion of Asian styles—from yoga classes at the incense-scented and bamboo-screen health club to bungalows (considered "standard rooms") with private Japanese gardens (and marvelous outdoor showers). In the evening, torches illuminate the paths, which meander through sand dunes. **Pros:** All rooms are spacious bungalows; fabulous, personalized service; on-site activities compensate for distance to sights and restaurants. **Cons:** Despite copious netting and bug spray, the mosquitoes can get out of hand; food quality is erratic; noisy Argentine families can infringe on romantic getaways. ⊠*Ruta 21, Km 262, Carmelo, 70100* ☎*54/29000* ⊕*www.fourseasons.com/carmelo* ⇆*20 bungalows, 24 duplex suites* ⌂*In-room: dial-up, safe, refrigerator, VCR. In-hotel: 2 restaurants, room service, golf course, tennis courts, pools, gym, spa, bicycles, children's programs (ages 5–12), laundry service, airport shuttle, executive floor, public Internet,, no-smoking rooms* ⊟*AE, DC, MC, V.* ⊙*CP*.

$ Posada Don Antonio. Rooms open onto long galleries that overlook an enormous split-level courtyard at Posada Don Antonio, the latest incarnation of a large, elegant building which housed one hotel or another for over a century. With their plain white walls and drab green carpets, the rooms lack the character promised by the architecture outside, but they're clean and functional and have comfy beds with wrought-iron bedsteads. **Pros:** The sparkling turquoise pool, surrounded by loungers; it's two blocks from the Barrio Histórico; rates are low but there are proper hotel perks like room service and poolside snacks. **Cons:** Staff are sometimes indifferent, at other times rude; plain, characterless rooms; ill-fitting doors let in noise from the courtyard. ⊠*Ituzaingó 232, 70000* ☎*52/25344* ⊕*www.posadadonantonio.com* ➥*38 rooms* △*In-room: refrigerator. In-hotel: room service, pool, no elevator, laundry facilities, public Internet* ⊟*AE, MC, V* ��❙*CP.*

$ Posada de la Flor. This colonial-style hotel is on a quiet street lead-
★ ing to the river, and is arranged around a sunny courtyard. Quilts and old china decorating the walls of the bright dining room announce a country-cottage vibe. You feel even more at home after attacking the unlimited breakfast spreads or gazing at the river over a glass of wine on the roof terrace—the owner's happy for you to bring your own. The simple, clean rooms have cheery quilts and are named after flowers: it's worth paying a few dollars extra for the more-spacious ones, like "Nomeolvides," or "Forget-me-not." The posada is a pleasant five-minute walk to Plaza Mayor. **Pros:** Peaceful location near the river and the Barrio Histórico; gorgeous breakfast area and roof terrace; great value. **Cons:** Standard rooms are a little cramped; damp spots on some ceilings; ground-floor rooms open onto the courtyard and can be noisy. ⊠*Calle Ituzaingó 268, 70000* ☎*52/30794* ⊕*www.hotelescolonia.com/posadadelaflor* ➥*14 rooms* △*In-room: safe, no phone. In-hotel: no elevator, laundry service* ⊟*No credit cards* ⓓ❙*CP.*

$$ Posada Plaza Mayor. A faint scent of jasmine fills the air at this lovely old hotel. All the rooms open onto a large, plant-filled courtyard complete with a bubbling fountain. The main building dates to 1840 (a part at the back is even older) and the original stone walls are visible in most rooms, which also have gloriously high ceilings. There are river views from the first-floor dining room and from the garden tucked behind the building, whose deck chairs rival those in the courtyard. **Pros:** Beautiful green spaces; on a quiet street of the Barrio Histórico; cheerful, accommodating staff. **Cons:** Cramped bathrooms; the three cheapest rooms are small and lack the atmosphere of the regular standard rooms; high price of deluxe rooms isn't justified by the amenities. ⊠*Calle del Comercio 111, 70000* ☎*52/23193* ⊕*www.posadaplazamayor.com* ➥*14 rooms* △*In-room: refrigerator. In-hotel: room service, no elevator, laundry service* ⊟*AE, DC, MC, V.* ⓓ❙*CP.*

$$$ Sheraton Colonia. This riverside hotel and spa, which opened in 2005,
★ is fast becoming a favorite with porteños on weekend escapes. It's easy to see why. Materials like copper, terra-cotta, and golden-color stone add warm touches to the airy, light-filled atrium. So does the massive wood-fronted fireplace, which is always lighted in winter. The rooms are just as inviting, with handmade woolen bed throws that take the edge off the

elegant, but rather generic, furniture. You can walk out straight onto the golf course and the sandy river beaches—who cares about the muddy water when you've got two gorgeous pools (one heated) to play in? Plan your visit midweek, when the rooms and spa packages are heavily discounted. **Pros:** Excellent value, considering the quality of accommodations; peaceful location with river views from many rooms; great spa. **Cons:** It's a 15-minute drive or taxi ride north of the Barrio Histórico; lots of noisy kids on weekends; staff are slow and sometimes unhelpful. ⊠*Cont. Rambla de las Américas s/n, 70000* ☎*54/29000* ⊕*www.sheraton.com* ➘*88 rooms, 4 suites* ⌂*In-room: safe, refrigerator, dial-up. In-hotel: 2 restaurants, room service, bar, golf course, pools, gym, spa, laundry service, no-smoking rooms* ⊟*AE, DC, MC, V* ⊺⦾*CP.*

AFTER DARK

Much of Colonia's nightlife centers on its restaurants, which become default drinking and bar-snacking spots after 11 or midnight. In summer, outdoor tables on the Plaza Mayor, which is often lighted with torches, are particularly atmospheric. Locals in their twenties and thirties rub shoulders with visitors at **Colonia Rock** (⊠*Misiones de los Tapies 157, 70000* ☎*52/28189*), a popular, laid-back bar on the Plaza Mayor. There's live music and even karaoke on Friday and Saturday.

BUENOS AIRES PROVINCE

Plains fan out where the city of Buenos Aires ends: this is the beginning of the pampas, which derive their name from the native Quéchua word for "flat field." This fertile earth is home to the cattle that make up the mainstay of Argentina's economy. All over are signs of active ranch life, from the grazing cattle to the modern-day gauchos. The region is also noted for its crops—alfalfa, sunflowers, wheat, corn, and soy.

While Argentina was still a Spanish colony, settlers gradually began to force indigenous tribes away from the pampas near Buenos Aires, making extensive agriculture and cattle breeding possible. (In 1880, during the bloody Campaign of the Desert, the southern pampas were also "cleared" of indigenous tribes.) By the latter half of the 19th century the region had become known as the grain supplier for the world. From 1850 to 1950 more than 400 important estancias were built in Buenos Aires Province alone. Some of these have been modified for use as guest ranches and provide the best glimpse of the fabled Pampean lifestyle.

TIGRE & THE PARANÁ DELTA

Tigre is 30 km (19 mi) northwest of Buenos Aires on the Ruta Panamericana, 35 km (22 mi) northwest of Buenos Aires on Avenida Libertador.

A coastal train ride or a drive through the shady riverside suburbs of Buenos Aires takes you to the river-port town of Tigre, the embarkation point for boats that ply the Delta del Paraná. Half a day is plenty of time to visit the town itself from Buenos Aires; allow a whole day if you

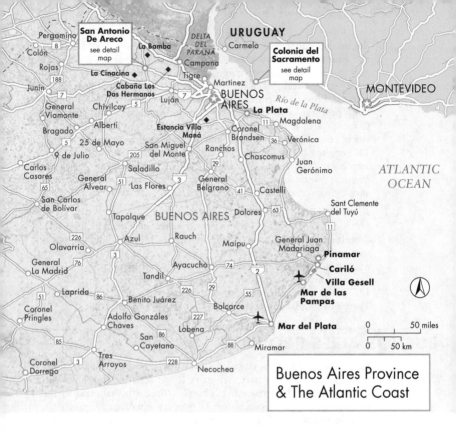

Buenos Aires Province & The Atlantic Coast

plan to explore the delta, too. The delta is a vast maze of canals, tributaries, and river expanding out like the veins of a leaf. Heavy vegetation and rich birdlife (as well as clouds of mosquitoes) make the network of rivers feel very tropical. The delta's many islands hide peaceful luxury getaways and cozy riverside restaurants accessible only by boat.

The waterways and close-packed islands that stretch northwest of Tigre are the most-accessible part of the 14,000 square km (5,400 square mi) that make up the delta, where roads are replaced by rivers. Churning brown waters and heavy vegetation are vaguely reminiscent of Southeast Asia, though the chichi houses and manicured gardens that line the rivers of the *Primera Sección* (the First Section, closest to Tigre) are a far cry from Mekong River settlements.

If you want to take in more of the delta than a short boat trip allows, do as the porteños do and combine it with a day's wining and dining at an island restaurant or a weekend at one of the luxury tropical lodges a little farther afield. Many offer private transport; otherwise inquire about which boat services take you there and check the timetables. The delta gets very hot and humid in summer, and the mosquitoes are ferocious; bring insect repellent.

GETTING HERE & AROUND

The cheapest way of getting to Tigre by train is on the suburban commuter train from Estación Retiro to Estación Tigre in the center of the town. There are about four departures an hour on the Línea Mitre, Ramal Tigre; a round-trip tickets costs 2.20 pesos. The slick, tourist-oriented Tren de la Costa was originally built in 1895 as a passenger train and refurbished in 1990. The train meanders through some of Buenos Aires' most-fashionable

> **WORD OF MOUTH**
>
> Just take a regular train to Tigre and the boats are across the street. No need for a tour. Try and arrive before 10 AM and take the boat that lets you get off at the islands. This trip takes all day, but it's so beautiful and very cheap. Have lunch at one of the islands.
>
> —Alana

northern suburbs and along the riverbank, stopping at nine stations before arriving at Estación Delta, right on the Río Luján. It starts halfway between Buenos Aires and Tigre, so you'll have to first take Línea Mitre to Mitre Station, where you can change to the Tren de la Costa's Maipú Station. Round-trip fare is 16 pesos. The center of Tigre is small enough to walk around easily, but there are taxis outside both train stations.

The most-comfortable—though touristy—way to travel the delta's waterways is aboard the two-story catamarans that leave from the docks on the Luján River, near the Tren de la Costa station. Rio Tur does two-hour round-trips; trips cost 30 pesos and leave on the hour 11–7 on weekends, and at 1, 3, and 5 PM on weekdays. ■TIP➜For an especially memorable ride, take a sunset cruise.

The low-slung wooden *lanchas colectivas* (boat buses) are the cheaper and more-authentic way to explore the waterways; locals use them to get around the delta. These leave from the Estación Fluvial (Boat Station), on the other side of the roundabout from Tigre Station. The main transport company for the delta is Interisleña, which serves all of the Primera Sección, the closest islands to the Tigre. Líneas Delta Argentino uses similar boats but is tourism-oriented—one- and three-hour trips cost 15 and 20 pesos. As the boats leave the delta, they pass the magnificent turn-of-the-20th-century buildings of Tigre's heyday and colorfully painted houses built on stilts to protect them from floods.

ESSENTIALS

Bank **Banco de la Nación** (⊠*Av. Cazón 1600, 1648* ⊕*www.bna.com.ar*).

Boat Contacts **Interisleña** (☏*11/4749–0900*). **Líneas Delta Argentino** (☏*11/4731–1236* ⊕*www.lineasdelta.com.ar*).

Medical Assistance **Hospital de Tigre** (⊠*Casaretto 118, 1648* ☏*11/4749–0876*).

Train Contacts **Trenes de Buenos Aires (Línea Mitre)** (☏*11/4317–4400* ⊕*www.tbanet.com.ar*). **Tren de la Costa** (☏*11/4732–6000* ⊕*www.trendelacosta.com.ar*).

Visitor & Tour Info **Rio Tur** (⊠*Sarmiento at Buenos Aires, 1648* ☏*11/4731–0280* ⊕*www.rioturcatamaranes.com.ar*). **Tigre Tourist Board** (⊠*Estación Fluvial, Mitre 305, Tigre 1648* ☏*11/4512–4497* ⊕*www.tigre.gov.ar* ⊙*Daily 9–5*).

EXPLORING

The focus of the action at Tigre is the picturesque **Puerto de Frutos** market. Hundreds of stalls selling furniture, home ware, and handicrafts fill the area around the docks along the River Luján, about eight blocks from the stations. It's a good place to find reasonably priced souvenirs and is particularly busy on weekends, the best time to visit it. ⊠*Sarmiento at Buenos Aires, 1648* ☏*No phone* ⊕*www.puertodefrutos-arg.com.ar* ⊙*Weekdays 10–6, weekends 10–7.*

⟳ **Parque de la Costa.** The devaluation of the peso forced rich porteños to abandon their annual Disney World expeditions. Instead, they come here, to Argentina's largest, most-modern amusement park whose main attractions are the two side-by-side roller coasters, *El Boomerang* and *El Desafío.* There's also a splashy river ride, swinging inverter ship, and a host of milder thrills, including a petting zoo. ⊠*Vivanco 1509, 1648* ☏*11/4002–6000* ⊕*www.parquedelacosta.com.ar* ⊠*38 pesos* ⊙*Jan. and Feb., Tues.–Sun. 11–9; Mar.–Nov., Fri.–Sun. 11–7.*

Italianate mansions, restaurants, and several rowing clubs dot the **Paseo Victorica,** a paved walkway that curves alongside the Río Luján for about 10 blocks. To reach it, cross the bridge next to the roundabout immediately north of Estación Tigre, then turn right and walk five blocks along Avenida Lavalle, which runs along the Río Tigre. ⊠*Along Río Luján between Río Tigre and Río Reconquista.*

WHERE TO EAT

PARANÁ DELTA ✕**El Gato Blanco.** It's easy to make a day out of lunch at El Gato Blanco,
$$–$$$ which is about 45 minutes from Tigre by boat—take any Interisleña service going to the Río Capitán. House specialties like *lenguado à la citron vert* (flatfish in a lime-and-champagne sauce) are served at tables arranged on huge wooden verandas, which have great views of the river. Weekends the place is incredibly popular with porteños and elbow room becomes scarce. After lunch, kids can play in the sweeping parkland behind the restaurant, while you relax in a riverside deckchair. ⊠*Río Capitán 80* ☏*11/4728–0390* ⌃*Reservations essential* ⊟*AE, MC, V* ⊙*No dinner Sun.–Fri.*

TIGRE ✕**Il Novo María del Luján.** An expansive terrace overlooking the river is
$$–$$$ the appropriate backdrop for the best fish dishes in Tigre. They favor elaborate preparations: some are so packed with unlikely ingredients that the fish gets lost; others, like the sole in champagne and wild mushroom cream, are spot-on. Crab ravioli in prawn sauce are another happy marriage. Both the terrace and the large inside room fill up on weekends, when harried waitstaff often take a long time to bring your orders or even the check. ⊠*Paseo Victorica 611, 1648* ☏*11/4731–9613* ⌃*Reservations essential* ⊟*AE, MC, V.*

WHERE TO STAY

It only takes a few hours to visit Tigre, and it's so close to Buenos Aires that there's no reason to relocate to a hotel there.

$$ ⌂**Alpenhaus.** Steeply sloping roofs and ornate wooden balconies are part of the Alpine theme at this little slice of Germany, delta-style.

Though the complex's exterior is slightly kitsch, the tiled floors and wooden furnishings of the bungalows are unassuming. Alpenhaus is on a small river, meaning you can enjoy the large lawns and swimming pool without the noise of too many boats. Everything served at the small restaurant–cum–beer garden from the fondues to the silky Sacher tortes (dark chocolate–and–nut cakes) is entirely homemade. To get here, take an Interisleña boat from Estación Fluvial going to Rama Negra. **Pros:** Homemade German food; friendly owners eager to please; good value for Delta accommodation. **Cons:** Plain rooms; it fills up with day-trippers on weekends; no other restaurants within walking distance. ⊠*Arroyo Rama Negra, 0.5 km (0.3 mi) from Río Capitán, 1648* ☎*11/4728–0422* ⊕*www.alpenhaus.com.ar* ⊷*1 room, 3 bungalows* ⚒*In-room: no phone, kitchen (some), refrigerator, Wi-Fi. In-hotel: restaurant, bar, pool, gym, no elevator* ⊟*No credit cards* ⦶*CP.*

PARANÁ DELTA
$$$
★

⊞**La Becasina Delta Lodge.** Wooden walkways connect the luxurious bungalows—each with a private riverside deck. Natural materials pervade the rooms, all of which have hardwood walls, jute rugs, and feather pillows in thick cotton cases. Comfort has been carefully thought out here: rooms have CD players, mosquito netting on the balconies, and reading lights over the bathtubs. You can get in touch with the delta by exploring in boats or kayaks, or soak up the jungle atmosphere by the lagoonlike pool, take a yoga class, or have a massage. As well as a dining room and a grill, nighttime entertainment options include a living-room-style bar serving top cocktails and a well-stocked library. The lodge is a bit out of the way to justify a night's visit: inquire about their two- and three-day all-inclusive packages. **Pros:** Total peace and quiet; lots of creature comforts; wild delta surroundings. **Cons:** The private boat is expensive; the public service is long and complicated; there's nothing else nearby so you're bound to the lodge; lots of mosquitoes. ⊠*Arroyo las Cañas, 1648* ☎*11/4328–2687* ⊕*www.labecasina.com* ⊷*15 bungalows* ⚒*In-room: no phone, no TV. In-hotel: 2 restaurants, pool, bar, no elevator, no kids under 14* ⊟*No credit cards* ⦶*AI.*

$$

⊞**Bonanza Deltaventura.** Thick vegetation surrounds the tomato-red 19th-century country house that's the center of the eco-action at Bonanza Deltaventura. The idea behind the establishment is to share the natural wonders of the area with visitors through organized nature walks, kayak expeditions, and horseback rides. Ten-foot ceilings, rustic furniture, and nothing but green outside the huge windows are some of the simple pleasures awaiting you. Hearty barbecues and drawn-out *mateadas* (mate tea and cake) are also highlights. Day packages are offered. **Pros:** Very back-to-nature; great home cooking; lots of sports. **Cons:** Rooms get hot in summer; no pool; minimum luxury. ⊠*Arroyo Rama Negra, 1648* ☎*11/4728–1674* ⊕*www.deltaventura.com* ⊷*4 rooms, 3 guesthouses* ⚒*In-room: no a/c, no phone, no TV. In-hotel: beachfront, bicycles, public Internet* ⊟*No credit cards* ⦶*AI.*

LA PLATA

55 km (35 mi) southeast of Buenos Aires via Autopista La Plata.

At the famous 1889 Paris Exposition (think Eiffel Tower), Jules Verne honored La Plata with a gold medal, citing the newly built city as a symbol of resplendent modernity. Accepting the medal was Dardo Rocha, the Buenos Aires governor who a few years prior assembled a team of architects and planners and created the provincial capital from the dust of semi-arid desert.

La Plata succeeds today from that creative genesis, a beautiful city of palatial estates on an ordered grid intersected by wide, diagonal boulevards and a rational scheme of parks and plazas every six blocks. The core of the city's planning is the "monumental axis" between 51st and 53rd streets, which contains most of the attractive churches, and government and cultural buildings. A stroll around the city and a visit to the *Museo de Ciencias Naturales* (Natural Science Museum) make a pleasant day trip from Buenos Aires. Streets have numbers instead of names, and though the city's perfect geometry makes it seem like a cinch to get your bearings, the diagonals can be quite disorienting, so keep your map at hand.

■TIP➜La Plata is so close to Buenos Aires that most people make it a day trip. That said, for a fabulous estancia experience, consider an overnight at Juan Gerónimo, a working ranch, close to the tiny village of Veronica, about 100 km (60 mi) south of La Plata. The ranch can arrange transportation; a car from Buenos Aires costs 270 pesos for up to four people each way.

GETTING HERE & AROUND

The Autopista La Plata connects Buenos Aires with La Plata (tolls of 4 pesos). Plaza and Costera Criolla Metropolitana run comfortable commuter buses between the two cities every 10 to 15 minutes. Both services leave from Dr. Martínez Zuviria, opposite Retiro station. Plaza also has stops (usually marked "129") at major intersections along Avenida 9 de Julio, and you can catch the Costera Metropolitana along Avenida Alem and Avenida Paseo Colón. Tickets for the 1¼-hour trip, which you need to buy from a vendor before getting on to the bus, cost 6.50 pesos. Take the buses labeled "La Plata x Autopista," which are the quickest.

Suburban trains run several times an hour on the Línea Roca from Buenos Aires' Constitución station to La Plata. It's slower than traveling by bus, and both the station and the ride itself can be dangerous, especially at night when muggers hang out around the station.

La Plata's city bus service is highly chaotic, and seems to baffle even locals. Thankfully, walking around the city center is both easy and pleasant. But, if you do get tired, flag down a black-and-white metered city taxi, which has a stop outside the bus terminal.

ESSENTIALS

Bank Banco de la Nación Argentina (⊠*Calle 7 No. 842, at Calle 48* ⊕*www. bna.com.ar*).

Bus Contacts **Costera Metropolitana** (📞800/222-6798 🌐www.costeramet
ropolitana.com). **Plaza** (📞800/333-1970 🌐www.grupoplaza.com.ar). **Terminal
de Ómnibus de La Plata** (📞221/421-0992). **Terminal de Ómnibus Retiro**
(📞11/4310-0700 🌐www.tebasa.com.ar).

Medical Assistance **Hospital San Martín** (✉Calle 1 No. 1791 📞221/425-
1717).

Taxi **Tele Taxi La Plata** (📞221/452-0648).

Train Contact **Estacíon de Trenes Plaza Constitución** (✉General Hornos 11, Plaza
Constitución, Buenos Aires). **Estacíon de Trenes La Plata** (✉Av. 1 at Calle 44).

Visitor Info **La Plata Tourist Board** (✉Palacio Campodónico, Diagonal 79 between Calles 5 and 56 📞221/422-9764 🌐www.laplata.gov.ar 🕐Weekdays 9–5).
Tourist Information Center (✉Pasaje Dardo Rocha, Calle 50 between Calles 6
and 7 📞221/427-1535 🕐Daily 10–5).

EXPLORING

🕐 In the northern portion of the city, the eucalyptus-shaded promenade,
★ **Paseo del Bosque,** is La Plata's biggest green space and a good place to
relax. Recreational options include a small zoo, a lake with paddleboat
rentals, an outdoor amphitheater, botanical gardens, an observatory, and
an equestrian center. In the middle of the Paseo del Bosque is the **Museo
de Ciencias Naturales** (✉Paseo del Bosque 📞221/425-7744 🌐www.
fcnym.unlp.edu.ar/museo 🖲12 pesos 🕐Tues.–Sun. 10–6; guided tours,
in Spanish, weekends on the half-hr), Argentina's only natural history
museum and the apple of La Plata's eye. Both the museum and the rambling building housing it date to 1889, and despite an ongoing renovation procedure the museum still seems eccentrically Edwardian. On
the ground floor, dusty glass cases display a host of bones, including a
substantial dinosaur collection and fossilized Argentinean megafauna
(think rodents the size of elephants). The freakishly large collection of
taxidermic animals, many rather moth-eaten, is eerie. Upstairs is a small
but strong display of Latin American archaeology.

The geographic center of the city is **Plaza Moreno,** where the Piedra
Fundacional (La Plata's Founding Stone) was laid in 1882. The graceful, pink-brick **Catedral de la Inmaculada Concepción** (✉Calle 14 between
Calles 51 and 53 📞221/427-3504 guided tours 🌐www.catedral
delaplata.com 🕐Museum daily 9–8) stands at the south end of Plaza
Moreno's tiled walkway. The neo-Gothic structure, inspired by cathe-
drals in Amiens and Cologne, was originally inaugurated in 1932 but
lacked the long double spires. During the past decade of restoration,
the monumental stained-glass window was completed and a museum
documenting the church's history was added in the crypt. Construction
wasn't complete until November 19, 1999—118 years to the day after
the city's foundation stone was laid. A carillon with 25 bronze bells
enlivens the western (51st Street) tower; the eastern (53rd Street) tower
has an elevator that rises to a lookout with the city's best views. At the
north end of Plaza Moreno is the 1883 German neoclassical **Palacio
Municipal** (✉Plaza Moreno s/n 🕐Daily 10–6), which is recognizable
by its central clock tower. The sumptuous interior is a quick wander,

especially the Salón Dorado (Golden Salon), with its marble staircase, painted ceilings, and mosaic tile floors.

The equestrian statue of South American liberator José de San Martín stands in the center of **Plaza San Martín**. On the north side of the square is the black slate roof of the French neoclassical Legislatura (provincial legislature) building. The cultural epicenter of La Plata is the **Pasaje Dardo Rocha** (⊠*Calle 50 between Calles 6 and 7* ☎*221/427–1843* ⏲*Tues.–Fri. 10–8, weekends 10–10*), housed in a massive Parisian-style building on the northwest side of Plaza San Martín. Once the city's main train station, it's now home to a small art-house theater, temporary exhibition and performance spaces, and several small art museums including the MACLA (Museum of Contemporary Latin American Art), a small collection of artworks by Argentinean masters. It occasionally hosts small-scale international exhibitions: Dalí and Goya shows are two recent examples.

Casa Curutchet. One of La Plata's architectural highlights is the only building designed by Le Corbusier in Latin America. The ultrageometric structure embodies all the modernist architectural principals the French master was famous for. ⊠*Bul. 53 No. 320, between Av. 1 and Calle 2* ☎*221/482–2631* ⊕*www.capba.org.ar/curutchet.html* ⏚*24 pesos* ⏲*Weekdays 10–2:30.*

WHERE TO STAY & EAT

$-$$
★
✕**Barra del Bosque.** When the Paseo del Bosque, La Plata's biggest green space, was designed in 1885, this diminutive stone building was the men's changing room for the now-defunct public pools. Two or three trim booths are squeezed into the cozy space, but the best seats are at the outdoor tables under the trees. The *rabas a la provenzal* (calamari rings sprinkled with garlic and parsley) come in deep white china bowls, and the steak sandwiches are juicy and well stuffed. A blackboard displaying the four daily main courses is tilted in your direction when you sit down—dishes like glazed *lomo* (filet mignon) with roast butternut squash are a welcome addition to La Plata's more-classic offerings. The Museo de Ciencias Naturales is a five-minute walk away. ⊠*Calle 57 at Calle 115, inside Paseo del Bosque, 1900* ☎*221/489–3115* ⊟*MC, V* ⏲*No dinner Apr.–Oct..*

¢–$
✕**Cervecería Modelo.** This alehouse restaurant opened its doors in 1892—10 years after the city was founded. The most-interesting tradition is tossing peanut shells to the floor. Pigeons, who have cleverly found a way inside, peck at them. But this spot isn't just about established quirkiness—it has what may be the largest menu in the country, which an exceptionally friendly and fast waitstaff guides you through it. The homemade pasta is a good bet; you'll have a choice of 25 sauces. The restaurant stays open late: until 2 AM weekdays and 3 AM weekends. ⊠*Calle 5 at Calle 54, 1900* ☎*221/421–1321* ⊟*AE, MC, V.*

$$$$
🛏**Juan Gerónimo.** For an authentic experience of a traditional working estancia, you can't beat this early 1920s ranch. It's said to have once belonged to a shipwrecked English bandit, but for several generations now it's been in the hands of the same family, who host your stay as well as running the estancia. Close to the tiny village of Veronica, south

CHOOSING THE RIGHT ESTANCIA

You can visit most estancias for the day—a *día de campo*—or stay for a day or two. How long you stay isn't the only thing you need to decide though. Estancias vary hugely in terms of price, luxury, and overall vibe. Here are a few helpful hints to help you choose:

Best for historical luxury: La Bamba

Best for all-out gaucho hokiness: La Cinacina

Best for horsing about on a budget: Cabaña Los Dos Hermanos

Best for getting back to nature: Juan Gerónimo

of La Plata, the ranch is set in the middle of a UNESCO World Biosphere Reserve known for its bird-watching. Horse enthusiasts love the grounds—there are 150 horses to choose from, and it's said that you can ride around the estancia for three days without covering the same terrain. The rather basic rooms are another hallmark of a real estancia—like the rest of the house, they're decorated with heavy antique furniture. **Pros:** Not at all touristy; huge portions of delicious homemade food; great for nature-lovers. **Cons:** Though charming, some rooms are small and rather basic, and not all have en suite bathrooms. ⊠*In Veronica, 100 km (63 mi) south of La Plata, 165 km (103 mi) south of Buenos Aires* ✆*Arroyo 873, Buenos Aires 1007* ☎*11/15–4937–4326 Buenos Aires reservations, 2221/481–414 estancia* ⊕*www.juangeron imo.com.ar* ⤳*11 rooms* &*In-room: no a/c, no phone, no TV. In-hotel: pool, no elevator, laundry service* ☰*No credit cards* ⊙|*AI.*

SAN ANTONIO DE ARECO

110 km (68 mi) west of Buenos Aires.

There's no better place to experience traditional provincial life in the pampas than this well-to-do farming town off RN 8. Grand *estancias* (ranches) dot the land in and around San Antonio. Many of the families that own them, which form a sort of local aristocracy, have switched from farming to estancia tourism. The gauchos who were once ranch hands now cook up huge asados (barbecues) and lead horseback expeditions for the ever-growing numbers of foreign tourists. You can visit one for a day—*un día de campo*—or immerse yourself with an overnight visit.

Porteño visitors tend to base themselves in the town itself, which is becoming known for its B&Bs. The fiercely conservative inhabitants have done a good job of preserving the turn-of-the-20th-century Italianate buildings that fill the sleepy *casco histórico* (historic center). Many contain bars and general stores, which maintain their original fittings; others are the workshops of some of the best craftspeople in the country.

In summer the Río Areco (Areco River), which runs through town, is teeming with swimmers—especially near the center of town, at the Puente Viejo (Old Bridge), which is overlooked by the open-air tables of various riverside parrillas. Nearby is the Museo Gauchesco y Parque

Criollo Ricardo Güiraldes, which celebrates historical gaucho life. During the week surrounding November 10, the *Día de la Tradición* (Day of Tradition), the town transforms into one long gaucho party, including shows, community barbecues, riding competitions, and a huge crafts fair. It's more fun to visit San Antonio on weekends, as many restaurants are closed Monday–Thursday.

GETTING HERE & AROUND

To drive to San Antonio de Areco, leave Buenos Aires on RN 9, crossing to RN 8 when it intersects at Km 35 (total tolls of 4.4 pesos). There are more than 20 daily bus services from Buenos Aires' Retiro bus station to San Antonio de Areco; most are run by Chevallier, and some by Pullman General Belgrano. Each company operates from its own bus stop in San Antonio de Areco. Once you've arrived, the best way to get around is on foot, but you'll need a *remis* (radio taxi) to get to most estancias (many also have their own shuttle service).

ESSENTIALS

Bank **Banco de la Nación Argentina** (⊠*Alsina 250, at San Martín* ☎*2326/42591* ⊕*www.bna.com.ar*).

Bus Contacts **Chevallier**(☎*2326/453–904 in San Antonio de Areco, 11/4311–0033 in Buenos Aires* ⊕*www.nuevachevallier.com*). **Pullman General Belgrano** (☎*2326/454–059 in San Antonio de Areco, 11/4315–6522 in Buenos Aires* ⊕*www. gralbelgrano.com.ar*). **Terminal de Ómnibus Retiro** (☎*11/4310–0700* ⊕*www. tebasa.com.ar*).

Medical Assistance **Farmacia Risolino** (⊠*Arellano at San Martín* ☎*2326/455–200*). **Hospital Emilio Zerboni** (⊠*Moreno at Lavalle* ☎*2326/452–759*).

Taxi **Remis Centro** (☎*2326/456–225*).

Visitor Info **San Antonio de Areco Tourist Board** (⊠*Bul. Zerboni at Arellano* ☎*2326/453–165* ⊕*www.pagosdeareco.com.ar* ⊘*Daily 8–8*).

EXPLORING

❶ **Museo Gauchesco y Parque Criollo Ricardo Güiraldes.** Gaucho life of the past is celebrated—and idealized—at this quiet museum on a small estate just outside town. Start at the 150-year-old *pulpería* (the gaucho version of the saloon), complete with dressed-up wax figures ready for a drink. Then head for the museum proper, an early-20th-century replica of a stately 18th-century *casco de estancia* (estancia house). Here, polished wooden cases contain a collection of traditional gaucho gear: *mates,* elaborately decorated knives, ponchos, and all manner of elaborate saddlery and bridlery. The museum is named for local writer Ricardo Güiraldes (1886–1927), whose romantic gaucho novels captured the popular imagination of the Argentinean people. Several rooms document his life in San Antonio de Areco and the real-life gauchos who inspired his work. ⊠*Camino Ricardo Güiraldes, 2760* ☎*2326/455–839* ⊕*www.museoguiraldes.com.ar* ▭*3 pesos* ⊘*Wed.–Mon. 11–5.*

❷ **Museo Taller Draghi.** San Antonio is famed for its silversmiths, and the late Juan José Draghi was the best in town. This small quiet museum adjoining his workshop showcases the emergence and evolution of

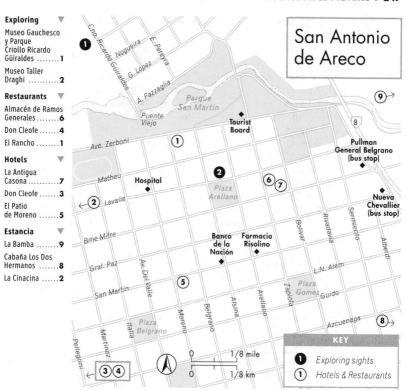

San Antonio de Areco

KEY

1 Exploring sights

(1) Hotels & Restaurants

the Argentine silver work style known as *platería criolla*. The pieces are mostly ornate takes on gaucho-related items: spurs, belt buckles, knives, stirrups, and the ubiquitous mates, some dating to the 18th century. Also on display is the incredibly ornate work of Juan José Draghi himself, which you can purchase in the shop. His son and a host of disciples keep the family business alive—they're often at work shaping new pieces at the back of the museum. ⊠*Lavalle 387, 2760* ☎*2326/454–219* ⊕*www.draghiplaterosorfebres.com* ₧*5 pesos* ☉*Daily 9–1 and 4–8.*

WHERE TO EAT

$ ✕**Almacen de Ramos Generales.** This old general store is airy and charming and its classic Argentine fare is consistently good. You can snack on *picadas* of salami, prosciutto, cheeses, olives, and eggplant *en escabeche* (pickled). The *bife de chorizo* (sirloin steak), meanwhile, is perfectly juicy, tender, and flavorful, all the more so when accompanied by wondrous french fries with basil. The atmosphere, too, is just right: it's country-store-meets-elegant-restaurant. Pleasant hues of light pour in from the plate-glass windows while you enjoy the impeccable service and memorable food. ⊠*Zapiola 143, between Lavalle and Sdo. Sombra, 2760* ☎*2326/456–376* ⊕*www.ramosgeneralesareco.com.ar* ▤*MC, V.*

$-$$ ✗**Don Cleofe.** Its peaceful setting—a century-old adobe house with but-
★ tercup-yellow walls hung with weavings and pottery from northwestern Argentina, where the chef is from—just out of town is not the only
thing that sets Don Cleofe apart from most San Antonio restaurants.
Forget about asado and milanesas: here the stars are *lomo* (tenderloin)
in a Malbec reduction and rabbit stew with *papines* (small potatoes
native to the Andes). Locals make the 10-block trek here on weekend
nights, but consider coming at lunch for the fabulous views over surrounding fields. Note that this restaurant is officially only open Friday through Sunday, but as it's in a hotel (that's always open), the
management has been known to open during off-hours (even for only
two people); just call ahead. ⊠*Guido s/n, west of town over old train
tracks, 2760* ☎*2326/455–858* ⊕*www.doncleofe.com.ar* ⊟*No credit
cards* ⊘*Closed Mon.–Thurs. except by reservation.*

$-$$ ✗**El Rancho.** San Antonio is famous for its parrillas, and the riverside
tables of this local favorite fill up fast on sunny weekends. Potbel-
lied stoves and an open fireplace keep the long thatched hut, with its
exposed beams and yellow-painted walls, toasty in winter. Cow-happy
porteño visitors inevitably order rounds of *asado* and *vacío* (beef on
and off the bone), cooked gaucho-style on a metal cross over hot coals.
Consider, at least, a break from the beef here: grilled *surubí* (catfish),
lenguado (sole), and *pacú* (a fish native to the Paraná River) are also
specialties. ⊠*Bul. Zerboni at Belgrano, 2760* ☎*2326/455–926* ⊟*No
credit cards* ⊘*No dinner Sun. –Thurs. No lunch Mon. –Thurs..*

WHERE TO STAY

B&BS 🛏**La Antigua Casona.** The dusky pink walls, brass bedsteads, antique
$ wardrobes, and embroidered linens of this small B&B make you feel
like you're staying in a Merchant Ivory film. The owner-architect renovated the 1897 house himself, and the fittings are as period as the
furnishings: think claw-footed bathtubs, vintage tiles, and doors and
floors rescued from demolition sites. Thankfully, old-world charm
comes with modern comforts like well-sprung beds and thick bath-
robes. **Pros:** Vintage furnishings; sunny, sheltered patio; two blocks
from the main square. **Cons:** High ceilings make some rooms drafty
in winter; getting to the bathroom of one room involves crossing the
(admittedly pretty) kitchen. ⊠*Segundo Sombra 495, at Bolívar, 2760*
☎*2326/456–600* ⊕*www.antiguacasona.com* ⇤*5 rooms* ⚬*In room:
no phone, no TV. In hotel: bicycles* ⊟*No credit cards* ⏁*CP.*

$ 🛏**Don Cleofe.** Rolling farmland spreads out before this family-run estab-
lishment, which is only a few blocks out of town but feels a million miles
from everywhere. Colorful cushions and bed throws from the north
of Argentina warm up the small, ultrasimple rooms, which each has
one wall painted a rich color like butter-yellow or crimson (but jarring
with the Formica wardrobes). The owners are happy to customize your
already generous breakfast, served in a sunny dining room that turns
into one of San Antonio's best restaurants on weekends. **Pros:** Fabulous
home cooking; fresh air and serious peace and quiet within walking distance of the main drag; friendly but nonintrusive owners. **Cons:** Small
rooms; only the best room has views of the fields; basic bathrooms.
⊠*Guido s/n, west of town over old train tracks, 2760* ☎*2326/455–*

858 ⊕*www.doncleofe.com.ar* ⊷*7 rooms* ⚒*In room: no a/c, no phone, no TV. In hotel: restaurant, bicycles* ▭*No credit cards* ⏏*CP.*

$$$ ⊞**El Patio de Moreno.** You might be in gauchoville but that doesn't mean you have to renounce creature comforts or slick design: hip hotel chain New Age has turned this 1910 town house into the coolest digs in town. You'll be loathe to get up from the comfy crimson sofas in the slate-gray atrium,

whose checkered floors, exposed beams, and stained-glass windows hint at the building's past. At night, the lights dim and it becomes a wine bar. Cow-skin rugs bring just the right dose of country to the minimal beige-painted rooms, which have huge beds. Some rooms open directly onto the sunny patio, where tables, chairs, and outdoor sofas overlook a tiny pool. **Pros:** Two blocks from the main street; beautifully designed rooms and lobby; most bathrooms have double sinks and shower heads. **Cons:** Rooms overlooking the street can be noisy; kids might be uncomfortable with the very adult vibe; service is professional but not very personal. ⊠*Moreno 251, at San Martín, 2760* ☎*2326/455–144* ⊕*www.patiodemoreno.com* ⊷*6 rooms* ⚒*In room: safe, no TV (some), Wi-Fi. In hotel: room service, bar, pool, no elevator, laundry service, public Internet* ▭*AE, MC, V* ⏏*CP.*

ESTANCIAS ⊞**La Bamba.** Nothing sums up aristocratic country splendor like the
$$$$ view you get of the stately main house as you sweep down the driveway. Visitors have been coming by here since the late 1700s, when the pulpería (where breakfast is served) was a stop-off on the viceroyal road to Peru. The main house dates to 1840, and has beautiful roofed verandas and a rear courtyard with a well. Inside, the heavy mismatched furniture, chintz curtains, handmade quilts, and enormous bathrooms feel like Argentina's take on Gosford Park. Although it's run like a business, the owners, the Aldao family, often preside over the communal dinners. La Bamba also organizes relaxed días de campo, which include riding, an asado and afternoon tea, and use of the swimming pool and grounds. A *día de campo* here costs 240 pesos per person; there's a 20% discount if you pay in cash. Lunch and drinks are included but transportation is not, though they will pick you up in San Antonio. **Pros:** Open views of the surrounding plains; elegant, old-worldly rooms and acres of bathroom with original fittings; relaxed vibe. **Cons:** You're paying for history, not luxury; the annex rooms, in the old servants' quarters, are much less atmospheric than those in the main house; you have to eat all meals with other guests. ⊠*Ruta 31, Cuartel IV, Villa Lía,1609* ☎11/4732–1269 Buenos Aires reservations, 2326/45–6293 estancia ⊕*www.la-bamba.com.ar* ⊷*12 rooms* ⚒*In room: no a/c, no phone, no TV. In-hotel: pool, bicycles, no elevator, laundry service* ▭*AE, MC, V* ⏏*AI.*

7

$$$ ⚑Cabaña Los Dos Hermanos. Horses—about 200 of them—are the focus of the action at this low-key estancia. There are no fancy shows on their día de campo, just great asados and lots of riding. The owners, Ana and Pancho Peña, welcome guests personally, while Don Juan, a gaucho with sideburns that rival Elvis, leads the lengthy horseback trips. If you're not up for the cowboy act, there are several sulkies in which to tour the land in style. You get unlimited riding if you stay over in one of their basic cabins, which are filled with an unharmonious hodgepodge of furniture but are clean and functional. Meals are homey, revolving around lots of beef. A *día de campo* here costs 200 pesos per person, including transport from Buenos Aires and lunch, but not alcoholic drinks. **Pros:** Unbeatably good value, especially the días de campo; loads of horsey action; gorgeous peaceful fields all around. **Cons:** Accommodation is basic and rather unwelcoming; no towns nearby; room TVs clash with the rootsy, country vibe. ⊠*Ruta 193, Km 10.5, Cuartel IV, Escalada, C.C. No. 50, Zárate 2800* ☎*11/4765–4320 in Buenos Aires, 3487/43–8903 estancia* ⊕*www.estancialosdoshermanos.com* ⇌*3 cabins* ⚑*In room: no a/c, no phone, kitchen, refrigerator. In-hotel: pool, laundry service* ⊟*No credit cards* ⦿*AI.*

$$$ ⚑La Cinacina. "Gauchodisney" is one way to describe this former dairy's *días de campo*, which routinely involve more than 200 tourists. You eat your lunchtime asado in a massive faux-rustic hall as an all-singing, all-dancing gaucho crew entertains you, then it's off to horseback riding and more shows. Still, what La Cinacina lacks in authenticity it makes up for in good old-fashioned fun. An overnight stay doesn't include the communal meals typical of estancias, but then La Cinacina's firm beds, monogrammed linens, and beautifully designed bathrooms aren't typical either. When the day visitors leave, the huge turquoise pool and the view over the fields are all yours. You can spend a *día de campo* here on Tuesday, Friday, and Sunday; they cost 170 pesos per person, including transport from Buenos Aires and lunch, but not alcoholic drinks. **Pros:** Better-appointed rooms than your average estancia; the conservatory-like breakfast room, with its comfy sofas and daylong supply of drinks and cakes; only two blocks from the town center. **Cons:** As representative of gaucho life as "Pirates of the Caribbean" is of buccaneers; unlike at most estancias, you pay extra for everything except breakfast; overrun with visitors during the day. ⊠*Western end of Lavalle, 300 m from Puente Viejo, 2760* ☎*2326/452–045* ⊕*www.lacinacina.com.ar* ⇌*12 rooms* ⚑*In room: safe, no TV. In hotel: restaurant, pool, bicycles, no elevator, laundry service* ⊟*AE, MC, V* ⦿*CP.*

AFTER DARK

Pulpería (tavern), *almacén* (general store), and *despacho de bebidas* (drinks counter) are some of the labels you might find on San Antonio's many traditional bars. Some genuinely haven't changed in 50 years (nor have their clientele), others are well-intentioned re-creations; all provide truly atmospheric surroundings for a coffee or a drink.

Candy jars, old bottles, and a gleaming antique cash register sit atop the decades-old zinc-topped bar of **La Esquina de Mertí** (✉*Arellano at Segundo Sombra., 2760* ☎*2326/456–705*), a gorgeous old café on Plaza Arellano. The owners seem more preoccupied with the charm of the building than that of the waitstaff, so stick with drinks—mugs of icy beer or Cinzano and soda are the local favorites.

La Ochava de Cocota (✉*Alsina at Alem* ☎*2326/452–176*) is a dim haunt, with old wooden tables and chairs, vintage photographs, and lamps that swing from the ceiling. In addition to being a laid-back place to down a couple of drinks, it makes great empanadas.

The guitars come out late on Friday and Saturday nights at **Puesto La Lechuza** (✉*Segundo Sombra at Bolívar, 2760* ☎*2326/454–542*). The traditional *pulpería* starts off the evening as a parrilla, but it's the drinks, picadas, and gaucho singsong that really make it special.

SHOPPING

San Antonio de Areco is an excellent place to pick up high-quality handicrafts and gifts, especially traditional silverware and leather goods. Workshops that double as shops fill the old houses lining Calle Alsina and other streets leading off Plaza Arellano, the main square.

The handwoven belts and ponchos **Cristina Giordano** (✉*Sarmiento 112, 2760* ☎*2326/452–829* ∰*www.telarcriolloypampa.com.ar*) creates in soft, naturally dyed fibers are fit to hang on the wall as art, and have justifiably made her San Antonio's best-known exponent of the traditional craft of weaving.

Gustavo Stagnaro (✉*Arellano at Matheu* ☎*2326/454–801* ∰*www.stagnaro.com.ar*) is a big name in San Antonio silversmithing. His majestic corner store sells gaucho knives, no-nonsense silver jewelry, and mate paraphernalia.

All of the mouthwatering chocolates and alfajores at **La Olla de Cobre** (✉*Matheu 433* ☎*2326/453–105* ∰*www.laolladecobre.com.ar*) are

Continued on page 259

THE COWBOYS at WORLD'S END

by Victoria Patience

Along a country road, you may come across riders herding cattle. Dressed in baggy pants and shirts, a knife stuck in the back of their belts, these are the descendants of the gauchos, Argentina's cowboys. These men of few words symbolize honor, honesty, and courage— so much so that a favor or good deed is known locally as a *gauchada*.

WHAT'S IN A NAME?

No one can agree on where the word "gaucho" comes from. Some say it's derived from the native Quechua-language word *guachu*, meaning "orphan" or "outcast"; others attribute similar meanings to the French word *gauche*, another suggested source. Yet another theory traces it (via Andalusian Spanish) to the Arabic word *chaouche*, a kind of whip for herding cattle.

Gauchos were the cattle-herding settlers of the pampas (grasslands), renowned for their prowess as horsemen. Most were criollos (Argentina-born descendants of Spanish immigrants) or mestizos (of mixed Spanish and native Argentine descent). They lived in villages but spent much of their time riding the plains, much like North American cowboys.

With the establishment of big estancias (ranches) in the early- and mid-19th century, landowners began taking on gauchos as hired hands. The sheer size of these ranches meant that the gaucho's nomadic lifestyle remained largely unchanged, however.

In the 1860s Argentina's president Domingo Faustino Sarmiento encouraged massive settlement of the pampas, and branded gau-chos as barbaric, potentially criminal elements. (Despite being of humble origins, Sarmiento was a snob about anything he saw as uncivilized.) Laws requiring travelers to carry passes ended the gaucho's right to roam. Many more than ever signed on as permanent ranch hands; others were drafted into military service, at times becoming deserters and outlaws.

Vindication came in the late-19th and early-20th century, when a wave of literary works like José Hernández's Martín Fierro and Ricardo Güiraldes's Don Segundo Sombra captured the national imagination with their dramatic, romantic descriptions of gauchos and their nomadic lifestyle. The gaucho—proud, brave, and melancholy—has been a national icon ever since.

Gaucho on an estancia near El Calafate, Patagonia, Argentina

GAUCHO GEAR

SOMBRERO:
Although a sombrero (flat-crowned, wide-brimmed hat) is the most typical style, conical felt hats (shown), berets, flat caps, and even top hats are also worn.

CAMISA:
Traditionally smocked shirt with baggy sleeves. Modern gauchos wear regular long-sleeved cotton shirts.

BOMBACHA:
Baggy pants cinched at the ankle; the story goes that after the Crimean War, surplus Turkish-style army pants were sold to Argentina by Britain and France. The fashion caught on: no gaucho is seen without these.

BOTAS:
Early gauchos wore rough, rawhide boots with open toes or a flip-flop-style thong. Today, gauchos in colder parts of Argentina wear flat-soled, tapered boots, usually with a baggy pirate-style leg.

CHIRIPÁ:
Before bombachas arrived, gauchos used to wind a large swathe of woven fabric (like an oversize loincloth) over thin, long underpants.

PAÑUELO:
Large, brightly colored kerchief, worn knotted around the neck; some gauchos drape them under their hats to protect their necks from the sun or cold.

CHAQUETA
Jacket; often kept for special occasions, and usually worn short and unbuttoned, to better display the shirt and waistcoat underneath.

FAJA:
A long strip of colorful woven fabric once worn to hold the pants up, now mainly decorative and often replaced by a leather belt. Either way, gauchos stick their knives in the back.

ESPUELAS:
Spurs; most gauchos favor those with spiked wheel-like designs.

Gaucho traditionally dressed

REBENQUE:
A short rawhide crop, often with a decorative metal handle.

PONCHO:
Woven from sheep's or llama's wool, usually long and often vertically striped. Some colors denote certain provinces.

ALPARGATAS:
Spanish immigrants in the 18th century popularized flat, rope-soled espadrilles in warmer parts of Argentina. Today, rubber-soled versions are more common.

BOLEADORAS:
Gauchos adopted this native Argentinian device for catching animals. It's made of two or three stones wrapped in cowhide and mounted at the end of a cowhide cord. You whirl the boleadora then release it at the animal's legs.

LAZO:
A braided rawhide lasso used for roping cattle.

CUCHILLO OR FACÓN:
No gaucho leaves home without his knife. Indeed, most Argentine men have one to use at barbecues (early gauchos used theirs for fighting, too). Handles are made of wood or horn, blades are triangular.

SUPER GAUCHOS

Unsigned mural of Gauchito Gil, a saint-like character in popular Argentine belief (supposedly a Robin Hood-type outlaw called Antonio Mamerto Gil Núñez).

EL GAUCHITO GIL: legend has it that this gaucho from Corrientes Province was hunted down by a sheriff over a woman. He was hung by his feet from a tree but, just before his throat was cut, he predicted that the sheriff would find his son at home mortally ill and only able to recover if the sheriff prayed to Gil. The prediction came true, and the repentant sheriff spread the word. Today, roadsides all over Argentina are dotted with red-painted shrines to this folk saint. Superstitious locals leave offerings, hoping for help with their problems.

MARTÍN FIERRO: the fictional hero of an eponymous 19th-century epic poem written by José Hernández. Fierro is a poor but noble gaucho who's drafted into the army. He deserts, and becomes an outlaw. His pride, independence, and love of the land embody the national ideal of what a man should be. Writer Jorge Luis Borges so loved the poem that he started a literary magazine with the same name.

JUAN MOREIRA: a real-life gaucho who married the daughter of a wealthy landowner, provoking the wrath of a jealous local judge. Wrongly accused of various crimes, Moreira became a fugitive and a famed knife-fighter, killing 16 men before eventually dying in a police ambush in 1874 in the town of Lobos in Buenos Aires Province. A 1973 biographical film by arty local director Leonardo Favio was a box-office smash.

UN DIA DE CAMPO

In the late 19th century, well-to-do European families bought huge blocks of pampas land on which to build estancias, often with luxurious houses reminiscent of the old country. The advent of industrial agriculture has led many estancias to turn to tourism for income; others combine tourism with small-scale farming.

The gauchos who once herded cows now have a new sideline shepherding visitors, putting on riding shows or preparing large-scale *asados* (barbecues). You can visit an estancia for a *día de campo* (day in the country) or to stay overnight or for a weekend. There are estancias for most budgets: some are ultraluxurious bed-and-breakfasts, others are homey, family-run farms.

A day at an estancia typically involves a late breakfast; horseback riding or a long walk; a full-blown asado accompanied by Argentine red wine; and afternoon tea. Longer stays at upscale establishments might also include golf or other sports; at working farms you

can feed animals or help with the milking. Estancia accommodation generally includes all meals, and although some estancias are close to towns, it's rare to leave the grounds during a stay.

HORSEMANSHIP

During a visit to an estancia, you may see gauchos demonstrating traditional skills and games such as:

Zapateo Criollo: a complicated, rhythmic, foot-stomping dance.

Jineteada or Doma: rodeo, gaucho-style.

La Carrera de Sortija: riders gallop under a bar from which metal rings are hung, trying to spear a ring on a stick as they pass.

Carrera Cuadrera: a short horseback sprint that riders start from a standstill.

Boleadas and Pialadas: catching an animal using boleadoras or a lasso, respectively.

La Maroma: participants hang from a bar or rope and jump onto a horse that gallops beneath them.

GAUCHO GRUB

When gauchos were out on the pampas for weeks, even months, at a time, their diet revolved around one food—beef—and one drink—mate (a type of tea). Times may have changed, but most Argentines still consume a lot of both.

MAKING THE MOST OF AN ASADO

Whether you're just at someone's home or out on an estancia, a traditional Argentine asado is a drawn-out affair. All sorts of meats go on the grill initially, including chorizo sausage, black pudding, and sweetbreads. These are grilled and served before the larger cuts. You'll probably also be served a pica-da (cheese, salami, and other snacks). Follow the local example and go easy on these starters: there's lots more to come.

The main event is, of course, the beef. Huge, grass-fed chunks of it, roasted for at least two hours over hot coals and flavored with little more than salt. While the asador (barbecuer) does his stuff, it's traditional to admire his or her skills; interfering (criticism, touching the meat, or the like) is not part of this tradition. The first meat to be served is often thick-cut ribs, accompanied simply by a mixed salad and bread. Then there will be a pause for digestion, and the asador will serve the choicest cuts: flank or tenderloin, usually. All this is washed down with a robust red wine and, not surprisingly, followed by a siesta.

THE COWBOYS AT WORLD'S END

7

MATE FOR BEGINNERS

Mate (mah-tay) is a strong tea made from the dried leaves of *Ilex paraguariensis*, known as yerba. It's drunk from a gourd (also called a mate) through a metal straw with a filter on the end (the *bombilla*).

Mate has long been a traditional drink for the Guaraní people native to Argentina's northeast. They introduced it to Jesuit missionaries, who learned to cultivate it, and today, most yerba mate is still grown in Misiones and Corrientes provinces. The drink eventually became popular throughout Argentina, Uruguay, and southern Brazil.

Much like tea in England, mate serves as the basis of social interaction: people drink it at any hour of the day. Several drinkers share the same gourd, which is refilled and passed round the group. It's often extended to strangers as a welcoming gesture. If you're shown this hospitality be sure to wait your turn, drink all the mate in the gourd fairly quickly, and hand the gourd directly back to the *cebador* (server). Don't pour yourself a mate if someone else is the cebador, and avoid wiping or wiggling the straw around. Also, you don't say "gracias" until you've had your fill.

WHAT'S IN A MATE?

Caffeine: 30 mg per 8-oz serving (versus 47 mg in tea and 100 mg in coffee)

Vitamins:
A, C, E, B1, B2, B3, B5, B complex

Minerals:
Calcium, manganese, iron, selenium, potassium, magnesium, phosphorus, zinc

Antioxidant properties:
similar to green tea.

SERVING MATE

1) Heat a kettle of water to just before boiling (176°F/80°C)—boiling water ruins yerba.

2) Fill ⅔ of the gourd with yerba.

3) Without the bombilla in place, cover the gourd with your hand, and turn it quickly upside down (to get rid of any fine yerba dust that can block the bombilla).

4) For some reason, yerba never sits flat in the gourd; pour some hot water in the empty space left by the slightly slanting yerba leaves. Let the yerba swell a little, cover the top of the bombilla with your thumb, and drive it firmly into the leaves.

5) Finish filling the gourd with water, pouring it in slowly near the bombilla's base. (Some people also add sugar at this point.)

6) Drink all the mate in the gourd (the cebador traditionally drinks first, so the mate isn't so bitter when brewed for others) and repeat Step 5, passing the gourd to the next drinker—and so on—until the yerba mate loses its flavor.

handmade on the premises. Best of all, you can sample at leisure before you buy. All the gaucho accessories you can think of—including knives, belt buckles, and kerchief rings—are exquisitely made in silver at **Platería del Campo** (⊠*Bolívar 66, 2760* ☎*2326/456–825*).

It's not surprising that the smell of leather hits you even before you go into **Talabartería El Moro** (⊠*Alsina at San Martín, 2760* ☎*2326/455–443*), as everything in this beautiful corner shop is made of the stuff.

THE ATLANTIC COAST

Southern Buenos Aires Province is synonymous with one thing—*la playa* (the beach). Every summer Argentines flock to the beaches at resort towns along the coast, many of which were originally large estates. Now they all hinge around a long *peatonal* (a pedestrians-only street) or central avenue. Nowadays it can be hard to see the sand in the summer months, when the towns are packed with porteños desperate to escape the city. However, by walking (or driving) a little farther, you can get some beach action in more-agreeable surroundings even in peak season. Locals prefer to be in the thick of things by renting a canvas tent at a *balneario* (beach club); weekly rents are extortionate but include access to toilets and showers, otherwise nonexistent on Argentine beaches. Happily, buying a drink at their snack bars earns you the same privilege.

Although the weather is usually hot and sunny December through February, the sea is usually bracing and temperatures drop in the evenings. Off-peak, the beaches tend to be deserted, and luxury accommodations are half price. Though the weather can get chilly, walks along the windswept sands—when followed by an evening in front of a warm log fire—can be very romantic. Bear in mind, though, that many hotels and restaurants only open on weekends April through November.

Busy resort town Pinamar has been *the* place for well-to-do porteños to buy holiday houses for decades. The nearby towns of Cariló and Mar de las Pampas are set among pine forests that have made their names as more-exclusive (and thus expensive) destinations. Although these three towns are self-contained, their beaches are actually one continuous stretch of sand.

GETTING HERE & AROUND
Comfortable long-distance buses connect Buenos Aires with the Atlantic Coast. Although extra services are added in January and February, tickets sell out fast. Pinamar's bus terminal also serves Cariló. Plusmar and El Rápido run numerous daily services; the five-hour trip costs 50–60 pesos.

Local bus company Montemar operates services every 15 minutes between Pinamar's bus station and Cariló and Villa Gesell, the closest town to Mar de las Pampas; as all services run along Avenida Bunge they are useful for getting around Pinamar, too.

Having your own wheels is a great boon on the coast. You can rent cars locally, or drive from Buenos Aires via Autopista La Plata and AU 2, a two-lane highway that continues straight to Mar del Plata. To reach the northern coast, come off AU 2 at Dolores, continue 30 km (20 mi) on RP 63 to Esquina de Crotto, then turn onto RP 56. This takes you the 110 km (70 mi) to Pinamar. The Pinamar turn-off also intersects with RP 11, also known as the Interbalneária, a two-lane coast road that connects Pinamar with Cariló and Mar de las Pampas.

ESSENTIALS

Bus Contacts **El Rápido Argentino** (☎11/4314–7999 ⊕www.rapido-argentino.com). **Plusmar** (☎810/999–1111 ⊕www.plusmar.com.ar). **Montemar** (☎2254/404–501). **Terminal de Ómnibus de Retiro** (☎11/4310–0700 ⊕www.tebasa.com.ar).

PINAMAR

342 km (212 mi) southeast of Buenos Aires via R2 and R11.

The resort town of Pinamar is a home away from home for wealthy porteños, including film and television stars, models, and politicians (those who haven't gone to the even snootier Punta del Este in Uruguay). Top local-brand boutiques compete for space with family-run shops along the otherwise unattractive main street, Avenida Bunge, which is usually packed with browsing teens during peak season. Pretty redbrick summerhouses with well-kept lawns line the un-tarmacked sand streets that make up the rest of the town; many follow curving lines inspired by the shapes of sea animals. The beach has pale sands, though to get a view of the dunes Pinamar was once famous for you need to go much farther north or south of the main drag. Some of the best sands in the area are in Ostende, a small town that is officially 5 km (3 mi) south of Pinamar, but effectively one of its suburbs—the half-hour walk along the beach from Pinamar is a pleasant way of reaching it.

ESSENTIALS

Bank **Banco de la Nación Argentina** (✉Av. Shaw 156, 7167 ☎2254/481–880 ⊕www.bna.com.ar).

Bus Contacts **Terminal de Ómnibus Pinamar** (☎2254/403–500).

Medical Assistance **Farmacia Bunge** (✉Av. Bunge 794 ☎2254/497–078). **Hospital de Pinamar** (✉Av. Shaw 255, at Las Medusas, 7167 ☎2254/491–670).

Taxi **Remises Pinamar** (☎2254/404–600).

Visitor Info **Pinamar** (✉Av. Bunge 654, 7167 ☎2254/491–680 ⊕www.pinamar.gov.ar ⊙Daily 8 AM–10 PM).

WHERE TO EAT

It's important to note that most restaurants only open on weekends during low season (April through November).

$$ ✗**Bar de Tapas.** This trendy beachfront restaurant's bite-size servings of pickled cuttlefish and octopus attract vacationing foodies looking to escape Pinamar's similar seafood menus. Their take on the seaside look is equally refreshing: the clapboard lining the walls and ceilings is painted a glossy white, as are the tables, chairs, and bar, punctuated by the occasional ultramarine tablecloth. During the day, huge plate-glass windows flood the airy, open-plan room with light. Candles, dimmed lights, and a great view of the moonlighted sea make for romance after dark. Although you could easily make a meal of tapas, it would be a shame to miss mains like the hake-and-salmon fillet in creamy leek sauce. Landlubberly standouts include garlicky lamb and sautéed vegetables brought to your table in a sizzling iron frying pan. ⊠*Av. del Mar at Los Tritones, 7167* ☎*2254/495–074* ⌂*Reservations essential* ▭*MC, V* ☉*Closed weekdays Apr.–June and Aug.–Nov.*

$$ ✗**Tante.** Though this restaurant's huge menu offers food from all over the world, it's the signature German dishes that keep Pinamar residents coming back for more. The elegant white house the restaurant occupies is a lonely historical orphan among glitzy car showrooms and 1970s tower blocks—it was the home of soprano Bruna Castagna. At lunch or dinner, there's classic Alpine fare like fondues (meat, cheese, and chocolate), smoked pork ribs, or goulash, all artfully presented. Alternatively, come for an afternoon tea of Tante's calorie-filled homemade cakes, strudels, and pastries, as you watch the world pass on Avenida Bunge through the restaurant's big windows or from the large wooden tables on the sidewalk. ⊠*De las Artes 35, 7167* ☎*2254/482–735* ▭*MC, V.*

$$ ✗**El Viejo Lobo.** Right on the beach, this has long been the most-popular seafood joint in town. The airy open-plan dining room doesn't offer intimacy, but the checkered tablecloths are as cheery as the waitstaff. *Gambas al ajillo* (deliciously garlicky chili prawns) are the must-have starter; follow them with a more-unusual fish dish like *pez lenguado con alcaparras* (flatfish in a browned butter-and-caper sauce). Reservations are a must if you want a table with a sea view. ⊠*Av. del Mar between Del Caracol and De las Almejas, 100 m from Av. Bunge, 7167* ☎*2254/483–218* ▭*MC, V.*

WHERE TO STAY

$$-$$$ ▤**Hotel del Bosque.** Two hectares (5 acres) of rolling parkland lie behind this solid redbrick hotel, giving all-green views to the pricier rooms. The mirrored lobby and shuddering elevator are the first signs that parts of the hotel haven't changed since it opened in 1981: even die-hard retro fans might balk at the scuffed furniture and closets, and rust-stained bathroom fixtures. All the same, the hotel is usually full of returning porteño families who value the friendly, efficient service over luxury. The parts that *have* been renovated are spot-on—sanded wood fittings, polished cement floors, and park views brighten the snack bar, minispa, and gym. Flowers from nearby trees drift into the irregular outdoor pool, while mosaic tiles and dark-wood paneling make the indoor pool warm and enticing. **Pros:** Beautiful grounds; great pools and sports facilities; good-value winter weekend packages include spa access and massages. **Cons:** Ten traffic-jammed blocks from the beach; run-down

rooms; high-season prices are exorbitant for the accommodation quality. ⊠*Av. Bunge 1550, at Jupiter, 7167* ☎*2254/482–480* ⊕*www.hotel-delbosque.com* ➥*46 rooms, 8 suites* ⌂*In-hotel: 2 restaurants, room service, tennis courts, pools, gym, spa, children's programs (ages 4–16; summer only), laundry service* ☰*AE, MC, V* ⊙*Closed weekdays Apr.–June and Aug.–Nov.* ⏀*CP.*

$$ 🖼**Hotel las Calas.** Detailed attention to design and a quiet adult atmosphere make this self-proclaimed boutique hotel the exception to Pinamar's family-oriented approach. Earth- and cinnamon-color stucco walls and sleek, polished wood furniture give you a warm welcome to the small lobby and bar. Plain white walls and drab linens mean that the rooms verge on the basic, though the bathrooms with their big bowl-style sinks are more of a step in the right direction. Avoid the four apartment-style suites, as their balconies look onto traffic-packed Avenida Bunge. Off-season the hotel is sometimes closed weekdays, so call ahead to check. **Pros:** Slickly designed, great for couples; lobby bar does good cocktails; wooden loungers in gravel-and-bamboo patio are great for sunbathing. **Cons:** Bang in the middle of Pinamar's busy main street; no pool; clueless (though amiable) staff. ⊠*Bunge 560, 7167* ☎*2254/405–999* ⊕*www.lascalashotel.com.ar* ➥*13 rooms, 4 apartments* ⌂*In-room: safe, refrigerator, dial-up, Wi-Fi. In-hotel: bar, gym, no elevator, parking (no fee)* ☰*AE, MC, V* ⊙*Closed weekdays Apr.–June and Aug.–Nov.* ⏀*CP.*

$$$$ 🖼**Terrazas al Mar.** Right in front of the beach, and only a block or two away from Pinamar's best restaurants and nightclubs, this huge hotel's location is its main draw. You can tell it's popular: guests file through the lobby continuously, flooding the willing but overworked staff with requests and lobbing their used towels at them. The rooms' plain ceramic floors, beige-and-slate walls, and rustic metal bedsteads are perfectly inoffensive, but they're not up to the hotel's high-season prices. Your own beach-club tent, the two pools, and small spa partly make up for it, as does the airy teal-wall restaurant where breakfast is served. Fully fitted apartments connecting to rooms on another floor are another boon for groups or families. **Pros:** Right on the beach; close to shops and restaurants; prices halve when summer finishes. **Cons:** Basic, uninspiring furnishings; unreasonably high prices and seven-night minimum stay in summer; pool-view rooms can be rowdy. ⊠*Av. del Mar and De las Gaviotas, 7167* ☎*2254/480–900* ⊕*www.terrazasalmar.com* ➥*76 rooms* ⌂*In-room: safe, kitchen (some), refrigerator, Wi-Fi. In-hotel: pools, gym, spa, beachfront, children's programs (ages 4–16; summer only), laundry service* ☰*AE, MC, V* ⏀*CP; MAP and FAP available in low-season.*

$$$ 🖼**Villa Ostende.** A block from the beach in a tranquil corner of Ostende, ★ this good-value hotel is a five-minute taxi ride from Pinamar's brash town center, but seems worlds apart. The breezy, uncluttered rooms and apartments have cream-color ceramic floors, simple wooden furniture, and crisp cotton bed linen. What rooms lack in serious luxury, the owners (themselves long-term Pinamar vacationers) have made up for in thoughtful attention to detail. One of Villa Ostende's two mock-Tudor buildings contains apartments with beach-view balconies.

Asado-addicted well-to-do Argentine families are especially grateful for the dishwashing service and private barbecue decks. These look onto the large, sloping garden, and deck-edged pool, which the hotel shelters from strong sea winds. Couples usually opt for the quieter block of double rooms. Its indoor pool has windows onto the lawn and a rock-grotto Jacuzzi; a sauna and steam room round off the cold-weather comforts. **Pros:** One block from a quiet stretch of beach; in summer, the already reasonable rates include your own tent at the beach club; well appointed for winter visits. **Cons:** No decent restaurants within comfortable walking distance; apartment bedrooms are slightly cramped; minimum seven-night stay in January and February. ☒*El Cairo at Biarritz, Ostende, 7167* ☎*2254/406–966.* ⊕*www.villaostende.com.ar* ⤶*8 rooms, 18 apartments* ♿*In-room: no a/c, kitchen (some), refrigerator, Wi-Fi. In-hotel: pools, gym, beachfront, no elevator, children's program (ages 6–12; summer only), public Internet* ☰*AE, MC, V* ⦿*CP.*

AFTER DARK

Seeing, being seen, and getting your photo in the social pages of a glossy mag is what Pinamar nightlife is all about. Most of it centers on the cafés, laid-back bars, and ice-cream parlors on Avenida Bunge and the streets branching off it. The vibe here is mostly laid-back and beachy, though it can feel like a frat party on weekends. Local guys often keep their board shorts on, although girls tend to doll up. The hottest bars belong to beach clubs north of Bunge—celebs are often present, but many events are invitation-only. Note that most people don't finish dinner until 1 or 2 AM, and clubs don't really fill up until 4 AM.

The long queues that form outside **Munchi's** (☒*Bunge at Av. Libertador, 7167* ☎*2254/481–015*) is a sign that the ultracreamy ice cream is worth waiting for. The seating area functions as a kind of boozeless pre-bar, where locals flirt before they hit nearby dance floors.

Dancers groove atop speakers at Pinamar's most-popular nightclub, **Ku–El Alma** (☒*Av. Quintana at Corso, 7167* ☎*2254/481–1314*). The seriously young and rowdy crowd don't seem to mind the wide variety of music—rock, techno, salsa, and cumbia—played on any given night. Local models and rock stars know that some of the best cocktails in town are at trendy beachfront bar **UFO Point** (☒*Av. del Mar y Tobís, 7167* ☎*2254/488–511*), which gets clubby later on.

CARILÓ

8 km (5 mi) south of Pinamar.

Cariló, the new darling of the summer resorts, represents an entirely new concept in Argentine beach tourism. Rather than a built-up town with a central square, a business center, and a bustling beach scene, Cariló is more like an exclusive seaside forest—a protected community with bungalows, hotels, and condos hidden in strategic places along a network of winding dirt roads. As a result, the beaches are pristine, the air is clean and quiet, and the beach experience is more intimate, but the experience is not steeped in Argentine history or culture. It's especially good for groups or families looking for an expensive bucolic getaway. There's an 18-hole golf course just outside town, and many companies offer outdoor activities like horseback riding and trekking— inquire at your hotel.

GETTING HERE & AROUND

Cariló's winding sandy streets are pleasant to walk along, but the main drag, Avenida Divisadero, is sufficiently far apart from the beach to make a car very appealing. The town's access road is 8 km (5 mi) south along RN 11 from Pinamar. Montemar buses connect the two towns via a less-direct route four times each hour; they arrive and depart from Avenida Divisadero and Cerezo.

ESSENTIALS

Bank **Banco de la Provincia de Buenos Aires** (⊠*Av. Divisadero 1500, 7167* ☎*2254/470–660* ⊕*www.bapro.com.ar*).

Bus Contacts **Montemar** (☎*2254/404–501*).

Medical Assistance **Farmacia Outóon** (⊠*Av. Divisadero at Avellano, Centro Comercial shop 17* ☎*2254/470–190*).

Taxi **Remis Cariló** (☎*2254/570–808*).

Visitor Info **Cariló** (⊠*Castaño at Benteveo* ☎*2254/570–773* ☉*Mar.–Nov., daily 9–7; Dec.–Feb., 8 AM–10 PM*).

WHERE TO STAY & EAT

Cariló has nothing in the way of budget accommodations, and meals and drinks here are some of the most expensive on the coast.

$$$ ✕**Burzako en el Mar.** The seaside outpost of Buenos Aires' most-inno-
★ vative Basque restaurant favors a hands-on approach to ingredients that's unusual in Argentina and unheard of in Cariló. Not content with merely cooking your sea bass, third-generation Basque-Argentine chef Koko Egozcue might well have caught it that morning himself, too. Other seafood standouts include perfectly battered *rabas* (calamari); octopus, anchovy, and cuttlefish *tapas*; and a perfectly gloppy black paella. All the same, few fish can upstage Burzako's original signature dish, *rabo de buey*, oxtail stewed for nine hours in red wine. The *crema fina de chocolate* makes an equally rich finish. The restaurant's all-white walls, tables, and floors are as plain as it gets, but with food this good, it's hard to care. ⊠*Avutarda at Cerezo, 7167* ☎*2254/572–123* ⚑*Reservations essential* ▤*MC, V* ☉*Closed weekdays Apr.–June and Aug.–Nov.*

$$$–$$$$ ✕**Camelia Sensi.** A modern take on traditional Swiss fare is the inspira-
tion behind the menu at Camelia Sensi. If you're feeling adventurous, go for the house specialty, *lomo à la pierrade*: a chef brings a hot slab of marble to your table and cooks the thinly sliced beef and vegetables on it, right under your nose. The fondues are drippingly delicious. ⊠*Boyero 1481, at Avellano, 7167* ☎*2254/571–157* ⚑*Reservations essential* ▤*AE, MC, V* ☉*Closed weekdays Apr.–June and Aug.–Nov.*

$–$$ ✕**La Pulpería.** A thatched roof, rustic tables and chairs, cast-iron grills, and big steaks might sound a bit too gaucho for Cariló's posh crowd, but this traditional parrilla is a firm local favorite. As well as the usual beef cuts, La Pulpería does great barbecued pork, chicken, and *achuras* (sweetbreads). ⊠*Av. Divisadero 1490, at Avellano* ☎*2254/470–296* ⌦*Reservations essential* ☐*MC, V* ⊘*Closed weekdays Apr.–June and Aug.–Nov.*

$$$$ 🍴**Casa Grande Cariló.** A faint scent of pine and eucalyptus wafting over your balcony sofa is as woodsy as it gets at Casa Grande, whose slick contemporary design is a world away from the Hansel-and-Gretel cabins most Cariló developers favor. The airy apartments are fitted with polished dark-wood furniture, cubey white sofas, and leather butterfly chairs. Pale stone fireplaces, in-room hot tubs, and touches of color like chocolate and pistachio prove that oh-so-cool can be warm, too. However, the real stroke of off-season genius is the huge plate-glass window that divides but unites the irregular outdoor pool and lawn and the heated, deck-edged indoor pool. It's worth paying a little extra for a two-room apartment, as the studios are much smaller. **Pros:** Gorgeous pool area; great contemporary design; very close to restaurants. **Cons:** Low ceilings mean if your neighbors are noisy, you'll hear them; snooty staff; seriously high prices in January and February. ⊠*Aromo 255, 7167* ☎*2254/470–739* ⊕*www.casagrandecarilo.com.ar* ⌦*12 apartments* ⌂*In room: no phone, kitchen, refrigerator, DVD, dial-up, Wi-Fi . In hotel: pools, gym, children's program (ages 6–16; summer only), laundry service* ☐*AE, MC, V* ⊚ICP.

$$$$ 🍴**Hostería Cariló.** This small hotel has put a lot of effort into creating an artsy vibe: the background music in the light-filled lobby is classic jazz, and there is a substantial DVD library from which you can borrow both classics and new releases to watch in your room. Terra-cotta floor tiles, pine furniture, and natural bedspreads suit Cariló's rustic atmosphere, though the cramped bathrooms are a bit *too* basic. They're back on track with the wooden tables and loungers scattered through the small garden which separates the hotel from the spa and pools. Antique soda siphons, old-fashioned liquor bottles, and retro ads decorate the hotel's restaurant, Tiramisú. At night, the lights are lowered and crisp white linen covers the simple wooden tables. The menu was designed by local celebrity chef Donato de Santis: his Italian classics are safe but very well executed. **Pros:** Two blocks from the beach; all-inclusive winter spa packages make for perfect winter escapes; warm, friendly staff. **Cons:** Not within comfortable walking distance of the main restaurant scene; low privacy in "duplex" apartments—open stairs separate the two sleeping areas; minimum seven-night stay in January and February. ⊠*Avutarda at Jacarandá, 7167* ☎*2254/570–704* ⊕*www.hosteriacarilo.com.ar* ⌦*16 suites, 4 duplexes, 12 apartments* ⌂*In-room: refrigerator, DVD, Wi-Fi. In-hotel: restaurant, room service, pools, gym, spa, bicycles, no elevator, laundry service* ☐*AE, MC, V* ⊚ICP; MAP in low season.*

AFTER DARK

An animated after-dinner discussion is the only nighttime noise Carilo's militant neighbors' committee allows. The nearest clubs and bars are in Pinamar, but there's plenty of squeaky-clean fun to be had at the quiet café-bars and ice-creameries along Boyero and Avenida Divisadero.

The richest, creamiest, most-natural ice cream on the Atlantic Coast comes from **Abuela Goye** (✉*Av. Divisadero at Cerezo, 7167* ☎*2254/531–710*). Patagonian berry sorbets are a specialty, and they do a roaring side business in handmade chocolates and jams.

On hot nights, young locals and older holidaymakers compete for an outside table at slick bar **La Confederada** (✉*Boyero at Cerezo, 7167* ☎*2254/572–333*). The drink of choice here is *clericó*, a sangria-like fruit drink made with cider and sold by the pitcher.

SHOPPING

You'd be hard-pressed to find a more-concentrated collection of souvenir and chocolate stores than Cariló has to offer. A series of *galerías, paseos,* and *ferias*—all euphemisms for tiny outdoor arcades—take up the whole of the large block bounded by Cerezo, Boyero, Avellano, and Avenida Divisadero. The corner of these last two streets houses the Centro Commercial, which contains a pharmacy, a general store, and most importantly, a good—but very pricey—supermarket and liquor store where you can stock up for picnics or (if you're renting an apartment) plan the night's cookout. Note that everything except breathing is cheaper in nearby Pinamar.

SPORTS & THE OUTDOORS

Cariló vacationers are typically a sporty lot. Expect lots of company on runs along the beach, not to mention competitive glances at your sports gear. The gorgeous golf club attracts players holidaying in other coastal towns.

You can rent well-maintained quad bikes by the hour from **Motorrad** (☎*2254/470–109*), which also organizes half-day adventure outings on them. Bicycles are available for the adrenaline-weary, but it's hard going on the sandy streets.

Cariló's best-established horse-riding outfit is **Palenque Maito** (☎*2254/1566–6363*). Their guided expeditions include night rides along the beach.

Sandboarding, sandsledding, and four-by-four expeditions across the dunes are some of the thrills available from **Wenner Adventure** (☎*2267/1567–6835*).

Narrow, doglegging fairways heavily lined with trees characterize **Links Cariló** (☎*2254/470–044*), the town's 73-par 18-hole golf course. The first 9 holes were designed by a Scotsman in the mid-1970s, and emulate a traditional British links. The club aimed for a more-modern, American style when they built the second part of the course in 1998. The club is open daily; access to greens costs 85 pesos Friday through Sunday, and 60 pesos Monday through Thursday. Club hire is also available.

MAR DE LAS PAMPAS

21 km (13 mi) south of Pinamar on RN 11.

The secret is out: this tiny town, once known only to campers and backpackers, has suddenly become the most sought-after vacation spot on the northern coast. Those willing to fork out the immense summer rents are generally rich, nature-loving porteños. They come here for the quiet sandy streets, heavily wooded lots, and stylish stone-and-wood cabins that have become Mar de las Pampas's trademark. Most of these are really glorified hotels, and include breakfast and maid service.

Huge dunes separate the town from the beach, and despite the fleets of new four-wheel drives that pack the few blocks around Avenida Cruz del Sur and El Lucero, the commercial center, the sands are wide and peaceful. Two smaller towns, Las Gaviotas and Mar Azul, lie south of Mar de las Pampas, and maintain an equally peaceful—if less-exclusive—back-to-nature vibe.

GETTING HERE & AROUND

The nearest long-distance bus station to Mar de las Pampas is in Villa Gesell, a crowded, unattractive resort town 6 km (4 mi) north of Mar de las Pampas. Taxis depart from an official taxi stand in the Villa Gesell terminal and cost around 15 pesos to Mar de las Pampas. Local bus company El Ultimo Querandí also connects the two: their groaning, sand-filled buses leave Avenida 3 in Villa Gesell every hour on the half hour, and return from Mar de las Pampas's main square on the hour. As Mar de las Pampas has no supermarket or bank (only an ATM), a car is useful for stays of more than a day or two. If you don't fancy the drive from Buenos Aires, you can rent a car in Pinamar or Villa Gesell, then continue along RN 11 until you reach the clearly labeled left-hand turnoff to Mar de las Pampas.

ESSENTIALS

Bank (ATM only) **Red Link** (⊠*Av. Lucero at Santa María, 7165* ⊕*www.redlink. com.ar*).

Medical Assistance **Farmacia Pujol** (⊠*In Paseo Sendas del Encuentro shopping center, Santa María between El Lucero and El Ceibo, 7165* ☎*2254/451–827*). **Hospital General de Agudos** (⊠*Av. 8 at Paseo 124, Villa Gese ll7165* ☎*2255/462–618*).

Taxi **Remises Sol** (⊠*Villa Gesell* ☎*2255/464–570*).

Visitor Info **Mar de las Pampas Tourist Board** (⊠*Av. 3 at Rotunda* ☎*2255/470–324* ⊕*www.mardelaspampas.info* ☉*Dec.–Mar. 10–8*).

EXPLORING

Picturesque **Faro Querandí** (Querandí Lighthouse) (⊠*Rte. 11* ☎*No phone*), about 24 km (15 mi) south of Mar de las Pampas, is surrounded by forest and sand dunes and can only be reached by quad-bike, which you can rent on the beach, or on organized four-wheel-drive excursion from Villa Gesell. The lighthouse itself is not open to the public.

Turismo Aventura (☎2255/466–797), based in Villa Gesell, organizes four-wheel-drive trips to the Faro Querandí and along the dunes south of Mar de las Pampas.

WHERE TO STAY & EAT

Mar de las Pampas has several different campsites, which the tourist office can direct you to. Be warned that in summer most campsites are packed to bursting with noisy teenagers. Most other accommodations here are cabins and apart-hotels (a cross between a furnished apartment and a hotel—breakfast is usually offered as is maid service and each room has a private kitchen and living room); breakfast and maid service are usually included in room rates. In January and February, the minimum stay is often one week.

$$–$$$ ✕**Amorinda.** Mom and dad are in the kitchen, and their grown-up daughters wait on the tables, but the real secret to this family-run restaurant are the killer pasta recipes grandma brought with her from Italy. The creamy whiskey-and-tomato sauce packs a punch, but it's not just flavors that knock you over here. Portions of pancetta-and-broccoli or ricotta ravioli easily serve two, while the mammoth lasagna, scattered with tiny meatballs, might fill even more. Their dense tiramisu might be too much to contemplate, but the trembling panna cotta in marmalade sauce is easier to deal with. ⊠*Av. Lucero at Cerchunoff, 7165* ☎*2255/479–750* ⚑*Reservations essential* ⊟*No credit cards* ☾*Closed weekdays Apr.–June and Aug.–Nov.*

$–$$ ✕**Heiwa.** Some say Heiwa does the best sushi and sashimi on the coast, others say it's the best in Argentina. It seems only fair, given the restaurant's fabulous setting on the ground floor of a small hotel by the same name right on the quiet sands of Las Gaviotas. Tempera, fish kebabs, and stir-fries are some of their other light but flavorful homemade dishes that go perfectly with beachy weather. As if the sight and sound of the real sea weren't enough, a huge Hokusai wave decorates one of the walls; mismatched crockery, paper lamp shades, and sandy floors complete the backdrop. The dessert *de rigueur* is the orange-and-ginger spring rolls. If you just want a drink, Heiwa makes delicious juices and cocktails under the white canvas awnings of their beach bar, which is lighted with flaming torches after dark. ⊠*Calle 34 at beachfront, Las Gaviotas 7165 (3 km from Mar de las Pampas)* ☎*2255/453–674* ⚑*Reservations essential* ⊟*No credit cards* ☾*Closed weekdays Apr.–June and Aug.–Nov.*

¢–$ ✕**Viejos Tiempos.** Teahouses abound in this area, but none have more-tranquil surroundings than Viejos Tiempos, which sits in a beautifully kept garden. In summer, hummingbirds hover over the flowers, while tea and cakes are served at heavy wood tables set with floral-patterned china. Inside, the chintz-and-lace drapes and cloying red cloths look like something your great-grandma would love, but at least the open fireplace keeps things toasty in winter. After years of making some of the best cakes in town, Viejos Tiempos has added (bizarrely) Mexican dishes to their menu, but it's the sweets that remain the main draw here. ⊠*Leoncio Paina at Cruz del Sur, 7165* ☎*2255/470–524* ⊟*No credit cards.*

$$ ⬛**Abedul.** Solid stone walls, oak fixtures, and handwoven drapes make the split-level cabins at Abedul very earthy. Outside each is a wooden deck with its own barbecue, and you can arrange for your breakfast to be brought here at the hour of your choice. The bedrooms look out over Mar de las Pampas's unspoiled woods, and the beach is only three blocks away. The sheltered indoor-outdoor pool is a boon when the wind whips up the sand and sea. **Pros:** Close to the beach and even closer to restaurants in the town center; lovely wooded grounds; low-key and laid-back but staff still try hard to please. **Cons:** In summer, four-wheel drives roar up and down the road outside; limited nearby grocery stores make the kitchen redundant; beds are on the hard side. ✉*Santa María between El Lucero and El Ceibo, 7165* ☎*2255/455-819* ⊕*www.mardelaspampas.com.ar/abedul* ⇆*7 cabins* ⌂*In-room: no a/c, kitchen, refrigerator, Wi-Fi. In-hotel: pool, bicycles* ⊟*AE, MC, V* ⊙*Closed weekdays Apr.–June and Aug.–Nov.* ⫟*CP.*

$$ ⬛**Heiwa.** The sea breezes that ruffle the cotton drapes at this beach-
★ front hotel are almost as calming as the owners' blissfully zenned-out approach. No wonder the low-key, simply furnished apartments are often booked up months in advance by returning devotees. With their colorful quilts, bright mosaic-tile bathrooms, and delicate table arrangements, the apartments are more reminiscent of staying with an attentive, arty relative than at a hotel. The incredible sea views more than compensate for the rather cramped bedrooms. The Japanese-Argentine couple who built the hotel have combined their heritages in the individual, bamboo-fenced patios, where solid-looking barbecues have pride of place. **Pros:** Any closer to the sea and you're in it; break-fast is served on the beach; incredible sushi restaurant by the same name and beach bar on-site. **Cons:** Far from other restaurants and the center of Mar de las Pampas; dead zone after midnight, aside from the in-house bar; tiny bedrooms. ✉*Calle 34 at beachfront, Las Gaviotas 7165 (3 km from Mar de las Pampas)* ☎*2255/453-674* ⊕*www.heiwa. com.ar* ⇆*5 apartments* ⌂*In-room: no a/c, no phone, kitchen, refrig-erator. In-hotel: restaurant, bar, beachfront, no elevator* ⊟*No credit cards* ⊙*Closed weekdays Apr.–June and Aug.–Nov.* ⫟*CP, MAP.*

LOS ESTEROS DEL IBERÁ

119 km (74 mi) northeast of Mercedes, Corrientes, on RP 40; 857 km (530 mi) northeast of Buenos Aires; 264 km (164 mi) southwest of Posadas, Misiones; 576 km (358 mi) southwest of Puerto Iguazú, Misiones.

Few places in Argentina are more peaceful, or more magical, than this vast wetland reserve, which stretches over 13,000 square km (5,000 square mi) of Corrientes Province (that's almost the size of Connecti-cut). "Iberá" is Guaraní (the local indigenous language) for "brilliant water," and the name couldn't be more apt. The wetlands are made of more than 60 shallow shimmering *lagunas* (lagoons), separated by sandy banks and punctuated by dense floating "islands" of vegetation.

Foz do Iguaçu
see detail map

Puerto Iguazú
see detail map

Esteros del Iberá &
Iguazú

Most are not fed by rivers; instead, the water seeps into them from the underground tables of the Paraná River basin.

The esteros are home to an incredible variety of wildlife, including two species of *yacaré* (Argentine alligators), capybara (the world's largest rodents), long-legged marsh deer, and around 400 species of birds. Small, flat-bottomed launches take you alongside these animals and the colorful vegetation they live among, into the heart of the Laguna Iberá, one of the biggest lagoons.

Although hunting is forbidden here, patrolling an area this size is almost impossible and some of the inhabitants, like the *aguará guazú* (maned wolf) and the *lobito de río* (neotropical otter), are close to extinction.

The tiny town of Colonia Carlos Pellegrini (population 800), on the eastern shore of Laguna Iberá, is the base for exploring the Esteros del Iberá. A handful of lodges and guesthouses are scattered about its dirt roads, most of which organize transfers, boat trips, hikes, and horse-back riding. Many operate all-inclusive packages, an advantage as the town's few restaurants have very limited offerings. Set between Buenos Aires and Puerto Iguazú, it makes a fascinating, albeit time-consuming, detour on trips to the falls. Note that there is no bank in the town, and no credit card facilities, so bring ample cash supplies with you.

GETTING HERE & AROUND

The unpaved, pothole-ridden Ruta Provincial 40 connects Colonia Carlos Pellegrini to Mercedes, a small city in Corrientes, and Posadas, the capital of Misiones. Flechabus operates four daily services to Mercedes (9–10 hours; 92 pesos). You can reach Posadas from Buenos Aires by bus with Vía Bariloche (12 hours; 135–155 pesos); or by plane on one of Aerolíneas Argentinas five weekly flights (1½ hours; 310 pesos).

Private **four-wheel-drive** transfers take two hours between Mercedes and Colonia Carlos Pellegrini; most accommodations in Colonia Carlos Pellegrini offer (or can arrange) transfers—expect to pay 240 pesos for up to four people. A cheaper option are the timetabled **four-wheel-drive** transfers run by Argentina Exploring, which connect Colonia Carlos Pellegrini with both Posadas and Mercedes several days a week and cost 90 pesos one-way.

ESSENTIALS

Bank **Banco de la Nación Argentina** (✉*Rivadavia 602, Mercedes 3470* ⊕*www. bna.com.ar*).

Bus Contacts **Argentina Exploring** (☎*3773/422–209*). **Flechabus** (☎*11/4000– 5200* ⊕*www.flechabus.com.ar*). **Vía Bariloche** (☎*11/4315–7700* ⊕*www.viabariloche.com.ar*).

Medical Assistance **Hospital Colonia Carlos Pellegrini** (✉*Aguará at Timbá, Colonia Carlos Pellegrini 3471* ☎*3773/422–040*).

SAFETY & PRECAUTIONS

Heavy rain can make the dirt road to Colonia Carlos Pellegrini treacherous. The alligators that live in the lagoon are all relatively young and are not big enough to harm a human (still, swimming is forbidden). Corrientes becomes unbearably hot and humid between December and February, and few visitors come during these months. The town is busiest during Argentinean winter holidays in July, when most accommodation is booked up. Whenever you come, be sure to bring plenty of mosquito repellent.

EXPLORING

The detailed, up-to-date displays at the **Centro de Interpretación** (visitor center) provide an excellent introduction to the local wildlife and the park's history. There's also a screening-room showing different short documentaries about the flora and fauna in the park. Families of capybara often sunbathe outside, sometimes joined by small alligators. ✉*Ruta Provincial 40, Km 118, Colonia Carlos Pellegrini* ☎*No phone* ⊕*www.camaraturismoibera.com* ⊗*Daily 8–noon and 4–6.*

Across the road from the visitor center is a short forest walk known as the **Sendero de los Monos** (Monkey Trail) for the families of howler monkeys that live high in its trees. It only takes 10 minutes to walk, but you'll need to linger longer (in patient silence) to see the monkeys. Early morning and evening are the best times to catch a glimpse of them.

⟳ The highlight of any visit to the Esteros is a boat trip to the **Laguna Iberá,**
★ home to more than 4,000 species of native plants and animals. The second-largest lagoon in the reserve, its incredibly still waters cover an area of 52 square km (20 square mi), but are on average only 10 feet deep. Every hotel and guesthouse in Colonia Carlos Pellegrini has its own small six- to eight-seater launch and arranges two- or three-hour guided trips (you can't visit the lagoon alone). Guides check in with the park rangers before speeding out into the center of the lake; when you're close to the floating islands of matted vegetation, they cut the motors and use long poles to maneuver the boat silently through the waters, gondolier-style. Among the rushes, ferns, floating hyacinths, and water lilies, you'll certainly see glistening, half-submerged *yacarés,* paddling *carpinchos* (capybara), and lots and lots of birds. Bring binoculars to see them and more-timid animals like the *ciervo de los pantanos* (marsh deer), which rarely come close to the boats. Thankfully, Colonia Carlos Pellegrini is remote enough to keep visitor numbers to a minimum, so you're unlikely to encounter other launches. You see different animals at different times of day, so try to visit the lake more than once. Afternoon visits are the most dramatic, however: you return to the shore at dusk, when the still waters seem to burn a brilliant orange as they reflect the setting sun.

WHERE TO STAY & EAT

¢ ✕**El Esquinazo.** The menu at this rough-and-ready *comedor* (canteen) runs to two dishes: empanadas and milanesas. Both are totally homemade—you can see the owners preparing them to order through a serving hatch—and go perfectly with the endless supplies of cheap beer from the shop they run in the other half of the house. ⊠*Curipí at Guaysú Virá, Colonia Carlos Pellegrini 3471* ☎*3773/1562–7548* ⊟*No credit cards.*

$$$ 🏠**Irupé Lodge.** If this thatched yellow lodge was any closer to the Laguna Iberá you'd be sharing your bed with an alligator. Half of the rooms look out over the water, and though they're fairly simple, the well-made wooden furniture, shining wood floors, and tangerine-painted walls mean they're still stylish. All-inclusive two-, three-, and four-night packages include guided walks, boat trips, horse riding, and all meals. These are served on the breeze-swept veranda overlooking the lagoon, and feature hearty, mandioca-based dishes typical of Corrientes. **Pros:** Location next to the lagoon; the pool; reasonably luxurious (for the town. **Cons:** In-house transfers are expensive; alcoholic drinks aren't included; portions can be small. ⊠*Capivára between Irupé and Ysypá, Colonia Carlos Pellegrini 3471* ☎*3773/1540–2193* ⊕*www.irupelodge.com.ar* �’*9 rooms* ⌂*In-room: no a/c, no phone, no TV. In-hotel: restaurant, pool, no elevator, some pets allowed* ⊟*No credit cards* ⊘*AI.*

¢ 🏠**Rancho Inambú.** Traditional materials—adobe, wooden beams, and thatching—were used to build this charming hostel, which is far and away the best budget accommodation in the Esteros. Hammocks swing from the veranda overlooking a lush garden. Local handcrafts decorate the white-walled rooms, which are plain but utterly spotless. The owner, Julieta Balparda, is a qualified guide and keen birdwatcher: fellow enthusiasts and nature-loving backpackers make up most of the guests. She organizes boat trips and leads many hiking expeditions herself (moonlight birding trips are a house specialty). Colonia Carlos Pellegrini's limited restaurants mean the large kitchen, living area, and on-site food shop are handy. **Pros:** Traditional Corrientes architecture; knowledgeable, attentive owner; great breakfasts included in the rock-bottom price. **Cons:** Shared bathroom; not right on the lake; beds are a bit hard. ⊠*Yerutí between Aguapé and Peguajó, Colonia Carlos Pellegrini 3471* ☎*221/15542–4692* ⊕*www.ranchoinambu.com.ar* ✇*3 rooms, 6 dorm beds, all without bath* ⏷*In-room: no a/c, no phone, no TV. In-hotel: laundry service* ▭*No credit cards* ◉*CP.*

> ## DOOR-TO-DOOR
>
> Argentinean travel agencies **Sol Iguazú Turismo** (☎*3757/421–008* ⊕*www.soliguazu.com.ar*) and **Caracol Turismo** (☎*3757/424–242* ⊕*www.caracolturismo.com.ar*) organize door-to-door transport to both sides of the falls, and can reserve places on the Iguazú Jungle Explorer trips. Both also run day trips to the Jesuit ruins in San Ignacio, the Itaipú Dam, and to other areas of Misiones Province.

IGUAZÚ FALLS

1358 km (843 mi) north of Buenos Aires; 637 km (396 mi) west of Curitiba, 544 (338 mi) west of Vila Velha.

Iguazú consists of some 275 separate waterfalls—in the rainy season there are as many as 350—that plunge more than 200 feet onto the rocks below. They cascade in a deafening roar at a bend in the Iguazú River (Río Iguazú/Río Iguaçu) where the borders of Argentina, Brazil, and Paraguay meet. Dense, lush jungle surrounds the falls: here the tropical sun and the omnipresent moisture make the jungle grow at a pace that produces a towering pine tree in two decades instead of the seven it takes in, say, Scandinavia. By the falls and along the roadside, rainbows and butterflies are set off against vast walls of red earth, which is so ubiquitous that eventually even paper currency in the area turns red from exposure to the stuff.

The falls and the lands around them are protected by Argentina's Parque Nacional Iguazú (where the falls are referred to by their Spanish name, the Cataratas de Iguazú) and by Brazil's Parque Nacional do Iguaçu (where the falls go by the Portuguese name of Foz do Iguaçu). The Argentine town of Puerto Iguazú and the Brazilian town of Foz do Iguaçu are the hubs for exploring the falls (the Paraguayan town of Ciudad del Este is also nearby).

Puerto Iguazú

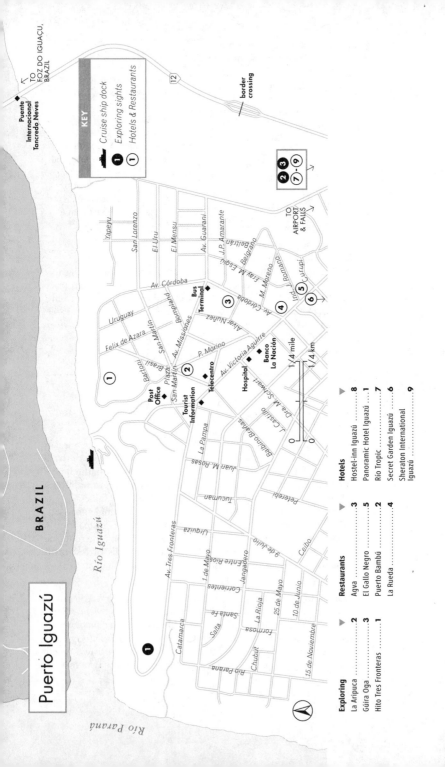

BRAZIL

Río Paraná

Río Iguazú

Puente Internacional Tancredo Neves

TO FOZ DO IGUAÇÚ, BRAZIL

TO AIRPORT & FALLS

border crossing

KEY
🚢 Cruise ship dock
1 Exploring sights
① Hotels & Restaurants

1/4 mile
1/4 km

Exploring
La Aripuca 2
Güira Oga 3
Hito Tres Fronteras 1

Restaurants ▶
Agva 3
El Gallo Negro 5
Puerto Bambú 2
La Rueda 4

Hotels ▶
Hostel-inn Iguazú 8
Panoramic Hotel Iguazú 1
Río Tropic 7
Secret Garden Iguazú 6
Sheraton International Iguazú 9

GETTING HERE & AROUND

ARGENTINA INFO

Aerolíneas Argentinas flies four to six times daily between Aeroparque Jorge Newbery in Buenos Aires and the Aeropuerto Internacional de Puerto Iguazú (20 km/12 mi southeast of Puerto Iguazú); the trip takes 1¾ hours. LAN does the same trip three to four times daily. Normal rates are about 350–400 pesos each way. Four Tourist Travel runs shuttle buses from the airport to hotels in Puerto Iguazú. Services leave after every flight lands and cost 12 pesos. Taxis to Puerto Iguazú cost 40 pesos.

> ### CROSS-BORDER BUS
>
> **Tres Fronteras** (☎3757/420–377 in Puerto Iguazú ⊕www.tresfronteras.com.ar) runs an hourly cross-border public bus service between the centers of Puerto Iguazú and Foz do Iguaçu. Locals don't have to get on and off for immigration but be sure you do so. To reach the Argentine falls, change to a local bus at the intersection with RN 12 on the Argentine side. For the Brazilian park, change to a local bus at the Avenida Cataratas roundabout.

Vía Bariloche operates several daily bus services between Retiro bus station in Buenos Aires and the Puerto Iguazú Terminal de Omnibus in the center of town. The trip takes 16–18 hours, so it's worth paying the little extra for *coche cama* (sleeper) or *cama ejecutivo* (deluxe sleeper) services, which cost 200–240 pesos one-way (regular semi-cama services cost around 180 pesos). You can travel direct to Rio de Janeiro (22 hours) and São Paolo (15 hours) with Crucero del Norte; the trips cost 250 and 200 pesos, respectively.

From Puerto Iguazú to the falls or the hotels along RN 12, take El Práctico from the terminal or along Avenida Victoria Aguirre. Buses leave every 15 minutes 7–7 and cost 8 pesos round-trip.

There's little point in renting a car around Puerto Iguazú: daily rentals start at 150–200 pesos, more than twice what you pay for a taxi between the town and the falls. A hire car is useful for visiting the Jesuit ruins at San Ignacio, 256 km (165 mi) south of Puerto Iguazú on RN 12, a two-lane highway in excellent condition.

ARGENTINA ESSENTIALS

Airline Contacts Aerolíneas Argentinas (☎800/2228–6527 ⊕www.aerolineas.com.ar). **LAN** (☎810/999–9526 ⊕www.lan.com).

Banks & Currency Exchange Argencam (⊠Av. Victoria Aguirre 1162). **Banco de la Nación** (⊠Av. Victoria Aguirre 179 ⊕www.bna.com.ar).

Bus Contacts Crucero del Norte (☎11/5258–5000 in Buenos Aires, 3757/421–916 in Puerto Iguazú ⊕www.crucerodelnorte.com.ar).**Four Tourist Travel** (☎3757/422–962 at airport, 3757/420–681 in Puerto Iguazú).**Vía Bariloche** (☎11/4315–7700 in Buenos Aires, 3757/420–854 in Puerto Iguazú ⊕www.viabariloche.com.ar).

Internet Telecentro (⊠Av. Victoria Aguirre 300 ☎3757/422–864).

Medical Assistance Farmacia Bravo (⊠Av. Victoria Aguirre 423 ☎3757/420–479). **Hospital Samic** (⊠Av. Victoria Aguirre 131, Puerto Iguazú ☎3757/420–288).

Taxis Remises Iguazú (⊠Puerto Iguazú ☎3757/422–008).

Visitor Info **Cataratas del Iguazú Visitors Center** (⊠*Park entrance* ☎*3757/420–180* ⊕*www.iguazuargentina.com* ⊘*Apr.–Sept. 8 AM–6 PM; Oct.–Mar. 7:30 AM–6:30 PM*). **Puerto Iguazú Tourist Office** (⊠*Av. Victoria Aguirre 311, Puerto Iguazú* ☎*3757/420–800* ⊘*Daily 7–1 and 2–9*).

BRAZIL INFO

There are direct flights between Foz do Iguaçu and São Paulo (1½ hours; R$380), Rio de Janeiro (2 hours; R$440), and Curitiba (1 hour; R$250) on TAM, which also has connecting flights to Salvador, Recife, Brasilia, other Brazilian cities, and Buenos Aires. Low-cost airline Gol operates slightly cheaper direct flights on the same three routes.

The Aeroporto Internacional Foz do Iguaçu is 13 km (8 mi) southeast of downtown Foz. The 20-minute taxi ride should cost R$35–R$40; the 45-minute regular bus ride about R$3. Note that several major hotels are on the highway to downtown, so a cab ride from the airport to these may be less than R$30. A cab ride from downtown hotels directly to the Parque Nacional in Brazil costs about R$90.

Via bus, the trip between Curitiba and Foz do Iguaçu takes 9–10 hours with Catarinense (R$90; R$180 for sleeper service). The same company operates the 17-hour route to Florianópolis (R$120). Pluma travels to Rio de Janeiro, which takes 11½ hours (R$130), and São Paolo, which takes 14 hours (R$130; R$205 for sleeper). The Terminal Rodoviário in Foz do Iguaçu is 5 km (3 mi) northeast of downtown. There are regular buses into town, which stop at the Terminal de Transportes Urbano (local bus station, often shortened to TTU) at Avenida Juscelino Kubitschek and Rua Mem de Sá. From here, buses labeled Parque Nacional also depart every 15 minutes (7–7) to the visitor center at the park entrance; the fare is R$4. The buses run along Avenida Juscelino Kubitschek and Avenida Jorge Schimmelpfeng, where you can also flag them down.

There's no real reason to rent a car in Foz do Iguaçu: it's cheaper and easier to use taxis or local tour companies to visit the falls, especially as you can't cross the border in a rental car. There are taxi stands (*pontos de taxi*) at intersections all over town, each with its own phone number. Hotels and restaurants can call you a cab, but you can also hail them on the street.

BRAZIL ESSENTIALS

Airline Contacts **GOL** (☎*300/115–2121 toll-free, 45/3521–4230 in Foz do Iguaçu* ⊕*www.voegol.com.br*).**TAM** (☎*800/570–5700 toll-free, 45/3528–8500 in Foz do Iguaçu* ⊕*www.tam.com.br*).

Bus Contacts **Catarinense** (☎*300/147–0470 toll-free, 45/3522–2050 in Foz do Iguaçu* ⊕*www.catarinense.net*). **Pluma** (☎*800/646–0300 toll-free, 045/3522–2515 in Foz do Iguaçu* ⊕*www.pluma.com.br*).

Banks & Currency Exchange **Banco do Brasil** (⊠*Av. Brasil 1377* ⊕*www.bb.com.br*).

Internet **Jinius** (⊠*Av. Brasil 34* ☎*45/3572–0078*).

Medical Assistance **FarmaRede (pharmacy)** (⊠*Av. Brasil 46* ☎*45/3572–1363*). **Hospital e Maternidade Cataratas** (⊠*Rua Santos Dumont 714* ☎*45/3523–*

Foz do Iguaçu

5200).

Taxis **Ponto de Taxi 20** (☎45/3523–4625).

Visitor Info **Foz do Iguaçu Tourist Office** (✉*Praça Getúlio Vargas 69, Brazil* ☎*45/3521–1455* ⊕*www.iguassu.tur.br* ⊙*7 AM –11 PM*).

EXPLORING

To visit the falls, you can base yourself in the small Argentine city of Puerto Iguazú, or its sprawling Brazilian counterpart, the city of Foz do Iguaçu. The two cities are 18 km (11 mi) and 25 km (15 mi) northwest of the falls, respectively, and are connected by an international bridge, the Puente Presidente Tancredo Neves. Another bridge links Foz do Iguaçu with Ciudad del Este in Paraguay. Together, the three cities form the *Triple Frontera* (Tri Border).

Originally a port for shipping wood from the region, Puerto Iguazú now revolves around tourism. This was made possible in the early 20th century when Victoria Aguirre, a high-society porteña, funded the building of a road to the falls to make it easier for people to visit them. Despite the constant stream of visitors from Argentina and abroad,

Puerto Iguazú is small and sleepy: there are only 32,000 inhabitants, and many of its roads still aren't paved.

The same was once true of Foz de Iguaçu, but the construction of the Itaipú dam (now the second largest in the world) in 1975 transformed it into a bustling city with 10 times more people than Puerto Iguazú. Many have jobs connected with the hydroelectric power station at the dam, while others are involved with trade (both legal and illegal) with the duty-free zone of Ciudad del Este, in Paraguay.

In general it makes more sense to stay in tourism-oriented Puerto Iguazú: hotels and restaurants are better, peso prices are lower, and it's much safer than Foz do Iguaçu, which has a bad reputation for violent street crime. There's also more to do and see on the Argentine side of the falls, which take up to two days to visit. The Brazilian side, though impressive, only warrants half a day.

Many travel agencies offer packages from Buenos Aires, São Paulo, or Curitiba that include flights or bus tickets, transfers, accommodation, and transport to the falls. These packages are usually more expensive than booking everything yourself but you do get round-the-clock support, which can be useful for rescheduling transfers around Argentina's delay-prone flights. WOW! Argentina's Iguazú packages include flights, two nights' accommodation at the Sheraton Iguazú, airport transfers, and a boat ride (but not transport to the Brazilian side), and costs around $700 per person. Buenos Aires Tours does a similar package but with accommodation in Puerto Iguazú; it includes transport to the Argentine side of the park (but not the Brazilian) and costs around $400 per person.

If you're staying in town, rather than at the hotels in the parks, you can easily reach the falls on your side of the border by public bus, private shuttle (most hotels work with shuttle company), or taxi. Travel agencies and tour operators in Puerto Iguazú and Foz de Iguaçu also offer day trips to the opposite sides of the border. Most are glorified shuttle services that save you the hassle of changing buses and get you through immigration formalities quickly. Use them to facilitate getting to the park, but avoid those that include in-park tours: most drag you around with a huge group of people and a megaphone, which rather ruins the fabulous natural surroundings.

Both parks are incredibly well organized and clearly signposted, so most visitors have no trouble exploring independently. Once in the park, be sure to go on a boat trip, an unmissable—though drenching—experience that gets you almost under the falls. You can reserve these through tour operators or hotels, or at booths inside the parks.

OTHER SITES TO SEE
Surprisingly, Iguazú is not the only site to see in these parts, though few people actually have time (or make time) to go see them.

IN ARGENTINA
Numbers in the margin correspond to numbers on the Puerto Iguazú map.

Continued on page 286

IGUAZÚ FALLS

By Victoria Patience

Big water. That's what *y-guasu*—the name given to the falls by the indigenous Guaraní people—means. As you approach, a thundering fills the air and steam rises above the trees. Then the jungle parts. Spray-soaked and speechless, you face the Devil's Throat, and it's clear that "big" doesn't come close to describing this wall of water.

Taller than Niagara, wider than Victoria, Iguazú's raging, monumental beauty is one of nature's most awe-inspiring sights. The Iguazú River, on the border between Argentina and Brazil, plummets 200 feet to form the Cataratas de Iguazú (as the falls are known in Spanish) or Foz do Iguaçu (their Portuguese name). Considered to be one waterfall, Iguazú is actually made up of around 275 individual drops, that stretch along 2.7 km (1.7 mi) of cliff-face. Ranging from picturesque cascades to immense cataracts, this incredible variety is what makes Iguazú so special. National parks in Brazil and Argentina protect the falls and the flora and fauna that surround them. Exploring their jungle-fringed trails can take two or three days: you get right alongside some falls, gaze down dizzily into others, and can take in the whole spectacle from afar. You're sure to come across lizards, emerald- and sapphire-colored hummingbirds, clouds of butterflies, and scavenging raccoonlike coatis. You'll also glimpse monkeys and toucans, if you're lucky.

GEOLOGY 101

Over 100 million years ago, lava surged up through cracks in the earth's crust near Iguazú. It spread out over the surrounding area, forming three layers of basalt (a dark, fine-grained rock) tens of meters high. The Iguazú River, which starts 1,200 km (745 mi) east, flowed over this. Later, the movement of tectonic plates raised parts of the surface, which became stepped. As the river flowed over these steps it eroded the rock surface it fell on even more, and over the next few million years, the waters carved out what are now the falls.

WHEN TO GO

Time of year	Advantages	Disadvantages
Nov.—Feb.	High rainfall in December and January, so expect lots of water.	Hot and sticky. December and January are popular with local visitors. High water levels stop Zodiac rides.
Mar.—Jun.	Increasingly cooler weather. Fewer local tourists. Water levels are usually good.	Too cold for some people, especially when you get wet. Occasional freak water shortages.
Jul.—Oct.	Cool weather.	Low rainfall in July and August—water levels can be low. July is peak season for local visitors.

WHERE TO GO: ARGENTINA VS. BRAZIL

Argentines and Brazilians can fight all day about who has the best angle on the falls. But the two sides are so different that comparisons are academic. To really say you've done Iguazú (or Iguaçu), you need to visit both. If you twist our arm, we'll say the Argentine side is a better experience with lots more to do, but (and this is a big "but") the Brazilian side gives you a tick in the box and the best been-there-done-that photos. It's also got more non-falls-related activities (but you have to pay extra for them).

IGUAZÚ FALLS

7

	ARGENTINA	BRAZIL
Park Name	Parque Nacional Iguazú	Parque Nacional do Iguaçu
The experience	Up close and personal (you're going to get wet).	What a view!
The falls	Two-thirds are in Argentina including Garganta del Diablo, the star attraction.	The fabulous panoramic perspective of the Garganta do Diablo is what people really come for.
Timing	One day to blitz the main attractions. Two days to explore fully.	Half a day to see the falls; all day if you do other activities.
Other activities	Extensive self-guided hiking and Zodiac rides.	Organized hikes, Zodiac rides, boat rides, helicopter rides, rafting, abseiling.
Park size	67,620 hectares (167,092 acres)	182,262 hectares (450,379 acres)
Animal species	80 mammals/450 birds	50 mammals/200 birds

VITAL STATISTICS

Number of falls: 160—275*	**Total length:** 2.7 km (1.7 mi)	**Average Flow:** 396,258 gallons per second **Peak Flow:** 1,717,118 gallons per second
Major falls: 19	**Height of Garganta del Diablo:** 82 m (270 feet)	**Age:** 120—150 million years

*Depending on water levels

IGUAZÚ ITINERARIES

LIGHTNING VISIT. If you only have one day, limit your visit to the Argentine park. Arrive when it opens, and get your first look at the falls aboard one of Iguazú Jungle Explorer's Zodiacs. The rides finish at the Circuito Inferior: take a couple of hours to explore this. (Longer summer opening hours give you time to squeeze in the **Isla San Martín**.) Grab a quick lunch at the Dos Hermanas snack bar, then blitz the shorter Circuito Superior. You've kept the best

for last: catch the train from **Estación Cataratas** to **Estación Garganta del Diablo,** where the trail to the viewing platform starts (allow at least two hours for this).

BEST OF BOTH SIDES. Two days gives you enough time to see both sides of the falls. Visit the Brazilian park on your second day to get the panoramic take on what you've experienced up-close in Argentina. If you arrive at 9 AM, you've got time to walk the entire trail, take photos, have lunch in the Porto Canoas service area, and be back at the park entrance by 1 PM. You could spend the afternoon doing excursions and activities from Macuco Safari

and Macuco EcoAventura, or visiting the Itaipú dam. Alternatively, you could keep the visit to Brazil for the afternoon of the second day, and start off with a lightning return visit to the Argentine park (half-price entrance on second visit) and see the **Garganta del Diablo** (left) with the sun rising behind it.

SEE IT ALL. With three days you can explore both parks at a leisurely pace. Follow the one-day itinerary, then return to the Argentine park on your second day. Make a beeline for the Garganta del Diablo, which looks different in the mornings, then spend the afternoon exploring the **Sendero Macuco** (and Isla San Martín, if you didn't have time on the first day). You'll also have time to visit Güira Oga bird sanctuary or La Aripuca (both on RN 12) afterwards. You could spend all of your third day in the Brazilian park, or just the morning, giving you time to catch an afternoon flight or bus.

IGUAZÚ FALLS

7

Estación
Cataratas

Estación
Central

Circuito
Superior

Parque Nacional Iguazú

Circuito
Inferior

Dos Hermanas

KEY

♿ *Wheelchair-accessible*

🍽 *Restaurant*

➚ *Scenic Viewpoint*

--- *Walking/Hiking Trails*

⛵ *Ferry Lines*

+++ *Rail Lines*

VISITING THE PARKS

Visitors gaze at the falls in Parque Nacional Iguazú.

Argentina's side of the falls is in the **Parque Nacional Iguazú**, which was founded in 1934 and declared a World Heritage Site in 1984. The park is divided into two areas, each of which is organized around a train station: Estación Cataratas or the Estación Garganta del Diablo. (A third, Estación Central, is near the park entrance.)

Paved walkways lead from the main entrance past the **Visitor Center,** called *Yvyrá Retá*—"country of the trees" in Guaraní (☎ 3757/49-1469 ⊕ www.iguazuargentina.com ✉ 40 pesos; 20 pesos on second day ⊗ Apr.–Sep 8–6; Oct.–Mar. 7:30–6:30). Colorful visual displays provide a good explanation of the region's ecology and human history. To reach the park proper, you cross through a small plaza containing a food court, gift shops, and ATM. From the nearby Estación Central, the gas-propelled Tren de la Selva (Jungle Train) departs every 20 minutes.

In Brazil, the falls can be seen from the **Parque Nacional Foz do Iguaçu** (☎45/3521–4400 ⊕ www.cataratasdoiguacu.com.br ✉ R$20.50 ⊗ Apr.–Sep 9–5; Oct.–Mar. 9–6). Much of the park is protected rain forest—off-limits to

visitors and home to the last viable populations of panthers as well as rare flora. Buses and taxis drop you off at a vast, plaza alongside the park entrance building. As well as ticket booths, there's an ATM, a snack bar, gift shop, and information and currency exchange. Next to the entrance turnstiles is the small **Visitor Center,** where helpful geological models explain how the falls were formed. Double-decker buses run every 15 minutes between the entrance and the trailhead to the falls, 11 km (7 mi) away; the buses stop at the entrances to excursions run by private operators Macuco Safari and Macuco Ecoaventura (these aren't included in your ticket). The trail ends in the **Porto Canoas** service area. There's a posh linen-service restaurant with river views, and two fast-food counters the with tables overlooking the rapids leading to the falls.

VISAS

U.S. citizens don't need a visa to visit Argentina as tourists, but the situation is more complicated in Brazil. ⇨ See the planning section at the beginning of the chapter.

EXCURSIONS IN AND AROUND THE PARKS

A Zodiac trip to the falls.

Iguazú Jungle Explorer (☎ 3757/42–1696 ⊕ www.iguazujungleexplorer.com) runs trips within the Argentine park. Their standard trip, the Gran Aventura, costs 100 pesos and includes a truck ride through the forest and a Zodiac ride to San Martín, Bossetti, and the Salto Tres Mosqueteros (be ready to get soaked). The truck carries so many people that most animals are scared away: you're better off buying the 50-peso boat trip—Aventura Nautica—separately.

You can take to the water on the Brazilian side with **Macuco Safari** (☎ 045/3574–4244 ⊕ www.macucosafari.com.br). Their signature trip is a Zodiac ride around (and under) the Salto Tres Mosqueteros. You get a more sedate ride on the Iguaçu Explorer, a 3½ hour trip up the river.

It's all about adrenaline with **Iguazú Forest** (☎ 3757/42–1140 ⊕ www.iguazuforest.com). Their full day expedition involves kayaking, abseiling, waterfall-climbing, mountain-biking, and canopying all within the Argentine park.

In Brazil, **Cânion Iguaçu** (☎ 045/3529–6040 ⊕ www.campodedesafios.com.br) offers rafting and canopying, as well as abseiling over the river from the Salto San Martín. They also offer wheelchair-compatible equipment.

Argentine park ranger Daniel Somay organizes two-hour Jeep tours with an ecological focus through his Puerto Iguazú–based **Explorador Expediciones** (☎ 3757/42–1632 ⊕ www.hotelguia.com/turismo/explorador-expediciones). The tours cost 50 pesos and include detailed explanations of the Iguazú ecosystem and lots of photo ops. A specialist leads the birdwatching trips, which cost 215 pesos and include the use of binoculars.

Macuco Ecoaventura (☎ 045/3529–6927 ⊕ www.macucoecoaventura.com.br) is one of the official tour operators within the Brazilian park. Their Trilha do Pozo Negro combines a 9-km guided hike or bike ride with a scary boat trip along the upper river (the bit before the falls). The aptly-named Floating trip is more leisurely; shorter jungle hikes are also offered.

ON THE CATWALK

You spend most of your visit to the falls walking the many trails and catwalks, so be sure to wear comfortable shoes.

IGUAZÚ FALLS

7

2 La Aripuca. It looks like a cross between a log cabin and the Pentagon, but this massive wooden structure—which weighs 551 tons—is a large-scale replica of a Guaraní bird trap. La Aripuca officially showcases different local woods, supposedly for conservation purposes—ironic, given the huge trunks used to build it, and the overpriced wooden furniture that fills the gift shop. ⊠*RN 12, Km 5, Puerto Iguazú* ☎*3757/423–488* ⊕*www.aripuca.com.ar* ☑*10 pesos* ⊙*Daily 9–7.*

3 Gúira Oga. Although Iguazú is home to around 450 bird species, the parks are so busy these days that you'd be lucky to see so much as a feather. It's another story at Gúira Oga, which means "house of the birds" in Guaraní, although "bird rehab" might be more appropriate. Injured birds, birds displaced by deforestation, and birds confiscated from traffickers are brought here for treatment. The large cages also contain many species on the verge of extinction, including the harpy eagle and the red macaw, a gorgeous parrot. The sanctuary is in a forested plot just off RN 12, halfway between Puerto Iguazú and the falls. ⊠*RN 12, Km 5, Puerto Iguazú* ☎*3757/423–890* ☑*Free* ⊙*Daily 8:30–6:30.*

1 Hito Tres Fronteras. This viewpoint west of the town center stands high above the turbulent reddish-brown confluence of the Iguacú and Paraná rivers, which also form the *Triple Frontera*, or Tri Border. A mini pale-blue-and-white obelisk reminds you you're in Argentina; across the Iguazú River is Brazil's green-and-yellow equivalent; farther away, across the Paraná, is Paraguay's, painted red, white, and blue. A row of overpriced souvenir stalls stands alongside it. ⊠*Av. Tres Fronteras, Puerto Iguazú.*

IN BRAZIL
Numbers in the margin correspond to numbers on the Foz do Iguaçu map.

1 Itaipú Dam and Hydroelectric Power Plant. It took more than 30,000 workers eight years to build this 8-km (5-mi) dam, voted one of the Seven Wonders of the Modern World by the American Society of Civil Engineers. The monumental structure produces 25% of Brazil's electricity and 78% of Paraguay's, and will be the largest hydroelectric power plant on Earth until China's Three Gorges (Yangtze) Dam is completed. You get plenty of insight into how proud this makes the Brazilian government—and some idea of how the dam was built—during the 30-minute video that precedes hour-long guided panoramic bus tours of

> **WORD OF MOUTH**
>
> We fell in love with Iguazú falls, even though we had a full day of rain. The falls are really breathtaking. We stayed at Sheraton. It's nothing special, but if you can afford it, stay here because the location is beyond amazing. And the food was actually very good. The must is the boat ride under the falls! So fun and a really great time! The people offering this tour are all over the place—so don't worry, you won't miss it. All the walks are really nice. We were lucky, we had no issues with mosquitoes. —jodicook

the complex. Although commentaries are humdrum, the sheer size of the dam is an impressive sight. To see more than a view over the spillways, consider the special tours, which take you inside the cavernous structure and includes a visit to the control room. Night tours—which include a light-and-sound show—begin at 8:30 Friday and Saturday.

2 At the **Ecomuseu de Itaipú** (Itaipú Eco-Museum) (⊠*Km 10, Av. Tancredo Neves* ☞*R$8* ☉*Daily 8–5:30*) you can learn about the geology, archaeology, and efforts to preserve the flora and fauna of the area since the dam was built. Note that it's funded by the dam's operator Itaipú Binacional, so information isn't necessarily objective. ⊠*Km 11, Av. Tancredo Neves* ☎*800/645–4645* ⊕*www.itaipu.gov.br* ☞*Panoramic tour R$13, special tour R$30* ☉*Panoramic tours Mon.–Sat. 8, 9, 10* AM*, 2, 3, 3:30* PM*. Special tours Mon.–Sat. 8, 8:30, 9:30, 10* AM*, 2, 2:30, 3:30* PM.

Flamingos, parrots, and toucans are some of the more-colorful inhab-
3 itants of the privately run **Parque das Aves** (Bird Park). Right outside the Parque Nacional Foz do Iguaçu, it's an interesting complement to a visit to the falls. A winding path leads you through untouched tropical forest and walk-through aviaries containing hundreds of species of birds. Iguanas, alligators, and other nonfeathered friends have their own pens. ⊠*Km 17, Rodovia das Cataratas* ☎*045/3529–8282* ⊕*www.parquedasaves.com.br* ☞*$10* ☉*Apr.–Sept., 8:30–5:30; Oct.– Mar., 8:30–6.*

WHERE TO EAT

Booming tourism is kindling the restaurant scenes of Puerto Iguazú and Foz do Iguaçu, and each has enough reasonably priced, reliable choices to get most visitors through the two or three days they spend there. Neither border town has much of a culinary tradition to speak of, though most restaurants at least advertise some form of the local specialty *surubí* (a kind of catfish), although it's frequently out of stock. Instead, parrillas or churrascarias abound, as do pizza and pasta joints.

PUERTO IGUAZÚ

$$ ✕**Aqva.** Locals are thrilled: finally, a date-night restaurant in Puerto Iguazú. Although the high-ceilinged split-level cabin seats too many to be truly intimate, they make up for it with well-spaced tables, discreet service, and low lighting. Softly gleaming timber from different local trees lines the walls, roof, and floor. Local river fish like *surubí* and *dorado* are the specialty: have them panfried, or, more unusually, as empanada fillings. Forget being romantic at dessert time: the chef's signature dessert, fresh mango and pineapple with a torrontés sabayon, is definitely worth keeping to yourself. ⊠*Av. Córdoba at Carlos Thays, 3370* ☎*3757/422–064* ▤*AE, MC, V.*

$$ ✕**El Gallo Negro.** A gaucho in full regalia mans the barbecue, which has
★ pride of place outside the hefty wooden cabin that houses this classy parrilla. The rustic-looking trestle tables on the wide veranda afford a great view of your sizzling steak; at night, they get the white table-cloth and candle treatment. It's not all barbecued beef: caramelized

suckling pig in an apple-and-honey sauce or lamb slow-cooked in red wine are some of the standouts from the kitchen. Their tempting take on Iguazú's only regional specialty, *surubi*, which they sauté in coconut milk, is sadly rarely available. ⊠*Av. Victoria Aguirre 773, at Curupí, 3370* ☎*3757/422–465* ▤*AE, MC, V.*

$ ✕**Puerto Bambú.** Iguazú's warm evenings make this popular pizzería's outdoor tables perfect for a casual meal. Their thin-crust pizzas are cooked *a la parrilla* (on a barbecue), so there's a pleasantly smoky edge to them. Reggae plays quietly in the background until around midnight, when they crank up the volume and bring out the cocktails as Puerto Bambú turns into a bar. ⊠*Av. Brasil 96, 3370* ☎*3757/421–900* ⌕*Reservations not accepted* ▤*No credit cards.*

$$–$$$ ✕**La Rueda.** This parrilla is so popular with visitors that they start serving dinner as early as 7:30 PM—teatime by Argentine standards. The local beef isn't quite up to Buenos Aires standards, but La Rueda's bife de chorizo is one of the best in town. Surubi is another house specialty, but skip the traditional Roquefort sauce, which rather eclipses the fish's flavor. They've stayed true to their rustic roots, however: hefty tree trunks hold up the bamboo-lined roof, and the walls are adorned by a curious wooden frieze carved by a local artist. ⊠*Av. Córdoba 28, 3370* ☎*3757/422–531* ⌕*Reservations essential* ▤*AE, DC, MC, V.*

FOZ DO IGUAÇU

$$ ✕**Búfalo Branco.** The city's finest and largest churrascaria does a killer *rodizio* (all-you-can-eat meat buffet). The picanha stands out from the 25 meat choices, but pork, lamb, chicken, and even—yum—bull testicles find their way onto the metal skewers they use to grill the meat. The salad bar is well stocked, a boon for vegetarians. ⊠*Av. Rebouças 530, 85851-190* ☎*45/3523–9744* ▤*AE, MC, V.*

$$–$$$$ ✕**Tempero da Bahia.** If you're not going as far as Bahia on your trip, you can at least check out its flavors at this busy tangerine-painted restaurant. It specializes in northeastern fare like *moquecas* (a rich seafood stew made with coconut milk and palm oil); their delicious versions are unusual for mixing prawns with local river fish. Spicy panfried sole and salmon are lighter options. The flavors aren't quite so subtle at the all-out seafood (and river food) buffets they hold several times a week, but they're tasty and cheap enough to pull in crowds. ⊠*Rua Marechal Deodoro 1228, 85851-030* ☎*45/3025–1144* ▤*AE, MC, V* ☾*No dinner Sun.*

$$–$$$$ ✕**Zaragoza.** On a tree-lined street in a quiet neighborhood, this traditional restaurant's Spanish owner is an expert at matching Iguaçu's fresh river fish to authentic Spanish seafood recipes. Brazilian ingredients sneak into some dishes—the *surubi à Goya,* catfish in a tomato-and-coconut-milk sauce—definitely merits a try. ⊠*Rua Quintino Bocaiúva 882, 85851-130* ☎*45/3028–8084* ▤*AE, DC, MC, V.*

WHERE TO STAY

Once you've decided which country to base yourself in, the next big decision is whether to stay in town or at the five-star hotel inside each park. If you're on a lightning one-night visit and you only want to see one side of the falls, the convenience of staying inside the park might offset the otherwise unreasonably high prices for mediocre levels of luxury. Otherwise, you get much better value for money at the establishments in town or on highways BR 489 (Rodavia das Cataratas) in Brazil, or RN 12 in Argentina. During the day you're a 20-minute bus ride from the falls and the border, and at night you're closer to restaurants and nightlife (buses stop running to the park after 7 or 8; after that, it's a 70-peso taxi ride into town from the park). Hotels in Argentina are generally cheaper than in Brazil. During low season (late September–early-November and February–May, excluding Easter), rooms are often heavily discounted.

⚠Staying on the Brazilian side (apart from at the Hotel das Cataratas in the park) is not recommended. It's dangerous, especially after dark, more expensive, and the hotels are worse.

PUERTO IGUAZÚ

¢ ⊞**Hostel-Inn Iguazú.** An enormous turquoise pool surrounded by classy wooden loungers and well-kept gardens lets you know this hostel is far from typical. Spacious double rooms with private bathrooms, huge windows, and lots of light attract couples and families. Partying backpackers love the great-value dorm accommodations (but be sure to book one with air-conditioning) and organized weekend bar expeditions. The Hostel-Inn is on the road halfway between Puerto Iguazú and the falls so you can get to the park early, but you're only a short bus or taxi ride from the restaurants and bars in town. You can sort out excursions, including visa-less visits to the Brazilian side, through the in-house travel agency. The kitchen churns out simple sandwiches, salads, and burgers, and there's an all-out asado several times a week. **Pros:** Beautiful pool area; rooms are simple but clean and well designed; location between town and the falls gives you the best of both worlds. **Cons:** Impersonal service from indifferent staff; lounge and kitchen are run-down; very basic breakfast. ⊠*Ruta 12, Km 5, 3370* ☎*3757/421–823* ⊕*www.hostel-inn.com* ⋑*52 rooms* ⌂*In-room: no a/c, no phone, no TV (some), Wi-Fi. In-hotel: restaurant, pool, bar, no elevator, laundry service, public Internet* ⊟*No credit cards* ⍟|CP.

$$$ ⊞**Panoramic Hotel Iguazú.** The falls aren't the only good views in Iguazú:
★ half the rooms of this chic hotel look onto the churning, jungle-framed waters of the Iguazú and Paraná rivers. The view inside the rooms is lovely, too. Taupe throws and ocher pillow shams offset the clean lines of the contemporary dark-wood furniture. You don't miss out on luxury by booking a standard, as all have king-size beds, flat-screen TVs, and hot tubs. Even the pool, set on a large terrace, looks over the river. The view gets seriously panoramic from the top-floor level, one of the best sundowner spots in town. **Pros:** River views; great attention to detail in the beautifully designed rooms; the gorgeous pool. **Cons:** The in-house casino can make the lobby noisy; indifferent staff aren't up to the price tag; it's a short taxi ride to the town center and in-house transport is overpriced. ⊠*Paraguay 372, 3370* ☎*3757/498–133* ⊕*www. panoramic-hoteliguazu.com* ⋑*91 rooms* ⌂*In-room: safe, refrigerator,*

Wi-Fi. *In-hotel: 3 restaurants, bar, pool, public Internet, no-smoking rooms* ☰*AE, MC, V* ¹⊙¹*CP.*

¢ ★ 🏠**Río Tropic.** Friendly owners Rémy and Romina give you a warm welcome at this rootsy B&B, which is surrounded by a lush garden. Rooms open onto a shady veranda that runs all the way along the wooden building; from there it's a couple of more steps to the pool. Pine paneling gives the rooms a country vibe, and though simple, they're spotlessly clean and have firm beds. **Pros:** The wonderfully helpful and attentive owners; peaceful surroundings; abundant homemade breakfasts served on a terrace in the garden. **Cons:** Too far from the town center to walk to; the rooms with no air-conditioning are stuffy in summer; low on luxury. ⊠*Montecarlo s/n, at Km 5, RN 12, 3370* ☎*3757/1541–6764* ⊕*www.riotropic.com.ar* ⟳*10 rooms* △*In-room: no a/c (some), no phone, no TV. In-hotel: bar, pool, bicycles* ☰*No credit cards* ¹⊙¹*CP.*

$ 🏠**Secret Garden Iguazú.** Dense tropical vegetation overhangs the wooden walkway that leads to this tiny guesthouse's three rooms, tucked away in a pale-blue clapboard house. There's nothing fancy about them, but the wood and wicker furniture and brightly painted paneling are cheerful and welcoming. So is the owner, John Fernandes. He's full of information and advice about Iguazú, which he shares with you over high-octane caipirinhas at the nightly cocktail sessions. **Pros:** Wooden deck overlooking the back-to-nature garden; knowledgeable owner John's charm and expert mixology; home-away-from-home vibe. **Cons:** The three rooms book up fast; no pool; comfortable but not luxurious. ⊠*Los Lapachos 623, 3370* ☎*3757/423–099* ⊕*www.secretgardeniguazu.com* ⟳*3 rooms* △*In-room: no phone, no TV, Wi-Fi. In-hotel: Public Wi-Fi.* ☰*No credit cards* ¹⊙¹*CP.*

$$$$ 🏠**Sheraton International Iguazú.** That thundering you can hear in the distance lets you know how close this hotel is to the falls. The lobby opens right onto the park trails and half the rooms have big balconies with fabulous falls views—be sure to reserve one of these well in advance (note that they're about 30% more expensive). The proximity is what you pay for: the rooms are perfectly serviceable, but the dated furniture, worn bathrooms, and drab linens aren't up to the price. And although the spa is a step in the right direction, with a gorgeous hot tub and treatment tents on an outdoor deck, you have to pay extra to use it. You can see the rising mist over the falls from the beautiful swimming pool, which is surrounded by palm trees and jungle. **Pros:** The falls are on your doorstep; great buffet breakfasts; well-designed spa. **Cons:** Drab rooms are in need of a complete makeover; mediocre food and service at dinner; other restaurants are an expensive taxi-ride away. ⊠*Parque Nacional Iguazú, Argentina 3370* ☎*3757/491–800* ⊕*www.sheraton.com* ⟳*176 rooms, 4 suites* △*In-room: safe, refrigerator. In-hotel: 2 restaurants, room service, pools, gym, spa, tennis courts, laundry service, public Internet, airport shuttle, no-smoking rooms* ☰*AE, DC, MC, V* ¹⊙¹*CP.*

FOZ DO IGUAÇU

$$$$ ⊤**Hotel das Cataratas.** Not only is this stately hotel *in* the national park,
★ with views of the smaller falls from the front-side suites, but it also provides the traditional comforts of a colonial-style establishment: large
rooms, terraces, vintage furniture, and hammocks. The main building,
surrounded by verandas and gardens, is almost 100 years old and is a
National Heritage Site. Although the rooms are comfortable, it's the
setting and atmosphere that you pay for, rather than luxury fittings.
Still, for many, the chance to wander the paths to the falls before and
after the hordes of day visitors arrive is priceless. The Itaipú restaurant serves traditional Brazilian dinners, including feijoada and a variety of side dishes. There's also an all-you-can-eat barbecue and salad
buffet each night in the Ipê grill near the pool. The hotel is undergoing extensive renovations through 2009: it will remain open, but
with fewer rooms. **Pros:** Right inside the park, a short walk from the
falls; serious colonial-style charm; friendly, helpful staff. **Cons:** Rooms
aren't as luxurious as the price promises; far from Foz do Iguaçu so
you're limited to the on-site restaurants; only the most-expensive suites
have views of the falls. ⊠*Km 28, Rodovia das Cataratas, 85853-000*
☎*045/2102–7000 or 0800/726–4545* ⊕*www.hoteldascataratas.com.
br* ⤸*198 rooms, 5 suites* ⌂*In-room: safe, refrigerator. In-hotel: 2 restaurants, tennis courts, pool, gym, laundry service, public Internet,
airport shuttle* ⊟*AE, MC, V* ⏇ICP.*

7

UNDERSTANDING BUENOS AIRES

Spanish Vocabulary

Menu Guide

SPANISH VOCABULARY

ENGLISH	SPANISH	PRONUNCIATION
BASICS		
Yes/no	Sí/no	see/noh
Please	Por favor	por fah-**vor**
Thank you (very much)	(Muchas) gracias	(**moo**-chas) **grah**-see-ass
You're welcome	De nada	deh **nah**-da
Excuse me	Con permiso	con pehr-**mee**-so
Pardon me	¿Perdón?	pehr-**don**
Could you tell me...?	¿Podría decirme...? ¿Podrías decirme...?	po-**dree**-ah deh-**seer**-me po-**dree**-as deh-**seer**-me
I'm sorry	Lo siento/Perdón	lo see-**en**-to/ pehr-**don**
Hello!/Hi!	¡Hola!	**o**-la
Good morning!	¡Buen día!	bwen **dee**-a
Good afternoon!	¡Buenas tardes!	**bwen**-as **tar**-des
Good evening/ Good night!	¡Buenas noches!	**bwen**-as **no**-ches
Goodbye!	¡Chau!/¡Adiós!	chow/a-dee-**os**
Mr./sir	Señor	sen-**yor**
Mrs./madam	Señora	sen-**yor**-a
Miss	Señorita	sen-yo-**ri**-ta
Pleased to meet you	Mucho gusto	**moo**-cho **goos**-to
How are you?	¿Cómo está usted?	**ko**-mo es-**ta** oos-**ted**
	¿Cómo estás?	**ko**-mo es-**tas**
Very well, thank you.	Muy bien, gracias.	mwee bi-**en**, **grah**-see-ass
And you?	¿Y usted?	ee oos-**ted**
	¿Y vos?	ee voss
Hello(on the telephone)	Hola	**o**-la

NUMBERS

0	Cero	**seh**-ro
1	Un, uno	oon, **oo**-no
2	Dos	doss
3	Tres	tress
4	Cuatro	**kwah**-troh
5	Cinco	**sin**-koh
6	Seis	**say**-iss
7	Siete	see-**yet**-eh
8	Ocho	**och**-oh
9	Nueve	**nweh**-veh
10	Diez	dee-**ess**
11	Once	**on**-seh
12	Doce	**dos**-seh
13	Trece	**tres**-seh
14	Catorce	kat-**or**-seh
15	Quince	**keen**-seh
16	Dieciséis	dee-**ess**-ee-**say**-iss
17	Diecisiete	dee-**ess**-ee-see-**yet**-eh
18	Dieciocho	dee-**ess**-ee-**och**-oh
19	Diecinueve	dee-**ess**-ee-**nweh**-veh
20	Veinte	**vain**-the
21	Veintiuno	**vain**-tee-oo-no
30	Treinta	**train**-tah
32	Treinta y dos	traint-tah-ee-**doss**
40	Cuarenta	kwah-**ren**-tah
43	Cuarenta y tres	kwah-**ren**-tah-ee-**tress**
50	Cincuenta	sin-**kwen**-tah
54	Cincuenta y cuatro	sin-**kwen**-tah-ee-**kwah**-tro
60	Sesenta	seh-**sen**-tah
65	Sesenta y cinco	seh-**sen**-tah-ee-**sin**-koh
70	Setenta	seh-**ten**-tah
76	Setenta y seis	seh-**ten**-tah-ee-**say**-iss

80	Ochenta	oh-**chen**-tah
87	Ochenta y siete	oh-**chen**-tah-ee-see-**yet**-eh
90	Noventa	no-**ven**-tah
98	Noventa y ocho	no-**ven**-tah-ee-**och**-oh
100	Cien	see-**en**
101	Ciento uno	see-**en**-to-**oo**-no
200	Doscientos	doh-see-**en**-toss
500	Quinientos	kin-ee-**en**-toss
700	Setecientos	set-eh-see-**en**-toss
900	Novecientos	nov-eh-see-**en**-toss
1,000	Mil	meel
2,000	Dos mil	doss meel
1,000,000	Un millón	un mi-**shon**

DAYS OF THE WEEK

Sunday	domingo	doh-**ming**-oh
Monday	lunes	**loo**-ness
Tuesday	martes	**mar**-tess
Wednesday	miércoles	mee-**er**-koh-less
Thursday	jueves	**hweh**-vess
Friday	viernes	vee-**er**-ness
Saturday	sábado	**sah**-bad-oh

MONTHS

January	enero	eh-**neh**-ro
February	febrero	feb-**reh**-ro
March	marzo	**mar**-soh
April	abril	ab-**reel**
May	mayo	**mah**-shoh
June	junio	**hoo**-nee-oh
July	julio	**hoo**-lee-oh
August	agosto	ah-**gos**-toh
September	septiembre	sep-tee-**em**-breh
October	octubre	ok-**too**-breh

| November | noviembre | nov-ee-**em**-breh |
| December | diciembre | diss-ee-**em**-breh |

USEFUL PHRASES

Do you speak English?	¿Habla usted inglés?	**ab**-la oo-**sted** ing-**less**
	¿Hablás inglés?	**ab**-las ing-**less**
I don't speak Spanish	No hablo castellano	No **ab**-loh cas-**teh**-sha-no
I don't understand	No entiendo	No en-tee-**en**-doh
I understand	Entiendo	en-tee-**en**-doh
I don't know	No sé	No seh
I am...	Soy...	soy
American	estadounidense	ess-**tah**-doh-oo-nee-**den**-seh
English	inglés(a)	ing-**less**(ah)
Scottish	escocés(a)	ess-koss-**sess**(-ah)
Irish	irlandés(a)	eer-lan-**dess**
Australian	australiano(a)	ow-stra-lee-**ah**-noh(nah)
from New Zealand	neo-celandés(a)	nay-oh-seh-lan-**dess**(ah)
What's your name?	¿Cómo se llama usted? ¿Cómo te llamás?	ko-mo seh **shah**-mah oo-**sted** ko-mo teh **shah**-mass
My name is...	Me llamo...	meh **shah**-moh...
What time is it?	¿Qué hora es?	keh **o**-rah ess
It's one o'clock	Es la una	ess la **oo**-na
It's two/three/four...o'clock	Son las dos/tres/cuatro	son lass doss/tress/**kwah**-troh
Yes, please/	Si, gracias.	see, **grah**-see-ass
No, thank you	No, gracias.	noh, **grah**-see-ass
How?	¿Cómo?	**ko**-mo
When?	¿Cuándo?	**kwan**-doh
This/next week	Esta semana/ La semana que viene	**ess**-tah sem-**ah**-nah la sem-**ah**-nah keh vee-**en**-eh

This/next month	Este mes/El mes que viene	ess-teh mess/el mess keh vee-**en**-eh
This/next year	Este año/El año que viene	**ess**-teh **an**-yoh/el **an**-yoh keh vee-**en**-eh
Yesterday/today/ tomorrow	Ayer/hoy/ mañana	**ah**-share/oy/ man-**yan**-ah
This morning/ afternoon	Esta mañana/ tarde	**ess**-tah man-**yan**-ah/ **tar**-deh
Tonight	Esta noche	**ess**-tah **noch**-eh
What?	¿Qué?	keh
What is this?	¿Qué es esto?	keh ess **ess**-toh
Why?	¿Por qué?	por keh
Who?	¿Quién?	kee-**yen**
Telephone	teléfono	tel-**eff**-on-oh
I am ill	Estoy enfermo(a)	ess-**toy** en-**fer**-moh(mah)
Please call a doctor	Por favor, llame a un médico	Por fah-**vor**, **shah**-meh a oon **meh**-dik-oh
Help!	¡Auxilio!	owk-**see**-lee-oh
Fire!	¡Incendio!	in-**sen**-dee-oh
Look out!	¡Cuidado!	kwee-**dah**-doh
I'd like...	Quiero...por favor	kee-**eh**-roh...por fah-**vor**
a room	un cuarto	oon **kwar**-toh
the key	la llave	la **shah**-veh
a newspaper	un diario	oon dee-**ah**-ree-oh
to send this letter to...	mandar esta carta a...	man-**dar** **ess**-tah **kar**-tah a...

OUT AND ABOUT

Where is...?	¿Dónde está...?	**don**-deh ess-**tah**...
the train station	la estación de tren	la ess-tah-see-**on** deh tren
the subway station	la estación de subte	la ess-tah-see-**on** deh **soob**-teh
the bus stop	la parada del colectivo	la pah-**rah**-dah del col-ek-**tee**-voh
the post office	el correo	el cor-**reh**-yoh

the bank	el banco	el **ban**-koh
the hotel	el hotel	el oh-**tel**
the store	la tienda	la tee-**en**-dah
the cashier	la caja	la **cah**-ha
the museum	el museo	el moo-**seh**-yoh
the hospital	el hospital	el oss-pee-**tal**
the elevator	el ascensor	el ass-**en**-sor
the bathroom	el baño	el **ban**-yoh
the entrance/exit	la entrada/salida	la en-**trah**-dah/**sal**-ee-dah
Here/there	acá/allá	ah-**kah**/ah-**shah**
Open/closed	abierto/cerrado	ab-ee-**er**-toh/seh-**rah**-do
Left/right	izquierda/derecha	iss-kee-**er**-dah/deh-**rech**-ah
Straight ahead	derecho	deh-**rech**-oh
Is it near/far?	¿Está cerca/lejos?	ess-**tah** ser-kah/**leh**-hoss
Avenue	avenida	av-en-**ee**-dah
City street	calle	**cah**-sheh
Highway	carretera/ruta	cah-ret-**eh**-rah
Waterfront promenade	costanera	cost-an-**eh**-rah
Cathedral	catedral	cat-**eh**-dral
Church	iglesia	ig-**less**-ee-ah
City Hall	municipalidad	moo-niss-ee-**pal**-ee-dad
Door, gate	puerta, portón	**pwer**-tah/por-**ton**
Tavern or rustic restaurant	bodegón	bod-eh-**gon**
Restaurant	restaurante/restorán	rest-ow-**ran**-teh/rest-oh-**ran**
Main square	plaza principal	**plass**-ah prin-see-**pal**
Market	mercado	mer-**kah**-do
Neighborhood	barrio	**bah**-ree-oh
Traffic circle	rotunda	rot-**oon**-dah

SHOPPING

How much is it?	¿Cuánto cuesta?	**kwan**-toh **kwes**-tah
It's expensive/cheap	Es caro/barato	ess **kah**-roh/ bah-**rah**-toh
A little/a lot	Un poquito/mucho	oon pok-**ee**-toh/ **mooch**-oh
More/less	Más/menos	mass/meh-noss
Enough/ too much/ too little	Suficiente/ dem asiado/ muy poco	soo-fiss-ee-**en**-teh/ dem-ass-ee-**ah**-doh/ mwee **poh**-koh
I'd like to buy...	Quiero comprar... por favor.	kee-**eh**-roh kom-**prar**... por fah-**vor**
cigarrettes	cigarrillos	sig-eh-**ree**-yoss
matches	fósforos	**foss**-for-oss
a dictionary	un diccionario	oon dik-see-on-**ah**-ree-oh
soap	jabón	hah-**bon**
sunglasses	anteojos de sol	an-tee-**oh**-hoss deh sol
suntan lotion	protector solar	proh-tek-**tor** sol-**ar**
a map	un mapa	oon **map**-ah
a magazine	una revista	oo-na rev-**eess**-tah
paper	papel	pap-**el**
envelopes	sobres	**sob**-ress
a postcard	una tarjeta postal	oo-na tar-**het**-ah **poss**-tal
I'd like to try on...	Me gustaría probarme...	meh goos-tah-**ree**-ah proh-**bar**-meh...
this T-shirt	esta remera	**ess**-tah rem-**eh**-rah
these trousers/jeans	este pantalón/jean	**ess**-teh pan-tah-**lon**/ sheen
this skirt	esta pollera	**ess**-tah posh-**eh**-rah
this shirt	esta camisa	**ess**-tah kam-**ee**-sah
this sweater	este suéter	**ess**-teh **swet**-er
this overcoat	este abrigo	**ess**-teh ab-**ree**-goh
this jacket	este saco	**ess**-teh **sak**-oh
this suit	este traje	**ess**-teh **trah**-heh

these shoes	estos zapatos	**ess**-toss sah-**pat**-oss
these sneakers	estas zapatillas	**ess**-tass sah-pat-**ee**-shass
Have you got it in a bigger/smaller size?	¿Lo tenés en un talle más grande/chiquito?	loh ten-**ess** en oon **tah**-sheh mass **gran**-deh/chee-**kee**-toh
Does it come in another color?	¿Lo tenés en otro color?	loh ten-**ess** en ot-roh kol-**or**
I'll take this.	Me llevo éste.	meh **sheh**-voh **ess**-teh

COLORS

Black	Negro	**neg**-roh
Blue/light blue/	Azul/celeste/	ah-**sool**/sel-**ess**-teh/
navy blue	azul marino	ah-**sool** mah-**ree**-noh
Brown	Marrón	mah-**ron**
Gray	Gris	greess
Green	Verde	**ver**-deh
Pink	Rosa	**ross**-ah
Purple	Violeta	vee-ol-**et**-ah
Orange	Naranja	nah-**ran**-hah
Red	Rojo	**roh**-ho
White	Blanco	**blan**-koh
Yellow	Amarillo	am-ar-**ee**-shoh

DINING OUT

Please could you bring me...	Me podrías traer... por favor	me pod-**ree**-ass trah-er... por fah-**vor**
a bottle of...	una botella de...	**oo**-na bot-**eh**-shah deh...
a cup of...	una taza de...	oo-na **tass**-ah deh
a glass of...	un vaso de...	oon **vah**-soh deh
an ashtray	un cenicero	oon sen-ee-**seh**-roh
the bill/check	la cuenta	la **kwen**-tah
some bread	pan	pan
some butter	manteca	man-**tek**-ah
the menu	la carta	la **kar**-tah

a knife	un cuchillo	oon koo-**chee**-shoh
a fork	un tenedor	oon ten-eh-**dor**
a spoon	una cuchara	oo-na koo-**chah**-rah
a napkin	una servilleta	**oo**-na ser-vee-**shet**-ah
salt/pepper	la sal/la pimienta	la sal/la pim-ee-**en**-tah
sugar	el azúcar	el ass-**oo**-kar
Breakfast	el desayuno	el dess-ah-**shoo**-noh
Cheers!	¡Salud!	sal-**ood**
Cocktail	un aperitivo/ un trago largo	oon ap-er-it-**ee**-voh/ oon **trah**-goh **lar**-goh
Dinner	la cena	la **sen**-ah
Dish	un plato	oon **plat**-oh
Enjoy!	¡Buen provecho!	bwen proh-**vech**-oh
Fixed-price menu	Un menú fijo/ ejecutivo	oon men-**oo fee**-hoh/ eh-hek-oo-**tee**-voh
Lunch	el almuerzo	el al-**mwer**-soh
Selection of cold cuts	una picada	oo-na pik-**ah**-dah
Tip	una propina	oo-na prop-**ee**-nah
Waiter/Waitress	mozo/moza	**moss**-oh/**moss**-ah

MENU GUIDE

With so much meat on the menu, you'll need to know how to order it: jugoso (juicy) means medium rare, vuelta y vuelta (flipped back and forth) means rare, and vivo por adentro (alive inside) is barely warm in the middle. Argentines like their meat bien cocido (well cooked).

aceite de olivo: olive oil

alfajores: Argentine cookies, usually made with dulce de leche and often covered with chocolate, though there are hundreds of varieties

arroz: rice

bife de lomo: filet mignon

bife de chorizo: like a New York strip steak, but double the size (not to be confused with *chorizo*, which is a type of sausage)

budín de pan: Argentine version of bread pudding

cabrito: roasted kid

cafecito: espresso

café con leche: coffee with milk

centolla: King crab, a Patagonian specialty

chimichurri: a sauce of oil, garlic, and salt, served with meat

chinchulines: small intestines

chorizo: thick, spicy pork-and-beef sausages, usually served with bread (*choripan*)

churros: baton-shaped donuts for dipping in hot chocolate

ciervo: venison

chivito: kid

cordero: lamb

cortado: coffee "cut" with a drop of milk

dulce de leche: a sweet caramel concoction made from milk and served on pancakes, in pastries, on cookies, and on ice cream

empanadas: pockets stuffed with meat—usually beef—chicken, or cheese

ensalada de fruta: fruit salad (sometimes fresh, sometimes canned)

estofado: beef stew

facturas: small pastries

huevos: eggs

humitas: steamed cornhusks wrapped around cornmeal and cheese

jamón: ham

lechón: roast suckling pig

lengua: tongue

licuado: milk shake

locro: local stew, usually made with hominy and beans, that's cooked slowly with meat and vegetables; common in northern Argentina

medialuna: croissant

mejillones: mussels

merluza: hake

milanesa: breaded meat cutlet, usually veal, pounded thin and fried; served as a main course or in a sandwich with lettuce, tomato, ham, cheese, and egg

milanesa a la napolitana: a breaded veal cutlet with melted mozzarella cheese and tomato sauce

mollejas: sweetbreads; the thymus glands, usually of the cow but also can be of the lamb or the goat

morcilla: blood sausage

pejerrey: a kind of mackerel

pollo: chicken

provoleta: grilled provolone cheese sprinkled with olive oil and oregano

puchero: boiled meat and vegetables; like pot-au-feu

queso: cheese

salchichas: long, thin sausages

sambayon: an alcohol-infused custard

tamales: ground corn stuffed with meat, cheese, or other fillings and tied up in a corn husk

tenedor libre: all-you-can-eat meat and salad bar

tinto: red wine

trucha: trout

Travel Smart
Buenos Aires

PLANNING TOOLS, EXPERT INSIGHT,
GREAT CONTACTS

"It's not bad form to wear a suit at all, but there's no problem if you dress a little more 'sport' as we say here, like a nice shirt and shoes and a good pair of jeans or light trousers. It cools down at night in Buenos Aires, but there're evenings in which you wish you left your jacket at home."

—mandeb

"Better yet, pack light and buy your clothes there (cheap if you carry U.S. dollars or euros)."

—siberia_BA

GETTING HERE & AROUND

Argentina measures around 3,650 km (2,268 mi) from tip to tail, and many of its attractions are hundreds of miles apart. Carefully planning how you're going to get around on your trip will help you save lots of time and money.

Buenos Aires lies about two-thirds of the way up Argentina's eastern side, on the banks of the Río de la Plata. It's the country's capital and its main transport hub. A well-developed network of long-distance buses connects it with cities all over Argentina; buses also operate between many cities without passing through Buenos Aires. Most domestic flights operate from Buenos Aires, so to fly from the extreme south of the country to the extreme north, you often have to change planes here.

Three of the country's main draws are around 1,000 km (621 mi) from Buenos Aires, as the crow flies: Puerto Iguazú, the base for exploring Iguazú Falls, in northeastern Misiones Province; Salta, the gateway to the Andean Northwest; and Mendoza, in the wine region, near the Chilean border. Slightly farther, this time southwest of Buenos Aires, is Bariloche, the hub for the Lakes District of northern Patagonia. The hub of southern Patagonia is El Calafate, close to the Perito Moreno glacier, a whopping 2,068 km (1,285 mi) southwest of Buenos Aires.

Flying within the country makes sense given these huge distances. That said, domestic flights are expensive, and at this writing, flight delays of two to six hours are regular occurrences. As a result, many visitors opt for the more-reliable overnight sleeper buses for trips of up to 1,000 km (621 mi; around 12 hours).

TRAVEL TIMES FROM BUENOS AIRES	BY AIR	BY BUS
San Antonio de Areco	n/a	2 hours
Atlantic Coast	1 hour	5–6 hours
Córdoba	1¼ hours	9–11 hours
Mendoza	1¾ hours	12–14 hours
Puerto Iguazú	1¾ hours	16–19 hours
Salta	2¼ hours	18–21 hours
Bariloche	2¼ hours	21–23 hours
El Calafate	3¼ hours	40 hours

▌BY AIR

TO ARGENTINA

There are direct daily services between Buenos Aires and several North American cities, with New York and Miami as primary departure points. Many airlines fly to Buenos Aires via Santiago de Chile or São Paulo in Brazil, which only adds a little to your trip time.

Aerolíneas Argentinas, the flagship airline, operates direct flights between Buenos Aires and New York JFK and Miami. Note that at this writing, Aerolíneas flights are frequently prone to chronic delays due to industrial disputes.

Chilean airline LAN is Aerolíneas's biggest local competition. LAN flies direct to JFK, Miami, and Los Angeles. There are direct flights from Los Angeles and Atlanta on Delta, and from Chicago on American. American also has nonstop service from JFK and direct service via Miami and Dallas from JFK, LaGuardia, and Newark. United flies from JFK via Washington D.C. Continental connects Buenos Aires with Houston, Dallas, and Newark, sometimes via Panama City.

Flying times to Buenos Aires are 11–12 hours from New York, 9 hours from Miami, 10½ hours from Dallas or Houston, and 13 hours from Los Angeles, via Santiago de Chile.

WITHIN ARGENTINA

Aerolíneas Argentinas and their partner Austral operate flights from Buenos Aires to more Argentine cities than any other airline, including daily services (often more than one) to Puerto Iguazú, Salta, Mendoza, Córdoba, Bariloche, Ushuaia, and El Calafate. The more-reliable LAN also flies to these cities and a few others.

Airline Contacts Aerolíneas Argentinas (⊕ www.aerolineas.com.ar). **American Airlines** (⊕ www.aa.com). **Continental Airlines** (⊕ www.continental.com). **Delta Airlines** (⊕ www.delta.com). **LAN** (⊕ www.LAN.com). **United Airlines** (⊕ www.united.com).

AIR PASSES

If you're flying into Argentina on Aerolíneas Argentinas, you're eligible for their Visit Argentina fares: these are regular tickets with a discount of 20%–30%. Be aware, however, that at this writing strikes and industrial disputes have made flight delays common.

Aerolíneas Argentinas also participates in the Mercosur Air Pass (together with Austral Líneas Aéreas, Aerolíneas del Sur, and Pluna) that allows you to visit Argentina, Brazil, Chile, Uruguay, and Paraguay. The price is based on your total mileage, and you must visit at least two countries to be eligible. Traveling up to 3,060 km (1,900 mi) costs $295, for example, and you can do up to 8,370 km (5,200 mi) for $695. Brazilian airline TAM's South America Pass works in a similar fashion but also includes Bolivia, Peru, and Venezuela, and is slightly more expensive.

If you plan to take at least three flights within Argentina or South America in general, the OneWorld Alliance's Visit South America pass can save money. Flights are categorized by mileage; most segments (both domestic and international) range from $100 to $240. The catch is that as most domestic routes only operate from Buenos Aires, so you always have to return there. Visiting Iguazú and Calafate from Buenos Aires would cost $560, for example.

Airlines & Airports Airline and Airport Links.com (⊕ www.airlineandairportlinks.com).

Airline Security Issues Transportation Security Administration (⊕ www.tsa.gov).

Air Passes Visit Argentina (Aerolíneas Argentinas, ☎ 800/333-0276 ⊕ www.aerolineas.com. ar). **Mercosur Air Pass** (Aerolíneas Argentinas ☎ 800/333-0276 ⊕ www.aerolineas.com.ar). **South America Pass** (TAM ☎ 888/235-9826 ⊕ www.tam-airlines.com). **Visit South America Pass** (OneWorld Alliance ☎ Lan: 866/435-9526 ⊕ www.oneworld.com).

Air Travel Resources in Argentina Organismo Regulador del Sistema Nacional de Aeropuertos (Regulatory Body of the National Airport System) (☎ 800/999-67762 ⊕ www.orsna.gov.ar).

AIRPORTS

Buenos Aires's Aeropuerto Internacional de Ezeiza Ministro Pistarini (EZE)—known simply as Ezeiza—is 35 km (22 mi) southwest of and a 45-minute drive from the city center. It's served by a variety of international airlines, along with domestic airlines running international routes.

⚠ **Ezeiza has been plagued by problems. Faulty radar has led to all air traffic being controlled manually, which has caused huge delays. Underpaid Aerolíneas Argentinas staff have been on strike repeatedly. Local police even uncovered a luggage-theft racket within the airport, run by employees. At this writing the situation seems to have calmed slightly, but you should still expect the unexpected, especially as work is slated to start on a new passenger terminal in 2008.** Aerolíneas Argentinas and its partner Austral operate out of the older Terminal B. All other airlines are based at Terminal A, a pleasant, glass-sided building. A covered walkway connects the two terminals. Each terminal has a few small snack bars, a small range of shops, a public phone center with Internet services, and a tourist information booth. The ATM, 24-hour luggage storage, and car-rental agencies are in Terminal A.

Most domestic flights operate out of Aeroparque Jorge Newbery (AEP). It's next to the Río de la Plata in northeast Palermo, about 8 km (5 mi) north of the city center.

Security at Argentine airports isn't as stringent as it is in the States—computers stay in cases, shoes stay on your feet, and there are no random searches. Air travel is expensive for Argentines, so airports are more likely to be crowded with foreigners than locals. Both Ezeiza and Aeroparque are run by the private company Aeropuertos Argentinos 2000 and are regulated by the Organismo Regulador del Sistema Nacional de Aeropuertos (Regulatory Body of the National Airport System), known as ORSNA.

Airport Information Aeropuertos Argentinos 2000 (⊕www.aa2000.com.ar). Aeroparque Jorge Newbery (☎11/5480–6111 ⊕www.aa2000.com.ar). Aeropuerto Internacional de Ezeiza Ministro Pistarini (⊕www.aa2000.com.ar). ORSNA (⊕www.orsna.gov.ar).

GROUND TRANSPORTATION

From Ezeiza the quickest way of getting into town is in one of the registered black-and-yellow city taxis that you can get at booths outside either terminal. The trip costs about 70 pesos (you pay the metered price and tolls) and takes 45–60 minutes.

Almost as fast are private shuttle buses run by Manuel Tienda León. Services to and from their terminal in the Retiro district leave roughly every half hour; some include free drop-off at downtown hotels. A one-way ticket costs 35 pesos, which you can buy from the ticket booths in the

arrival halls of both terminals and in the covered walkway connecting the two.

The only public transport that connects Buenos Aires and Ezeiza is Bus 86. It leaves from a shelter in the parking area opposite the Aeropuertos Argentinos 2000 building (turn left out of Terminal B). You need change for the 1.50 peso ticket and patience for the two to three hours it takes to reach San Telmo and Plaza de Mayo (it runs along Avenida Paseo Colón).

The highway connecting Ezeiza with the city is the Autopista Ricchieri, which you can reach by taking either Autopista 25 de Mayo out of the city or the Avenida General Paz, which encircles the city. ■TIP→**Note that most flights to the United States depart Buenos Aires in the evening, so plan to offset afternoon traffic snarls by allowing at least an hour of travel time to Ezeiza.**

Aeroparque Jorge Newbery is actually inside Buenos Aires, on the Costanera Norte in northeast Palermo. A taxi to Microcentro or San Telmo costs 10–15 pesos and takes anything from 15 to 45 minutes depending on downtown traffic. Manuel Tienda León also operates shuttle buses to and from their terminal and to downtown hotels, but as a ticket costs 14 pesos, it makes more sense to take a taxi. Several city buses run along Avenida Rafael Obligado, outside the airport: the 160 and 37 go to Plaza Italia, and the 33 and 45 go to Retiro and the Microcentro. All cost 90 centavos.

There are several routes to Aeroparque from downtown—about a 15-minute trip. The easiest way is to take Avenida Libertador north to Avenida Sarmiento, and then take a right and follow it until Costanera Rafael Obligado. The airport will be on your left. Traffic can be heavy between 6 and 8 PM.

TRANSFERS BETWEEN AIRPORTS

A taxi ride between Ezeiza and Aeroparque costs 80–90 pesos and takes an hour in normal traffic. Manuel Tienda León shuttles make the same trip for 38 pesos; there are usually two departures per hour in each direction.

Shuttle **Manuel Tienda León** (☎11/4383–4454 or 810/888–5366 ⊕www.tiendaleon.com.ar).

▌ BY BOAT

There are frequent ferry services across the Río de la Plata between Buenos Aires and the Uruguayan cities of Colonia and Montevideo. Buquebus operates direct services to both cities on large car-and-passenger ferries, which take three hours (return tickets cost 169 pesos to Colonia and 451 pesos to Montevideo). Both Buquebus and Colonia Express also run faster catamarans to Colonia, which take an hour or less, and cost 219 pesos and 234 pesos return, respectively. The two companies also sell packages that include bus tickets to La Paloma, Montevideo, and Punta del Este on services direct from Colonia's ferry terminal. You can order tickets by phone or online. The more-modest Ferrylíneas also serves the Buenos Aires–Colonia route on a smaller scale with fewer boats per day.

Buquebus and Ferrylíneas both leave from terminals at the northern end of Puerto Madero. The Colonia Express terminal is in the port area near Retiro, a five-block walk from long-distance bus station.

Contacts **Buquebus** (☎11/4316–6500 ⊕www.buquebus.com). **Colonia Express** (☎11/4313–5100 in Buenos Aires, 52/29676 in Colonia ⊕www.coloniaexpress.com). **Ferrylíneas** (☎11/4314–2300 ⊕www.ferrylineas.com.ar).

▌ BY BUS

TO & FROM BUENOS AIRES

A fabulous range of frequent, comfortable, and dependable long-distance bus services connects Buenos Aires with cities all over Argentina, and to neighboring countries. Bus travel is substantially cheaper than flying, and far less prone to delays. Both Argentineans and visitors often choose overnight sleeper services for trips up to 12 hours long.

Most major bus companies have online timetables; some allow you to buy tickets online or over the phone. Web sites also list *puntos de venta* (sales offices)—in many cases you don't need to go all the way to the bus terminal to buy tickets, though you can usually buy them at the terminal right up until departure time. Arrive early to get a ticket, and be prepared to pay cash. During January, February, and July, buy your ticket as far in advance as possible—a week or more, at least—and arrive at the terminal extra early.

Most long-distance buses depart from the Terminal de Omnibus de Retiro, which is often referred to as the Terminal de Retiro or simply Retiro. Ramps and stairs from the street lead you a huge concourse where buses leave from more than 60 numbered platforms. There are restrooms, restaurants, public phones, lockers, news kiosks, and a tourist office on this floor.

You buy tickets from the *boleterías* (ticket offices) on the upper level; there are also two ATMs here. Each company has its own booth; they're arranged in zones according to the destinations served, which makes price comparisons easy. The bus terminal's excellent Web site lists bus companies by destination, including their telephone number and ticket booth location.

All long-distance buses have toilets, air-conditioning, videos, and snacks like sandwiches or cookies. The most-basic service is *semi-cama*, which has minimally reclineable seats and often takes a little longer than more-luxurious services. It's worth paying the little extra for *coche cama*, sometimes called *ejecutivo*, where you get large, business-class-style seats and, sometimes, pillows and blankets. The best rides of all are on the fully reclineable seats of *cama suite* services, which are often contained in their own little booth. Bus attendants and free drinks are other perks. The more expensive the service, the cleaner and newer the bus.

Contacts **Terminal de Ómnibus Retiro** (⌧Av. Antártida Argentina at Av. Ramos Mejía, Retiro ☎11/4310-0700 ⊕www.tebasa.com.ar).

WITHIN BUENOS AIRES

City buses, called *colectivos* connect the city's barrios and greater Buenos Aires. Stops are roughly every other block (656 feet apart). Some are at proper shelters with large numbered signposts, others are marked by small, easy-to-miss metal disks or stickers stuck on nearby walls, posts, or even trees. Buses are generally safe, and run 24 hours a day, although service is less frequent at night.

A few routes have smaller, faster *diferencial* buses (indicated by a sign on the front) as well as regular ones; they run less frequently and are more expensive, but you usually get a seat on them.

Hail your bus and tell the driver the value of the ticket you want (all fares within the city are 90¢, so say "*noventa*"); then insert your coins in the machine (exact change isn't necessary, but coins are), which will print your ticket. Fares outside the city are 1.35–1.75 pesos; diferenciales cost 2 pesos. There are no daily or weekly discount passes.

Once on board, head for the back, which is where you exit. A small button on the grab bar lets you signal for a stop. Don't depend on drivers for much assistance; they're busy navigating traffic. You can purchase a *Guia T,* an essential guide to the routes, at any news kiosk, or visit the Spanish-language colectivo Web site for info.

Information **Los Colectivos** (⊕www.loscolectivos.com.ar).

▌BY CAR

Having a car in Buenos Aires is really more hassle than it's worth; there are ample taxis and public transportation options. A more- convenient option than driving yourself is to have your travel agent or hotel arrange for a *remis* (car and driver), especially for a day's tour of the suburbs (⇨*By Remis, below*). However, a car can be useful for longer excursions to the Atlantic Coast or interior towns of Buenos Aires Province.

Porteño driving styles range from erratic to downright psychotic, and the road mortality rate is shockingly high. Drive defensively.

Avenida General Paz is Buenos Aires' ring road. If you're driving into the city, you'll know you're in Buenos Aires proper once you cross it. ⚠Be cautious when approaching or exiting overpasses on General Paz where there have been incidences of *ladrillazos* (brick throwing): you stop the car to examine your broken windshield, at which point thieves appear.

If you're entering from the north, chances are you'll be on the Ruta Panamericana, which has wide lanes and good lighting. The quickest way from downtown to Ezeiza Airport is Autopista 25 de Mayo to Autopista Ricchieri. The R2 (Ruta 2) takes you to the Atlantic beach resorts in and around Mar del Plata.

City streets are notorious for potholes, uneven surfaces, and poorly marked lanes and turnoffs. Rush hour traffic affects the roads into Buenos Aires between 8 and 10 AM, and roads out between 6 and 9 PM; the General Paz ring road and Panamericana are particularly problematic.

PARKING

On-street parking is limited. Some neighborhoods, such as San Telmo and Recoleta, have meters: you pay with coins (50¢ per 30 minutes) then display the ticket you receive on your dashboard. In popular meter-free spots, there's often a self-appointed caretaker who guides you into your spot and charges 2–3 pesos to watch your car: it's best to pay.

Car theft is fairly common so many rental agencies insist you park in a guarded lot—Buenos Aires is full of them. Look for a circular blue sign with a white E (for *estacionamiento* [parking]). Downtown, expect to pay 6–8 pesos per hour, or 25 pesos for 12 hours. Illegally parked cars are towed only from the Microcentro. Getting your car back is a bureaucratic nightmare and costs around 200 pesos. Most malls have garages, which are usually free or give you a reduced rate with a purchase.

RULES OF THE ROAD

Buenos Aires has a one-way system where parallel streets run in opposite directions: never going the wrong way along a street is one of the few rules that Argentines abide by. Where there are no traffic lights at an intersection, you give way to drivers coming from the right, but have priority over those coming from the left.

Most driving rules in the United States theoretically apply here (although locals flout them shamelessly). However, keep in mind the following: right turns on red are not allowed; never park on the left side of avenues, where there's a yellow line on the curb, or near a bus stop; and turning left on two-way avenues is prohibited unless there's a left-turn signal. During the week, the Microcentro, the bustling commercial district bounded by Carlos Pellegrini, Avenida Córdoba, Avenida Leandro Alem, and Avenida de Mayo, is off-limits to all but public transit vehicles.

The legal blood-alcohol limit is 500 mg of alcohol per liter of blood, but breathalyzing is rare. In Buenos Aires, a 40-kph (25-mph) speed limit applies on streets, and a 60-kph (37-mph) limit is in effect on avenues. However, locals take speed-limit signs, the ban on driving with cell phones, and drinking and driving lightly, so drive very defensively indeed.

Local police tend to be forgiving of foreigners' driving faults and often waive tickets and fines when they see your passport or driver's license. If you do get a traffic ticket, don't argue. Most traffic tickets are not payable on the spot, but some police officers offer "reduced" on-the-spot fines in lieu of a ticket: it's out-and-out bribery and you'd do best to avoid it by insisting on receiving the proper ticket.

CAR RENTALS

Daily rental rates range from around 150 pesos to 280 pesos, depending on the type of car and the distance you plan to travel. This generally includes tax and 200 free km (125 mi) daily. Note that nearly all rental cars in Argentina have manual transmissions, so if you need an automatic, be sure to request one in advance.

Reputable firms don't rent to drivers under 21, and those under 23 often have to pay a daily surcharge of 10–15 pesos. In general, you cannot cross the border in a rental car. Children's car seats are not compulsory but are available for 7–10 pesos per day. Some agencies charge a 10% surcharge for picking up a car from the airport.

Collision damage waiver (CDW) is mandatory in Argentina and is included in standard rental prices. However, you're still responsible for a deductible fee—a maximum amount that you'll have to pay if damage occurs. The amount of this deductible is generally around 3,000 pesos for a car, and can be much higher for a four-wheel-drive vehicle. You can reduce the figure substantially by paying an insurance premium (usually 30–60 pesos per day); some companies have lower deductibles than others.

Many rental companies do not insure you for driving on unpaved roads. Discuss your itinerary carefully with the agent to be certain you're always covered.

Major car-rental agencies with branches in Buenos Aires include Avis, Budget, Hertz, Alamo, and Dollar, and Latin American agency Localiza. You can rent cars at both airports and through many hotels. If the rental agency has a branch in another town, arrangements can usually be made for a one-way drop-off, for a hefty surcharge.

Automobile Association **Automóvil Club Argentina** (ACA 🕾11/4808-4000 ⊕www.aca. org.ar).

Rental Agencies **Alamo** (🕾810/999-25266, 11/4322-3320 in Buenos Aires ⊕www.alamoargentina.com). **Avis** (🕾810/999-12847, 11/4326-5542 in Buenos Aires ⊕www.avis. com.ar). **Budget** (🕾810/444-2834, 11/4314-7577 in Buenos Aires ⊕www.budget.com. ar). **Dollar** (🕾800/555-3655, 11/4315-8800 in Buenos Aires ⊕www.dollar.com.ar). **Hertz** (🕾810/222-43789, 11/4816-8001 in Buenos Aires ⊕www.hertzargentina.com.ar). **Localiza** (🕾800/999-2999, 11/4813-3184 in Buenos Aires ⊕www.localiza.com.ar).

▌ BY REMIS

An alternative to renting a car is to hire a *remis,* a car with a driver, especially for day outings. Hotels and travel agents can make arrangements for you. You'll have to pay cash, but you'll often spend less than you would on a rental car or hiring cabs for whole days. Remis service costs about 35–50 pesos per hour, sometimes with a three-hour minimum and an additional charge per kilometer (0.5 mi) if you drive outside the city limits. If your driver is helpful and friendly, a 10% tip is appropriate. Some local car agencies offer chauffeur-driven rentals as well. *Refer to individual chapters for more information on hiring remises.*

Remises **Abbey Rent-A-Car** (🕾11/4924-1984). **Annie Millet Transfers** (🕾11/4816-0101). **Remises Full-Time** (🕾11/4775-1011). **Remises Traslada** (🕾11/5128-8888). **Universal Vans** (🕾11/4315-6555).

▌ BY SUBTE

The subway is one of the quickest ways to get from one part of Buenos Aires to another. Packed trains mean it's not always the most comfortable, though it's generally fairly safe. The stations are well patrolled by police and many are decorated with artworks, including murals by Argentine artists. You'll likely hear musicians and see actors performing on trains and in the stations.

Single-ride tickets cost 90¢ to anywhere in the city; you can buy passes in stations for 1, 2, 5, or 10 trips or a rechargeable contact-free card. The subte shuts down around 11 PM and reopens at 5 AM.

Línea A travels beneath Avenida Rivadavía from Plaza de Mayo to Primera Junta in Caballito and is serviced by handsome antique wooden cars. At this writing four new stations in Flores were almost complete.

Línea B begins at Leandro Alem Station, in the financial district, and runs under Avenida Corrientes to De los Incas Station in Parque Chas, and will soon continue on to Villa Urquiza.

Línea C, under Avenida 9 de Julio, connects the two major train stations, Retiro and Constitución, making stops along the way in Centro and San Telmo.

Línea D runs from Catedral Station on Plaza de Mayo to Congreso de Túcuman in Belgrano.

Línea E takes you from Bolívar Station, at Plaza de Mayo, to Plaza de los Virreyes, in the neighborhood of Flores.

Linéa H, the subte's newest line, is only partially open. It will eventually run from Retiro to Pompeya, crossing lines A, B, D, and E.

Information **Metrovías** (🕾800/555-1616 ⊕www.metrovias.com.ar).

▌BY TAXI

Taxis in Buenos Aires are cheap and plentiful. All have black-and-yellow tops. An unoccupied one will have a small, red LIBRE sign on the left-hand side of its windshield. Local wisdom has it that the safest taxis to hail on the street are those with a light on the roof that says RADIO TAXI, which are part of licensed fleets and are in constant contact with dispatchers. If you phone for a taxi, you'll have to wait a few minutes, but you can be sure of its origin and safety. Legally, all taxis are supposed to have working seatbelts, but this isn't always the case.

Meters start at 3.10 pesos and charge 22¢ per 200 meters (650 feet); you'll also end up paying for standing time spent at a light or in a traffic jam. From downtown, it will cost you around 10 pesos to Recoleta, 8–10 pesos to San Telmo, 15 pesos to Palermo, and 20 pesos to Belgrano. Drivers don't expect tips; rounding up to the next peso is sufficient.

Taxi Companies **City Tax** (☎11/4585–5544). **Del Plata** (☎11/4505–1111 ⊕www.del-plataradiotaxi.com). **Pídalo** (☎11/4956–1200 ⊕www.radiotaxipidalo.com.ar). **Premium** (☎11/4374–6666). **Radio Taxi Ciudad** (☎11/4923–7007 ⊕www.radiotaxiciudad.com.ar). **Su Taxi** (☎11/4635–2500).

▌BY TRAIN

Commuter rail lines provide extensive service from the city proper to the suburbs for low prices. A network of lines operated by six companies—Ferrobaires, Ferrovías, Metropolitano, Metrovías, Trenes de Buenos Aires, Tren de la Costa—spreads out from five central stations in Buenos Aires. Lines to the north tend to work fairly well; other lines are seriously run down and dangerous after dark. In 2007 protesting passengers even set a wagon on fire.

Most trains leave at regular 7- to 20-minute intervals, though there may be less frequent service for trains traveling long distances. Fares range from 60¢ to 1.85 pesos. Purchase tickets before boarding the train at ticket windows or through coin-operated machines at the stations. Hold on to your ticket until you reach the end of the line. If an official asks for it and you don't have it, you'll have to pay a 3.50–6.50 pesos on-the-spot fine.

Commuter trains to the southern suburbs and La Plata leave from Estación Plaza Constitución. Ferrobaires also runs between here and Mar del Plata twice a week, and to Pinamar once a week. Extra services are put on in summer. Note that Constitución is a very sketchy neighborhood, especially after dark.

Estación Federico Lacroze, in Chacarita, provides train service to the northeastern part of the city and greater Buenos Aires. You can also reach Posadas in Misiones province on the Gran Capitán, Trenes del Litoral's twice weekly service from here. You can reach the western parts of the city and greater Buenos Aires from Estación Plaza Once, in the city center.

Trains running out of Estación Retiro, across from Plaza San Martín, serve Belgrano and Núñez neighborhoods in the northern part of the city. Trains also run to greater Buenos Aires' well-to-do northern suburbs, including Tigre. Ferrocentral runs two services each week from the Mitre section of Retiro to Córdoba, and to Tucumán. Both services stop at Rosario Norte station in Rosario.

Contacts **Ferrobaires** (☎11/4304–0028 ⊕www.ferrobaires.gba.gov.ar). **Ferrocentral** (☎800/777–8736). **Tren de la Costa** (☎11/4732–6000 ⊕www.trendelacosta.com.ar). **Trenes del Litoral** (☎11/4554–8018 ⊕www.trenesdellitoral.com.ar).

ESSENTIALS

▌BUSINESS TRAVEL

DOING BUSINESS

Suits are definitely still the norm for Argentinean men in the office. Local businesswomen are usually immaculately groomed, and wear either skirt or pants suits with high heels; they often wear sexier or more-revealing clothing than their North American counterparts might. Arriving late for social occasions may be normal and acceptable among porteños, but arriving late for a business appointment is not, even though proceedings may take a while to get going. Business cards are always appreciated.

Argentinean businesspeople are mostly direct and to the point. Giving someone your word or shaking hands on something don't carry the same weight in Argentina as in the United States. If you want something set in stone, get it down on paper and signed.

Most local businesspeople eat lunch out, but meals are often a break from the boardroom, not an extension of it. At a typical business dinner, the flow of conversation is much like it is in the Unites States—discussing common interests such as sports, hobbies, family, travel, and even politics are all part of the ritual of getting to know and trust an individual. Spouses may or may not be included in post-business socializing.

Porteño businesspeople tend to use first names in all but the most-formal meetings; some professions use their jobs as titles: *doctor/a* is a catchall used by medical and legal professionals; *ingeniero/a* for engineers; and *arquitecto/a* for architects.

BUSINESS SERVICES

Ambito Financiero is Argentina's leading financial daily. You can get information on business opportunities through the Cámara Argentina de Comercio, the Argentine chamber of commerce, as

GREAT READS
Sample the work of Argentina's greatest writers with Jorge Luis Borges's *Labyrinths: Selected Stories and Other Writings* and Julio Cortázar's *Blow Up: And Other Stories*. You get a decidedly lighter take on the city in Jessica Morrison's chick-lit best seller, *The Buenos Aires Broken Hearts Club*. Spanish detective novelist Manuel Vázquez Montalbán set his *Buenos Aires Quintet* on the city streets.

well as the Fundación Invertir, which has useful information on investing in Argentina.

Stationery stores (*papeleris*) are easy to find in Buenos Aires—most offer photocopying and binding services. For special printing and document design, ask your hotel to recommend a *gráfica* (print and design company). Regus is an international business services company with serviced office, meeting, and conference facilities in four Buenos Aires office blocks. Contact Virtual Assistance Argentina for secretarial services. In Touch Languages and OutLoud offer reliable translation and interpretation services. Buenos Aires' flagship convention center is enormous La Rural, which has event-organizing services.

Contacts Ambito Financiero (⊕www.ambitoweb.com). **Cámara Argentina de Comercio** (⊕www.cac.com.ar). **Fundación Invertir** (⊕www.invertir.com). **In Touch Languages** (☏11/4307–1064 ⊕www.intouchlanguages. com.ar). **OutLoud** (☏11/4783–6916 ⊕www. outloud.com.ar). **Regus** (☏888/271–4615 from U.S. ⊕www.regus.com). **La Rural** (☏11/4777–5500 ⊕www.la-rural.com.ar). **Virtual Assistance Argentina** (☏11/5353–9851 ⊕www. vaargentina.com).

▌ COMMUNICATIONS

INTERNET

Inexpensive Internet access is widely available in Buenos Aires. Top-end hotels tend to have high-speed in-room data ports, while lower-budget establishments (including many hostels) have free Wi-Fi. Many hotels have a PC in the lobby for guests to use.

If you're traveling without a laptop, look for a *ciber* (Internet café) or *locutorios* (telephone and Internet centers). It's hard to walk more than a block without coming across one. Expect to pay between 2 and 5 pesos per hour to surf the Web. Broadband connections are common.

In Buenos Aires, many bars and restaurants have free Wi-Fi—look out for stickers on their windows. In general, these are open networks and you don't need to ask for a password to use them. You can also find Wi-Fi in many hotel lobbies, libraries, business and event centers, some airports, and in public spaces—piggybacking is common practice.

Contact **Cybercafes** (⊕ www.cybercafes.com) lists over 4,000 Internet cafés worldwide.

PHONES

The country code for Argentina is 54. To call landlines in Argentina from the United States, dial the international access code (011) followed by the country code (54), the two- to four-digit area code without the initial 0, then the five- to eight--digit phone number. For example, to call the Buenos Aires number (011) 4123–4567, you would dial 011 54 11 4123–4567.

Any number that is prefixed by a 15 is a cell phone number. To call cell phones from the United States, dial the international access code (011) followed by the country code (54), Argentina's cell phone code (9), the area code without the initial 0, then the seven- or eight-digit cell phone number without the initial 15. For example, to call the Buenos Aires cell phone (011) 15 5123–4567, you would dial 011–54–9–11–5123–4567.

CALLING WITHIN ARGENTINA

Argentina's phone service is run by the duopoly of Telecom and Telefónica. Telecom does the northern half of Argentina (including the northern half of the city of Buenos Aires) and Telefónica does the south. However, both companies operate public phones and phone centers, called *locutorios* or *telecentros*, throughout the city.

Service is generally efficient, and direct dialing—both long-distance and international—is universal. You can make local and long-distance calls from your hotel (usually with a surcharge) and from any public phone or locutorio. Public phones aren't particularly abundant, and are often broken. All accept coins; some have slots for phone cards, but now most phone cards can be used from both public and private phones by calling a free access number and entering the card code number. *See also Calling Cards below.*

Locutorios are useful if you need to make lots of calls or don't have coins on you. Ask the receptionist for *una cabina* (a booth), make as many local, long-distance, or international calls as you like (a small LCD display tracks how much you've spent), then pay as you leave. There's no charge if you don't get through. Note that many locutorios don't allow you to call free numbers, so you can't use prepaid calling cards from them.

All of Argentina's area codes are prefixed with a 0, which you need to include when dialing another area within Argentina. You don't need to dial the area code to call a local number. Confusingly, area codes and phone numbers don't all have the same number of digits. The area code for Buenos Aires is 011, and phone numbers have eight digits. Area codes for the rest of the country have three or four digits, and start with 02 (the southern prov-

LOCAL DO'S & TABOOS

CUSTOMS OF THE COUNTRY

Welcoming and helpful, porteños are a pleasure to travel among. They have more in common with, say, Spanish or Italians, than other Latin Americans. However, although cultural differences between here and North America are small, they're still palpable.

Porteños are usually fashionably late for all social events—don't be offended if someone keeps you waiting over half an hour for a lunch or dinner date. However, tardiness is frowned upon in the business world.

Fiercely animated discussions are a national pastime, and locals relish probing controversial issues like politics and religion, as well as soccer and their friends' personal lives. Political correctness isn't a valued trait, and just about everything and everyone—except mothers—is a target for playful mockery. Locals are often disparaging about their country's shortcomings, but Argentina-bashing is a privilege reserved for Argentineans. That said, some anti-American feeling—both serious and jokey—permeates most of society. You'll earn more friends by taking it in stride.

GREETINGS

Porteños have no qualms about getting physical, and the way they greet each other reflects this. One kiss on the right cheek is the customary greeting between both male and female friends. Women also greet strangers in this way, although men—especially older men—often shake hands the first time they meet someone. Other than that, handshaking is seen as very cold and formal.

When you leave a party it's normal to say good-bye to everyone in the room (or, if you're in a restaurant, to everyone at your table), which means kissing everyone once again. Unlike other Latin Americans, porteños only use the formal "you" form, *usted,* with people much older than them or in very formal situations, and the casual greeting ¡Hola! often replaces *buen día, buenas tardes,* and *buenas noches.* In small towns, formal greetings and the use of *usted* are much more widespread.

SIGHTSEEING

You can dress pretty much as you like in Buenos Aires: skimpy clothing causes no offense.

Argentinean men almost always allow women to go through doors and to board buses and elevators first, often with exaggerated ceremony. Far from finding this sexist, local women take it as a god-given right. Frustratingly, there's no local rule about standing on one side of escalators to allow people to pass you.

Despite bus drivers' best efforts, locals are often reluctant to move to the back of buses. Pregnant women, the elderly, and those with disabilities have priority on the front seats of city buses, and you should offer them your seat if these are already taken.

Children and adults selling pens, notepads, or sheets of stickers are regular fixtures on urban public transport. Some children also hand out tiny greeting cards in exchange for coins. The standard procedure is to accept the merchandise or cards as the vendor moves up the carriage, then either return the item (saying no, gracias) or given them money when they return.

Most porteños are hardened jaywalkers, but given how reckless local driving can be, you'd do well to cross at corners and wait for pedestrian lights.

OUT ON THE TOWN

A firm nod of the head or raised eyebrow usually gets waiters' attention; "disculpa" (excuse me) also does the trick. You can ask your waiter for la cuenta (the check) or make a signing gesture in the air from afar.

Alcohol—especially wine and beer—is a big part of life in Argentina. Local women generally drink less than their foreign counterparts, but there are no taboos about this. Social events usually end in general tipsiness rather than all-out drunkenness, which is seen as a rather tasteless foreign habit.

Smoking is very common in Argentina, but anti-smoking legislation introduced in Buenos Aires in 2006 has banned smoking all but the largest cafés and restaurants (which must have extractor fans and designated smoking areas). Smoking is prohibited on public transport, in government offices, in banks, and in cinemas.

Public displays of affection between heterosexual couples attract little attention in most parts of the country; beyond downtown Buenos Aires, same-sex couples may attract hostile reactions.

All locals tend to make an effort to look nice—though not necessarily formal—for dinner out. Older couples get very dressed up for the theater; younger women usually put on high heels and makeup for clubbing.

If you're invited to someone's home for dinner, a bottle of good Argentinean wine is the best gift to take to the hosts.

LANGUAGE

Argentina's official language is Spanish, known locally as *castellano* (rather than *español*). It differs from other varieties of Spanish in its use of *vos* (instead of *tú*) for the informal "you" form, and there are lots of small vocabulary differences, especially for everyday things like food. Porteño intonation is rather singsong, and sounds more like Italian than Mexican or peninsular Spanish. And, like Italians, porteños supplement their words with lots and lots of gesturing. Another porteño peculiarity is pronouncing the letters "y" and "ll" as a "sh" sound.

In hotels, restaurants, and shops that cater to visitors, many people speak at least some English. All the same, attempts to speak Spanish are usually appreciated. Basic courtesies like *buen día* (good morning) or

buenas tardes (good afternoon), and *por favor* (please) and *gracias* (thank you) are a good place to start. Even if your language skills are basic and phrasebook bound, locals generally make an effort to understand you. If people don't know the answer to a question, such as a request for directions, they'll tell you so. ■TIP➜**Buenos Aires' official tourism body runs a free, 24-hour tourist assistant hotline with English speaking operators, ☎0800/999-2838.** Many local language schools offer quick Spanish immersion courses in Buenos Aires. *For more information,* ⇨*the Master Class section of Chapter 1*

inces) or 03 (the northern provinces); phone numbers have six or seven digits.

For local directory assistance (in Spanish), dial 110.

Local calls cost 23¢ for two minutes at peak time (weekdays 8–8 and Saturday 8–1) or four minutes the rest of the time. Long-distance calls cost 57¢ per *ficha* (unit)—the farther the distance, the shorter each unit lasts. For example, 57¢ lasts about two minutes to places less than 55 km (34 mi) away, but only half a minute to somewhere more than 250 km (155 mi) away.

To make international calls from Argentina, dial 00, then the country code, area code, and number. The country code for the United States is 1.

CALLING CARDS

You can use prepaid calling cards (*tarjetas prepagas*) to make local and international calls from public phones, but not locutorios. All cards come with a scratch-off panel, which reveals a pin number. You dial a free access number, the pin number, and the number you wish to call.

Most kioscos and small supermarkets sell a variety of prepaid calling cards from different companies: specify it's for *llamadas internacionales* (international calls), and compare each card's per-minute rates to the country you want to call. Many cost as little as 9¢ per minute for calls to the United States. Telecom and Telefónica also sell prepaid 5-, 10-, and 20-peso calling cards from kioscos and locutorios. They're called Tarjeta Países and GeoDestino, respectively. Calls to the United. States cost 19¢ per minute using both.

Calling card information **Telecom** (☎0800/555–0030 ⊕www.telecom.com.ar). **Telefónica** (☎0800/333–9000 ⊕www.telefonica.com.ar).

Two local hustlers try to out-con each other in the Fabián Bielinsky's fabulous *Nine Queens,* mostly filmed in Puerto Madero. A gay Cantonese art-house road movie filmed in Buenos Aires? Wong Kar-Wai pulls it off brilliantly in *Happy Together.* A psychologist and a jealous neurotic boyfriend: it doesn't get any more porteño than Damián Szifrón's *The Bottom of the Sea.* A gloriously retro Buenos Aires is one of the stars of *Valentín,* a moving comedy about a young boy directed by Alejandro Agresti.

MOBILE PHONES

Mobile phones are immensely popular; all are GSM 850/1900 Mhz. If you have an unlocked dual-band GSM phone from North America and intend to call local numbers, it makes sense to buy a prepaid Argentinean SIM card on arrival—rates will be cheaper than using your U.S. network or renting a phone. Alternatively, you can buy a basic pay-as-you-go handset and SIM card for around 110 pesos.

All Argentinean cell phone numbers use a local area code, then the cell phone prefix (15), then a seven- or eight--digit number. To call a cell phone in the same area as you, dial 15 and the number. To call a cell phone in a different area, dial the area code including the initial 0, then 15, then the number.

Local cell phone charges vary depending on certain factors, such as the company and time of day, but most cost between 50¢ and 90¢ per minute. If you call from a pay phone, the fee is charged to the recipient.

There are three main mobile phone companies in Argentina: Movistar, owned by Telefónica, CTI, and Personal. Their prices are similar but CTI is said to have better coverage, Movistar has the most users, and Personal is the least popular service, so cards can be harder to find. All three companies have offices and sales stands all over the country. You only pay for outgoing calls, which cost between 25¢ and 1 peso a minute. You can buy a SIM card (*tarjeta SIM*) from any of the companies' outlets; pay-as-you-go cards (*tarjetas de celular*) are available from kioscos, locutorios, supermarkets, and gas stations.

Cellular phones can be rented at the airport from Phonerental. A basic phone costs 20 pesos a week, outgoing calls are reasonable, but you pay 60¢ per minute to receive calls. For very short stays, however, they can be good value.

Contacts **Cellular Abroad** (☎800/287–5072 ⊕www.cellularabroad.com). **CTI** (⊕www.cti.com.ar). **Mobal** (☎888/888–9162 ⊕www.mobalrental.com). **Movistar** (⊕www.movistar.com.ar). **Personal** (⊕www.personal.com.ar). **Phonerental** (☎11/4311–2933 ⊕www.phonerental.com.ar). **Planet Fone** (☎888/988–4777 ⊕www.planetfone.com).

▌ CUSTOMS & DUTIES

Customs uses a random inspection system that requires you to push a button at the inspection bay—if a green light comes on, you walk through; if a red light appears, your bags are X-rayed and (very occasionally opened). In practice, many officials wave foreigners through without close inspection. Officially, you can bring up to 2 liters of alcoholic beverages, 400 cigarettes, and 50 cigars into the country duty-free. However, Argentina's international airports have duty-free shops after you land, and customs officials never take alcohol and tobacco purchased there into account. Personal clothing and effects are admitted duty-free, provided they have been used, as are personal jewelry and professional equipment. Fishing gear and skies present no problems.

Argentina has strict regulations designed to prevent the illicit trafficking of antiques, fossils, and other items of cultural and historical importance. For more information, contact the Dirección Nacional de Patrimonio y Museos (National Heritage and Museums Board).

Information in Argentina **Dirección Nacional de Patrimonio y Museos** (☎11/4381–6656 ⊕www.cultura.gov.ar).

U.S. Information **U.S. Customs and Border Protection** (⊕www.cbp.gov).

▌ ELECTRICITY

The electrical current is 220 volts, 50 cycles alternating current (AC) so most North American appliances can't be used without a transformer. Older wall outlets take Continental-type plugs, with two round prongs, whereas newer buildings take plugs with three flat, angled prongs or two flat prongs set at a "V" angle.

Electricity is a hit-and-miss thing in Argentina. Brief power outages (and surges when the power comes back) are fairly regular occurrences, so it's a good idea to unplug your laptop when leaving your hotel for the day.

▌ EMERGENCIES

In a medical emergency, taking a taxi to the nearest hospital—taxi drivers usually know where to go—can sometimes be quicker than waiting for an ambulance. If you do call for an ambulance, it will take you to the nearest hospital—possibly a public one that may well look run down; don't worry, though, as the medical attention will be excellent. Alternatively you can call a private hospital directly.

For theft, wallet loss, small road accidents, and minor emergencies, contact the nearest police station. Expect all dealings with the police to be a lengthy, bureaucratic business—it's probably only worth bothering if you need the report for insurance claims.

American Embassy **American Embassy** (✉Av. Colombia 4300, Palermo ☎11/5777–4554, 11/5777–4873 after hours ⊕http://argentina.usembassy.gov).

General Emergency Contacts Ambulance & Medical (☎107). **Fire** (☎100). **Police** (☎101). **All Buenos Aires Emergency Services** (☎911).

▌ HEALTH

No specific vaccinations are required for travel to Argentina. However, the Centers for Disease Control (CDC), recommend vaccinations against hepatitis A and B, and typhoid for all travelers. Yellow fever is also advisable if you're traveling to the Iguazú area. Children traveling to Argentina should have current inoculations against measles, mumps, rubella, and polio.

▌TIP➜Argentina has free national health care that also provides foreigners with free outpatient care. Although the medical practitioners working at Buenos Aires' *hospitales públicos* (public hospitals) are usually first rate, the institutions themselves are often underfunded: bed space and basic supplies are at a minimum, and except in emergencies, you should consider leaving these resources for the people who really need them. Private consultations and treatment at Buenos Aires' best private hospitals are reasonably priced compared to those in North America (so much so that medical tourism is booming). All the same, it's a good idea to have some kind of medical insurance. Doctors at the Hospital Británico and Hospital Alemán generally speak English; indeed, so do staff at most private hospitals.

You might want to consider buying trip insurance with medical-only coverage. Neither Medicare nor some private insurers cover medical expenses anywhere outside of the United States. Medical-only policies typically reimburse you for medical care (excluding that related to pre-existing conditions) and hospitalization abroad, and provide for evacuation. You still have to pay the bills and await reimbursement from the insurer, though.

Another option is to sign up with a medical-evacuation assistance company. A membership in one of these companies gets you doctor referrals, emergency evacuation or repatriation, 24-hour hotlines for medical consultation, and other assistance. International SOS Assistance Emergency (www.intsos.com) and AirMed International (www.airmed.com) provide evacuation services and medical referrals. MedjetAssist (www.medjetassist.com) offers medical evacuation.

People in Buenos Aires drink tap water and eat uncooked fruits and vegetables. However, if you're prone to tummy trouble, stick to bottled water, which can be found throughout the city for about 2.50 pesos for 2 liters.

You wouldn't know it from locals' intense love of sunbathing, but the sun is a significant health hazard in Argentina. Stay out of the sun at midday and, regardless of whether you normally burn, wear plenty of good-quality sunblock. A limited selection is available in most supermarkets and pharmacies, but if you use high SPF factors or have sensitive skin, bring your favorite brands with you. A hat and decent sunglasses are also essential.

Health Warnings National Centers for Disease Control & Prevention (⊕ www.cdc.gov/travel). **World Health Organization (WHO;** ⊕ www.who.int).

HEALTH CARE

Hospitals Hospital Británico (British Hospital) (✉Pedriel 74, Barracas ☎11/4309–6500 ⊕www.hospitalbritanico.org.ar). **Hospital Alemán** (German Hospital) (✉Av. Pueyrredon 1640, Recoleta ☎11/4827–7000 ⊕www.hospitalaleman.com.ar).

Medical Assistance Companies AirMed International (⊕ www.airmed.com). **International SOS Assistance Emergency** (⊕ www.intsos.com). **MedjetAssist** (⊕ www.medjetassist.com).

Medical-Only Insurers International Medical Group (☎ 800/628–4664 ⊕ www.

imglobal.com). **International SOS** (⊕ www. internationalsos.com). **Wallach & Company** (☎ 800/237–6615 or 540/687–3166 ⊕ www. wallach.com).

OVER-THE-COUNTER REMEDIES

In Buenos Aires, *farmacias* (pharmacies) carry painkillers, first-aid supplies, contraceptives, diarrhea treatments, and a range of other over-the-counter treatments, including drugs that would require a prescription in the United States (antibiotics, for example). Note that acetominophen—or Tylenol—is known as "paracetamol" in Spanish. If you think you'll need to have prescriptions filled while you're in Argentina, be sure to have your doctor write down the generic name of the drug, not just the brand name.

Farmacity is a supermarket-style drugstore chain with stores all over town; many of its branches are open 24 hours and have a delivery service.

24-Hour Pharmacies Farmacity (⊠Florida 474, Centro ☎11/4322–6559 ⊠R.M. Ortíz 1861, Recoleta ☎11/4514–3231 ⊠Scalabrini Ortíz 3149, Palermo ☎11/4809–0666 ⊕www. farmacity.com).

▌ HOLIDAYS

January through March is summer holiday season for Argentines. Winter holidays fall toward the end of July and beginning of August.

Año Nuevo (New Year's Day), January 1. **Día Nacional de la Memoria por la Verdad y la Justicia** (National Memory Day for Truth and Justice; commemoration of the start of the 1976–82 dictatorship), March 24. **Día del Veterano y de los Caídos en la Guerra de Malvinas** (Malvinas Veterans' Day), April 2. **Semana Santa** (Easter Week), March or April. **Día del Trabajador** (Labor Day), May 1. **Primer Gobierno Patrio** (First National Government, Anniversary of the 1810 Revolution), May 25. **Día de la Bandera** (Flag Day), June 20. **Día de la Independencia**

(Independence Day), July 9. **Paso a la Inmortalidad del General José de San Martín** (Anniversary of General José de San Martín's Death), August 17. **Día de la Raza** (European Arrival in America), October 12. **Inmaculada Concepción de María** (Immaculate Conception), December 8. **Christmas,** December 25.

▌ HOURS OF OPERATION

Banks in Buenos Aires are only open weekdays 10–3 all over the country. Government offices are usually open to the public on weekday mornings from 7 to noon or 1. Government offices, banks, and post offices close on all public holidays, but malls and supermarkets generally only close on Christmas, New Year's day, and Labor Day (May 1).

Private businesses are generally open weekdays 9–7. Malls and clothes and souvenirs shops 10–8 or 9; and supermarkets 8:30 AM–9 or 10 PM. Shops that aren't part of chains or in malls are often closed Saturday afternoon and Sunday, except in Palermo Viejo, where Monday is often the day they close.

Post offices are open weekdays from 9 to 5 or 6 and Saturday 9–1. Telephone centers generally stay open daily 8–8 or later. Most gas stations are open 24 hours.

Museums usually close one day a week (Tuesday is common), and often shut their doors for a whole month in summer. Restaurants generally don't open for dinner until 8:30 or 9 PM but stay open until midnight or 1 AM. Most bars don't get going till midnight, and often open right through the night. There's no official last call.

▌ MAIL

Correo Argentino, Argentina's mail service, has an office in most neighborhoods; some *locutorios* (phone centers) serve as collection points and sell stamps. Mail delivery is far from dependable: it can take 6–21 days for standard letters and postcards to get to the United States. Regular airmail letters cost 4 pesos for up to 20 grams.

If you want to be sure something will arrive, sent it by *correo certificado* (registered mail), which costs 10.75 pesos for up to 20 grams. Postboxes are dark blue and yellow, but there are very few that are not directly outside—or even inside—post offices. Valuable items are best sent with private express services such as DHL, UPS, or FedEx—delivery within one to two days for a 5 kilogram package starts at 490 pesos.

Argentina's post code system is based on a four-digit code. In 1998 each province was assigned a letter (the city of Buenos Aires is "C," for instance), which goes before the number code, and each city block is identified by three letters afterward (such as ABD). In practice, however, only very big cities use these complete postal codes (which look like C1234ABC), whereas the rest of Argentina uses the basic number code (1234, for example).

You can receive mail in Buenos Aires at the Correo Central (Central Post Office). Letters should be addressed to your name, A/C Lista/Poste Restante, Correo Central, 1000 Ciudad Autónoma de Buenos Aires, Argentina. You will be asked to present an ID and pay 1.50 pesos for handling when recovering your mail. American Express cardholders can have mail sent to American Express. If you're receiving anything other than a letter, ask the sender to mail it registered: incoming packages disappear with alarming frequency.

Contacts **American Express** (⊠Arenales 707, Retiro, C1061AAA ☎11/4310-3535 ⊕www.americanexpress.com.ar). **Correo Argentino** (⊠Correo Central, Sarmiento 151, fl. 1, Microcentro, C1000ZAA ☎11/4316-3000 ⊕www.correoargentino.com.ar). **DHL** (⊠Moreno 927, Microcentro ☎0800/222-2345 ⊕www.dhl.com.ar). **Federal Express** (⊠25 de Mayo 386, Microcentro ☎0810/333-3339 ⊕www.fedex.

com). **UPS** (⊠Pte. Luis Saenz Peña 1351, Constitución ☎0800/2222-2877 ⊕www.ups.com).

∎ MONEY

Although prices in Argentina have been steadily rising, Buenos Aires is still surprisingly cheap if you're traveling from a country with a strong currency. Eating out is very good value, as are mid-range hotels. Room rates at first-class hotels approach those in the United States, however.

You can plan your trip around ATMs—cash is king for day-to-day dealings. U.S. dollars can be changed at any bank and are widely accepted as payment. Note that there's a perennial shortage of change. Hundred-peso bills can be hard to get rid of, so ask for tens, twenties, and fifties when you change money. Traveler's checks are useful only as a reserve.

You can usually pay by credit card in top-end restaurants, hotels, and stores; the latter sometimes charge a small surcharge for using credit cards. Some establishments only accept credit cards for purchase over 50 pesos. Outside big cities, plastic is less widely accepted.

Visa is the most widely accepted credit card, followed closely by MasterCard. American Express is also accepted in hotels and restaurants, but Diners Club and Discover might not even be recognized. If possible, bring more than one credit card, as some establishments accept only one type. Note that, throughout this guide, the following abbreviations are used: **AE**, American Express; **DC**, Diners Club; **MC**, MasterCard; and **V**, Visa.

Nonchain stores often display two prices for goods: *precio de lista* (the standard price, valid if you pay by credit card) and a discounted price if you pay in *efectivo* (cash). Many travel services and even some hotels also offer cash discounts—it's always worth asking about.

ITEM	AVERAGE COST
Cup of Coffee and Two Medialunas (croissants)	5–6 pesos
Glass of Wine	11–16 pesos
Liter Bottle of Local Beer	8–14 pesos
Steak and Fries in a Cheap Restaurant	12–15 pesos
One-Mile Taxi Ride in Buenos Aires	3.10 pesos
Museum Admission	Free–5 pesos

Prices throughout this guide are given for adults. Substantially reduced fees are almost always available for children, students, and senior citizens.

ATMS & BANKS
There are ATMs, called *cajeros automáticos* all over Buenos Aires. There are two main systems. Banelco, indicated by a burgundy-color sign with white lettering, is used by Banco Francés, HSBC, Banco Galicia, Banco Santander, and Banco Patagonia. Link, recognizable by a green-and-yellow sign, is the system used by Banco Provincia and Banco de la Nación, among others. Cards on the Cirrus and Plus networks can be used on both networks.

Many banks have daily withdrawal limits of 1,000 pesos or less. Breaking large bills can be tricky, so try to withdraw change (for example, 490 pesos, rather than 500). Make withdrawals from ATMs in daylight, rather than at night.

ATM Locations **Banelco** (⊕http://w3.banelco.com.ar). **Link** (⊕www.redlink.com.ar).

CURRENCY & EXCHANGE
Argentina's currency is the peso, which equal 100 centavos (100¢). Bills come in denominations of 100 (violet), 50 (navy blue), 20 (red), 10 (ocher), 5 (green), and 2 (blue). Coins are in denominations of 1 peso (a heavy bimetallic coin); and 50, 25, 10, and 5 centavos. U.S. dollars are widely accepted in big city stores, supermarkets, and at hotels and restaurants (usually at a slightly worse exchange rate than you'd get at a bank). You always receive change in pesos, even when you pay with U.S. dollars. Taxi drivers may accept dollars, but it's not the norm.

At this writing the exchange rate is 3.15 pesos to the U.S. dollar. You can change dollars at most banks (between 10 AM and 3 PM), at a *casa de cambio* (money changer), or at your hotel. Forex and Cambio America are two reliable downtown exchange services. All currency exchange involves fees, but as a rule, banks charge the least, and hotels the most. You need to show your passport to complete the transaction.

Contacts **Banco Francés** (⊠Av. Córdoba 631, Microcentro ☎11/4314–8720 ⊕www.bancofrances.com.ar). **Banco de la Nación** (⊠Bartolomé Mitre 343, Microcentro ☎11/4331–2961 ⊕www.bna.com.ar). **Cambio America** (⊠Sarmiento 501, Microcentro ☎11/4393–0081). **Forex Cambio** (⊠M.T. de Alvear 540, Microcentro ☎11/4010–2000 ⊕www.forexar.com.ar). **HSBC** (⊠Florida 201, Microcentro ☎11/4320–2800).

Exchange-Rate Information **Oanda.com** (⊕www.oanda.com). **XE.com** (⊕www.xe.com).

∎ PACKING

Porteños are an appearance-conscious bunch who choose fashion over comfort any day. But though locals are stylish, they're usually fairly casual. Your nicer jeans or khakis, capri pants, skirts, and dress shorts are perfect for urban sightseeing. Combine them with stylish walking shoes or leather flats; sneakers are fine if they're out-about-town and hip (leave the beat-up runners behind). In summer many local women seem to live in nice flip-flops or sandals. With the exception of truly posh establishments, a dirty look is usually the only punishment restaurants give the underdressed; refusing entry is almost unheard of. A jacket and tie or stylish dress are only necessary if you plan on some seriously fine dining.

Trendiness takes the backseat in most smaller towns and villages, where dress is more practical and sometimes more conservative. Wherever you go in the country, take good-quality sunglasses, sunblock, and a cap or hat: the sun can be strong, and you're close to the ozone hole, whatever sun-mad locals tell you. A good insect repellent is useful in Buenos Aires in summer, and invaluable in Iguazú year-round.

For beach vacations, bring lightweight sweaters, a windbreaker, or a jacket for evenings when the temperatures drop. Temperatures rarely drop below freezing in the northern half of Argentina, including Buenos Aires, but a heavier coat or jacket is still a must in winter. Temperatures drop dramatically at night in the high-altitude towns of the northwest, so bring a jacket even in summer.

Pharmacies in Buenos Aires stock a good range of toiletries, including some international brands, and hygiene products (note that only nonapplicator tampons are available, however). Pharmacies, supermarkets, and kiosks sell condoms (*preservativos*), and oral contraceptive pills are available over the counter.

Toilet paper is a rare find in public restrooms, but you can buy pocket packs of tissues (known by their brand name, *Carilinas*) in kiosks. Antibacterial wipes and alcohol gel, available in pharmacies, can make bathroom trips more pleasant in remote areas. Don't forget to check camera batteries or chargers and bring along ample memory (or your favorite film).

▌ PASSPORTS & VISAS

As a U.S. citizen, you only need a passport valid for at least six months to enter Argentina for visits of up to 90 days—you'll receive a tourist visa stamp on your passport when you arrive. You should carry your passport or other photo ID with you at all times. If you need to stay longer, you can apply for a 90-day extension (*prórroga*) at the Dirección Nacional de Migraciones. The process takes a morning and costs about 100 pesos. Alternatively, you can exit the country (by taking a boat trip to Uruguay from Buenos Aires, or crossing into Brazil near Iguazú, for example); upon reentering Argentina, your passport will be stamped allowing an additional 90 days. Overstaying your tourist visa is illegal, and incurs a fine of $50, payable upon departure at the airport. If you do overstay your visa, plan to arrive at the airport several hours in advance of your flight so that you have ample time to take care of the fine.

Officially, children visiting Argentina with only one parent do not need a signed and notarized permission-to-travel letter from the other parent to visit Argentina. However, as Argentine citizens *are* required to have such documentation, it's worth carrying a letter just in case laws change or border officials get confused. Single Parent Travel is a useful online resource that provides advice and downloadable sample permission letters.

For information on passport and visa requirements to visit the Brazilian side of Iguazú Falls, see the Planner pages at the start of Chapter 7, Excursions from Buenos Aires.

Contacts **Dirección Nacional de Migraciones** (✉Av. Antártida Argentina 1355, C1104ACA ☎11/4317–0237 ⊕www.mininterior.gov.ar/migraciones). **Embassy of Argentina** (⊕www.embassyofargentina.us). **Single Parent Travel** (⊕www.singleparenttravel.net).

U.S. Passport Information **U.S. Department of State** (☎877/487–2778 ⊕http://travel.state.gov/passport).

▌RESTROOMS

Argentinean restrooms have regular Western-style toilets, but cleanliness standards of public facilities vary hugely. You can find public restrooms in shopping centers, gas stations, bus stations, and some subway stations. Restaurant proprietors often don't complain if you ask to use the facilities without patronizing the establishment, but buying a coffee or a drink is a nice gesture.

There's no guarantee of toilet paper, so carry tissues in your day pack. Alcohol gel and antibacterial hand wipes are also useful for sanitizing you or the facilities.

Restrooms are usually labeled *baño* or *toilette*. Men's toilets are typically labeled *hombres*, often shortened to "H" (men), *caballeros* (gentlemen) or *ellos*. Don't get caught out by an "M" on a door: it's short for *mujeres* (women), not "men." *Damas* (ladies) and *ellas* are other labels for female facilities.

Find a Loo **The Bathroom Diaries** (⊕www.thebathroomdiaries.com) is flush with unsanitized info on restrooms the world over—each one located, reviewed, and rated.

▌SAFETY

CRIME

Argentina is safer than many Latin American countries. However, recent political and economic instability has caused an increase in street crime—mainly pickpocketing, bag-snatching, and occasionally mugging—especially in Buenos Aires. Taking a few precautions when traveling in the region is usually enough to avoid being a target.

Attitude is essential: strive to look aware and purposeful at all times. Don't wear any jewelry you're not willing to lose. Even imitation jewelry and small items can attract attention and are best left behind. Keep a very firm hold of purses and cameras when out and about, and keep them on your lap in restaurants, not dangling off the back of your chair.

Always remain alert for pickpockets. Try to keep your cash and credit cards in different places, so that if one gets stolen you can fall back on the other. Tickets and other valuables are best left in hotel safes. Avoid carrying large sums of money around, but always keep enough to have something to hand over if you do get mugged. Another time-honored tactic is to keep a dummy wallet (an old one containing an expired credit card and a small amount of cash) in your pocket, with your real cash in an inside or vest pocket: if your "wallet" gets stolen you have little to lose.

Women can expect pointed looks, the occasional *piropo* (a flirtatious remark, usually alluding to some physical aspect), and some advances. These catcalls rarely escalate into actual physical harassment—the best reaction is to make like local girls and ignore it; reply only if you're really confident with Spanish curse words. Going to a bar alone will be seen as an open invitation for attention. If you're heading out for the night, it's wise to take a taxi.

There's a notable police presence in barrios popular with visitors, such as San Telmo and Palermo, and this seems to deter potential pickpockets and hustlers. However, porteños have little faith in their police forces: many officers are corrupt and involved in protection rackets or dealing in stolen goods. At best the police are well meaning but under-equipped, so don't count on them to come to your rescue in a difficult situation. Reporting crimes is usually ineffectual and is only worth the time it takes if you need the report for insurance.

The most-important advice we can give you is that, in the unlikely event of being mugged or robbed, do not put up a struggle. Nearly all physical attacks on tourists are the direct result of them resisting would-be pickpockets or muggers. Comply with demands, hand over your stuff, and try to get the situation over with as quickly as possible—then let your travel insurance take care of it.

PROTESTS

Argentines like to speak their minds, and there has been a huge increase in strikes and street protests since the economic crisis of 2001–2. Protesters frequently block streets and squares in downtown Buenos Aires, causing major traffic jams. Most of them have to do with government policies. Trigger-happy local police have historically proved themselves more of a worry than the demonstrators, but though protests are usually peaceful, exercise caution if you happen across one.

SCAMS

Taxi drivers in Buenos Aires are usually honest, but occasionally they decide to take people for a ride, literally. All official cabs have meters, so make sure this is turned on. Some scam artists have hidden switches that make the meter tick over more quickly, but simply driving a circuitous route is a more-common ploy. It helps to have an idea where you're going and how long it will take. Local lore says that, if hailing taxis on the street, those with lights on top (usually labeled RADIO TAXI) are more trustworthy. Late at night, try to call for a cab—all hotels and restaurants, no matter how cheap, have a number and will usually call for you.

When asking for price quotes in touristy areas, always confirm whether the price is in dollars or pesos. Some salespeople, especially street vendors, have found that they can take advantage of confused tourists by charging dollars for goods that are actually priced in pesos. If you're in doubt about that beautiful leather coat, don't be shy about asking if the number on the tag is in pesos or dollars.

Advisories & Other Information **Transportation Security Administration** (TSA ⊕www.

tsa.gov). **U.S. Department of State** (⊕www.travel.state.gov).

▌TAXES

Argentina has an international departure tax of $18, payable by credit card or in cash in pesos, dollars, or euros. There's an $8 domestic departure tax, but this is often included in the price of tickets. Hotel rooms carry a 21% tax. Cheaper hotels and hostels tend to include this in their quoted rates; more-expensive hotels add it to your bill.

Argentina has 21% V.A.T. (known as IVA) on most consumer goods and services. The tax is usually included in the price of goods and noted on your receipt. You can get nearly all the IVA back on locally manufactured goods if you spend more than 70 pesos at stores displaying a duty-free sign. You're given a Global Refund check to the value of the IVA, which you get stamped by customs at the airport, and can then cash in at the clearly signed tax refund booths. Allow an extra hour to get this done.

Tax refunds **Global Refund** (☎11/5238–1970 ⊕www.globalrefund.com).

▌TIME

Argentina is three hours behind G.M.T., or three hours ahead of U.S. central standard time. Daylight saving was introduced in 2007: clocks go forward one hour between December 31 and March 21. Because Argentina and the United States are in opposite hemispheres, this means that in January and February Buenos Aires is four hours ahead of CST, but three hours ahead in November, December, and part of March, and two hours ahead the rest of the time.

Time-Zone Information **Timeanddate.com** (⊕www.timeanddate.com/worldclock).

∎ TIPPING

Propinas (tips) are a question of reward-ing good service rather than an obli-gation. Restaurant bills—even those that have a *cubierto* (bread and service charge)—don't include gratuities; locals usually add 10%. Bellhops and maids expect tips only in the very expensive hotels, where a tip in dollars is appreci-ated. You can also give a small tip (10% or less) to tour guides. Porteños round off taxi fares, though some cabbies who fre-quent hotels popular with tourists seem to expect more. Tipping is a nice gesture with beauty and barbershop personnel—5%–10% is fine.

TIPPING GUIDELINES FOR BUENOS AIRES	
Bellhop at top-end hotels	$1 to $5 per bag, de-pending on the level of the hotel
Hotel Maid at top-end hotels	$1–$3 a day (either daily or at the end of your stay, in cash)
Hotel Room-Service Waiter	$1 to $2 per delivery, even if a service charge has been added
Taxi Driver	10%, or round up the fare to the next full peso amount
Tour Guide	10% of the cost of the tour if service was good
Waiter	10%–15%, depending on service
Restroom attendants	Small change, such as 50¢ or 1 peso.

∎ VISITOR INFORMATION

The Buenos Aires city government oper-ates tourist information booths around the city and an excellent Web site that includes downloadable maps, free MP3 walking tours, hundreds of listings, and insightful articles on porteño culture. Each Argentine province also operates

a tourist office in Buenos Aires, usually called the Casa de (Province Name Here) en Buenos Aires; that is, for information about Salta, you'd go to the Casa de Salta en Buenos Aires, for Mendoza, the Casa de Mendoza en Buenos Aires, and so on. The government umbrella organization for all regional and city-based tourist offices is the Secretaría de Turismo (Secre-tariat of Tourism). Their no-frills Web site has links and addresses to these offices, and lots of other practical information. Limited tourist information is also avail-able at Argentina's embassy and consul-ates in the United States.

Contacts **Argentine Secretariat of Tourism** (☎800/555–0016 in Argentina ⊕www.tur-ismo.gov.ar). **Dirección de Turismo del Gobi-erno de la Ciudad de Buenos Aires** (Turismo Buenos Aires) (☎0800/999–2838 in Argentina ⊕www.bue.gov.ar). **Embassy of Argentina** (⊕www.embassyofargentina.us).

ONLINE RESOURCES

The like-minded travelers on Fodors.com are eager to answer questions and share information. Several Web sites have infor-mation that will supplement or comple-ment that on tourist board sites. Atlas Ambiental de Buenos Aires is part atlas, part environmental encyclopedia. It's a well-designed site that has detailed back-ground information about the city. Mapa de Buenos Aires is an interactive online map run by the city government. It allows you to search for specific addresses. Wel-come Argentina has good overviews of Argentina's different regions, and lots of articles on Buenos Aires.

BA Expats has lots of insider tips on life in Buenos Aires in its searchable forums. The Museo Nacional de Bellas Artes, which contains the world's biggest collection of Argentine art, has lots of information about Argentine artists on its Web site. Tangodata, the official tango site of the Buenos Aires city government, has lots of practical information and listings. Todo Tango is an excellent bilingual tango site with tango lyrics, history, and free downloads. *What's Up Buenos Aires is* a slick bilingual guide, run by American expats, to contemporary culture in the city. Argentine Wines is overflowing with information about Argentina's best tipple. The Web site of *Guía Óleo* has searchable listings and user reviews of restaurants in Buenos Aires. For everything you always wanted to know about mate (a type of tea) but were afraid to ask, check out the site of Mundo Matero. Saltshaker, American food writer Dan Perlman's blog, is packed with insight on local cooking and ingredients.

The English-language daily *Buenos Aires Herald* has a Web site that's worth checking out before and during your trip.

All About Buenos Aires **Atlas Ambiental de Buenos Aires** (⊕www.atlasdebuenosaires.gov.ar). **Fodors.com** (⊕ www.fodors.com/forums). **Mapa de Buenos Aires** (⊕www.mapa.buenosaires.gov.ar). **Welcome Argentina** (⊕www.welcomeargentina.com.ar).

Argentina-Based Travel Agents **Argentina Escapes** (☎11/5032–2938 ⊕www.argentinaescapes.com). **Buenos Aires Tours** (⊕www.buenosaires-tours.com.ar). **Limitless Argentina** (☎202/503–5812 in U.S., 11/4772–9309 in Buenos Aires ⊕www.limitlessargentina.com). **Wow! Argentina** (☎11/5239–3019 ⊕www.wowargentina.com.ar).

Culture & Entertainment **BA Expats** (⊕www.baexpats.com). **Museo Nacional de Bellas Artes** (⊕www.mnba.org.ar). **Tangodata** (⊕www.tangodata.gov.ar). **Todo Tango** (⊕www.todotango.com.ar). **What's Up Buenos Aires** (⊕www.whatsupbuenosaires.com).

English-Language Newspaper **Buenos Aires Herald** (⊕www.buenosairesherald.com).

Food & Wine **Argentine Wines** (⊕www.argentinewines.com). Guía Óleo (⊕www.guiaoleo.com.ar). **Mundo Matero** (⊕www.mundomatero.com/yerba). **Saltshaker** (⊕www.saltshaker.net).

Weather **Accuweather.com** (⊕www.accuweather.com). **Servicio Metereológico Nacional** (National Meteorological Service) (⊕www.meteofa.mil.ar). **Weather.com** (⊕www.weather.com).

INDEX

PHOTO CREDITS

5, *Ken Welsh/age fotostock.* **Chapter 1: Experience Buenos Aires:** 7, *Jeremy Hoare/age fotostock.* 8, *Christopher Pillitz/Alamy.* 9 (left), *Craig Lovell/Alamy.* 9 (right), *Tony Morrison/South American Pictures.* 12, *Jason Friend/Alamy.* 13, *Thomas Cockrem/Alamy.* 14 (left), *Giulio Andreini/age fotostock.* 14 (top center), *Jon Hicks/Alamy.* 14 (top right), *Natalie Pecht/Alamy.* 14 (bottom right), *Wim Wiskerke/Alamy.* 15 (top left), *Frank Nowikowski/South American Pictures.* 15 (bottom left), *Enrique Shore/Woodfin Camp/Aurora Photos.* 15 (top right), *Apeiron-Photo/Alamy.* 15 (bottom right), *Pictorial Press Ltd/Alamy.* 16, *Alvaro Leiva/age fotostock.* 17 (left), *Michel Friang/Alamy.* 17 (right), *David R. Frazier Photolibrary, Inc./Alamy.* 18, *Wim Wiskerke/Alamy.* 19 (left), *Chad Ehlers/Alamy.* 19 (right), *PhotoLatino/eStock Photo.* 20, *Alvaro Leiva/age fotostock.* 21 (left), *Craig Lovell/Alamy.* 21 (right), *Maggie Birkner/age fotostock.* 22, *Peter M. Wilson/Alamy.* 23, *Per Karlsson-BKWine.com.* 24, *El Universal/Newscom.* 25, *Jorge Royan/Alamy.* 26, *Beverly Logan/SuperStock.* 27 (left), *Michael Obert/age fotostock.* 27 (right), *AFP Photo/Newscom.* 27 (bottom), *South American Pictures.* 28, *Frank Nowikowski/South American Pictures.* 29 (left), *Marcelo Gabriel Domenichelli/Shutterstock.* 29 (right), *Tony Morrison/South American Pictures.* 30, *Amado Group.* 31, *Homer Sykes/TravelStockCollection/Alamy.* 32, *Eduardo Dreizzen/age fotostock.* 33 (left), *Image Asset Management/age fotostock.* 33 (right), *José Francisco Ruiz/age fotostock.* 34 (left), *Eduardo M. Rivero/age fotostock.* 34 (bottom right), *Jordi Cami/age fotostock.* 35 (left), *Apeiron-Photo/Alamy.* 36 (left and top right), *A.H.C./age fotostock.* 36 (bottom right), *Pictorial Press Ltd/Alamy.* 37 (top), *Roger Bamber/Alamy.* 37 (bottom), *Tramonto/age fotostock.* 38 (left), *Christopher Pillitz/Alamy.* 38 (top right), *AFP Photos/Newscom.* 38 (bottom right), *DYN/Getty Images/Newscom.* 39 (top), *Roberto Fiadone.* **Chapter 2: Buenos Aires Neighborhoods:** 41, *John Hicks/Alamy.* 46, *Bernardo Galmarini/Alamy.* 49, *John Hicks/Alamy.* 58, *Kobi Israel/Alamy.* 61, *Nick Baylis/Alamy.* 64, *Alfredo Maiquez/age fotostock.* 67, *Frank Nowikowski/South American Pictures.* 69, *Thomas Cockrem/Alamy.* 74, *Anthony Arendt/Alamy.* 76, *Giulio Andreini/age fotostock.* 79, *Michele Molinari/Alamy.* 81, *Christian Kapteyn/Alamy.* 84, *Zuma Press/Newscom.* 86, *Wim Wiskerke/Alamy.* 89 (top), *Network Photographers/Alamy.* 89 (bottom), *Adrian Lascom/Alamy.* 90 (top), *Visual Arts Library (London)/Alamy.* 90 (bottom), *P. Narayan/age fotostock.* 91 (top), *Tramonto/age fotostock.* 91 (bottom), *A.H.C./age fotostock.* 92 (top), *Keystone/Getty Images/Newscom.* 93 (left), *Bruno Perousse/age fotostock.* 93 (right), *Beth/Queen/Zuma Press/Newscom.* 94 (top), *Christopher Pillitz/Alamy.* 95 (top left), *Odile Montserrat/Sygma/Corbis.* 95 (top right), *Universal/Newscom.* 96 (top left), *Interfoto Pressebildagentur/Alamy.* 96 (top right), *SuperStock/age fotostock.* 96 (bottom), *G. Sioen/DEA/age fotostock.* 97 (top), *MRP Photos/Newscom.* 97 (bottom), *Picture-Alliance/DPA/Newscom.* **Chapter 3: Shopping:** 99 and 108, *Susan Seubert/drr.net/Digital Railroad.* 100, *Jochem Wijnands/age fotostock.* 109, *Jon Hicks/Alamy.* 116, *Nick Baylis/Alamy.* 117, *Juncal/Alamy.* 122, *Jeremy Hoare/Alamy.* 123, *Jeremy Hoare/age fotostock.* 130, *P. Narayan/age fotostock.* 131, *Jeremy Hoare/Alamy.* **Chapter 4: After Dark:** 135, *Jorge Royan/Alamy.* 138, *Miguel Mendez/AFP/Newscom.* 143, *Ernesto Rios Lanz/age fotostock.* 144, *flickr.com.*145, *eyalos.com/Shutterstock.* 146 (top), *Picture Contact/Alamy.* 146 (2nd from top), *Christina Wilson/Alamy.* 146 (3rd from top), *Michel Friang/Alamy.* 146 (bottom), *Jason Howe/South American Pictures.* 147 (top), *South American Pictures.* 147 (bottom), *Danita Delimont/Alamy.* 148, *Christina Wilson/Alamy.* **Chapter 5: Where to Eat:** 159, *Adrian Reynolds/age fotostock.* 160, *Nick Baylis/Alamy.* 164, *Wim Wiskerke/Alamy.* 165 (top), *Alan Howden-Argentina Stock/Alamy.* 165 (bottom), *Fabricio Di Dio.* 166, *Sergio Pitamitz/age fotostock.* 167 (top), *Picture Contact/Alamy.* 167 (bottom), *Francis Mallman.* 168, *Orient-Express Hotels, Trains & Cruises.* 169 (top), *Jeremy Hoare/Alamy.* 169 (bottom), *Hyatt.* 170, *Angel Terry/Alamy.* 171 (top), *Eduardo Dreizzen/age fotostock.* 171 (bottom), *Harriet Cummings/Alamy.* 172 and 173 (top), *Fabricio Di Dio.* 173 (bottom), *Mashe/Shutterstock.* **Chapter 6: Where to Stay:** 201, *Home Hotel Buenos Aires.* 202, *Panamericano Buenos Aires.* **Chapter 7: Excursions from Buenos Aires:** 225, *David Lyons/Alamy.* 226, *Dario Diament/Shutterstock.* 227 (top), *Adrian Reynolds/age fotostock.* 227 (bottom), *Carla Antonini.* 252-53, *Jeremy Hoare/Alamy.* 254, *Chris Sharp/South American Pictures.* 255, *Pablo D. Flores.* 256, *Jeremy Hoare/Alamy.* 257, *SuperStock.* 258 (top), *Hughes/age fotostock.* 258 (bottom), *Johannes Odland/Shutterstock.* 279, *Ken Welsh/age fotostock.* 280, *Javier Etcheverry/Alamy.* 281, *Sue Cunningham Photographic/Alamy.* 282-83 (bottom), *Fritz Poelking/age fotostock.* 282 (top), *David R. Frazier Photolibrary, Inc./Alamy.* 283 (top), *PCL/Alamy.* 284, *travelstock44/Alamy.* 285, *Vittorio Sciosia/age fotostock.*

NOTES

NOTES

NOTES

NOTES

ABOUT OUR WRITERS

Brian Byrnes (www.brianbyrnes.com.) lives in Buenos Aires, where he reports in print, on-air, and online for media outlets like *CBS News, Newsweek magazine, CNN, The Hollywood Reporter, Fodors.com,* and others. He first arrived in Argentina in 2001 to update the Patagonia chapter of Fodor's Argentina and has worked on every edition of the guide since. He's married to a porteña and has a young son, to whom he is teaching the ways of the Argentine asado. He wrote the Where to Stay and Where to Eat chapters.

Andy Footner, who updated the After Dark chapter, completed a Philosophy degree in Leeds, gained office experience in London, started a record company in Sofia, Bulgaria, and edited *Time Out Istanbul* magazine in Turkey and a guidebook in Rio de Janeiro. He came to South America with his Patagonian wife, with whom he produced a documentary about a women's gym in Iraq. They're now living in Buenos Aires, writing stories from the country and the continent, and dreaming up new projects.

Although Victoria Patience grew up in Hong Kong, crowded buses and cranky old cars have taken her thousands of miles through Latin America over the last decade or so. She's been hooked on Argentina since the moment she arrived. Buenos Aires—first the city, then the province—has been her home for several years. This served her well during her work on the Buenos Aires Experience, Neighborhoods, Side Trips, and Travel Smart chapters. Victoria focused on Hispanic Studies at the University of London, and her ongoing fascination with Latin American literature and culture came in handy when she penned the features "The Dance of Buenos Aires," "Un Dia de Campo," "Argentine Icons," "A Passionate History," and "Iguazú Falls." She's a freelance contributor to many Fodor's guidebooks and also runs her own translation company.